The Politics of Realism

The Politics of Realism

Thomas Docherty

BLOOMSBURY ACADEMIC
LONDON • NEW YORK • OXFORD • NEW DELHI • SYDNEY

BLOOMSBURY ACADEMIC
Bloomsbury Publishing Plc
50 Bedford Square, London, WC1B 3DP, UK
1385 Broadway, New York, NY 10018, USA
29 Earlsfort Terrace, Dublin 2, Ireland

BLOOMSBURY, BLOOMSBURY ACADEMIC and the Diana logo are trademarks
of Bloomsbury Publishing Plc

First published in Great Britain 2022
This paperback edition published 2023

Copyright © Thomas Docherty, 2022

Thomas Docherty has asserted his right under the Copyright, Designs and
Patents Act, 1988, to be identified as Author of this work.

For legal purposes the Acknowledgements on p. vii constitute an extension
of this copyright page.

Cover design by Eleanor Rose
Cover image: *The Pretty Pastry Cook* (oil on canvas) by Joseph Bail (1862-1921) / French
© Archives Charmet / Bridgeman Images

All rights reserved. No part of this publication may be reproduced or transmitted
in any form or by any means, electronic or mechanical, including photocopying,
recording, or any information storage or retrieval system, without prior
permission in writing from the publishers.

Bloomsbury Publishing Plc does not have any control over, or responsibility for, any
third-party websites referred to or in this book. All internet addresses given in this book
were correct at the time of going to press. The author and publisher regret
any inconvenience caused if addresses have changed or sites have ceased to
exist, but can accept no responsibility for any such changes.

A catalogue record for this book is available from the British Library.

A catalog record for this book is available from the Library of Congress.

ISBN: HB: 978-1-3502-2853-5
PB: 978-1-3502-2857-3
ePDF: 978-1-3502-2854-2
eBook: 978-1-3502-2855-9

Typeset by Deanta Global Publishing Services, Chennai, India

To find out more about our authors and books visit www.bloomsbury.com
and sign up for our newsletters.

For the University of Glasgow

Contents

Introduction	1

Part I Controlling the real and its representations

1	Assembly: Reality and the commerce of censorship	23
2	A present and private reality: Labour, sex and death in Courbet's painting	48
3	Grotesque Realism: Flaubert, Baudelaire, impropriety and decorum	70
4	Legislating reality: Law, religion and education	87

Part II Making the real

5	Science and modernity: Vision, force, Turgenev and Russian Formalism	119
6	Realism changes reality: Revolution, documentary and socialist realisms	149

Part III Making the unreal

7	Naked propaganda: 'The intimate things of common life'	175
8	Neorealism: The real as resistance	197
9	The politics of fact, and the danger of totalitarian Realism	227

Bibliography	265
Index	274

Introduction

1

'What happened? . . . No; what *really* happened?'

The history of criticism is written into the relation between these two phrases. It is the critical intellectual who interjects the ellipsis here, as the space of a fundamental scepticism or doubt about the constitution of reality. That is accompanied by a further doubt: the critical intellectual is disinclined to believe what she or he is told, disinclined to accept the world as presented or represented. This is perhaps especially true of the contemporary critical intellectual. At an earlier stage in the institutional formation, history and development of literary criticism, the critical act was primarily an act of judgement. 'Criticism', we knew, was a term derived into English from the ancient Greek, '*krinein*', meaning to judge or to decide. More recently, however, and no doubt because of a historical political culture in which the laboratory sciences have been deemed to be more 'realistic', more useful in real and material terms than poetry, criticism has concerned itself with questions of evidence. The critic operates increasingly as a forensic detective – sometimes as a political paranoiac – seeking out 'what *really* happened' or what is *really* going on in a work of art; and this in turn provokes a curiosity (the word is cognate with 'care') about the conditions in which the art itself exists. The critical intellectual, we might say, is fundamentally curious about the real conditions in which we engage with a text or other cultural activity. In short, our work is always conditioned not just by the realities of politics but also by the politics of realism.

This attitude opens criticism to a world beyond the aesthetic, and, indeed, it insists that the aesthetic cannot be isolated from the conditions of its existence. In *The People's Republic of Amnesia*, Louisa Lim tells the story of Chen Guang. Chen was born and raised in Shangqiu, in Henan, but now lives in Beijing. He is a painter, but 'he creates whole collections [of paintings] that he knows cannot be shown in mainland China'.[1] The paintings cannot be shown because Chen is a former soldier in the Chinese military, whose duties in that role included

---

[1] Louisa Lim, *The People's Republic of Amnesia: Tiananmen Revisited* (Oxford University Press, Oxford, 2014), 8.

working as a military photographer in Tiananmen Square on 4 June 1989; and his art is haunted by the events that he witnessed that day. For the Chinese State, these events did not happen and so, from the official point of view of the Chinese State, Chen is making a representation of an unreal event: his figurative paintings have no original in empirical reality. They are, as it were, illegitimate as far as the official State is concerned; yet they are realist paintings, and they do exist, even if in clandestine, unshown fashion.

Chen described to Louisa Lim his memory of the days in and around the event in Tiananmen. Bored by barracks life in Zhangjiajkou, Chen saw the call to go to the capital as an exciting adventure, something that would be a moment of fun that would break the harsh routines on his days. Indeed, in the days immediately prior to the military attack on the protesting students, the general mood – shared by both sides, students and military in and around Beijing – was extremely positive, congenial and comradely. Soldiers and citizens were relaxed and friendly with each other, exchanging food and songs. The citizens offered food to the hungry soldiers, who had been in Beijing for longer than expected, and so their rations were therefore low. The soldiers engaged in a kind of sing-off against the citizens, military songs in a contest for volume against the Internationale sung by the students. This mood, and the entire situation, changed once the military were given their orders – and their ammunition, 'four clips per person, each carrying around 50 or 60 bullets'.[2] The soldiers were driven in buses towards the Square, but 'each time they nosed forward, a new wave of people crested around them' and they 'were hemmed in by this outpouring of humanity whose aim was to block the troops' advance into the city'. This was a significant moment for Chen, and indeed a turning point in his comprehension of what was happening. Lim quotes him: '"It didn't feel fun anymore," he remembered. "It felt real."'[3]

Chen's paintings are representations of reality, then; but they represent a reality that 'officially' does not exist and never has existed. 'What happened' in Tiananmen Square? 'Over the course of the past quarter-century, in an extraordinary sleight of hand, China's rulers have managed to transform this site of national shame into one of national pride,'[4] writes Lim. 'What *really* happened' is here displaced in two ways. From the point of view of the State, the act of political violence is airbrushed from history: it is displaced as if into an Orwellian memory hole, with documentary evidence of actual historical events

[2] Ibid., 17.
[3] Ibid., 11.
[4] Ibid., 1.

being systematically destroyed, and it therefore never happened. From Chen's angle, it is displaced into art, via the mechanism of a representation that is, first of all, explicitly memorial: Chen's memory of the day is present and re-presented to him at all times.

There is a contestation at stake here, and it is one that sits at the core of a politics of realism. Lest one think that this situation pertains solely to totalitarian regimes, we can consider the way in which the same tension actually marks the architecture of urban space. A good example is present-day Berlin. If one walks from the Brandenburg Gate in a southerly direction, along Ebertstrasse, one will arrive at a field of *steles*, concrete blocks of varying sizes, arranged in what looks like a geometric pattern, albeit a somewhat irregular one. The 'Field of Steles' is the main architectural form that occupies the site of the 'Monument to the Murdered Jews of Europe', often simply referred to as the 'Holocaust Memorial'. Walk further south from the Memorial, and proceed along Hannah-Arendt-Strasse, to a municipal car park. There is no particular signification openly given to this car park: it is simply where you might leave your car. However, it is the site of Hitler's bunker, the place where the primary instance of the Nazi project ostensibly died along with its leader, in May 1945.

The near-collocation of these two sites, symbolically linked by a memory of Arendt, is remarkable for what it says about the power of memory. In the Field of Steles, we find memory stirred, the dead evoked and, in the underground Room of Names (*Raum des Namen*), the dead brought back to identity. This is an almost literal act of remembering, bringing the dead back to life and placing them at the heart of a city, at the core of a civilization. Yet the city and the site remain haunted also by that which cannot be commemorated, even if it cannot also be forgotten: Hitler's bunker.

Memory is itself tied firmly to representations; and to representations that have a relation to empirical realities. St Augustine, in his *Confessions*, described memory as being 'like a great field', saying that 'When I use my memory, I ask it to produce whatever it is that I wish to remember'. The Field of Steles is metaphorically a field such as this; and, as a field, it is a place of fecundity and of potential growth. Closer to our own historical moment, Walter Benjamin also considered memory, writing that 'Language shows clearly that memory is not an instrument for exploring the past but its theatre. It is the medium of past experience, as the ground is the medium in which dead cities lie interred.' Memory is a theatre, tied to a polity. Benjamin goes on: 'He who seeks to approach his own buried past must conduct himself like a man digging. This confers the tone and bearing of genuine reminiscences'; and in this, we find the aspect of curiosity – that fundamental care – that I indicate as central to criticism. 'He must not be afraid again and again to return to the same matter; to scatter it as one scatters earth, to turn it over as one turns over soil. For the matter itself is only a deposit, a stratum, which yields only to the most meticulous examination what constitutes the real treasure hidden within the earth'. The investigator here asks 'No, what *really* happened?'. Benjamin concludes that what we find through our critical digging, now an insistent and ever-deepening archaeology, is 'images, severed from all earlier associations, that stand – like precious fragments or torsos in a collector's gallery – in the prosaic rooms of our later understanding'.[5] These images are, of course, representations that are themselves entirely conditioned by what we can now call the polity of memory.

Both of these metaphorical descriptions – Augustine's and Benjamin's – work to suggest that memory operates in a mode akin to archaeology: experiences occur but then are buried, covered and hidden, but to be discovered later as memories, in an act that quickens to life the dead and buried. This is important for my argument here, which is that memory operates as a bridge between the public and private spheres, and that it does so precisely as an act of quickening the dead. It is therefore shaped by politics, and haunted by the bio-political certainty of human death, of the death of its very subject and agent.

Every representation of reality is, in one way or another, configured first of all as a memory. It is apotropaic, striving to ward off death yet inevitably marked by the bio-political fact that dying – passing away from real and material existence, occupying the ghostly terrain of Chen Guang's paintings – is what human subjects inevitably do. Contemporary studies of how memory operates show that there is often a narrative drive that informs and shapes how we represent the world to ourselves and others. 'To remember the past, you tell a story about it. And in recalling the memory, you tell the story again.' But the repetition can operate like the fabled 'Chinese whisper'; and the story changes. 'Memory fits in with the demands of the present as much as it tries to remain faithful to the facts of what happened. It incorporates new ideas, including snippets of information that have nothing to do with the original events.'[6] Representation, we might say more generally, is subject to political conditions; and those political conditions bring into question the status of 'what happens' and of how we represent the reality of what happens.

---

[5] Augustine, *Confessions* (trans. R. S. Pine-Coffin; Penguin, London, 1961), 222; Walter Benjamin, 'A Berlin Chronicle', in *Selected Writings*, vol. 2, ed. Michael W. Jennings, Gary Smith and Howard Eiland (Harvard University Press, Cambridge, MA, 2005), 314.
[6] Charles Ferneyhough, *Pieces of Light: The New Science of Memory* (Profile, London, 2013), 113–14.

The political dimension of this is clarified for us by Walter Benjamin when he offers us what he calls a basic truth: 'nothing that has ever happened should be regarded as lost for history'.[7] At the same time, he adds that 'To articulate the past historically does not mean to recognize it "the way it really was"... It means to seize hold of a memory as it flashes up at a moment of danger'.[8] Following this, we might say that 'what really happened' is not in fact limited to 'what happened' or 'the way it really was'. In short, we can say firmly that there is a deep engagement between the ways in which we represent the world and the political situation of those representations. When we suggest that the representation has a firm and basic intimacy with empirical realities, then we must acknowledge that there is no realism without a politics of realism.

2

This book proceeds by understanding the example of Chen Guang as theoretically paradigmatic: the State has always had an interest in how we memorialize the past, with the consequence that it has a vested interest in representation. It is this fact that shapes virtually all 'public art', especially when that art is figural or representational. The politics of realism shapes the contestations that are at the core of the various 'must fall' movements around the world, and the politics of realism is equally at the heart of the various fundamentalist iconoclasms that we have historically witnessed, from the European Reformation right through to contemporary acts like the destruction of the Tetrapylon in Palmyra.

This, however, is not how the usual histories of literary or cultural realism begin. The classic version indicates that Realism begins as a reaction against a prevailing dispensation of more or less genteel politeness in the arts. The reaction is one that renders visible a number of elements that politeness had ignored: the conditions of real workers struggling for subsistence, say, or dirt and squalor in newly emergent cities, or the existence of prostitution, of crime, of a violent tenor in many actual and daily social relations in the world beyond the boudoir and salon. It is very important to stress that these more or less standard views

---

[7] Walter Benjamin, 'Theses on the Philosophy of History', in Benjamin, *Illuminations*, ed. Hannah Arendt (trans. Harry Zohn; Fontana, Glasgow, 1973), 256 (Thesis III).
[8] Ibid., 257 (Thesis VI). Benjamin's quoted phrase is from Leopold von Ranke, the historian who is credited with the prioritization of primary and documentary sources and an attendant empiricism in our historical attitude.

are not in the least wrong. On the contrary, they are extremely accurate. What I want to add in this book is a more sustained engagement with the consequences that follow from this understanding of the literary and cultural history. In doing so, we will discover that there has been a massive historical shift in the politics of realism – and it is this that forms the substructure of the present work. Further, the analysis will show not just that Realism is an active response to the politics of its prevailing moment, but also that Realism works to expose the false assumptions – and, indeed, the fundamental unreality – of those prevailing conditions.

The historical shift can be traced developmentally as one that has some devastating consequences for our contemporary predicaments in culture and society. What has happened is that, over time and with the emergence and normalization of new technologies, the politics of realism has itself been upended, such that the real question that literature and the arts pose for us now is the question regarding the reality or unreality of politics as such. Further, this shift is one that has increasingly evacuated politics itself – as the site of an Aristotelian 'association' of citizens – of real substance. It is a cliché (but no less meaningful for that) that many people in the advanced economies are politically disenchanted, and they increasingly support those politicians who pose as anti-politicians, to the extent even, paradoxically, of voting for them – a political act carried out by people who eschew politics, and exploited by politicians who represent themselves falsely as non-politicians.

There is an issue of real importance behind this; and the investigation here will help to reveal what it is. The argument is that, in our contemporary predicaments, politics itself – as both discursive and general activity – has been essentially censored out of our polities; and it has been replaced by something else that we can call identity. I do not mean by this that we are in the era of identity politics: that much is clear and has been clear for some time. Rather, I want to show that in this shift there is a massive evisceration of political life itself. Our expression into the public sphere of an identity that is also given as a fundamentally private and embodied self has become more important than – indeed has replaced entirely – the idea of the political citizen or subject, and has disrupted the productive functioning of social association. This is an act of censorship of the highest order, for it essentially eradicates the very category of the citizen as such, precisely at the moment when it appears to celebrate the very identity of the citizen; and it is one, therefore, that – as we can increasingly now see – obviously helps to establish and then normalize the totalitarian State.

3

I have indicated the importance, for criticism, of the sceptical doubt marked by the pause and ellipsis between the questions of 'what happened' and 'what really happened'; but that doubting pause is itself also marked by a moment of negation: no. This, with its intrinsic questioning of reality – of that which is a given, of that which is data – is a founding impetus that informs and guides a politics of realism, as my argument in this book should demonstrate.

It is a superb paradox that the word 'no' turns out to be one of the most affirmative in English. To say no is a gesture that goes well beyond a mere disagreement. We can here test an ostensibly grand proposition: saying no is the condition of what we have learned to call 'modernity'. Modernity – and, indeed, modernism as its aesthetic counterpart – rests upon a gesture of refusal, a denial and a negation. It says 'no' to all that is 'now', and 'no' to all that is 'here'. Modernity – like the critical intellectual – rejects the 'given' nature of our present and our presence.

This is a simple way of rehearsing Marx's observations at the opening of the *Eighteenth Brumaire*. There, Marx famously notes that, while men and women make their own history, they do not do so under conditions of their own making or choosing. We do not choose the circumstances in which we act; but rather have to live and work 'under given circumstances directly encountered and inherited from the past'.[9] On the one hand, Marx is here asserting human and individual autonomy: we make our own laws and are answerable to them; and, for this, we must assume the full responsibilities of our agency. We intervene in the workings of nature; and in doing this, we stand at an angle to history, adjacent to it and, from that position, able to steer its forward motion. At the same time, however, we do not have a completely free and undetermined hand in doing this: we have to negotiate between what we want as futurity and what we have been dealt as our given reality. He observes that 'The tradition of all the generations of the dead weighs like a nightmare on the brain of the living'.[10]

In explaining this, Marx has recourse to a literary trope, and he conjures up a metaphor. He writes that it is precisely at the moment when the revolutionary figure believes that she or he is genuinely creating something new, something un-preprogrammed and absolutely original that 'they anxiously conjure up the spirits of the past'[11] to structure and to explain their present actions. Although he

---

[9] Karl Marx, *The Eighteenth Brumaire of Louis Bonaparte* (Foreign Languages Press, Peking, 1978), 9.
[10] Ibid.
[11] Ibid., 9–10.

opens his study of Marx from another text, *The Communist Manifesto*, Derrida notes this haunting as *his* own point of origin, in a book that makes much of the difficulty of beginning things, of being autonomous or of 'learning how to live, finally'.[12] For Marx, the free autonomy that conditions the very possibility of our doing something new – intervening in history, making a moment that is explicitly and constitutively 'modern' as such – depends upon a kind of negation of that novelty. In short, we might say that our freedom is itself not free. The subject of a modern moment – the I that gives 'now' its substance or that makes the here and now what it is – is itself the very negation of the modern. Whatever I affirm – my 'yes' to a present agency – depends upon a negation – my saying 'no' to its pre-determination. The modern is born out of that struggle with tradition, that seemingly self-defeating demand for complete autonomy. In this (limited) regard, 'no' pre-dates and conditions 'yes', and configures the character of the self-consciously here-now that is the modern subject or the subject of modernity as such.[13]

Perhaps the clearest philosophical demonstration of this paradox – or aporia as we now call it – is found in Descartes, whose *Méditations* and the slightly earlier *Discours de la méthode* are often advanced as the foundational moment of modernity. The opening sentences of the First Meditation are a very clear moment of saying no, in precisely the manner of the critic as I have described it: 'I must once for all seriously undertake to rid myself of all the opinions which I had formerly accepted.' Descartes describes his current position as one where he can 'freely' negate all that has gone before: 'since I have procured for myself an assured leisure in a peaceable retirement, I shall at last seriously and freely address myself to the general upheaval of all my former opinions.' These statements – through which he begins his dismantling of the reality of his existing or given world – form the ground from which the first positive assertion – the yes – arises, when he can 'commence to build anew from the foundation'.[14]

What follows from this is not simply that Descartes divests himself of his former opinions; rather, he strips away the reality of the world around him, up to and including the material reality of his own body. As the First Meditation gets under way properly, Descartes seems to insist on the positive existence of these

---

[12] See Jacques Derrida, *Spectres de Marx* (Galilée, Paris, 1993), 22, 13. I will return to this in a later chapter, when I come to address the issue of representation and the various ways in which modern culture seeks to ban or prohibit representation as such.

[13] I want to stress that this is of *limited* applicability. There are, and must be, real world conditions in which 'no' means 'no', and can in no way be construed as preliminary to or implying a 'yes'.

[14] René Descartes, *Philosophical Works* (trans. Elizabeth S. Haldane and G. R. T. Ross; Cambridge University Press, Cambridge, 1969), 144.

things. Noting 'the fact that I am here, seated by the fire, attired in a dressing gown, having this paper in my hands. . . . And how could I deny that these hands and this body are mine'.[15] Yet this denial – this initial great 'upheaval of all my former opinions' – is exactly what follows, as Descartes, now retired from the labours of his life, argues that everything that he has taken for reality may in fact be no more substantial than a dream, a semblance or representation, a 'delusion' as he calls it, that has no actual and material reality. The logic takes him to a position where 'I shall consider myself as having no hands, no eyes, no flesh, no blood, nor any senses',[16] in a whole series of nos that lead him into the Second Meditation where he can argue that 'I persuade myself that nothing has ever existed of all that my fallacious memory represents to me. . . . I imagine that body, figure, extension, movement and pace are but fictions of the mind'.[17] The past is as unreal as Tiananmen Square for the Chinese State; the present body may itself not exist, or may be as if dead.

The standard reading of Descartes is that two things follow that will get him out of his predicament, the predicament in which he has said no to existence. First, no matter the content of his doubting – be it his eyes, his senses, the world – nonetheless he can always be sure that he is doubting. 'Dubio', 'I doubt', becomes the first certainty. Secondly, doubting is but one instance of a more general thinking; and thus we get the famous Cogito and its intrinsic logic that yields an identity and a certainty of being: I am a thing that thinks.[18]

This, however, misses one key turn; and it is a linguistic turn that takes his initial act of nay-saying and reverses it into a yea-saying, with the *saying* or declaration being the key element in that turn. We come, he argues, to a moment of certainty that rests upon a *proposition*: 'I am, I exist, is necessarily true *each time that I pronounce it*'.[19] [stress added] The 'I am' – that 'sum' that follows logically upon the 'cogito' – is first and foremost a statement and an affirmation. Technically, what Descartes has shown here is not that 'cogito ergo sum'; rather it is 'loquor ergo sum', or 'I speak therefore I am'. 'Loquor', of course, exists only in the passive voice: 'I speak' is the same as 'I am spoken'. As the great modernist Beckett will rewrite this, 'A voice comes to one in the dark. Imagine.'[20]

---

[15] Ibid., 145.
[16] Ibid., 148.
[17] Ibid., 149.
[18] Ibid., 152.
[19] Ibid., 150; stress added.
[20] Samuel Beckett, *Company* (John Calder, London, 1979); repr. in Dirk van Hulle, ed., *Samuel Beckett: Company / Ill Seen Ill Said / Worstword Ho / Stirrings Still* (Faber and Faber, London, 2009), 3.

We might summarize this by suggesting that it is the initial act of negation that reveals an utterance; and that utterance is nothing more or less than the affirmation of a voicing of the word 'yes'. In this respect, Beckett is indeed the heir to Joyce, who 'closes' *Ulysses* with the feminine word, 'yes I will Yes I said yes'. It takes Joyce a long time to get to that word, of course, for he, too, has begun in an act of nay-saying. As Joyce comes to be a writer, in *A Portrait of the Artist as a Young Man*, he first has to go through his own act of negation: 'non serviam', I will not serve. The first time Stephen hears the phrase comes in the midst of an explicit withdrawal from material realities: the retreat. Stephen and his fellow-pupils have been advised to 'Banish from your minds all worldly thoughts'.[21] Like Descartes, Stephen distances himself from the reality of even his own body:

> He, he himself, his body to which he had yielded was dying. Into the grave with it! Nail it down into a wooden box, the corpse. . . . Thrust it out of men's sight into a long hole in the ground, into the grave, to rot, to feed the mass of its creeping worms and to be devoured by scuttling plumpbellied rats.[22]

It is in the midst of this that Stephen hears the non serviam attributed to Lucifer, in an 'instant that was his ruin'. This theological no, according to Catholic theology, damns Lucifer in one shocking instant. The young Stephen is much impressed, and fears the possibility of such an act of defiance.

Some time later, of course, he himself utters the phrase. Explaining to his friend, Cranly, that he has refused to satisfy his mother's wishes to make his Catholic Easter duties, his reason is Lucifer's: 'I will not serve.'[23] This is an act of negation that, for Cranly, is overblown; and it is also one that is born out of protest. Thus it is that Cranly asks Stephen if he intends to become a protestant. Stephen's reply is witty; but at the same time it is also what we have learned to call, after Hegel, the negation of the negation: 'I said that I had lost the faith, Stephen answered, but not that I had lost self-respect. What kind of liberation would that be to forsake an absurdity which is logical and coherent and to embrace one that is illogical and incoherent?'[24]

In this 'negation of the negation' moment, Stephen claims his autonomy: the freedom to look at himself, to assume self-consciousness regarding his actions and beliefs, literally to 'respect himself' as if looking into a mirror. That mirror, of course, is something that operates as a dominant metaphor to help explain literary

---

[21] James Joyce, *A Portrait of the Artist as a Young Man* (1916; Granada, London, 1977), 103.
[22] Ibid., 105.
[23] Ibid., 215.
[24] Ibid., 220.

and other modes of realism. It has an initial moment in Hamlet's determination to make Gertrude reflect upon herself via the images that he shows her of her dead husband and her living one (a move that is more important in this book than the more obvious comparison he makes suggesting that art is a mirror held up to reflect nature). King Lear will use it to try to believe that Cordelia still lives, searching for a trace of her breath on it. More famously and directly, it appears in Stendhal as he describes how fiction works, the mirror going for a walk along a road and revealing the world as it is. It persists right through to the work of contemporary artists such as Cindy Sherman, whose poses yield images of her 'reflecting' various iconic figures. All such mirrors, of course, affect the reality that they reflect: they affirm it through a kind of simultaneous reversal or negation. It was the same with Descartes in the seventeenth century; and it was the same with Marx in the nineteenth, as Marx tries to wrest control of history from the farceurs.

There are numerous other such moments in which we can find a no becoming substantiated as a kind of affirmation. Consider the withholding of the mother's kiss at the opening of Proust's *A la Recherche du temps perdu*. But what will we say about a text like Virginia Woolf's *To the Lighthouse*? For Joyce, 'yes' was the feminine word; and here we have a text, by a woman, whose very opening word is indeed yes: 'Yes, of course' is how the novel opens. That yes is immediately qualified, however, not just with the emphatic 'of course' but then with a completely undermining 'if': 'Yes, of course, if it's fine tomorrow.' A paragraph later, Mr Ramsay crushes the yes with a very definitive: 'But . . . it won't be fine.'

The trip to the lighthouse is deferred; but, in this opening no that occasions the deferral, we get the time opening up that makes possible the entire novel itself, a novel that, appropriately for present purposes, hinges upon an opening section called 'The Window'. We will see these metaphors – windows, mirrors, distorted reflections, openings to the world and closing of sight – at work through the political inflections of realism in the pages that follow in this study.

4

Perhaps we might be more acquainted with the affirmative no – if I can call it thus – from the discourses and activities around real world politics. *No pasarán!* shouted La Pasionaria: 'they shall not pass.' 'No surrender!' shouted Ian Paisley during the Irish Troubles of the 1970s and beyond. We now know, as Naomi Klein has pointed out to us, that *no is not enough*. That text by Klein, written in haste after the Trump election, is clear. If we would work as a critical intellectual at all, then it is clear that we must indeed say no to Trump and the by now domesticated and near normalized shock doctrine of the political right-wing; but that is only useful as a preliminary to a yes. As Klein puts it, 'saying no to bad actors is not enough. The firmest of no's has to be accompanied by a bold and forward-looking yes. . . . No . . . may be what initially brings millions into the streets. But it is *yes* that will keep us in the fight.' She almost immediately reinforces that further:

> that *No* on the cover [of her book] is not just to an individual or even a group of individuals. . . . We're also saying no to the *system* that has elevated them to such heights. And then let's move to a *yes* – a yes that will bring about change so fundamental that today's corporate takeover will be relegated to a historical footnote, a warning to our kids.[25]

When Aristotle wrote *Politics*, he began from a consideration of the polity as such, as a community of citizens. There are three crucial founding elements in such a polity. The first is the fundamental relation that binds people together; and here, he focuses on the relation that promises futurity. The sexual relation of male to female, he argues, is basic to a society that envisages an existence beyond the immediately present. The logical next issue is that of self-preservation and security, for any such future generation depends on the present generation being safe from inimical elements that would endanger its life. How, though, is this present set of relations to be organized? For Aristotle, the basic axiom that governs this is the pursuit of the good, and a significant element within this is the pursuit of wealth. For this, productive work is required; and Aristotle focuses his immediate attention on the relation of master to slave in this regard.[26]

In the politics of realism, we can discover similar concerns. I have already indicated, through the example of Chen Guang and Tiananmen, the centrality of a bio-political concern with the simple real fact of death: dying is, in a fundamental way, what humans do, and it remains always an inescapable reality that governs a good deal of our activities, which are designed as far as possible to 'negotiate' the terms of each individual real death. In addition to this, the history of realism as I delineate it here is shaped also – as in Aristotle – by a concern with sex and with labour. These three basic realities – sex, labour, death – all exist in various forms of contestation as the underpinning not just of realistic

---

[25] Naomi Klein, *No Is Not Enough* (Allen Lane, London, 2017), 9, 11–12.
[26] Aristotle, *Politics* (trans. Ernest Barker, revised R. F. Stalley; Oxford University Press, Oxford, 1998), 7–12.

representations but also as the constituent elements that govern the political constitutions of realism in its various historical moments and in its different aesthetic modes.

It will be useful here, in this Introduction, to give some sense of the general trajectory of my argument. The investigation in what follows in this book takes, as its first point of reference, events in France and in England in 1857. This is the year in which the French State moves against Flaubert and Baudelaire, prosecuting these writers for offences against public morals and charging them with obscenity. Exactly coterminous with this, England passes legislation – the Obscene Publications Act – designed to curb what the State there sees as the threat of moral corruption and 'disease' arising from the availability of cultural representations of sexual activity. A censorious drive, governed by the powers of the State, intervenes into an emergent realist aesthetic. In showing how this happens, we can see that this emergent realism gets its basic significance from a politics that is concerned with an account, in both jurisdictions, of the ideal 'national character'. That character, as far as the State has any say in its configuration, will indicate that sexual activity will be regulated and policed.

The regulation in question here is proposed ostensibly for the good of all citizens; but analysis of the political shape of the trials in France and the legislation in England shows that the State is primarily interested in protecting existing privileges, privileges especially of wealth that are themselves dependent upon a differentiation of social classes. What is going on at this historical moment in these jurisdictions is something that we recognize in its much more developed form in contemporary political conditions. Timothy Snyder considers this in the case of Putin's Russia, where we see 'the stabilization of massive inequality' which is brought about in manoeuvres where we see 'the displacement of policy by propaganda'.[27] The roots of this contemporary political condition – a condition that is currently spreading right across the advanced world economies and jurisdictions – has its roots in the nineteenth-century policing of sexual activity. Its sexual dimension is apparent in the way in which Putin, for the clearest example, deploys a rhetoric about sexuality to retain his power. Snyder points out that, after 2012, Putin pitched himself as a standard-bearer against a new enemy of the State: the enemy included the European Union and the democratic States. Democracy protesters 'were mindless agents of global sexual decadence'; Medvedev called one of the leaders 'a stupid cocksucking sheep'; Putin said that the white ribbons worn by democracy protesters 'made him

[27] Timothy Snyder, *The Road to Unfreedom* (Bodley Head, London, 2018), 8.

think of condoms'. Snyder goes on: 'The purpose of the anti-gay campaign was to transform demands for democracy into a nebulous threat to Russian innocence: voting = West = sodomy' and Putin presented himself as one who 'was offering masculinity as an argument against democracy'.[28]

The precedent for this kind of politics is set in European laws in the nineteenth century. In fact, however, the censorious attitude of the nineteenth-century State (and in totalitarian States ever since) is deployed in the interests of constructing an account of sexual life that actually runs counter to the empirical realities of everyday life. The legislation does not deal with reality; rather, it strives to censor the reality of sexual activities (including adultery, homosexuality, feminist demands) out of account. The reason for this is that the State believes that sex threatens a disordering of the established polity, a polity governed by intrinsic inequalities based in its class stratification. This is especially the case when sex becomes a matter of public interest and discussion, as it does with its appearance in literature, for example.

The real concern here, as far as the State is concerned, is the fear that if a significant number of 'ordinary people' meet in a free assembly – the space or forum for a discussion around a text, say – then it is possible that this emergent mass will act collectively to change the way in which the socio-sexual organization of the polity protects existing privilege, including above all financial privilege. Central to this is the determination of the State to insist, explicitly if need be, on a polity that establishes a normative idea of biological man as heterosexual and as the agent of sexual activity, and woman as an always passive recipient of such activity. Baudelaire's lesbians, or Flaubert's adulterous Emma, as also Courbet's paintings of prostitutes, driven as they are by a desire that stands outside of this order, must be rendered invisible. At the very least, they cannot be validated in the accepted forum of public art; and, in this way, Courbet's Realism, for instance, becomes marked by its opposition to existing social norms and is viewed as material that, at best, will be kept private.

This is why something like Courbet's painting of *L'Origine du Monde* is utterly and intrinsically shocking: a painting commissioned as erotic art for a private individual (though an individual in a political role), Khalil Bey, displays in as public a manner as possible that which the society requires us not to see: female genitalia. The performance artist, Deborah De Robertis, has highlighted this attitude in recent times. In 2014, she sat before Courbet's painting, with her genitals entirely exposed; in 2016, she 'performed' a live version of Manet's

---

[28] Ibid., 51–3.

Olympia, lying down entirely nude in front of the painting. In both cases, she was making some explicit political arguments about sexual hypocrisies; but she was also exhibiting very clearly a concern with how such a politics can be siphoned off into an ostensibly discrete world of aesthetics, and her performance was determined to reintroduce such aesthetics back into material political realities. She was arrested.

The issue of law and legislation becomes instrumental not just in determining what can be seen or read by the general assembly of public associations, but also in allowing the State essentially to decide on what it is that constitutes reality itself. That is to say, we find a distinction between 'legitimate' reality, a reality that can be acknowledged as such and therefore represented, and an 'illegitimate' account of the world, one whose illegitimacy must eventually be pronounced not just illegitimate but also illegal. Censorship of various representations of reality starts to become censorship of reality itself. This takes its place not just in terms of the law regarding burials, say, but also the laws that are developed to police sexual activity and, above all, in this period – the age of Proudhon, Marx, Engels, Dickens, Martineau, Zola, Turgenev – labour.

As with sex, then, so also with the movement of labour. The first realist paintings, on the easel of Courbet as he worked under the influence of Proudhon, for instance, often will depict labour in a somewhat abstract form. When he shows men at work, for example, the individuality of the men is less important than the actual work being carried out in the images. That is to say, realist painting in the latter half of the nineteenth century concentrates attention on labour-as-such. By doing so, it can attend to the real conditions under which ordinary people work. There is no deviation from that realism into a sentimental attachment to individuals (such as we would see in Dickens, say), nothing that might divert attention from the real facts of work or conditions of labour onto the 'spirit' of an individual character or figure.

As Marx and others knew, all societies structured around forms of class inequality must find a means through which to conserve and protect their own structure and ideology. The key to this is education; and an education that can be underpinned by legal means within a State is an education that itself becomes committed to presenting a specific ideology as somehow natural, incontestable: 'realistic'. Between *Hard Times* and *Bleak House*, we find this played out in Dickens. Behind these texts, however, there lie very profound political determinations of the condition of education in England, and also in France. In both jurisdictions, the State strives to find methods that will ensure that the political realities that govern everyday life will persist beyond the present moment. In France, State education, via the Falloux Laws, comes under the guidance of eternity: the Church becomes the fundamental 'law' that will prioritize the life beyond the grave over existing conditions of life, especially for the poor. There is a direction of the eyes of citizens away from the realities of labour, sex and death towards instead a law that claims to transcend those conditions, and to find reality elsewhere.

The importance of Dickens to our case is that his writing contests this, not just in terms of content, but in terms of the newer experimental form in which he presented *Bleak House*. Against the norms of an omniscient narrator, he offers a fiction with explicitly competing points of view: the intercalated chapters hovering between Esther's voice and that of the narrator. Falloux – and the State – wanted a univocal and unquestionable account of reality. Dickens proposes a fiction, exposing the conditions of a totalizing legal system, in which such a unified account of the world can no longer stand. Once this is done, he is able also to present labour in a similar fashion: no longer simply the story told by a master or factory owner, but now a story with a different voice or point of view.

In 1854, Dickens visited Preston, a town where a strike would give him material for his novel. Thirty years later, Zola visited Anzin, where a prolonged miners' strike gave him not just material but also *documents*. Here, for Zola, was something that would allow his novels to assume the status that was now being afforded to the laboratory sciences: the documents grounded his fictions in the real world. It is also at this moment that novels start themselves to assume a new 'documentary' status; for it is at this moment that the advanced economies inaugurate an institutionalization of some forms of writing as 'literature', and begin formally to teach them in the schools and universities. Crucially, the State also now intervenes and explains *how* the new documents of literature will be taught: that is to say, they legislate in order to educate the emerging civic masses in what can be regarded and accepted as valid representations of the world as it should *really* be. Education in the documents is an education in realism, and considers itself to be a window on the ideal world, a mirror in which the citizen can examine herself or himself with a view to ensuring that they conform to that ideal.

The issue for the politics of realism, of course, is that not every citizen does indeed conform to the ideal. That is precisely what makes the citizen interesting, noteworthy. Most typically, she or he stands at an angle to the world, and finds the mirror to be a distortion. If these citizens do not then modify themselves, they do not 'fit in'; and, in 'standing out' they also start to speak out. This is the emergence, in fiction, of the figure of the critical intellectual; and its primary appearance is in Turgenev. In the latter decades of the nineteenth century, Russia witnesses a series of political struggles that will eventuate in a full revolution in 1917. In the hinterland of those struggles, we find the emergence of a new theoretical proposition, one that suggests that the function of art is not at all to give a faithful representation of reality, but rather to 'de-familiarize' the world. Russian Formalism, considering itself to be scientific and therefore determined to locate the precise occurrence of 'literariness', will focus on how it is that texts revitalize perception by making the world seem strange. That is to say: they indicate that the world 'as it is' can *really* be different. Such manoeuvring is itself strongly contested, of course; and, once again, the role of education in literature as a key foundation for the existence of the State and its polity comes into view. Further, education now starts to come under the jurisdiction of 'the people', a process in which 'the people' must itself be constructed as a real entity, and as an entity that will determine the real conditions of everyday life.

That construction of 'the people', of course, is not without controversy. People themselves do not often get much say in what 'the people' wants, for 'the people' is made by those who would usually exclude themselves from the category. Politicians, as we know, routinely call upon such a construct: in one way, they 'occupy' the space of 'the people', taking it over, giving it its direction; and they do so in the name of authenticity and truth. Yet, as Hannah Arendt has repeatedly shown, the relation of politics to truth is not and never has been straightforward.

She put the basic proposition here most succinctly when she argued that political lying is bound, more intimately than we might wish, to political action. She disturbs a clichéd view of political virtues by a straightforward observation that truth does not have any prime place in politics. If politics is concerned with the fruition of debate into actions, then it is lying that has a more privileged place here. One reason for this is that in order to bring about change, an existing state of affairs must be dismantled. 'Such change would be impossible', she argues 'if we could not mentally remove ourselves from where we are physically located and *imagine* that things might as well be different from what they actually are'. Thus it is, logically, that 'the deliberate denial of factual truth – the ability to lie – and the capacity to change facts – the ability to act – are interconnected'.[29]

The new development in all of this has become troublingly apparent. To lie, in the historical conditions described by Arendt, requires nonetheless a belief

---

[29] Hannah Arendt, 'Lying in Politics', in Arendt, *Crises of the Republic* (Harcourt Brace & Company, New York, 1972), 5.

that there remains some relation between a political (lying) statement and a (genuine) reality. Now, however, political discourse increasingly removes itself from reference to material realities completely; and so, lying has become not just so routine but, much more significantly, so *brazen* that it destroys the democratic function of debate entirely. 'Tiananmen did not happen; nothing to discuss, and nothing to represent.' Snyder describes the phenomenon through the example of Putin, who, according to the journalist Charles Clover, 'has correctly surmised that lies unite rather than divide Russia's political class. The greater and more obvious the lie, the more his subjects demonstrate their loyalty by accepting it, and the more they participate in the great sacral mystery of Kremlin power.'[30] We are operating in an environment 'where lies are accepted enthusiastically precisely because they are lies.'[31] What began as a political ideal of transparency has become simple brazenness, a mockery of the idea of the citizen engaged in serious debate as a means of finding the best form of Aristotelian association.

These various strands in the historical politics of realism now also confront new media: film and television above all. John Grierson coins the term 'documentary' to describe a very specific kind of realist film. The core of Grierson's work, in terms of the content of his first films, is in what he considers to be the pure dignity of labour as such. In terms of purpose, the core is found in education, a term that he insists is close to propaganda. Combined, Grierson takes these aims in order to make the real and underlying conditions of modern and contemporary life available to a general public, a people, to whom such access is structurally denied. The same manoeuvre was undertaken, with equally controversial consequences, by Anatoly Lunacharsky, Lenin's first Commissar for Education after the Revolution. It is obvious, of course, that documentary is not intrinsically governed by any one political persuasion. Against the kind of drive that we see in Grierson and his followers, there is also the prime example of Leni Riefenstahl. The whole philosophy of documentary, in terms of its relation to realism, pays substantial dividends; and, through it, we see not necessarily a 'triumph of the will' but certainly the rise of 'the will of the people' as a will that underpins the realist impetus. There is, as it were, a new popular account of realism.

That account makes its way into British culture in a new way after 1968 when the Theatre Act is passed, ostensibly releasing theatre from the shackles of the State censor, the Lord Chamberlain. The first response to this is one that

---

[30] Snyder, *Road to Unfreedom*, 163. For the original, see Charles Clover, *Black Wind, White Snow: The Rise of Russia's New Nationalism* (Yale University Press, New Haven, 2016), 19.
[31] Clover, *Black Wind, White Snow*, 19.

witnesses a crude sense of realism as a 'stripping bare' of all that is decorous; and that stripping is realized in literal form with the eruption of stage and staged nudity. Suddenly, what Grierson referred to as 'the intimate things of common life' are revealed. However, the period also seems the emergence of new forms of documentary realism, some involving narrative, with a genuinely serious political drive and energy. By this stage, it is clear that the purpose of documentary realism is less to 'reveal' reality and more to change the existing conditions of life in a society. Yet, even prior to this 1968 moment, we have seen in Italy precisely this same determination. Neorealist cinema, made under difficult work conditions and in the face of potential murder at the hands of Nazis and Fascists, is exemplary in its determination to focus on the ways in which the control and regulation of sex, labour and bio-politics conditions everyday life. More than this, the films have a clear message; and it is one that is, in some ways, also the message of this argument as a whole. Up until now, the artists have tried to represent the world and its reality; the point, however, is to change it.

That desire for change is sometimes crudely conceived as utopian. My closing chapter examines two ostensibly dystopian novels, Orwell's *Nineteen Eighty-Four* and Eggers's *The Circle*. These texts encourage an analysis of totalitarian realism; and their conclusions are indeed bleak. The kind of change demanded by neorealism becomes less and less available, these novels suggest. The reason – and the warning – is clear. In our moment, the real question that needs to be addressed is not just the politics of realism, but also the way in which contemporary societies and cultures have embraced the unreality of politics, making any action in the political sphere at best limited and at worst impossible. Censorship of texts becomes less important when the State can effectively censor the very idea of citizenship.

In his 1996 novel, *Reading in the Dark*, Seamus Deane recounts 'The Facts of Life'. The young Deane is being given an education in the facts of sex by the priest at his school. When the priest gets to the bit about intercourse, 'here my curiosity did light up, for I didn't know, though I had heard much, what this was. What I had heard was certainly improbable. It sounded like a feat of precision engineering', against which the character scented the reality of 'lust, which seemed wild, fierce, devil-may-care, like eating and drinking together while dancing to music on top of the table'. The basic curiosity here is what informs the critical attitude. The clash between scientific-engineering fact and reality is clear. Above all, however, there is the boy's attitude: 'I knew, but did not know. I wanted to know, but did not want to find out that I already knew. I wanted to know something different'.[32] The relation of education to reality, and the purpose to change reality, through the body itself, is at the core of this.

Deane makes it comic; but he knows, too, of the political reality that haunts such a critical attitude. In our time, the predicament is severe: to reveal and even change the real is made difficult when the advanced political economies find themselves governed by demagogic oligarchs whose determination now is not just to keep things the way they are, but actually to wage war against reality itself. Peter Pomerantsev, from whom I here borrow the phrase 'war against reality' has recently shown how 'More information was supposed to mean more freedom to stand up to the powerful, but it's also given them new ways to crush and silence dissent'. It was once the province of journalists, writers, artists to get to the heart of the real world's action and, from there, 'to report information on reality'; however, 'information itself is now where the action is'.[33] The very surfeit of information is what increasingly diverts attention to the realities of politics.

How we got here is the substance of this book's argument.

---

[32] Seamus Deane, *Reading in the Dark* (Jonathan Cape, London, 1996), 150.
[33] Peter Pomerantsev, *This Is Not Propaganda: Adventures in the War against Reality* (Faber and Faber, London, 2019), 4, 21.

Part I

Controlling the real and its representations

1

Assembly

Reality and the commerce of censorship

1

What is it that lies behind a recurring and insistent fear over representations? Why is it that some cultures fear representation so much that they determine to prohibit it, or at least to circumscribe it? In many cultures, at many historical moments, there has been an insistence on taming the power of representation, as if representation as such poses a fundamental and even an existential threat. Why is that so?

An anxiety about the power of the image has been with us for a long time, both in advanced and in developing economies. This extends beyond the visual image, and includes the imagining of speech or behaviour. The image has always been considered as something that exerts power or that is the source of a power that is mysterious, not immediately available to consciousness or to linguistic explanation. We have thus been suspicious of its ability to enchant us, to charm or seduce us, perhaps against our conscious or rational will. At the same time, aware of such power, we have often tried to overcome our anxiety by harnessing images – manipulating and controlling them – to make them instrumental in the furthering of our own ends, and to make use of them to exert our own power over others.

It is often mooted, further, that images have come more and more to dominate our culture and our social and political lives. W. J. T. Mitchell rightly reminds us that 'it is a commonplace of cultural criticism that images have a power in our world undreamed of by the ancient idolaters'. Historically, one way of dealing with these anxieties has been to attack images directly; and it is pretty clearly true to say that 'iconoclasm has a history at least as old as idolatry'.[1] With this in mind, we might even suggest that one way of

---

[1] W. J. T. Mitchell, *Iconology* (University of Chicago Press, Chicago, 1986), 7–8, 198. See also David Freedberg, *The Power of Images* (University of Chicago Press, Chicago, 1989) for another history of how images have operated as sources of power.

understanding history – at least in its cultural manifestations – is to see it as being primarily a constant battle between rival images. If we want to be more precise and specific, we might say that the history of culture is the history of struggles over rival images and their respective power, and that material history is really the history of representations of what constitutes the realities of the world and of our lives. A contestation around images is also, intrinsically, a contestation over the status of reality itself: the image is an instrument in the determination of an individual or group to control historical realities. There can be little doubt that our anxieties about representation are really the symptomatic evidence of a much more fundamental issue regarding the way we construct our polities.

Famously, Plato exiles the poets from his ideal Republic on the stated and entirely clear and simple grounds that they are good at representing things. Indeed, the ostensible logic of Socrates's argument in *Republic* is that the better the poets are at representation, the more dangerous they become in the ideal State. The Guardians of the ideal State – who turn to poetry for their education – 'should neither do a mean action, nor be clever at acting a mean or otherwise disgraceful part on the stage for fear of catching the infection in real life', argues Socrates.[2] The power of the image and of representation poses an especial risk, it might seem from this, to our processes of education and of acculturation. Such thinking reveals a good deal about what we consider to be the purposes of education, of course; but it also reveals an intrinsic link between education and modes of censorship.

As Plato's argument develops in *Republic*, Socrates 'proves' that it is imitation as such (*mimesis*) – as opposed to narration (*diegesis*) – that is inherently risky. That is an important distinction, not always adequately noted in the standard understanding of this ancient text. Socrates/Plato does not, in fact, banish the poets as such; rather, he argues that while *narrative representation* might be useful, *mimetic representation* poses a threat. In narrative, there is a significant aesthetic distance between the reader/listener and the actions that the narrative describes: the actions are events carried out by others. Narratives yield descriptions of events over which we can stand in detached judgement. By contrast, in imitated speech, an intimacy is achieved, through which the reader/audience can identify with the author/speaker of a text or an individual speech. There is therefore the strong possibility, in mimetic modes of representation, that we will suffer from what Dominick LaCapra has usefully characterized – following Socrates in this,

---

[2] Plato, *Republic* (trans. Desmond Lee; Penguin, London, 1976), 153 (Book III; §395d).

even if he does not explicitly note the fact – as a form of 'mimetic contagion'.³ If we repeat – or represent – an immoral character, say, then we run the risk of so imbibing the immorality that we in turn become 'really' immoral, not in a fiction but in material living. The representation, via mimetic imitation, of anything other than the good (or even perfection), is thus to be forbidden in the logic of Plato's account of Socratic teaching.

Plato is not unique, of course, in raising these or similar fears. Some of the world's major religions express, deep in their early formulations, a similar concern about representation. There is an anxiety that 'false gods' and any other figural representations might supplant the supposedly 'real thing', and lead people into iconophilia or idolatry. In Judaism, for instance, the logic can be straightforwardly expressed. By definition in Judaism, first and foremost God is incorporeal: spirit in the purest form. God, in this logic, exceeds the bounds of space and time, since these are things that can be understood materially. If we hold these two things together, we find that God cannot be represented, since there is no bounded 'presence' there to be re-presented in the first place; and therefore, any claim to represent that which has no initial bounded presence must be, intrinsically, a falsification. Representation is therefore prohibited, quite simply because it would be a falsification of the very essence of God and thus tantamount to the undermining of divine being. From this, a generalized anxiety – about the validity of representation and the possibility that it will always be tinged not just by falsehood but also by the very denial of the reality that it purports to represent – becomes more widespread.

Representations, in the kind of logic that shapes such religious or philosophical beliefs, need to be policed in some ways: we need the imposition of laws, or at least of shared norms, if we are to establish the priority of the correct over the wrong, and the good over the bad. In fact, the proposition is even greater than this: we need such laws if we are to hang onto reality itself, to prioritize the claims of 'how things really are' over 'how things might be' or 'how they are not'. Laws – and censorship – become fundamental to the 'protection' of something that asserts its logical priority. In religions, that prior reality is spiritual; but, once we leave the sphere of religion, this changes. We remain influenced by the logic, but in the secular condition – beyond religion – laws and censorship operate to protect the very priority of material and historical reality itself over the ostensibly immaterial 'unreality' of imagination in its

---

³ See Dominick LaCapra, *Madame Bovary on Trial* (Cornell University Press, Ithaca, 1982), 28.

literal sense as image-making. As we will see in this book, the consequence is that we enter the domain in which reality itself is intrinsically politicized, such that we have, for the first time, a politics of realism. The politics of realism is basic to a culture in which there is a struggle over representations of the world, for those representations are a vehicle for the gaining and retention of political power. Representations 'of' the real become central to a struggle for control 'over' the real, by the indirect means of aesthetic images.

2

The Judaic injunction against 'graven images' – like the Koranic suspicion of figural representations – leads religiously inspired thought to move away from sensuality to abstraction, from sensibility to sense, or from emotional engagement to detached reasoning. One reason why Judaism is considered by many to be so centred on 'the book' is because of the Mosaic necessity of translating sensual figural representations into the abstraction of words.

A proscription against images similar to that which exists in Judaism – or at least a warning regarding their power – appears to be advanced also in the Koran, in Surah 21, verses 52–69, where the worship around images is described as a 'manifest error'. However, in this case, the logic is that the images and idols are themselves intrinsically weak, indeed so weak that they cannot protect themselves against their own destruction. Yet the images and idols are seductive nonetheless; and to be seduced by them is to be diverted from attending to the reality of a deity and thus to be led astray from a supposed path of truth and reality.

As in Plato, it is as if perfection – here, theologically considered in Islam and Judaism – is itself negated, demeaned and denigrated by representation, because a representation can never be the original, even and especially as it aspires to yield up, or pretends to yield up, that very original and make it available to us in material terms. This is all the more the case when the original is itself materially absent (like the supposed perfection of a hidden god, say), and when all that we might have to go on to warrant its existence is, indeed, a representation.

Although Christianity too is suspicious of idolatry, it has nonetheless historically demonstrated a complex relation to images, hovering uncertainly between Calvinist Presbyterian austerity and gorgeous Roman luxuriousness. Historically, many wars of religion are wars that are fundamentally conditioned by the status that we give to bodily sensuality. A Christian crusade, for example, is fought literally under the leading sign of a body on a cross, whose complex iconography is intended not just to signify a religious responsibility but also literally to embody it. Signification invites words and disputed meanings; the sensuous immediacy of the body on a cross is intended to deny the very possibility of disputed meaning; and this is because what is at stake here is not discursive meanings but rather the supposed facts that underpin and justify faith and of a felt and experienced immediacy of belief, a belief immediately given through the image itself. Such wars are centred on the relative status that a religion gives to the power of the senses and to the attitudes that we might have to the primacy of sensuality over abstraction, emotion over reason, bodily feeling over rational thinking. That is to say – and this is a significant logical corollary of the foregoing observations – such wars are conditioned by our attitude to aesthetics itself, by our attitudes to bodily perceptions and sensualities.

War itself, historically, has been shaped by a very specific priority of aesthetics. Virtually all war strategy is conditioned by one dominant feature: the determination to make oneself unseen or invisible, occluding one's physical presence, while simultaneously trying to reveal, as clearly as possible, the body of the enemy. It is a struggle over transparency, we might say, or over the control of appearance and disappearance. Camouflage enables a soldier to disappear or to have no representation of herself or himself. The self in camouflage – while actually being there – is not represented, instead merging into a 'natural' background that renders a military threat invisible. Paul Virilio, urbanist and theorist of war, cites the case of the French Maquis during the Second World War. The *maquisard*, he writes, has to melt into a general topography; and so 'he sits under the cover of grass and tree, atmospheric disturbances, night itself',[4] and in this way the maquisard 'self-censors', as it were, merging the presentation of herself or himself into a background.

Indeed, Virilio mounts an entire model of society based on this foundational observation. It is an observation that illustrates the primacy of war or struggle – themselves based upon the *representability* of the military – as fundamental to the politics of realism. The whole of society, he argues, depends upon the regulation of what he calls 'the aesthetics of disappearance': our daily human and socio-political relations depend on the play of appearance and disappearance, in the establishment of a kind of society of strategic subterfuge. Such strategic subterfuge depends on a mode of censorship: the rendering invisible of that whose presence might change our social hierarchies. The intrinsic war-mentality

---

[4] Paul Virilio, *L'Horizon négatif* (Galilée, Paris, 1984), 100 (trans. mine).

underlying this – that play of forces that regulates all social relation – has its roots in a logic of aesthetics, or the play of appearance and disappearance.

Controversially, Virilio writes that, in the guise of war, we find a basic socio-sexual relation. War-paint or camouflage is a model for the daily presentation of the body and face under make-up, such that war becomes a precedent for love. It follows, in his logic, that

> the seduction of the disguised warrior is . . . the characteristic of the male, and thus the homosexuality of the duel is the foundation of the beautiful, the beautiful that is itself but the first degree of torture inflicted upon the body, in marks and scarifications, scars, up to and including mutilation and death. Perhaps the beautiful is the first *uniform*.[5]

In this respect, war links censorship to matters as fundamental as the religious veil, or religious ritual, or any forms of official ceremony and pageantry; and many of these, of course, are also fundamental to the ways in which we represent to ourselves our political States, and the place of our bodies within those States.

I have grounded some of this introductory section on Plato; but modern and contemporary Greece is also illustrative of some of the issues here around the censorship of the image and of its place in politics. David Runciman describes the way in which a more or less 'standard' coup d'état happened in mid-twentieth-century democracies, and points out that when the colonels effected their coup in 1967 Greece, it was imperative to their success in taking power not only that the coup was quickly carried out but also that it was made very visible. The military took control of radio and TV stations, and broadcast the fact of their coup and its consequences: 'The colonels marked their coup by making sure everyone understood what had changed'; and a part of that was the broadcasting of an image, that of the Greek flag, on TV screens across the nation.[6]

The interesting thing, however, is what has happened in Greece more recently. After the financial crisis of 2008, Greece entered a difficult social and political period. By 2011, there was a stand-off between the Greek government and the European troika of financial and political institutions (European Central Bank, European Commission and the International Monetary Fund). Yanis Varoufakis, as Greek finance minister, decided that it was imperative that Greece stood firm against the various economic demands that were being made by the troika as a

---

[5] Ibid., 101–2 [trans.mine]. For more on the logic underpinning Virilio's argument here, see, alongside *L'Horizon négatif*, his *Défense populaire et luttes écologiques* (Galilée, Paris, 1978), *Esthétique de la Disparition* (1980; Galilée, Paris, 1989), and his work with Sylvère Lotringer, *Pure War* (trans. Mark Polizotti; Semiotext(e), New York, 1988).

[6] David Runciman, *How Democracy Ends* (Profile Books, London, 2019), 35.

condition of securing financial support; and his prime minster, Alexis Tsipras, disagreed – and Tsipras prevailed. Varoufakis considered this to be another kind of coup, this time led by the finance institutions and the banks. As Runciman puts it, Varoufakis, who had been a child when the colonels took power, saw one fundamental difference. Then, in 1967, the colonels were open about what they were doing. Now, though, in 2011, 'television stations still play an important propaganda role, but what matters is what is kept *off* the screens. The government and the banks do what they can to prevent the spread of bad news.'[7]

In 1967, we had a kind of explicit iconography of the coup; in 2011, a kind of silent iconoclasm is at work. In both cases, Plato's concern about representation operates; and in both cases, the issue of censorship becomes a crucial determining force. In 1967, the display of an image – the Greek flag – becomes a marker that initiates a process of explicit political and social censorship, including the repression of dissident ideas. In 2011, the coup 'censors' itself, and the banks assume a power precisely by eliminating the image of themselves doing so.

It may turn out to be the case that the organization of any society requires censorship to be in play, as an intrinsic requirement of the regulation of norms that allow individuals to live socially at all. It may further be the case that censorship is best understood in terms of its relation to the logic of both war and aesthetics, while the case of 2011 Greece indicates that we will also have to consider the place of economics in the structures that govern the legitimacy and legality of representations in our societies.

3

Cultural history, then, is full of instances of fears around representation; and these fears historically have led to various forms of suppression, repression and oppression as we entered into various modulations of social, cultural and political modernity. During the sixteenth century, for example, the Office of the Master of the Revels, for instance, assumed a growing importance for the English State, and operated as an initial vehicle of State censorship of theatre. At that historical moment, it is not a simple question of direct censoring, in the sense that we might give that word today: determined prohibition of particular writings or statements by a heavy-handed surveillance- or police-State whose offices subject citizens to constant monitory audit. According to some accounts

---

[7] Ibid., 34.

that scholarship has given of this period, writers are extremely aware of the presence and functions of the Office; and some of them essentially internalize its workings such that their works do not need overt censoring, because they have self-censored.[8] Others have pointed out that the Office was rather haphazard in its workings, leading to a condition in which writers and the Master's Office were engaged together, really working tacitly as partners, in a form of 'editorial' activity, in which the content of writings was negotiated, almost as if there were a kind of collaboration going on between the writer and the State in order to determine what would be 'speakable', even comprehensible.[9]

Regardless of where we stand on this spectrum of scholarly understanding, the rationale that guides such censorship is not always philosophically straightforward. Ostensibly, the establishment of the Office of the Master of the Revels, with its attendant quasi-censorship duties, suggests that State authorities are concerned about the representation of immorality, specifically on the theatrical stage; and the stated fear is that the representation of immorality on the stage might work to legitimize immoral actions outside of the theatre. This is all the more likely, it is felt, if the audience enjoys watching the action, or if they sympathize with its actors and agents as they imitate their engagement in illicit or immoral activities.

As in Socrates's argument, as represented by Plato, representation operates as a kind of disease, threatening us with the contagious spread of illness, an illness that will breed corruption in the otherwise supposedly healthy State. It is perhaps worth indicating at this point that 'health' in these terms means the extent to which an individual acts in conformity with what the State-powers decide as the operative norms of the State as such, and conformity with what such State power legislates for as acceptable living and thinking.

The intricacy of Plato's text, however, should also be clarified definitively at this point. In the argument in Book III of *Republic*, Socrates makes that basic distinction I adverted to earlier between *mimesis* (the imitation of spoken words by an actor) and *diegesis* (the more neutral narration of 'what happened' in a story, without direct speeches being imitated or represented). *Diegesis* is permitted; but *mimesis* is dangerous and threatening.

So far, so clear, we might think. However, in *Republic* Book III, Plato proposes an argument that bans mimetic imitation; but he does so through a dialogue

---

[8] This is the case argued by Janet Clare, *Art Made Tongue-tied by Authority* (Manchester University Press, Manchester, 1999). Clare takes a robust absolutist line regarding State censorship, stressing its fundamental and systemic grounds in State authoritarianism.
[9] See Richard Dutton, *Mastering the Revels* (Macmillan, London, 1981).

that is constituted entirely by precisely the kind of mimetic imitation that it ostensibly banishes. The ironic logic here is one that provides us with a logical impasse, well known in our time as a kind of deconstructive aporia, or what in the seventeenth century Thomas Browne would have declared as a moment when reason has been pursued to the point where we must exclaim 'O altitudo!'.[10] If we subscribe to Socrates's argument regarding the danger of *mimesis*, then we must dismiss Socrates's argument because it is itself mimetic; but, having dismissed his argument and, with it, the entirely mimetic text of *The Republic*, we can now happily and logically reinstate once again the mimetic text of *The Republic* which, again, requires that we dismiss it; and so on, without resolution. The point about *Republic* is that it raises the question of censorship, fails determinedly to resolve it and drives us instead into a quandary through which we can start to explore its fundamental structure and function.

'Mimetic contagion' leads us into this obvious post-Platonic and quasi-deconstructive impasse. For the Master of the Revels in the sixteenth-century English State – and, indeed, for the organization of any political State – such an impasse must be overcome; and a formal position must be decided, and must be adopted as a matter of policy. In this early modern period, there is another element that enters the calculations and that helps give a definitive form to the meaning of State censorship. The ostensible moral stance advertised by the Office of the Master of the Revels is, in fact, actually a cover for something else. We can consider this more fully by exploring one seeming extremist and intrinsically fundamentalist censorious position: the formal closure of theatres in 1642.

One standard understanding of the closure has been that it was a Puritan-inspired stance against drama as a matter of religious or, more broadly, ethical principle. If that were the case, then it would seem to be a real-world realization of the primary and superficial meaning of Socrates's argument in Plato's *Republic*: imitation – acting out something that does not stem from the spontaneity of authentic selfhood – breeds a menacing corruption in the State. The facts, however, do not bear this out. As Margot Heinemann pointed out long ago, in her 1980 study *Puritanism and Theatre*, the assault upon theatre was not necessarily driven by any residual Platonic anxiety about 'the wickedness of disguise or impersonation'. In matter of documented fact, it was 'primarily though not exclusively an attack on the common players as idlers and vagabonds'; and the primary concerns of the State and civic authorities who enforced the ban derived

---

[10] Thomas Browne, 'Religio Medici', in *Sir Thomas Browne: The Major Works*, ed. C. A. Patrides (Penguin, London, 1977), 69: 'I love to lose myself in a mystery, to pursue my reason to an O altitudo!'.

from their sense that theatre presented a 'danger to law and order' because of the 'social atmosphere in the commercial theatres'.[11]

The period around 1642 was one in which crowds were making their presence felt in that newly emergent form of assembly – the innovation of a 'citizens' assembly' – that we now identify as 'the modern city'; and these crowds were often made up of individuals whose roots were in the country, where populations had been more widely dispersed spatially and practically. As internal migrants, many erstwhile rural people had come to the cities in search of financial security or advancement; and, as such, they were somewhat uprooted individuals, individuals seeking a new identity, new affiliations, and the security of higher income and wealth. That is to say, to the civic authorities they presented an obvious threat to the existing social and civic order of things, perhaps especially to the existing uneven distribution of the wealth that was being hoarded in these new civic spaces and institutions. The suppression of theatre, in fact, was largely driven by social and economic priorities rather than purely or even primarily ethical concerns about representations.

Heinemann notes that 'hostility to plays' was not by any means limited to Puritans and their religious ideology. She notes its prevalence elsewhere in Catholic Europe; and so, the driving force behind the closure of theatres must be considered as more complex than any simple ban based on a belief that 'disguise is sinful and imitation a form of lying'.[12] In the new growing cities across Europe, plays 'caused traffic jams and spread infection in time of plague'. In doing so, they threatened the growing spread of commercial transactions, which depended on the speedy transportation of goods, and upon safety in public health.

The rhetoric concerning the intrinsic menace of representation – around plague, infection, contamination and disease – continues until our present time. When she considers the state of political debate after 9/11, Judith Butler finds that social norms, based upon a mode of representation, preclude the possibility of us hearing the voices of non-US nationals. The representation of the meaning of 9/11 always seems to have to begin from what she calls a 'first-person' narrative point of view, centred upon the first-person I that is the United States: the United States as subject and simultaneously as victim. While she accepts that the United States is a victim in the events of that day, 9/11, she asks that we also hear narratives and representations of the event from others, from second- and third-person narratives. Instead of this, we get a deep disavowal of the

---

[11] Margot Heinemann, *Puritanism and Theatre* (Cambridge University Press, Cambridge, 1980), 27.
[12] Ibid., 31.

possibility of such representations, 'as if to explain these events would involve us in a sympathetic identification with the oppressor'. We are in a position where 'our fear of understanding a point of view [other than that of ourselves, as "first-person" narrators] belies a deeper fear that we shall be taken up by it, find it is contagious, become infected in a morally perilous way by the thinking of the presumed enemy'.[13]

With respect to questions about the threats and dangers of permitted representations, we are still operating today within the rhetoric that shaped seventeenth-century oppressive attitudes to crowds, and to theatrical representation. Then, above all, theatres 'gave an opportunity for the unemployed and idle to meet in riotous assemblies'.[14] This is the fundamental sequence of reasoning that lies behind the closure of the theatres. They represent a threat to commerce, a threat that derives from the fact that a developing civic culture itself generates not only wealth but also the exclusion of some individuals from that wealth. That is to say, modernity and the emergence of the city here are tied to what we have since come to call – in our own contemporary moment – growth in GDP: the stimulation of commercial and financial activities. That growth, however, is not evenly distributed among its agents and among citizens (either now or in the seventeenth century's emergence into civic modernity); and the result is some disaffection among those who do not benefit from it or participate in its spread.

The real disease that threatens the modern city with its contagion is not plague, but money. However, for those who stood to gain increases in personal and individual wealth, it is crucial to re-describe wealth as health, and to recast the opposition among the poor to its unjust distribution as an infestation, plague or disease. Thus it is that actors themselves become recast as unclean and menacing vagabonds. That rhetorical move is important if the already privileged are going to protect their properties, wealth and social position. It is a rhetorical move, further, that allows the privileged to present themselves as morally upright and healthy, concerned with social and public health in every sense, and not simply or crudely as selfishly interested in preserving their existing privileges.[15]

---

[13] Judith Butler, *Precarious Life* (Verso, London, 2003; 2006), 8.
[14] Heinemann, *Puritanism and Theatre*, 33.
[15] Precisely the same rhetoric shapes contemporary conservative attitudes to migration. Migrants are recast as disease-ridden threats allegedly infecting the purity of the host nation; but that host nation is invariably one that is in the position of an advanced economy; and the conservative is simply trying to ensure that her or his existing wealth privilege will not be threatened, and that she or he will not have to share their wealth more equally with those from less prosperous conditions. To state this baldly would make the host appear to be mean-spirited, unethical; and so the question of wealth preservation is recast in terms of public health – as if the wealthy individual conservative in the host nation really cared about her or his own domestic poor.

Indeed, in some ways this goes towards offering an explanation as to why it is the case that the arts in general have historically been seen as a threat of some kind. That attitude pertains, as we know, right up to our own contemporary moment. The arts in general are presented to us as incipiently a drain on a State's resources. However, that economic case is bolstered by a demand that the arts be kept under a particular kind of review, making them subject to censorship in ways that the laboratory sciences are not. This, of course, is not to imply that the sciences are themselves totally free of censorship; but regulation in the laboratory differs markedly from what is a more suspicious attitude regarding the arts. Increasingly, in the advanced economies, it is funding that is the mechanism for the control of scientific research. The fact that governments sometimes hold the purse strings for the funding of research has led many governments to arrogate to themselves the supposed right to intervene to establish scientific research priorities. It is in this way – when it happens – that scientific research is politicized. It is not censorship as such; but it does form an intervention of the State into the field of what can be known and discussed.

The disenfranchised in our modern cultures have time and energy – frustrated energy seeking an outlet and expression – to gather around places where 'the public' can assemble and share their time and speech, and where they can experiment with how to frame their shared voice. The theatre provided such an opportunity, and even a model for the trying on of new voices; and in this respect it is the freedom of assembly that the State and civic authorities fear – and perhaps have always feared – more than anything to do with the spread of immorality. What the State has historically always actually feared was and remains the uprising of disenfranchised people. Heinemann rightly indicates that, beyond London itself, 'the opposition of the city authorities in the main towns to performances by touring companies was demonstrably more marked in times of economic crisis'.[16]

Censorship is tied firmly to economic conditions – and, perhaps above all, to underlying suspicions about the power that lies vested in a free assembly of the disadvantaged – as this period finds itself emerging into new and modern polities.

---

[16] Heinemann, *Puritanism and Theatre*, 33.

4

Such an attitude informs more recent models of censorship, models whose effect persists until the present day in some of our cultural states. An important year in the history of this is 1857. That year saw the passing, in the UK, of the Obscene Publications Act in legislation that, although updated in 1959, persists even now, in the early twenty-first century, as a determining force in how we think of censorship and its purposes in the UK. In that same year, 'literature' itself went directly on trial, in the French jurisdiction and law courts of Paris. Between January and August that year, the French courts provided the setting for a high cultural and political drama: Flaubert found himself arraigned in January that year, on allegations that his novel, *Madame Bovary*, constituted an offence against public morality; and Baudelaire faced similar charges in August, when six poems in *Les Fleurs du Mal* were deemed to have caused similar offence.

Perhaps the first thing to note here relates to technology, and to the modes of distribution of literature. This takes us back to the earlier days of print, and to another court judgement, in England this time. In 1579, John Stubbs wrote and published *The Discovery of a Gaping Gulf*, 'an outspoken attack on Elizabeth's intended marriage' to Francis of Anjou and Alençon. The proposed marriage was highly controversial among many, and 'was widely regarded as grounds for popular rebellion'. Cyndia Susan Clegg cites the Spanish Ambassador's notes that a number of 'sermons preached before the Queen' spoke 'very violently about this marriage'.[17]

In response to the sermons, preached orally and directly in her presence, the Queen sought quiet advice. By contrast, the response to Stubbs's written tract was brutal. Alongside his publisher and printer, he was tried for seditious libel, found guilty, and suffered the penalty of amputation: his right hand was chopped off. The difference here lies in the fact that speech is local to and purely of its own occasion, while print is widely distributed and dispersed beyond the initial moment of writing. Technology changes things here, because it offers a putative assembly whose members are not even visible (readers elsewhere), an assembly that at least potentially opened the Queen and the State to troubles on the national and international stage.

Print technology makes it possible to establish an 'immaterial' assembly, a kind of potential or virtual assembly. The eighteenth century saw the development

---

[17] Cyndia Susan Clegg, *Press Censorship in Elizabethan England* (Cambridge University Press, Cambridge, 1997), 124–5.

of this, with the spread of newspapers; and this spread was mobilized largely in the middle-class milieu of the coffee-house – with its political and cultural debates, fuelled by the new drug of caffeine, quickened and further excited by the ingestion of sugar from the colonies – that helped to shape what might be thought and said as legitimate thought and speech. Cultural norms start to be established; and they work not by explicit censorship, but through this cultural complex of a relation between a somewhat nebulous immaterial community, or what Habermas thought of as 'the public sphere', and real material action.

By the time of the nineteenth century, this has taken a further turn. Some writings are now becoming described as being of a different status from the generality of the printed word: they are designated as being of lasting value and are described as 'literature', in our contemporary sense of that term, for the first time. As such – that is to say, as 'literature' – they are deemed intrinsically to find an audience beyond their immediate occurrence, an assembly that, because it cannot be precisely identified, can certainly therefore not be controlled, its actions resistant to predictability. Thus it is that Flaubert and Baudelaire found themselves in court; and thus it is that, at exactly this same time, in England, the Lord Chief Justice John Campbell takes a particular interest in printed material whose obscene contents shocked him. It was not only the content that shocked him, however; it was the ready availability of the printed matter, available for widespread distribution among the generality of the population that frightened him most.

However, it is important to ask what it was, exactly, that Campbell feared. On 9 May 1857, he heard a case in his court in which two men were being prosecuted for the sale of obscene materials. Shocked by the case, he told the House of Lords at its next sitting two days later that the city was facing infection from 'a poison more deadly than prussic acid, strychnine, or arsenic'. He would later extend the metaphor and would go on to describe the effects of the sale of obscene materials as being like the spread of leprosy. In this, we see the familiar line regarding a threat to the health of the nation. At this historical moment, the potential spread of leprosy was one of the prime concerns of the Royal College of Physicians in London. The fear was itself conditioned by colonial and imperial attitudes, in that leprosy was also being specifically associated with concerns over the health of British people in the British colonies; and so the fear here is also a fear of a foreign culture, the fear that, in taking control of foreign people, 'we' might become infected and afflicted by 'their' bad health and disease.

The specifics of Campbell's case make clear, however, the precise nature of his own personal – and political – fear. It relates directly to social class and to the protection of class privilege (themselves surely related to issues of Empire and political inequality more generally). He took the classic conservative line that the lower social classes have a kind of uncultivated and untrammelled animality, referring in his speeches directly to 'the potential animality of the working classes'.[18] The alleged animality arises from the sexually active body; and the suggestion is the classic one that working-class people are themselves not in control of their sexual energies. What he thought of as 'respectable society' needs to be protected from this. The logic is that sexual energy and activity can easily be re-channelled into generally disruptive social behaviour; and obscene *publications* encourage the assembling of that energy and its widespread distribution.

In this case, it is almost as if sex itself is the disease, and publication the vehicle through which the disease is transmitted. The published representation of sexual activity menaces not society as such, but rather only the upper and middle classes, because the working classes in their alleged animality have already fully internalized the disease; and, indeed, this class supposedly therefore actually embodies disease as such. It is not so much that the working classes are thereby inoculated against this supposed personal impairment-by-sex; rather, they have found a way of living with it – even if that mode of life is characterized as one of squalor. The point for Campbell is that if the disease spreads elsewhere, then comfortable middle-class life can itself become squalid; and who in their right mind, he thinks, would want to sacrifice their real-world privileges and comfort for the consequences that momentary sexual indulgence and pleasure might give? The argument is one that has its roots in the Faust legend. The whole question informing the logic of censorship in this argument, then, is a question about the 'moral character' of the nation, as allegedly embodied (literally) in the upper and middle classes. Censorship of the real conditions of everyday life for many people – 'the masses' – is important if we are to protect the existing privileges of that specific minority that we identify as the elite few.

Importantly, however, potential political unrest here is being tacitly construed as a 'representation' of sexual unrest; and the logic is that such representation must be curtailed, prohibited and censored. Campbell feared that individuals in the upper and middle classes might be 'seduced' by the obscene materials that he had seen, and that their own civic selfhood would have to deal with the potentially unsettling realization that they, too, have animal spirits that lie,

---

[18] See M. J. D. Roberts, 'Morals, Art, and the Law: The Passing of the Obscene Publications Act 1857', *Victorian Studies*, 28:4 (1985), 609–29. Campbell's words quoted here come from p 609, and are sourced by Roberts from *Hansard Parliamentary Debates*, 3rd series, vol. 145 (11 May 1857).

restrained, under their polished exterior.[19] In the sphere of imperialism, the grand-scale version of this is that of the Britisher who 'goes native'.

For Campbell, more immediately, disruptive animality, as it were, was assembling on the streets, via the distribution of printed obscene materials. The assembling of words is seen as preliminary to the assembling of people. Campbell's fear is that the widespread distribution, via print, of these materials is akin to the widespread distribution of 'animality'; and this assembling of animality – an attention to the physical and immediately sensual drives of the body, the sexualized body in particular – around the printed matter is thus the source of a threat to the existing privileges of the upper and middle classes.[20]

Campbell started to think about the legislation for an Obscene Publications Act, then, on a precise date: 9 May 1857. The following day – that is, on the Sunday between Campbell hearing the case and Monday, 11 May 1857, when he spoke about it in the House of Lords – in Meerut, Uttar Pradesh, a group of sepoys launched a revolt against the East India Company's militarized commercial rule in India, the initial move in what became known as the Indian Mutiny. There had been a growing sense that the Company was incrementally extending an imposition of Western and Christian values on a population – and, more specifically, an army – that was predominantly Hindu and Muslim. There was some truth in this, of course, at least in the sense that the rulers wanted to prioritize their own ideological sense of what constituted the proper protocols and codes of social, cultural and political life: 'public health'. It was, as it were, a part of the incipiently missionary zeal of the British themselves.

What might this have to do with Campbell and the Obscene Publications Act; and why might it have helped him to harden in his resolve to propose and pass the legislation? Ostensibly, very little, for it seems to be an entirely different issue; but in fact, it had a great deal to do with the fundamental ideology governing Campbell's thinking, and it helped shape the debate around this specific censorship. Ralph Crane and Radhika Mohanfram have pointed out that the Anglo-Indian representation of the events around the Mutiny 'are frequently

---

[19] His anxiety raises the obvious question, often repeated in debates around censorship. Is it the case that his fear that the middle classes might be seduced is based on the fact that he himself had been tempted? If so, how come he is so exceptional that he alone manages to resist the temptation? Intrinsic, if tacit, exceptionalism such as this is simply another way of describing a claimed individual superiority, which nonetheless rests in class hierarchies.

[20] Although there had been numerous forms of animal enclosure in Britain for centuries, the first 'scientific' zoo – the Zoological Society of London's official institution – opened to the public for the first time in 1847, displaying animals as 'exotic' creatures and as objects of study. There is no doubt that this has an influence on the presentation of social classes that had not previously been properly represented in 'respectable' or privileged social circles.

articulated in terms of masculinity: as the need for British soldier heroes to protect British women from the savagery of Indian men'. Further, 'While the Mutiny was undoubtedly traumatic for the Anglo-Indian population in India, it was also deeply disturbing for the general public in Britain. It shook their belief, both in their racial superiority and in the Empire'.[21] This damage to self-belief is key to understanding British elite society at this time.

It is also the case that the recurrent motif of disease and contamination finds another expression here. As is well known, one incident that helped give motivation to the Mutiny of 1857 was the deployment of the Enfield rifle, ammunition for which required the soldier to bite the tip off the cartridge; and this is controversial because, although not an issue for a Christian, the fact that the tip was made of grease from pig and cow fat made it objectionable, on religious grounds, for Muslims and Hindus. As Robert Darnton has argued, 'the sepoys thought the sahibs were trying to defile them in order to make them lose caste and convert to Christianity'.[22] The various caste systems that ran in India alongside the class system that structured society in England required a sense of purity: the mixing of castes, like the mixing of classes, was construed as a form of dangerous defilement or contamination. Any such mixing, or hint of defilement, is seen in both places as taboo; and taboo, by definition, is that which is intrinsically subject to censorship.

The kind of censorship proposed in the Obscene Publications Act depends precisely upon the idea that the State has some superior qualities in, or capacities for, judgement. That idea rests upon an assured self-belief, especially an assuredness that it is this that gives the censor the authority to legislate on behalf of others and in the interests of others, even when those others feel that their interests may differ from those underpinned by the values of the censors and judges. During the summer of 1857, 'while the fighting continued, explicit and invariably emotive descriptions of the Mutiny kept Britain at once spellbound and horrified'.[23] This response – being 'spellbound and horrified' – might equally accurately describe Campbell, as he surveyed the obscene publications that he had to judge on 9 May. It constitutes the scene of a kind of Mephistophelean seduction.

---

[21] Ralph Crane and Radhika Mohanfram, *Imperialism as Diaspora* (Liverpool University Press, London, 2013), 2, 29.
[22] Robert Darnton, *Censors at Work: How States Shaped Literature* (The British Library, London, 2014), 102.
[23] Ibid., 29.

Indeed, as M. J. D. Roberts points out, Campbell's bill is 'a clear example of that recurrent Victorian pastime – the attempt to legislate morals', and it shows the Victorians grappling 'with one of the most intractable ethical problems of their time – the problem of reconciling the claims of a libertarian ethic of individual responsibility with the claims of an ethic of paternalistic social concern'.[24] One means of effecting such a resolution lay in a religious impulse. Roberts argues that the Mutiny 'strengthened the resolve of Evangelical interventionists to purify the home society to make it worthy of its imperial mission. It also immensely hardened the general public mood against "sentimentality" in matters of social control, including the sexual'.[25] That motif – associating censorship with purgatorial purification – is absolutely to the point here; and it underpins the cliché from Wesley's sermons, emerging with the (false) authority of quasi-biblical authority in Victorian England, that 'cleanliness is next to godliness'. The censor is doing the work of God, in the sphere of politics.

It becomes clear that domestic politics in England and the UK is here informed by foreign policy. In both instances, issues of criminality and law become central to the establishment of what we can call 'policed' norms. The police themselves become the instruments through which matters pertaining to moral conduct become subject to law, and brought under the sign of potential criminality. The root for this, as Pablo Mukherjee has compellingly argued, lies in attitudes to Empire. 'Domestic compliance with colonial expansionism in the subcontinent,' he argues 'was secured at the material level with the lure of enormous profits and on the ideological level with the moral appeal of the "rule of law"'. Such a mentality rests on the ideological understanding that 'the degenerate Indians would wake up to the blessings of civilization with the introduction of British law and education'.[26]

Indians, in the political imagination of Britain at this moment, are always intrinsically potentially criminal, while yet being also susceptible to 'improvement' and 'civilization' – being brought into what the political establishment in Britain describe as the norms of civilized conduct – through a British education. 'Frequently, Indians would be seen simultaneously as "natural criminals" who only merited capital punishment *and* as candidates for reform through the enlightened policing of the colonial regime', as Mukherjee puts it.[27] However, the key thing here is that the British under-educated classes are

---

[24] Roberts, 'Morals, Art, and the Law', 611.
[25] Ibid., 626.
[26] Upamanyu Pablo Mukherjee, *Crime and Empire* (Oxford University Press, Oxford, 2003), 8.
[27] Ibid., 126.

seen themselves as mirror images of the allegedly degenerate colonial subject. The 'rule of law' becomes the conservative means and rhetoric through which imperial power – with all its intrinsic class and economic privileges and injustices – is to be maintained. In the domestic sphere within English law, this means that the 'native' lower social classes must become subjected to a version of law that is incipiently racist. That law, with an unstated eugenicist mentality at its root, will focus attention specifically on the material – 'animal' – body, and will then home in on what it sees as the body's most intimate work: sex and biology. At the cornerstone of this is the protection of privilege and of financial standing among the wealthier classes. Further, law has by now tacitly and surreptitiously entered the domain of a normative education – and there it will stay until our own contemporary moment.[28]

The initial thrust of modern censorship legislation, then, derives from a moment of imperialist politics mixed with evangelical religion. The Indian Mutiny initiates that moment when the British State essentially supplants the East India Company, making what was ostensibly a commercial arrangement into a fully operationalized and ideologically determined imperialist determination. At the same time, what is happening here is a proto-financialization of the State as such. Censorship is tied, at least covertly, with commercial interests and the control of financial wealth – giving a yet more concrete form to what we had seen in earlier centuries, with their attacks on theatre.

Underpinning this is a clear sense that 'the British' will assume a position of moral superiority; and central to that is the idea that they must therefore be presentable as pillars of moral virtue. That very terminology – 'virtue' – owes a good deal to the Latinate root known to the upper and educated classes in the House of Lords; and it thus influences a sense that a kind of 'upright manliness' stands at the core of political and social values, the very values that will be imposed not just on the Indians but also on the lower classes in the domestic UK population. Virtue – as seen in Campbell's moral crusade implicit in his bill, and thus coextensive with the need for censorship – is set here as a bulwark against the savagery of a race and of a class. The Obscene Publications Act of 1857 is instrumental in helping British men (and the primary addressee of the legislation is indeed thus gendered) remain 'British', which here now translates

---

[28] I explore this more fully later in this study, when I attend to issues around documentary realism. In this chapter, I look later at some instances of this operating in the field of French primary and secondary level education.

as pure, unsullied by the infectious savagery or animality of the lower classes and of colonized peoples, such as the Indians.[29]

5

France in 1857 was also in the process of extending significantly its imperial presence across the world. Napoleon III had established a solid military alliance with Britain between 1854 and 1856 when both joined forces against the Russian Empire in the Crimean War; and Napoleon was keen to extend the presence and image of France across the world. There are some remarkable similarities between the construction of French legislation and what we have already seen in Britain at this time; and these affect the shape of what is a fundamentally censorious culture, one that, between January 1857 and August 1857, puts both Flaubert and Baudelaire in the dock in the Paris courts.

For Napoleon III to assume the position of Emperor and thus launch France's Second Empire, it would be imperative that the kind of unrest that had marked the Second Republic should be forestalled. There were two key methods for doing this in France (operating here as a paradigmatic example): control of the press, and the co-opting of education as a mechanism for conservative political quietism.

Roger Price notes that 'The establishment of effective control over the press would become a major preoccupation of government' in this period.[30] Instead of direct oppressive measures, however, Napoleon's government deployed financial measures. It was the widespread distribution of 'cheap printed materials' that had been responsible, in the eyes of the emergent imperial administration, for the troubles that marked the later years of the Second Republic. The low price had made printed matter accessible, with widespread distribution offering the kind of free assembly that had also been seen as a root cause of unrest by Campbell in England. In France, the government re-imposed stamp duty, the effect of which

---

[29] For a nuanced view of how this plays out, see Mukherjee, *Crime and Empire*, 123–57, the chapter on 'Representing the Mutiny'. The chapter explores the consequences of the observation that 'In a time of an acute crisis of legitimacy like 1857, [a] fracture in the vital instrument of rulership could become the site of the radical questioning of authority both at "home" and [in] the colony' (ibid., 126).

[30] Roger Price, *The French Second Empire: An Anatomy of Political Power* (Cambridge University Press, Cambridge, 2001), 171.

would be to hike up significantly the price of any newspaper, thereby reducing circulation.[31]

A reduced circulation brings about a significant reduction in the public membership or participation in an assembly of individuals who can discuss and debate their interests. An assembly of establishment politics that calls itself 'virtuous' outplays a 'virtual' assembly, as it were. The State uses its financial instruments here in order to protect the privileges of those whose personal and individual financial interests are now aligned with the policies of the State. The means of achieving this involve a subtle and indirect form of censorship, through the reduction in the possibilities of underprivileged people constituting a free assembly. In addition, the government imposed a huge rise in 'deposit caution money', as a fund that would be there to pay the fines that would be imposed should any materials unacceptable to the government actually see the light of printed day; and this measure effectively co-opts the bourgeois classes – printers and publishers – for the interests of the State and those whose wealth is aligned with it.

The belief that underpins these moves is that printed materials are dangerous, but only or primarily if they are in the hands of the poor or disenfranchised. As Price describes this situation: 'Officials celebrated the disappearance of the newspapers, which had often served as the bases of republican organisation in the provinces', and the key self-justification for that celebration was that 'Once again political debate was safely restricted to "the serious, conscientious and enlightened", to the exclusion of that "illiterate class unable to understand serious social questions"'.[32] The bureaucracy of the State – those officious officials – operates here as a means of preventing debate, and through that, preventing also the extension in real terms of the franchise. This is so even despite Napoleon III's avowed claim that he is actually re-introducing a widened suffrage.

We might expect that, where there is a class that is deemed to be illiterate and unable to understand serious issues, education ought to step in to alleviate the consequent difficulties. Education, however, was itself also thoroughly politicized, and with a more or less explicit aim to consolidate State power and thus further constrain the spread of reliable information among the lower classes. An 'extra-parliamentary commission', chaired by Alfred de Falloux (Napoleon III's nominated 'Minister of Public Instruction', with Adolphe Thiers as its deputy chair) was set up in 1849, and its findings informed the Falloux

---

[31] For an interesting exploration of how similar structures affect our contemporary moment, especially in Anglophone cultures, see Alan Rusbridger, *Breaking News* (Canongate, Edinburgh, 2018).
[32] Price, *French Second Empire*, 176.

Law of March 1850. This Law shaped education across France, and in the most fundamental ways, for decades to follow. One of its fundamental principles was to reinstate the central position of the Church within education, and to place religious observance at the core of all learning. The fear of representation with which I opened this study is obviously alive, well, and thriving in 1850s France and England, the two major advanced economies of the period.

Schooling was essentially co-opted for conservative politics and culture, and the reason for this is again clear: it is a determined plan to prohibit political or any other social unrest that might jeopardize or in any way question Napoleon's ascent to imperial rule. As Laura Strumingher points out, by 1850 when the Falloux Law was passed, 'whatever liberal opposition to Catholic influence over primary education had existed as a residue from the eighteenth century enlightenment ideas had been overcome by the fear of the uncontrolled mob'.[33] A key figure whose input helped to shape Falloux and the subsequent character of educational and social norms was Adolphe Thiers; and his cynicism is thoroughly clear. Thiers argued that 'I regard the curé as an indispensable arbiter of the people's ideas; it is he who will teach them, at least in the name of Christ, that suffering is a condition of life. Therefore, when the poor catch cold, they will no longer think it was the rich who gave it to them.'[34] At the same time, Thiers also 'insisted on protecting the classical and secular bases of secondary education for the upper and middle classes on the grounds that groups which were not a threat to social order had less need of religion'.[35] In this respect, Thiers is accurately described as 'a deist…whose attitude toward organized religion is best described as Voltairean, as he believed that religion was and should remain the opiate of the masses'.[36]

To sum up where we are now with this argument, we can see that, through the ostensibly indirect control of the newspapers and the co-opting of education for religious and social conservatism, Napoleon III was able to lay the terrain for the cultural norms after the imperial coup of 2 December 1851. It is those norms that shape the censorious and prohibitive conditions that make the prosecution of a novel (*Madame Bovary*) and of some six poems (from *Les Fleurs du Mal*) not only possible but also inevitable. It is also those norms – the fact that such

---

[33] Laura S. Strumingher, *What Were Little Boys and Girls Made of?: Primary Education in Rural France 1830–1880* (SUNY Press, Albany, 1983), 40–1. On the importance of Roman Catholicism – in its contemporary condition as 'zombie Catholicism' – to French attitudes to issues of State censorship, see Emmanuel Todd, *Qui est Charlie?* (Seuil, Paris, 2015).
[34] Strumhinger, *What Were Little Boys*, 41.
[35] Price, *Second French Empire*, 195.
[36] Christopher Guyver, *The Second French Republic 1848–1852: A Political Reinterpretation* (Palgrave, London, 2016), 183.

constraining, proscriptive and narrow-minded conservatism has become normative – that make such a prosecution able to win significant support, even – and perhaps especially – among those co-opted bourgeois classes that include the publishers, printers and other writers.

The established political powers and authorities in 1850s France, then, had an analysis of their social structures that significantly resembled those in England. Poverty was a problem, because the poor had legitimate reasons to gather together in free assembly and to unite their forces in an effort to redistribute wealth and privilege more equitably. Instead of addressing that problem, the upper and middle classes preferred to work to prohibit the exercising of that right, first by describing it as 'unrest', next by legislating against it, and finally by co-opting the media, social institutions, legal institutions and bourgeois class interests to consolidate the norms that guaranteed their existing privileges.

The French established a 'commission du colportage', whose duty was to monitor the distribution of print and other street-trading, with particular emphasis on restraining the spread of any remaining 'cheap and accessible materials' that could be distributed or that could form the focal point for assembly not just in the major urban centres but also in 'small-town and rural France'. The commission prepared lists of titles that could be approved; and they were ready and primed to prosecute distributors and peddlers whose bags of goods contained any materials that were not thus approved. Its explicit aim was to 'control publications intended for the lower classes' because 'Peddling is the instrument by which one can corrupt or moralise the popular classes'.[37]

The peddler is construed here as the central actor in the making of a kind of public theatre. If peddlers are selling cheap printed matter, they become a magnet for the poorer and underprivileged classes. These classes then assemble, essentially around a text of some kind; and it is this that must be curtailed if the upper classes are to protect the existing privileges that they enjoy. A text, once printed and thus distanced from the voice of its author, is at once the subject of discussion and debate: it stimulates the widening of an assembly – a proto-Habermasian 'public sphere' – primarily through linguistic and interpretive suggestions that are made and disputed among different readers. Nowadays, we might recognize this quite simply as the business of literary criticism, of course. Later in this study, we will revisit this in order to demonstrate the ways in which both official and clandestine literary criticism relates to the State and to the

---

[37] Price, *Second French Empire*, 188, 189.

censorship or proliferation of ideas and debate. Literary criticism, as this early moment shows, is intrinsically related to democracy.

In 1850s France, emerging into the Second Empire, it is a logical extension of the work of the 'commission du colportage' that censorship extends directly into the actual theatre, given that the peddler is seen as a centripetal force around whose printed texts assembled debates can occur, especially among the underprivileged who might stand to gain from such debates and who might freely (or cheaply) assemble as a political force. In theatre, explicitly, the censor's role was 'to "prevent representation of the antagonism between the lower and upper classes . . . attacks on the principle of authority, against religion, the family, the magistrature, the army, in a word all those institutions on which society reposes; the more or less bold depiction of the depraved morals of amorous women"'.[38] One can see, immediately, that Emma Bovary is going to be regarded with some suspicion; and, in fact, it is once again matters relating to sexual mores (as in England) that will inform the legal proceedings against both Flaubert and, later, Baudelaire.

A further threat to State control develops, however, with the extension of the postal service; and, with this threat, we see the consolidation of the powers of the 'commission du colportage' into what is essentially full-blooded State censorship, where the opening of letters in transit became almost routine practice. Censorship here is entering the private space itself, not simply the public domain of the street-peddler and the open assembly of the poor. This is the start of the invasion of surveillance directly into the private and personal life; and it is key to the policing of a State that will be grounded in self-censorship. It is a logical extension of a normative State surveillance of a private life that the private individual starts to keep herself or himself under surveillance too (the name for which, in modern times, is Kafka; and in the contemporary moment, Facebook and 'social media' generally). It is, as it were, the ultimate schooling of the citizen, who learns not just to keep her or his thoughts to themselves, but actually to erase those thoughts and to substitute for them the thoughts that are regarded as officially acceptable to the State, 'authorized' by established figures of power.

In short: censorship in this way does indeed retain a fundamental aspect of representation, in that the citizen has to become the perfect embodied representation of the State itself. In some ways, this takes us right back to Plato's *Republic*. It is not the case, as I noted at the outset earlier, that all representation

---

[38] Ibid., 192.

is banned; rather, it is simply the actual case that some representation must be permitted and, indeed, endorsed as the purveyor of norms. As Socrates has it, 'we shall for our own good employ story-tellers and poets who are severe rather than amusing, who portray the style of the good man and in their works abide by the principles we laid down for them when we started out on this attempt to educate our military class.'[39]

That reference – to 'our military class' – is directly to the guardians of the allegedly ideal State. Yet it shows that what is at stake in this is the incipient militarization of the State as such. In the nineteenth-century examples I have been discussing in this chapter, what is at issue is the tacit militarization of the individual citizen. This is how modern censorship emerges, and it helps explain its particular condition and configuration.

We can now explore the specific examples of this work in practice, in the cases of Flaubert and of Baudelaire in France.

---

[39] Plato, *Republic*, Book III, § 398b, 157.

2

A present and private reality
Labour, sex and death in Courbet's painting

1

Censorship opens itself to resistance when and almost as soon as it becomes overt. If an individual or a population believes that its freedom to express itself is being hampered, there is a clear invitation to protest and to demand that any such constraints be removed. Those who would censor have found different ways of overcoming what they would see as this intrinsic problem. At one extreme, in the authoritarian and totalitarian State, there is simply a brutal exertion of force and power, including jailing or murdering those who refuse to be bound by the constraining powers of the State. In recent times, this has become shockingly common: journalists have 'disappeared' or been jailed in a very large number of jurisdictions, including many that present themselves as political democracies where freedom of expression is supposedly guaranteed by the State.

Often, the issue in such cases relates specifically to the questions around what constitutes the real conditions of public and private life in a jurisdiction. A good example is the case of Ahmet Altan, the Turkish novelist and journalist. Altan was first charged in July 2016 with sending 'subliminal messages' to the organizers of the alleged coup d'état against the Turkish president, Recep Tayyip Erdoğan; and he was subsequently jailed for life without parole, in 2018, by which time the charge had changed – with no evidence having been provided – to one of actually participating in the (failed but still alleged) coup.[1] When he was arrested in 2016, a police officer offered Altan a cigarette. He refused it,

---

[1] At the time of writing (December 2019), Altan has finally been released, but under very strict conditions. On 4 November 2019, he was sentenced to ten and half years in prison, but he was simultaneously provisionally released, as he had already been imprisoned for over three years. He is now formally 'under judicial control'. See https://pen.org/advocacy-case/ahmet-mehmet-altan/ for updated details (accessed 4 December 2019). Some eight days later, he was arrested again (for updates, see: https://pen.org/advocacy-case/ahmet-mehmet-altan/, accessed 12 August 2020).

saying 'I only smoke when I am nervous'. This single sentence becomes almost talismanic for Altan. He has no idea where it came from, and he realizes that 'Nowhere in my mind had I chosen to make such a declaration. It was a sentence that put an unbridgeable distance between itself and reality. It ignored reality, ridiculed it. . . . It divided reality in two'.[2]

This situation is one in which Altan is able – indeed almost required – to see reality as at once incontrovertible – as a state of affairs that is self-evident and undeniably itself – and yet also and simultaneously as something whose self-evidencing is profoundly resistible. It yields a situation in which he knows that 'when you are faced with a reality that can turn your life upside down, that same sorry reality will sweep you away like a wild flood only if you submit to it and act as it expects you to do'. The secret of survival, then, against such a seemingly unanswerable force of reality is precisely and determinedly to answer it, but to answer it with the unexpected sentence, a sentence that intrinsically ridicules it because it seems to come from an entirely different place.

Altan's observations go further than this, in fact. He essentially calls into question those who will too easily succumb to an existing tyranny through their suggestions that reality cannot be changed, or that there is an absolute and unquestionable ground of political reality that intrinsically resists the possibility of becoming different. 'As someone who has been thrown into the dirty, swelling waves of reality, I can say with certainty that its victims are those so-called smart people who believe that you have to act in accordance with it,' he writes. It is by an act of criticism – by the introduction of the unforeseen and unpredictable word or sentence – that we can not only resist the force of a reality that claims complete and absolute ontological certainty for itself, but also that we can break it and forge a new world.[3]

Along the spectrum from the extreme example of the jailed writer – or, worse, the murdered writer, such as Jamal Khashoggi, the dissident journalist murdered in October 2018 by Saudi Arabian agents – there are many other much less dramatic means by which censorship can be enforced, without becoming obviously, or in the first instance, authoritarian; and these are, in some ways, more troubling in that they do not immediately invite resistance. By operating insidiously, or by securing social or ideological compliance and by co-opting a generalized 'public opinion', censorship can progress inexorably,

---

[2] Ahmet Altan, *I Will Never See the World Again* (trans. Yasemin Çongar; Granta, London, 2019), 10–11.
[3] Ibid., 12. For a fuller engagement with the faults of those 'smart people' described here, see my *Complicity* (Rowman & Littlefield, London and New York, 2016).

and can essentially delegitimize the semantic content of many kinds of speech or expression.[4]

Often enough, this connivance with a normative censorship is simply a matter of making any alternative to a prevailing view of the world seem invisible, such that the prevailing view assumes the right to call itself 'real' or 'realistic'. It is obviously prima facie difficult to argue for an alternative to this, because it is obviously difficult to set an agenda for a resistance that is intrinsically deemed to be 'unrealistic'. T. J. Clark put it succinctly in *Image of the People*, his study of Gustave Courbet and the 1848 Revolution in France, where he argues that what we see or comprehend within the material world depends on conventional norms of belief, or what John Berger in 1972 famously called 'ways of seeing'. 'The way we see things,' wrote Berger in his influential observations, 'is affected by what we know or what we believe'.[5] Clark writes, the following year, 1973, that 'the question becomes: in order to see certain things, what should we believe about them?'. Glossing that further, he argued that 'one must ask ... what kind of "visibility" a certain symbolic system made possible; and in what specific circumstances one artist could take advantage of this, and another fail to'.[6]

The previous chapter showed how commerce-censorship (a censorship designed to protect the privileges accorded to one social class because of the uneven distribution of shared wealth) can work in a similar and specific way – and not just in the sphere of the visual arts. What is at issue is how a society establishes certain positions as 'realistic', and, primarily, as 'legitimately held'. A society might claim to base its legitimacy on the free and open exchange of all views, and might even propose this as the basis for its self-description as democratic. It might claim that nothing in its political or judicial norms prevents or precludes the frank expression of any views; and it assures its citizens that no such freely expressed view will be subject to legal proscription.

Were we to find this in the constitution of the United States, for example, we might characterize it as a kind of 'First Amendment Absolutism'. At the same time, however, you put a price on speech in economic terms, under which the costs of presenting one's views may themselves become prohibitive. The licensing of print, for example, is one way in which, historically, the basic 'publication' – making available to a public – of an individual's views may be circumscribed, in

---

[4] I will engage the arguments over the relation of realism to 'public opinion' in much more substantial and historical detail in Chapter 9.
[5] John Berger, *Ways of Seeing* (Penguin, London, 1972), 8.
[6] T. J. Clark, *Image of the People* (Thames and Hudson, London, 1973), 16–17. See also Berger, *Ways of Seeing*: 'The way we see things is affected by what we know or what we believe'.

ways that I described in Chapter 1. In this way, you limit the range of opinions – you reduce the number of 'ways of seeing' – and ensure that the opinions expressed are consistent with those that the State regards as supportive.

The issue here can be neatly summed up in a succinct phrase. Ideology, we might say, is the confusion of belief with reality. Consider the classic liberal view of freedom. According to this, considered socially, we are all equal before the law and, indeed, equal before the realities of the world. However, when we really stand outside the real three-star Michelin restaurant, say, we become radically economically unequal. Ideology confuses social liberalism with economic; and, in this example, it would argue that the problem of inequality here is not systemic, but really a problem regarding the individuals concerned: one has 'realized' her, his or their talents or potential, as seen clearly in an economic advantage that yields many possible real-life activities; the other has failed in such a task of 'realization' of themselves in some way.

The restaurant is (socially) open to all, while being (economically) exclusive of many. Ideology conspires to ignore that systemic difference, and to displace its terms onto an argument about how individuals 'realize' themselves and their world. It thus limits the number of ways of looking at and understanding the reality of the world as it materially exists. This restaurant silently 'selects' its diners, while officially opening its doors to all; by analogy, some jurisdictions offer an open platform for any and all voices, while finding means – through economic and other criteria – to select those whose voices will be heard. Some jurisdictions enact this exclusivity through cultural means: the establishment of a literary or aesthetic 'canon' of great works, say; or the validation of certain very specific ethical values as normative for a whole culture or society. The beneficiaries are Altan's 'so-called smart people' who act in conformity with the norms of what passes as 'reality' in a world that is regulated by wealth or other similar exclusive structural criteria. Those criteria select what is sayable; and, often, the extent of one's wealth is what the criteria measure and evaluate.

There is, so to speak, a fee that must be paid if you are to be granted access and legitimate rights to assemble in this restaurant or polity. In the political sphere in the UK, for example, an individual who wishes to stand for election to the UK Parliament must place a deposit (currently, £500) to their local Returning Officer for elections. Entitlement to speak within this domain, like that to eat in other social settings, can be circumscribed by indirect means, allowing us to proclaim the free liberality of the State while, simultaneously, the State stands over norms, systems and rules that deny many individuals a voice. This is not to suggest, of course, that there can be no barriers whatsoever to standing for election, say; but it does draw attention to the fact that, in the UK at least, such an example of 'free' speech is or can be determined by financial interests: it is a sum of money or, more broadly, the economic conditions that govern the polity – that will grant access to the domain of 'freedom of expression'. In the United States, of course, anyone can run for president; but, in fact, if you want to be taken seriously, you will need to find very substantial sums on which to build your base and secure serious standing.[7]

There is a question of how we legitimize authority in all of this, a question of how we grant an audience to a specific individual's political views. In the professional sphere, it is accreditation of some kind that usually grants such authority. For example, it is my own academic credentials that will help this very book to gain whatever audience it might reach. One danger arises when that authority is financialized: that is, when we grant authority to an individual simply because of her or his financial standing and ability to pay the required social 'deposits'. In this state of affairs, we rapidly discover that speech is far from 'free' in most political jurisdictions: it costs money to have one's views put forth for serious consideration in the polity.[8]

There are many other similar indirect and subtle mechanisms, besides the norms of individual capital, through which the State can exercise control over which representations of reality might be permitted to become widespread, or which representations can be broadcast. In the following pages, I will explain how one of these in particular works, typically to powerful and even devastating effect. I will look, in this first section of this book, at the cases of Flaubert and Baudelaire as particular examples of a more general trajectory for modern censorship, and we will see that censorship can work by the legitimization of cliché, in which this cliché operates as an adequate and therefore unquestionably accurate representation of the real conditions of life (even if, as we may rightly suspect, 'clichés are where truth goes to die').[9] It is as if we are living in Flaubert's world of a *Dictionnaire des Idées Reçues*, as I will show.

---

[7] President Obama, for instance, raised well in excess of $750 million in 2012; and, although the trend seems to have stalled a little since then (Hillary Clinton spending around $750 million in 2016, but the eventual incumbent, Trump, having seemingly only spent some $350 million), nonetheless the fact remains: finances determine standing.
[8] One emerging problem in many democracies is that *all* such accreditation is being financialized. Even academic qualifications are subject in our time to financial considerations; and the damaging consequence is that 'wealth' is often associated with 'rights'. For more on this, see the first chapter of my *Political English* (Bloomsbury, London, 2019). For the extended sociological exploration of how this works, see Pierre Bourdieu, *Homo Academicus* (1984; trans. Peter Collier; Polity Press, Cambridge, 1990).
[9] David Runciman, *How Democracy Dies* (Profile Books, London, 2019), 11.

This operates also beyond the printed word; and I shall consider the operation of censorship in the visual field as well, and will consider the meaning of some paintings by Courbet, often considered to be a great progenitor of realism in the visual arts.

2

What is of most interest in all of this is the simple fact that, at a specific point in cultural history, Realism itself was claimed precisely as resistance. In the mid-nineteenth century, especially in France, we can witness 'a time when art and politics could not escape each other', a moment when 'the State, the public and critics agreed that art had a political sense and intention', and thus also a moment when 'painting [and, as I will add, literature] was encouraged, repressed, hated and feared' as a result.[10] At this moment, we see the emergence of a new attitude to the form and function of arts; and that attitude identified itself as 'realist', with the consequence that we now understand that 'Realism is an episode against the grain of French art; and therefore its forms have to be extreme, explosive'.[11] What, then, is the status of 'realism' with respect to aesthetic and political representation: is it a repetition that endorses the values of the materially real, or a resistance to it? On what side of Altan's divide does it stand?

In French literature, the key location for the debate around this is in Stendhal, with his celebrated description of the author of a novel as one who holds a mirror up to the world.[12] Stendhal's first full deployment of the idea comes in 1830, in an epigraph at the start of chapter 13 in the first book of *Le Rouge et le noir*, where he cites César Vichard de Saint-Réal: 'Un roman: c'est un miroir qu'on promène le long d'un chemin' [a novel: it's what you get when you take a mirror for a walk along a road].[13] The phrase has not ever been found in the works of Saint-Réal; but, as P.-G. Castex notes in his edition of the novel, it is in Saint-Réal's *Discours sur l'usage de l'histoire* of 1671 that we find the argument that history makes readers see the very image of their faults, as in a mirror.[14]

---

[10] Clark, *Image of the People*, 9.
[11] Ibid., 19.
[12] F. W. J. Hemmings traces the first use of this to Stendhal's review of L.-B. Picard's novel, *L'Honnête homme ou le niais*, in *New Monthly Magazine*, 1 August 1825, and in a note Stendhal wrote on seeing Rossini's opera, *La Donna del lago* in 1826.
[13] Stendhal, *Le Rouge et le noir*, ed. P.-G. Castex (trans. mine; Garnier, Paris, 1973), 72.
[14] Ibid., 540.

The better-known reference comes in *Le Rouge et le noir* book 2, chapter 19, when a narratorial voice intervenes to tell the reader that

> a novel is a mirror going for a walk along a broad road. Now it reflects the azure of the sky, now the mud clogging up the gutters on the road. And you accuse the man humping the mirror on his back of being immoral? The mirror shows the muck, and you accuse the mirror? You'd be better attending to the road with its mucky puddles, or, better, attending to the inspector of roads who lets the water become a sludge and lets the puddles form ['un roman est un miroir qui se promène sur une grande route. Tantôt il reflète à vos yeux l'azur des cieux, tantôt la fange des bourbiers de la route. Et l'homme qui porte le miroir dans sa hotte sera par vous accusé d'être immoral! Son miroir montre la fange, et vous accusez le miroir! Accusez bien plutôt le grand chemin où est le bourbier, et plus encore l'inspecteur des routes qui laisse l'eau croupir et le bourbier se former'].[15]

Stendhal uses these images, both in *Armance* and in this better-known passage in *Le Rouge et le noir*, as a means of 'excusing' his presentation of vulgarity, arguing that the novelist cannot be held responsible for what passes before the mirror. On the one hand, the mirror renders visible that which 'respectable' society prefers to ignore, thus endorsing the material facts of reality; and on the other hand and simultaneously, the novelist disavows responsibility for revealing such a material reality, and attends instead on the broad – and real – social conditions that underlie the apparent or obvious (but merely superficial) reality of the material condition of the world.

The mirror – like all mirrors – both shows and reverses the real at once. The real becomes itself the site of a sceptical questioning; and it asks, among other things, whether the material reality that we see is itself the totality of historical real conditions of life (the mud, the filth), or whether it is merely the effect or product of a reality that lies hidden under the surface appearance (the inadequacy of the polity with its failing inspectors and authorities). Can we trust our own eyes, or should we realize that the image in the mirror has a source elsewhere that must be witnessed, even if only indirectly? Is the mirror itself a kind of censor, or a translucent but distorting veil that simultaneously reveals and occludes the world as it is?

There is here a fundamental issue regarding the representation of the material world. As soon as reality is imaged, it is doubled. Simultaneously, the most fundamental thing about a real object or event is that it is irreducibly itself: intrinsically, it is singular. Almost by definition, therefore, an art form that

---

[15] Ibid., 342 (translation mine).

predicates its own realization upon some pre-existing reality must be marked either by imperfection or duplicity. It necessarily misrepresents; and, at the same time and even more fundamentally, it calls the substance of a singular reality into question. As Altan said, from prison, a phrase can divide reality in two, and can do so with potentially liberating and devastating effect. This is one reason why any 'realism' must also be founded upon a politics of some kind.

With respect to the representation of a historical event, this issue is extremely fundamental: representation of an event or of a sequence of events necessarily calls the very essence of history itself into some doubt; and doubt introduces into the question, by default, its opposite: belief. In turn, this takes us back to my observation that ideology as such is founded upon the confusion of belief and factual reality; and criticism, almost by its very nature, must therefore be founded upon doubt. It follows that any criticism of a politics of realism that is 'fundamentalist' or governed by a totalizing theory of some kind is, ipso facto, the very antithesis of criticism. This situation makes censorship itself open to a new form of examination, a form that asks questions not about the substance of what may or may not be censored and permitted, but that rather attends to issues of what it is that censorship legitimizes as credible, and, in the final analysis, what censorship legitimizes in the sphere of an underlying economics as creditable.

3

The most effective modern forms of censorship operate by narrowing the scope of what might be regarded as 'legitimate' in any speech or writing or aesthetic representation, by determining and circumscribing with laws the scope and ambit of what is 'visible'; and this, the 'visible' is, in Clark's terms, the equivalent of what is believable. Altan's jailers in Turkey use – abuse – the law in order to make him invisible, and to make what he says inaudible, illegitimate. Yet such a rendering invisible is often done in a less obvious manner. When I argue that censorship works most effectively when it is surreptitious, I mean that it is most fully operative when it produces beliefs that become accepted as not only normative, but also 'realistic' or 'just the way things are' in what we can call a kind of ontological tyranny.

In this regard, censorship can have an intimate relation with the operations of both philosophical and literary realism, especially in the looser and more casual or vulgar sense of giving credence to 'what is realistic' or 'what is possible, and even likely to the point of being probable'. It is in this state of affairs that censorship disables resistance: it makes resistance literally incredible. It renders the world that the critic envisages as simply so unbelievable as to be invisible, literally unimaginable or unable to be imaged – *as if* the critic who proposes such a presentation of the world is behind bars. The real in its form as 'just the way things are', we might say, can be deployed against its representations by a State or indeed any other power in order to legitimize censorship by that State. The immediate obvious questions arise: to whose benefit does this work; and who operates the mechanisms of this covert censoring?

Ideologically speaking at least, it is a truth universally acknowledged that there is nothing more legitimate than the real itself; and thus the control of what constitutes reality in the public mind (or what passes as credible, or economically 'credit-worthy') is entirely consonant with the control of what constitutes legitimacy in the public sphere. When we consider the real as simply 'what is the given', or 'what can be taken for granted, precisely because it is granted or a given', then the real legitimizes itself. However, and at the same time, legitimacy can become subservient to legality; and both legitimacy and legality become subservient to the laws of finance or capital. The reason for this is straightforward, though usually never fully exposed or acknowledged.

The issue here is that what is 'given' or 'taken for granted' as reality is never genuinely and simply given at all; rather, it is the product of a series of regulated controls. The 'given' is shaped by whoever it is that controls what passes for reality in the public mind or public sphere; and, in modernity, that control is itself shaped by those who are in control of capital, because the credible is confounded with the 'credit-worthy'. One reason why Austen can offer her famous opening to *Pride and Prejudice* – 'It is a truth universally acknowledged, that a single man in possession of a good fortune, must be in want of a wife' – is quite simply ascribable to this intimate tie between truth and money. We will see later how the 'realism' of this is also tied to issues of the regulation of sexuality, and to matters of the organization of labour as that relates to sexuality and gender.

Law and the entire legal system – embracing judiciary in the grip of the executive in thrall to legislature, all validated through bureaucracy – is one place where this confluence of realism with credibility and thus also with credit becomes mainstream; and it is also here that we see an illuminating relation between the operation of the law and the aesthetics of literary and visual realism.

We saw in my previous chapter the source and origin of the 1857 Obscene Publications Act in England. It was in this same year – 1857 – that France also drove the question of alleged literary obscenity into the Law Courts. That year, the French State moved against two writers whose work would come to be emblematic of a new kind of modernity. Both writers were also associated at the time of their legal difficulties with specific (but very different) new 'realisms': Flaubert found himself in court in January 1857; and Baudelaire was charged in August the same year. Just two years before this, in 1855, Gustave Courbet had submitted a series of paintings for exhibition in the *Exposition Universelle* on the Champs-Elysées in Paris. Finding that some were rejected (some were too big, he was told), Courbet set up what might be the first ever 'pop-up art gallery', right next to the *Exposition*, where he displayed all his work, under the deliberately provocative and polemical title 'Pavillon du Réalisme'.

Courbet made a self-promoting drama out of the circumstances of the 1855 Exhibition. There had been over 8,000 paintings submitted for exposition; and the organizers simply had to ration the amount of wall-space given to each artist. Courbet had submitted fourteen canvasses, but three of the largest of them had been rejected. That three included some that are now regarded as central to an understanding of Courbet's entire development as a painter, and crucial to the emergence of his account of Realism. The jury decided against mounting *Burial at Ornans* and *The Artist's Studio* – both of which were immense pictures in sheer physical size. However, Courbet decided to present this as a decision motivated by other than purely practical issues about the amount of wall-space available for exhibition and hanging. He wrote to Alfred Bruyas, on 5 April 1855, saying 'I am at my wit's end! Terrible things are happening to me. They have just refused my *Burial* . . . and my latest painting, the *Atelier*. . . . They have made it clear that at any cost my tendencies in art must be stopped as they are disastrous for French art'.[16]

In these years, not only the aesthetic or other value of realism, but also in fact the very idea of realism was itself a matter of contentious cultural argument. Courbet here presents himself in the figure of the artist who resists established norms. In response to the jury's decision on his paintings, he mounted a rival exhibition, in a building directly opposite the main exposition, calling his show and building the 'Pavillon du Réalisme', and thereby implying that the paintings in the official exhibition were not 'realistic', not attentive to the realities of contemporary human or social life. In these ways, he turned a historical circumstance into a major statement of cultural resistance, and insisted that his paintings stand proud and unashamed before the forces of a surreptitious cultural

---

[16] Gustave Courbet, letter 55-4 to Alfred Bruyas, dated 5 April 1855, in Petra ten-Doesschate Chu, ed. and trans., *Letters of Gustave Courbet* (University of Chicago Press, Chicago, 1992), 139. The *Burial* had, in fact, already been shown before, at a Salon of 1851.

censorship. In doing so, he claims that it is he who is in possession of 'Realism' (now with its provocative upper-case R). In this way, Courbet politicized his 'way of seeing', and he provided a new linguistic term to indicate what that new visibility would be: 'realistic'.

4

How, then, should we understand Courbet's Realism? Within this question there lurks another, about 'ways of seeing' and about what we may be 'permitted' to see by the dominant beliefs, credibilities (and credit-worthiness) of an existing political system and social condition. In everyday discourse, 'realism' might simply suggest seeing the world as it actually is, as it 'really' exists; but the simple fact that Realism (with its upper-case R and its political dimension) stands in opposition to the existing art-world, when Courbet opens his Pavillon, indicates that something else is at stake. 'Realism' sets itself up in explicit opposition to the established understanding of how we see reality: the '-ism' indicates a specific determination to contest 'the establishment' of painting as such – to contest the accepted norms of what constitutes good visual art – and also to challenge what that establishment understands as the fundamental constituent elements of the real world. In effect, Realism indicates that all previously established painting actually hides the real from its viewers, precisely at the moment when it claims to reveal it.

Following Michael Fried, who has written expertly and in extended manner on Courbet, we might say that Courbet's Realism involves a specific kind of 'absorption', as the structural counter to something that Fried describes as 'theatricality' in painting. The distinction in question here – between absorption and theatricality – needs some clarification for readers unacquainted with Fried's highly original work. When he makes use of this conceptual opposition, Fried is essentially following an argument that he derives from the aesthetic of Diderot in the mid-eighteenth century.

Fundamentally, the distinction can be explained in terms of the way in which the frame of a painting operates. In the absorbed aesthetic, the subject of the painting is, as it were, entirely enclosed: it has little interest in the fact that it is being seen or watched by an observer. The first clear example that Fried proposes is *The Card Castle*, a painting done by Jean-Baptiste Siméon Chardin around 1737. This canvas shows a young man sitting at his table and arranging his cards into the figure of a castle. Fried writes that it is clear that the young man 'can plainly be described as absorbed in what he is doing'.[17] His attention is entirely concentrated on the cards, his gaze entirely focused on his own world within the frame; and it is as if he is oblivious to everything else, above all to the fact that there is a viewer of the painting. In this kind of work in the painting of absorption, 'the persuasive representation of action and expression entailed evoking the perfect obliviousness of a figure or group of figures to everything but the objects of their absorption, including – or especially – the beholder standing before the picture'.[18] Chardin figures absorption here by a straightforward faithful recording of a young man caught up entirely in the trivial action that engages his attention within the frame. The young man is not 'for show'.

Fried then adds, as a second example, Jean-Baptiste Greuze's *Filial Piety* of 1763. Here, some decades later, we have a different determination of absorption. While absorption can be established, for Chardin, simply by having the subject of the painting (the young man) focusing on an essentially trivial activity, Salon exhibition protocols by the mid-1750s had to assume the absolute necessity of a viewer. Thus, for Greuze, a structural absorption has to be engineered. *Filial Piety* depicts a dying man, surrounded by family, and attended primarily by his son. Once again, the attention of everyone *within* the painting is focused internally, on the dying man. Here, absorption is intensified by an implicit *narrative* that pre-exists the painting's scene – a narrative that involves the family and its history – a narrative that prioritizes sentimentality by asking us to consider what is going on here and how the characters arrive at this moment and in this scene. It is this foregrounding of sentiment that, once again, essentially alienates the viewer from the primary involvement *within* the scene, while engaging her as a distanced viewer *of* the scene, but, crucially, a viewer of whose presence the family remain determinedly unaware.[19]

Against this is the tradition that is associated more fully with 'theatricality', in which the figures within the painting know that they are there to be seen, with the consequence that their 'essential' being is that of a performance. In the terms that are central to the present book and argument, the presence of the subject or figure within the painting is already a re-presentation of themselves. The logic of the argument that I am presenting here – what makes Courbet different and

---

[17] Michael Fried, *Courbet's Realism* (University of Chicago Press, Chicago, 1990), 8–9. See also his earlier *Absorption and Theatricality: Painting and Beholder in the Age of Diderot* (University of California Press, Berkeley & Los Angeles, 1980) for the full account of the argument.
[18] Fried, *Courbet's Realism*, 10.
[19] Ibid., 10–11.

shockingly disturbing in the 1850s – is that Courbet can bring us a real that lies behind any intrinsic tendency to theatre and to representation. If there is a mirror somewhere in which this world is being reflected, the subjects of the painting are themselves completely unaware of it. It operates like a two-way mirror, as it were, and permits the artist and viewer to survey a reality without that reality being affected one way or another by the fact of being surveyed.

Yet, as Fried has shown with the examples taken from the previous century, there is nothing especially new here in any aesthetic of absorption that might be engaged by Courbet: there is a long tradition – at least a century old – of 'anti-theatricality' in French painting into which he fits comfortably. So how is Courbet different? This becomes the key issue. The answer lies in what we must now identify as the *politics* of Courbet's Realism. It is explicitly in the wake of 1848's political turmoil that Courbet makes what is usually considered to be the most significant new turn in his work, the Realist turn itself. This Realism is shaped by the political moment, and its intrinsic 'anti-theatrical' structure is determined by Courbet's attitudes to material conditions in his world.

As is well known, Courbet was influenced by Proudhon and by socialist political philosophy. In his painting, the 'reality' that interested him was one that was identified politically with this way of seeing the world. The key things that emerge from this include, first, his deep interest in *physicality*, as the most direct expression of an interest in material facts. This concentration on the physical as such will show itself in three themes in his work: labour; death (and/or the unconscious associated with sleep); and sex. In these three crucial interests, we will get to the root of how Courbet's Realism engages with 'the structure of beholding'; and we will find a way of working through the relation of this Realism to an emergent mode of censorship in the middle of the nineteenth century in Europe and in European art. In fact, as we will see, these three elements become completely determining for the politics of all realism in the emergence of modernity, and remain central to realism in our own contemporary moment.

5

The painting that marks Courbet's Realist turn most significantly perhaps is *The Stone Breakers*. This is one of three paintings that he made in an extraordinary period between October/November 1849 and mid-1850: *The Stone Breakers, A Burial at Ornans* and *The Peasants of Flagey Returning from the Fair*. The source of *The Stone Breakers* lies in his incidental sighting of two stonebreakers near

Maisières, which he called an 'encounter with the most complete expression of wretchedness'.[20] This is the historical original that gave Courbet the impetus to make the painting. However, the substance of the image is better described as the fact of the physical and material reality of labour as such.[21]

There can be few things more obviously physical than the breaking of stones: the utter concreteness of solidity faced by the precariousness of human flesh in a play of force. Neither an idea nor a thought can do the necessary work; rather, the force of the human body is needed, and that force has to be almost primordial, brutal. There is, in Courbet's Realist work – and this is perhaps the first utterly clear example of his new practice – little room for the presentation of anything that can be called ideal or idealized, or shaped by a presiding 'idea' as such. In these new paintings of the mid-1850s, the idea of the image itself is given from the material reality, such as that shock that Courbet has when he sees the physical labour of the two men stone-breaking in Maisières. The work of the painting – what the painting has to do – is to yield that real force in its most basic physical form.

Clark is clear, noting that the 'physical presence' of the two men in the picture 'has been set down with the utmost care'. He attends to the way in which Courbet paints the details of the boy's clothing (leather strap across shoulder, puckering of the shirt), noting 'the way these details register the substance of the body beneath them'. This, he says 'is painting whose subject is the material weight of things, the pressure of a bending back or the quarter-inch thickness of coarse cloth'.[22] The image is of the body-at-work, in which the body-as-such is realized precisely through that work-as-such. The body as we see it is the product of the physical labour, the product of that play of force between malleable human body and rebarbative solidity of stone. Clark essentially finds the same kind of absorption that Fried describes. Here, Clark argues that Courbet painted 'assertion turned away from the spectator'. It is an image, he argues, 'of labour gone to waste, and men turned stiff and wooden by routine'.[23]

This, then, is an image of labour in its pure form. The men are themselves incidental to it, every bit as much as are the rocks that they break: they are all simply 'there'. The fact that the two workers are anonymous, their faces averted or hidden, and their backs turned to us, allows the viewer to understand that it

---

[20] Clark, *Image of the People*, 79. See also Jack Lindsay, *Gustave Courbet: His Life and Art* (Adams and Dart, London, 1973), 59 (where the French original, given as 'wretchedness' by Clark, has instead been translated as 'poverty').
[21] To view an image of this painting, see: en.wikipedia.org/wiki/The_Stone_Breakers.
[22] Clark, *Image of the People*, 79.
[23] Ibid., 80.

is the work itself that is the focus, not the specific identity of the workers. The real centre of the painting is physical labour, and the labourers are themselves an effect of that, brought into being by it. The worker is the product of the primacy of labour itself; and this allows the viewer to focus on the material actuality of work in the painting. That is where the painting becomes 'Realism', for it is attending to the political reality of the human body, as it is realized in work, even 'manufactured' by physical force itself. There is nothing 'idealized' in these bodies; the idea of labour is itself generated from the fact of the work; and it is the fact of the work that leads to the damaged and stressed bodies that are merely implied, as it were, by the painting. Courbet 'gets the moral down in paint, and does not lean on anecdote or pathos'.[24]

The picture is controversial precisely because it focuses primarily on the reality of labour as such. It shows the effect of labour on the human body, rather than showing the human body 'posed' in the figure of the labourer. There is nothing 'representational', about this painting, in the sense that it does not aim to '*re*-present', and thus give a potentially 'theatrical image' to the idea of labour or of the dignity of the worker. On the contrary, the danger that lurks in this painting, as far as establishment politics is concerned, is that it shows that it is labour itself that is the determining force that shapes human being and human history. This is the reality that establishment politics needs to circumvent, the reality against which political power seeks to protect itself by forcing us to avoid looking at it. That reality is, in a specific sense, literally unbearable: established privilege and power cannot bear the thought that citizens might see through the veneer offered by 'representations' of workers, in all their theatricalized dignity. Courbet's Realism aims to give the real thing, no matter how unbearable it is.

Having made this picture, Courbet turned next to another literally unbearable reality: the physical fact of the human body as it is realized in death. Mortality is what makes us a physical being. Once again, the specific body in question in the painting is hidden or occluded. In *A Burial at Ornans*, the body is in the coffin that is entering the frame from the left.[25] The pall-bearers themselves are averting their eyes from it, for it is probably so rancid with the smell of rotting flesh that they have to turn away. But we don't see the rotting corpse itself. At the centre of the image is the hole into which the invisible body will become doubly invisible, as it is buried. As with *The Stone Breakers*, our attention is directed towards the physical condition of mortality itself, and not on the individual whose burial this is. Once again, the people are 'absorbed' – although they are fully 'there', and fully

[24] Ibid.
[25] To see an image of this painting, see: en.wikipedia.org/wiki/A_Burial_At_Ornans.

'in the picture', they are not there as objects to be seen by us or by Courbet. These people are not on display: they stand as *present*, but they are not *representations*.

For Clark, *A Burial at Ornans* of 1850 is a 'counterweight' to *The Stone Breakers*. Yet, if it is a counterweight, it functions nonetheless in precisely the same mode. Courbet gives us 'worship without worshippers . . . not exactly an image of disbelief, more of collective distraction; not exactly indifference, more inattention'. In what Clark calls 'the careful, ambiguous blankness of a public face',[26] we find the same kind of absorption and thus the same determined accent on a kind of anti-anthropomorphic reality as was there in *The Stone Breakers*.

The burial has clearly been preceded by a procession. This is why the women in the back of the painting look as if they are staring right outside and beyond the frame, looking to our right and away from the centre of the work. They are making their way round, in the procession, to where we as viewers are already standing, to complete the circle of mourners around the grave. We occupy – or preoccupy – the place of the mourners here. And we await their arrival. This painting, therefore, is also a moment in time, its temporality stressed not just by the fact of the procession taking its slow time to complete the picture, but also because the presiding religious official has not yet found his place in the funeral liturgy, and is thumbing through the Bible to find it. The painting shows a certain unreadiness, a certain unpreparedness – which is itself a motif of human mortality, of the body as a physical entity in the face of death. Dying, of course, is our meaning. It is what 'completes' us, completes our very existence, completes or fulfils our being, in a certain (proto-Heideggerian) sense. It is what – physically, as physical human beings – we are here to do, unarguably, and is the one thing that is guaranteed as a condition of life.[27] It is also what 'calls us to responsibility', as Derrida argued; and, here in this painting, this is exactly what is at work.[28]

Yet dying, in 1849, is something that is itself mired in politics, and most especially so in terms of the ritual of burial that it usually entails. France – like many jurisdictions – faced a burial crisis in the late 1840s. For close on a century, a number of cities across the world had faced a simple logistical issue: there was a lack of space in which to bury the dead. By the early nineteenth century in France, this had passed beyond the point of being an issue and was now a major

---

[26] Ibid., 81.
[27] This is so, even if, for Ludwig Wittgenstein, 'Death is not an event in life. It is not lived through'. See his *Tractatus Logico-Philosophicus* (trans. D. F. Pears and B. F. McGuinness; Routledge, London, 1961), proposition 6.4311.
[28] See Jacques Derrida, *The Gift of Death* (trans. David Wills; University of Chicago Press, Chicago, 1995), 41.

crisis. It was exacerbated by the emerging awareness of the buried dead as a public health issue, as the civic authorities related plague and disease increasingly to 'miasma' around graveyards. Overcrowded church graveyards, at the centre of towns and villages, were increasingly seen – and feared – as the primary locus of the spread of disease in the proximity of death. The graveyards were thought to be spreading death, distributing it widely. The graveyard, close to home and to where people prayed, was thus thought to be inviting death prematurely into the private home or into the individual body of the worshipper or villager. Laws are now made, therefore, requiring that people bury their bodies beyond the city walls in an effort to ghettoize death and to protect the living against this infection. It is from this period that we see the emergence of cemeteries, as repositories of dead bodies placed at the outskirts of cities or beyond the city walls.

This explains the fact that there is a procession in *A Burial at Ornans*, as the people have made their way out to what is clearly a place in the countryside, with the hills of the Roche du Château and the Roche du Mont in the background. And the final part of this procession – now a fully political event in that it is best understood as an event shaped by politics and law – is what we see as the women make their way round the canvas to arrive in our place, where they will again turn their backs to us so that they can face the fact and the reality of death.

When Courbet makes this painting, he is placing ordinary citizens into the law. He is painting the law in action; and this is a law that governs how we engage with the physical ending of human life. The women will eventually encircle the grave; they will enclose it – but not yet. For it is we who stand there, and we who gaze upon the empty hole, a void or emptiness that awaits a human presence so that it, too, can fulfil its existence. But we are already there. This is a painting to be viewed, as it were, from beyond human existence, from beyond the very point of death and burial itself; and that is where Courbet locates the viewer.

As in *The Stone Breakers*, the task here – the political dynamic of Realism in Courbet – is to avoid representation and to give instead an unbearable reality in all its sheer presence. Much later, in 1935, the Anglo-American poet T. S. Eliot will write in the first of his 'Four Quartets' that 'human kind / Cannot bear very much reality'. One of the concerns of that poem is precisely to ask how we live with the unbearable presence of the present moment, a moment whose full significance comes about only when both past and future collapse into the present itself: the moment of dying: 'What might have been and what has been / Point to one end, which is always present'.[29] Courbet's painting, a

---

[29] T. S. Eliot, *Complete Poems and Plays* (Faber and Faber, London, 1969), 172.

painting that is itself concerned with time, is one that brings us to a moment when the subject is fully present-to-itself, a moment when there can be no future and thus no imagination or imaging. Such a moment is itself the unbearable reality of the physicality of the human body, a body made for dying. A politics that ignores this simple fact is a politics that is concerned merely with images, with representations and imaginings. Courbet asks us to see reality instead.

Part of this reality relates to the political situation regarding burial, which, as I noted earlier, has become a matter of law. It is also worth noting in this context that, in August 1850, Louis Napoleon had visited Besançon, near Ornans, where he expected to be received hospitably, given that the area had strongly backed him after 1848. However, he was instead met by protests, his procession through the streets heckled and jeered by crowds of Republicans. Louis Napoleon responded to this very directly: he ordered the closing of the local newspaper, the *Démocrate Franc-Comtois*.[30] This was also the newspaper that advertised Courbet's local exhibitions. Censoriousness was strong, and immediate; and it is in this context that we need to understand how sensitive establishment politics are at this time to controversy around the realities for which these politicians are responsible.

Obviously, there is a clear sense in which the dead, as in *A Burial at Ornans*, must be unaware that they are being looked at, for they are unaware of everything.[31] The fact of the matter is that they have no consciousness at all. This might help explain Courbet's interest in sleep, as also in painting figures – including sleeping figures – from the back. Sleeping figures, however, figure in Courbet in a way that attends to the third political issue regarding human physicality: sex and sexual being. It is here, perhaps, that we see most clearly of all the unease with which establishment politics regards his work in the mid-1850s, for it is here that censoriousness enters very directly into the reception of his paintings.

It was in 1857 – the year that saw both Flaubert and Baudelaire in the dock, charged with offences against public morality – that Courbet was able to complete his *Demoiselles de La Seine*. This canvas shows two prostitutes dozing on the banks of the river, a small boat in the background with a man's hat clearly visible, and thus suggestive of the sexual liaison that has taken place. The theme of this painting recurs in Courbet's work a decade later, with three remarkable

---

[30] For fuller details, see Clark, *Image of the People*, 100–9.
[31] In passing, it is worth noting the resemblance between Courbet's depiction of the burial in this painting and Flaubert's description of Emma's burial in *Madame Bovary*. See especially Gustave Flaubert, *Madame Bovary*, ed. Claudine Gothot-Mersch (Garnier Frères, Paris, 1971), 344–5.

canvasses: *Venus and Psyche*, *Sleep*, and *L'Origine du Monde*, all made in 1866. *Venus and Psyche* was rejected at the 1866 Salon, which considered the painting to be 'an offence against morals'. Precisely the same censorious attitude that had caused Flaubert and Baudelaire their difficulties in 1857 was alive and well, in the world of the visual arts, in 1866. Yet it is probably the other two – *Sleep* and *L'Origine du Monde* – that are more obviously driven by erotic or sexual interest, given the more explicit nudity of the figures. *Sleep* is clearly erotic, with its two nude figures interlaced on a bed; and *L'Origine* is clearly pornographic – or, at least, was seemingly intended to be so, given its commission by Khalil Bey for his own purposes of private viewing.

Indeed, these paintings, prefigured by Courbet's works on labour and on death a decade earlier, can be usefully considered under the terms of a general condition of 'the privatization of viewing', a form of 'absorption' that now includes the viewer as well. We have seen that explicitly prefigured in my description of *A Burial at Ornans*, where the viewer stands in the position that is about to be occupied by the women who come to mourn and grieve at the graveside. In these later paintings, that viewing position becomes itself taken as an intrinsic element of the work: the viewer herself or himself is called upon to become absorbed in the content of the work.

Sleep is a good example of how this operates.[32] Here, the two women are absorbed in each other. At the same time, however, they are nonetheless there to be viewed, their bodies – and, indeed, their erotic desires for each other – sexually displayed. This combination of display and innocence (they are as if unaware of being viewed in their absorption with each other) is what constitutes the erotic aspect of the work and is also what calls upon the viewer's own involvement or absorption in the scene. This, in turn, makes the scene of *Sleep* into one of privacy, in which the viewing becomes an act of voyeurism. It is taboo, because it involves the invasion of a privacy, as it were – the viewer knows that she or he should not be seeing what is before them; the subjects within the painting would be shocked if they knew that they were being watched. Their absorption, which is at the core of the reality of their situation, would immediately become one where they are aware of themselves, and thus forced to 're-present' themselves theatrically, with the corresponding loss of all real being or ontological substance: they would become a mere painting, and they themselves 'for show'.

The viewer, then, is brought into a private view and becomes part of the world of the painting. This is – presumably – the desired aim in Khalil Bey's famous

---

[32] To see an image of this painting, see: petitpalais.paris.fr/en/oeuvre/sleepers.

commission of *L'Origine du Monde*. The trajectory across these painting becomes one that is shaped by an idea of 'transgression': the transgression of a boundary between public and private realms, followed by the transgression of the space of a bedroom, culminating finally in the invitation to transgress the private space of a human body itself. It is transgression that makes these paintings revealing of a taboo: the taboo of human sexual being, especially the sexual being of the female body and of female desire. And this, in 1866, brings us back once again to Emma Bovary a decade earlier.

It is worth considering Courbet's own clear political position when he made these paintings, for he was explicit in his agreement with the logic of Proudhon. As James Henry Rubin has argued, the rejection of Courbet's *Atelier* painting reveals what it is that is absolutely determining of a very specific and prevailing anxiety in 1855 France. Rubin points out that 'the cultural conditions of artistic production in the mid-nineteenth century... were determined by a contradiction between, on the one hand, the ideal of artistic creativity as unfettered subjective expression, and, on the other, the reality of concrete economic and social structures that invariably governed artistic success and survival in Paris'.[33]

Courbet sits at the centre of this, and had to think his way through the relations between economic necessities and aesthetic freedom. His way of resolving the contradiction here depended on his understanding of the conditions of labour, especially as described by Proudhon, for whom 'man worked from inner necessity for material satisfaction, and the value of the product thus depended on labor as *the expression of man's physicality*'.[34] Indeed, Proudhon himself argued that 'the constitutive element of society is the atelier', and that it was only through work – in the workshop, however realized – that freedom, and especially freedom from social injustices, could be attained.[35] Rubin goes on to say that 'Because of the physical and economic nature of man, then, artistic and intellectual freedom were economic matters. And because the artist had to contend with both the aesthetic and the economic constraints of governmental institutions, they were political matters'.[36]

Given all of this, it follows for Courbet also that 'to recognize work as man's means to survival was to recognize his mortality as well (as in Courbet's *Burial*), and vice versa'.[37] Proudhon also contended that the forces that give value to labour

---

[33] James Henry Rubin, *Realism and Social Vision in Courbet and Proudhon* (Princeton University Press, Princeton, 1980), 5.
[34] Ibid., 31 (stress added).
[35] Ibid., 36. Rubin quotes Proudhon from a statement made to Pierre Leroux in *La Voix du peuple*, no. 74 (13 December 1849).
[36] Rubin, *Realism*, 36.
[37] Ibid., 33.

are essentially the same as those that drive sexual desire. Because the motivations for labour and sex are similar, Courbet is able – especially in paintings such as the *Demoiselles* – to paint an essential component of the economic politics of the period, especially in high society: prostitution, or literally sex-work. The shock of his realism is actually a shock that the State feels at the fact that he is laying bare not the naked body, but the naked conditions of social and political life in all their material reality. As Rubin puts it, 'many men of the 1850s understood only too well the artist's intentions as having profound socio-political ramifications. These intentions were socialist and working class – that is, they represented the deepest and most permanent opposition to the higher classes that had, at least since 1852, become the solid base of Napoleon III's power'.[38]

6

We can now see what is the real object of censorship at this time in two of the world's most advanced economies: France and England. In the case of England, we saw that the State was concerned by two interlinked things: the possibility of an uprising in its empire that would question England's moral standing; and the fear that it might lose a normative control over what constituted legitimate sexual activity. Sexual activity was to be a private matter, and the public display of it was to be described as inherently obscene. Worse, because it was linked with the possibility of infection and disease, sexual activity outside the private domain was seen as potentially life-threatening. Sex and death become jointly taboo. That taboo, however, is also to be dealt with under the terms of a construction of the idealized English national (manly) character; and it is thus that this collocation of sex and death becomes instrumental in a determination of English superiority over other cultures and other races, in which imperialism is itself construed as a form of labour. Sex, death and labour all become inserted into a hierarchy; and anything that menaces the superior position in that hierarchy – occupied by the privileged English upper-class male, with a sexual life that is essentially privatized through the domestication of female sexuality – is to be censored, rendered both illegitimate and invisible.

The French position is similar, if expressed more directly via the sphere of aesthetic culture. The French State – like the English in this regard – feels the need to censor three very specific realities: the material reality of labour as that

[38] Ibid., 100.

which produces the reality of the bodies of human beings; the physical fact of death as the necessary fulfilment of human secular life and the confirmation of the primacy of secularism over the sacred or religious; and sex as the potential power of woman within a society that requires female submission to a masculinist ideology. These are the realities – the political realism – that the French State cannot easily accommodate and which it feels the need to censor.

To combat these, as we will see in more detail later, the State invokes the principle of 'the people', in the form of what it will call public morality; and it thereby co-opts the people as a mass into the express repression of the real and material conditions of everyday life. This is what informs the logic behind the prosecutions of both Flaubert and Baudelaire.

3

Grotesque Realism
Flaubert, Baudelaire, impropriety and decorum

1

Two years after Courbet had politicized Realism in his 1855 Pavillon, Flaubert was prosecuted in relation to the serial publication of *Madame Bovary* in the *Revue de Paris*. The prosecution's case was that the work 'offended public morality and religion'. The public, it was alleged, faced a fundamental threat to the codes by which people in general (though no one in particular) existed: morals and religion. It was probably fortunate for Flaubert that the court did not have access to his private notebooks, where he had recorded, in crude and direct language, some of the daily events and his intimate thoughts and experiences in the preceding years. The *Carnets* describe, among many other things, some of the sexual experiences Flaubert had when he travelled in Egypt and elsewhere in 1849–50. As private notebooks, our governing assumption is surely that they describe real historical events in all their material factuality, even if the pages are written by the pen of a great fiction-novelist. The assumption is that he is not intending to fool himself; and the remarkable improprieties of his language tend to suggest that these comments were, indeed, for entirely private consumption. He is perhaps amusing himself, but not lying to himself.

In March 1850, Flaubert visited a brothel, and had sex with a woman called Kuchuk-Hanem, noting that, in his 'second shot' with her, 'as I kissed her shoulder I could feel her necklace against my teeth – her cunt milking me was just like rolls of velvet – I felt ferocious'.[1] He is not alone on his travels here, either: 'Scarcely had we set foot on land when the infamous Du Camp [with whom he was traveling] experienced an erection at the sight of a negress drawing water from a fountain. He is equally excited by negro boys. By whom is he not excited?

---

[1] Geoffrey Wall, *Flaubert: A Life* (Faber and Faber, London, 2001), 174.

Or rather, by what?'.² In El Fayoum, Flaubert came across a priest and noted that the priest was 'quite obviously getting it up the lady of the house', before Flaubert himself engaged in sex with a prostitute 'with a pair the size of pumpkins'.³ In Athens, on the way back, 'I'm about to join the ranks of the men that whores wince at when it comes to the shagging'.⁴

Alongside the notebooks, ostensibly intended only for himself to read and thus for private delectation and not public consumption, Flaubert's letters during this same period also sometimes refer to this kind of event, thereby evidentially corroborating the realities and factual substance of the descriptions in the notebooks. In those letters to his correspondents – which are semi-public in that they do have an intended audience, however intimate, we find the usually more decorous language – the public language, as it were – in which he talked about his writing plans. Impropriety for private consumption, decorousness when the communication is with someone else, and thus at least partly public: both suggest realism, but with very different attitudes, and with different politics as a consequence.

In the preceding chapters, we were able to examine a particular inflection in realism. In the sphere of painting, a context arose in which the real is first of all identified with labour, death and sex: in all cases, the material production and condition of the human body is at the centre of realism's concern. In one specific turn, this body's reality is itself identified with the naked body, or even with the parts of the body that are most usually decorated – decorously covered up – in society. Thus, the naked body – and its privacy – becomes confused, in the mind of a collector such as Khalil Bey, with desire itself, and in that turn, realism opens itself to impropriety. It is from the contest of impropriety and decorousness that the collector commissions *L'Origine du Monde*. From that, we derive also an impetus for the collector towards the structural *privatization* of the real world – fundamentally tied to an economics of privatization or of capital acquisition and accumulation – as the painting makes its way into a private collection. Like Flaubert's *Carnets*, it there enjoys its status as realistic impropriety, and realistic because of its impropriety.

In this chapter, we can explore further this problematic relation of public realities with the private sphere; and we will see a new inflection of the aesthetics and politics of realism, particularly in the domain of language and literature. Flaubert will provide the first test case. In Flaubert, we find the relation of

---

² Ibid., 163.
³ Ibid., 172.
⁴ Ibid., 185.

realism to cliché in language and to a specific kind of impersonality in literature. This, indeed, is something that Flaubert – at least momentarily – shared with Courbet's friend, Baudelaire, as my next chapter will show in detail. What links the two writers in this, of course, is their linguistic impropriety with respect to society's preferred decorousness. That lies behind the fact of their prosecutions in the French courts – both of them for offences against public morals – during 1857, the same year that the legislation for the Obscene Publications Act is being carried through Parliament in England.

2

By November 1850, Flaubert had moved on from Egypt and found himself in Damascus, accompanied still by Maxime Du Camp on this next stage of his travels through what is now the Middle East and North Africa. Du Camp had just inherited the vast sum of some 200,000 francs, following the death of his grandmother. This was the money that largely funded the trip for both men. Both of the men were recently bereaved, in fact. Apart from his grandmother, Du Camp had just also suffered the death of his mother, while Flaubert was in mourning for the death of his close friend, Alfred du Poittevin. Flaubert was also in some despair after what he perceived as the failure of his *Tentation de Saint Antoine*. Indeed, his fellow Rouennais, the poet-dramatist Louis Bouilhet – essentially Flaubert's literary mentor as well as good friend – told him directly and without cushioning the blow, that his *Tentation de Saint Antoine* was a complete failure. Flaubert's poor mood and state of mind – occasioned by his grief over Poittevin – now worsened further when he heard this valuation of his writing, from one whose judgement he valued.

Flaubert had begun the trip with Du Camp reluctantly, then, feeling bereft and anxious; but, by the time they reached Damascus, having sailed up and down the Nile, partaking promiscuously in as many sexual adventures as he could, he was feeling ready to write again. In July, he had written to Bouilhet to say that 'I have been feeling myself bursting with intellectual intensity. The pot suddenly began to boil! I felt a burning need to write!'[5] It seems clear that his extraordinary libidinal (and libidinous) sexual energy would now be displaced and condensed into work – a literary project – accompanied by this somewhat

[5] Francis Steegmuller, ed. and trans., *The Letters of Gustave Flaubert 1830–1857* (Belknap; Harvard University Press, Cambridge, MA, 1980), 122; letter of 27 June 1850.

more decorous (if still emotive and raw) language. He also sees the activity of writing as itself a kind of turn away from the materiality of his sexual adventures and fleshly engagement with the world. Yet he does not turn completely into a world of supposed privacy, for his concentration will be on language itself, and on the public deployment of everyday speech.

Shortly after his July letter, he indicates what this new writing might be. 'You do well', he tells Bouilhet in a letter dated 4 September 1850, 'to think about the *Dictionary of Accepted Opinions*'. This projected book was one with which Flaubert would dally for the next two decades, while he was in fact publishing his most celebrated fiction. In these years, he made a series of notes towards the proposed Dictionary; and, in one plan, he intended it as an appendix to *Bouvard et Pécuchet*, which was itself to be left unfinished at the time of his eventual death. It is in the context of *Bouvard et Pécuchet* that it makes most sense to consider the entries that do in fact exist for the Dictionary, and also to consider what the real point and purchase of the Dictionary project might actually be. More specifically still, it is important to grasp the relation of these projects to the fundamental principles of realism.

It is difficult to imagine that, when Flaubert came up with the idea of making a *Dictionnaire des Idées Reçues*, he could not also have had in mind previous controversial 'dictionaries' or similar texts in French culture, including the revised sixth edition of the *Dictionnaire de l'Académie française* of 1835, a controversial edition whose aim was to re-purpose the dictionary for a republican and no longer monarchical age. The year 1842 saw the publication also of the *Complément du Dictionnaire de l'Académie française*, under the direction of Louis Barré. In his introduction to this supplement, Barré argued that languages can fall into decadence, vocabulary into desuetude. But, he asks 'who will judge whether language has become decadent or not? It is the genius of the *littérateur,* who alone sees how the relation of word to idea starts to alter, how words become more vague or abstract, floating around their idea instead of seizing it and dressing it with an elegant clarity'.[6] This – a succinct problematization of a realist aesthetic – is exactly Flaubert's quarry: the 'proper' functioning of language, a functioning that (it turns out) may well be conditioned by impropriety.

Given, further, that Flaubert's proposed dictionary would be focused on ideas as such, we can surely see the shadow more specifically of Voltaire, whose *Lettres philosophiques* of 1734 had caused its writer immense problems and difficulties.

---

[6] Louis Barré et al., *Introductory Materials Prefacing the Complément du Dictionnaire de l'Académie française* (trans. mine; Firmin-Didot, Paris, 1881 edition), 10, available at: https://gallica.bnf.fr/ark: /12148/bpt6k5834322m/f8.item.r=langue (accessed 11 July 2019).

Voltaire's book was burnt in public, and banned; and Voltaire went into exile – as he had had to do on previous occasions – in the face of State censorship and persecution. Voltaire's text had criticized French political conditions; but had done so very indirectly. The *Lettres* were a series of commentaries on British political systems; but the implicit comparison with the French was obvious, even if Voltaire had 'self-censored' by avoiding a direct critique of France. Flaubert's proposed text was planned as something much more direct, and more pointedly aimed at the real conditions of everyday life, as evinced through the clichés of thought and speech that governed real and material society.

As in those of his writings that can be straightforwardly described as 'fiction', Flaubert's eye in the *Dictionnaire* project was on the relation of language to realities; and his aesthetic was one that was couched in this 'linguistic realism'. By exposing cliché through the most realistic representation of it, without critical commentary or undermining, Flaubert would show that clichéd speech – which often constituted the accepted social decorum and etiquette of the day – constituted the 'way of seeing' that his fellow citizens regarded as legitimate. However, the straightforward and realistic representation would show that cliché in language is that which in fact limits our view of actual material reality, and that even misrepresents the world as it is. In this way, the project would be a systematic undermining of the work of the Académie on their Dictionary, and thereby profoundly controversial to the State and its cultural establishment. In fact, the unstated claim is that the Académie's hold on – and control of – what constitutes reality and its proper linguistic description is entirely bogus.

In an astute reading of Flaubert's realist predecessor, Balzac, Sandrine Berthelot proposes a useful consideration of realism as such as it emerged and flourished in the French nineteenth century. She gives an account that is completely relevant also to any serious consideration of Flaubert's attitude to representation. She argues that 'far from a serious conception of *mimesis*, we can propose the hypothesis that realism is better thought of in fact as a literature of denunciation and derision'. Realism offers a writing that is constitutionally and aesthetically 'violently opposed to bourgeois values, making a break with classical representations of the world, and tending towards the supreme – or grotesque – derision, one that laughs at the most serious things, one that plays with death, one that denies all values and opens itself instead to the unknown'.[7]

---

[7] Sandrine Berthelot, 'Balzac et le réalisme grotesque. Lecture de *La Cousine Bette*', in *La Pensée du paradoxe: approches du romantisme*, eds Didier Philippot et Fabienne Bercegol (trans. mine; PUF, Paris, 2006), 147–8: 'Loin d'une conception sérieuse de la *mimesis*, nous posons l'hypothèse que le réalisme serait au contraire une littérature de dénonciation et de dérision, violemment opposée

The immediate appropriateness of this in relation to Flaubert is clear as soon as we look at his letters, in which he considers his own aesthetic. In a letter to Louise Colet on 9 October 1852, he describes writing a passage concerning a meeting between Léon and Emma in *Madame Bovary*: 'It is something that could be taken seriously, and yet I fully intend it as grotesque. This will be the first time, I think, that a book makes fun of its leading lady and its leading man.'[8]

This attitude – the real as grotesque, at least in its translation into aesthetic representation – is, in fact, a staple element in the emergence of realism as an explicitly 'modern' aesthetic.[9] For example, it is a truism of literary criticism to see the emergence of the specific eighteenth-century form of the novel – if not also its earlier fictional precursors – as work that focuses attention on so-called 'low life', on that which is 'vulgar' or, literally, of the people and of the crowds. The focus is on what polite society regards as the usually and preferably invisible, the undesirable: that merging of human and animal (as described in Chapter 1) that constitutes the 'grotesque' as such. The intimacy between this new fictional form and the real-life discourses of criminals and outlaws (what such individuals actually said on their way to the gallows) has been well-charted, by Lennard J. Davis, among others.[10] Yet the impulse driving this phenomenon is more fundamental than the mere presentations or operations of literary 'character'.

In order to 'emerge' and to identify itself as a specific aesthetic, realism has to present itself as constitutively different from the prevailing modes of its moment – as we saw Courbet suavely doing with the setting up of his Pavillon du Réalisme in 1855. It rejects – resists – the priorities of the normative values surrounding writing or painting; and, in doing so, it constructs its aesthetic enemy, in order the better to declare war on it and to emerge, victorious, as a new value system. What, then, is it that realism rejects; and what does it contest?

Realism, we might now venture to say, is that aesthetic form that opposes a certain established notion of 'propriety' or decorousness, or that at least opposes the idea that such propriety is normative within a social formation. It resists the coercion that operates under the sign of what is 'proper' and decorous to existing social contracts and settlements. To cut to the chase here, what this means is that realism as it emerges through this cultural moment essentially

---

aux valeurs bourgeoises, en rupture avec les représentations classiques du monde, et tendant à la dérision suprême – ou grotesque –, celle qui rit des choses les plus graves, celle qui joue avec la mort, celle qui nie les valeurs et ouvre à l'inconnu'.

[8] Steegmuller, *Letters of Flaubert*, 171.
[9] For an account of the persistence of the 'grotesque real' through to the contemporary moment, see Robert Duggan, *The Grotesque in Contemporary British Fiction* (Manchester University Press, Manchester, 2013).
[10] See Lennard J. Davis, *Factual Fictions* (Columbia University Press, New York, 1983).

calls into question the idea of property as such, and of private property in particular. Realism wants to present life in the manner in which (as we saw in my quoted passages at the opening of this chapter) Flaubert presented it to himself, privately, in his *Carnets*: unfurnished, unvarnished – the human as animal, the real itself precisely as grotesque. The governing assumption is that aesthetic representation, prior to the new norms of realism, must have been concerned to present the world or reality in an artificially edifying manner. That is to say: all previously existing and normative modes of representation were necessarily and intrinsically misrepresentation, and were founded upon an aversion to the real as such.

Philosophically, this falls into alignment with attitudes to the status of 'truth', especially in the European eighteenth century. Hans Blumenberg persuasively argued that 'truth' itself undergoes a significant change in the eighteenth century.[11] Philosophy had traditionally associated the true with *eudaemonia*, with well-feeling and well-being. For Aristotle, famously, truth made you happy in that it helped to rid you of misunderstandings and falsehoods, such falsehoods leading to error in our understanding of what is for the best. Truth unmasked harmful falsehood; and, in clearing things up, made us intrinsically happier as individuals. However – or so the Blumenberg argument goes – truth starts to assume a major new evaluative significance in the emergence of social and political modernity. It becomes something that is not only argued about, but that is also absolute. Scientific endeavour tends to prioritize among possible variant 'interpretations' of the real, and then edges thereby towards a hierarchy in which truth itself is validated in absolutist terms. As a result, the 'homage' that we pay to truth is measured now in the amount of discomfort it provokes in us, including the discomforts that we undergo in seeking it out. For the first time in philosophical history, truth becomes 'painful', and we start to measure its validity not in terms of the pleasure that it provokes but rather in terms of how disconcerting it is for us.

In the literary domain, the idea of representation as a specific structural misrepresentation had already found its legitimation in Sidney's 1595 'Apology for Poetry'. There, Sidney argued, first of all, that poetry is the fundamental condition of all existing knowledge of the world. There are diverse disciplines, certainly; and they all take the world of nature as their object. Poetry, however, goes beyond mere description of nature. 'Only the poet,' writes Sidney, 'doth

---

[11] The argument I present here derives from Hans Blumenberg, *The Legitimacy of the Modern Age* (trans. R. M. Wallace; MIT Press, Cambridge, MA, 1983).

grow in effect another nature.' The poet is free, not tied to the world of things as they are or have been, because the poet has the power of imagination and invention. The poet, therefore, can improve upon nature: 'Nature never set forth the earth in so rich tapestry as divers poets have done. . . . Her world is brazen, the poets only deliver a golden'.¹² This understanding of the nature of art continues, in literature at least, through to the celebrated formulations given by Alexander Pope in 1711, arguing that *'True Wit* is *Nature* to Advantage drest, / What oft was *Thought*, but ne'er so well *Exprest*'.¹³

Against this, however, the nineteenth century sees a different attitude to representation. The new form of realism – a form that interested Flaubert in fiction and Courbet in painting – will focus attention instead on all that the existing arts and fiction have covered up: the 'brazen' world of material and natural realities and conditions that have been dressed in fine and edifying ornament by 'art', and which existing art forms have thus hidden from view and consideration. This realism's aim is not to present an 'improved' world, a world that takes the brazen and enhances its price by rendering it in more valuable gold; rather, the aim is to be yet more brazen in fact, and to 'undress' the world of any gloss at all.

Realism will be 'revelatory'; it will be a formal 'unveiling'; it will strip away the gloss to reveal the underlying ostensibly naked reality of things. In some instances, as with Courbet's *L'Origine du Monde*, this will be an extreme stripping away of any and all ornament, in the genre of the nude but done in that painting without even a human face that might divert attention away from the most intimate focus upon the female genitals.

In 1859 (by which time he had distanced himself from Courbet, with whom he had enjoyed an earlier close friendship and affinity), Baudelaire could describe realist painting as devoid of the human subject entirely: not just a universe without a model's face (as in the case of *L'Origine*), but entirely without humanity at all. The artist who self-describes as realist, he writes, is the artist who says 'I intend to represent things just as they are, or as they would be, as if I myself did not exist'; and this gives us 'the universe without humanity'.¹⁴ Realism here answers the question that had been implied by the 'immaterialist' philosophy

---

¹² Philip Sidney, 'An Apology for Poetry', in *English Critical Essays: Sixteenth, Seventeenth and Eighteenth Centuries*, ed. Edmund D. Jones (Oxford University Press, Oxford, 1975), 7.

¹³ Alexander Pope, 'An Essay on Criticism', in *The Poems of Alexander Pope*, ed. John Butt (Methuen, London, 1975), 153.

¹⁴ Charles Baudelaire, 'Salon de 1859', in Baudelaire, *Critique d'art* (trans. mine, Gallimard, Paris, 1992), 187: 'celui-ci, qui s'appelle lui-même *réaliste* . . . dit: "Je veux représenter les choses telles qu'elles sont, ou bien qu'elles seraient, en supposant que je n'existe pas." L'univers sans l'homme'.

of George Berkeley, a philosophy that asks what a tree might be like if there is no one to perceive it; but the answer contradicts the fundamental principles of Berkeley's philosophy, for Baudelaire's real world is thoroughly material, in ways that I will indicate later.

The governing assumption that drives and motivates the new form of realism in the mid-nineteenth century has to be that the gloss was always there in order to occlude something that the society did not like to consider: the real must, almost by definition now, be disturbing in some way, like the muddy or filthy gutters that overflow onto Stendhal's road, made visible by his mirror. It is the sense that the real has been not just 'to advantage drest' but rather the sense that it has been fundamentally 'censored' by that dressing, its brazen condition polished to burnished golden, that realism will challenge. Realism presents itself as a resistance to censorship – to 'polishing' and to the 'polite', to anything dressed in service of decorous social etiquette – as such.[15] For this reason, it will always face fundamental difficulties – due to its perceived impropriety – in any censorious State, or in any jurisdiction where the established powers are determined to retain existing privileges (and private property, or commonly shared wealth that has been transferred systematically into a small number of private hands) without the threat of any possible questioning of the legitimacy by which those privileges (or that wealth) might be held.

For Flaubert, the gloss in question lies within language itself, and perhaps especially within the vernacular of everyday speech: cliché. He is as aware as the makers of the French Dictionary and its Supplements that the relation of words to worlds is always contentious. He is deeply conscious of the fact that words are often used not to reveal ideas or thought but to prevent individual and critical thought from occurring in the first place. His task, then, is to provoke thought in his reader by showing, in words, how words themselves are often a barrier to thought. The intention is to demonstrate that words themselves can be devoid of any authentic and spontaneous idea at all in the speaker. When used thoughtlessly in this way, the words that a speaker utters are, in fact, the ventriloquized expression and validation of the thoughts of others, others who are determined to ensure that the meanings and values that they espouse will not be troubled by the critical thinking or thoughtful opposition of anyone else. This is the start of mass mediation; and it is intrinsically censorious, not in a moral

---

[15] For Baudelaire in 1859, the objection to realism derives from Baudelaire's own revalorization of the imagination and its status as the 'queen of the faculties'. See Baudelaire, *Critique*, 280.

but in a political sense. This is the framework into which Flaubert intends to launch his *Dictionnaire des Idées Reçues*.

3

Yet it does not follow for a demystifying realism that the artist or writer simply 'records' material realities in some supposedly neutral fashion. In realism, the artist and writer exert a specific pressure upon the presentation of those realities. Courbet himself, in his succinct 'Manifesto', stresses that, though he knows both the traditional and modern art of his time, his intention was not to follow them, nor even to follow the emergence of aestheticist 'art for art's sake'. Instead, he wanted to use his knowledge and expertise in order to 'mine . . . the reasoned and independent understanding of my own individuality', and 'to translate the customs, ideas and appearance of my times in accordance with my evaluations'.[16]

Realism in this vein permits of individual expression, as well as choice or prioritization of subject matter. It is as much a matter of the artist's *attitudes* to the world – a specific and literal 'disposition' with respect to the world – as of her or his technical abilities to represent a recognizable material reality. The entire problem, as contemporary philosophy today will tell us, relates to what Quentin Meillassoux has labelled 'correlationism'. The correlationist believes that we cannot conceive of external realities apart from our human consciousness of them, and nor can we conceive of human consciousness divorced from the pressures exerted upon it by external realities. That is to say: correlationism tries to calibrate the respective demands of a determining consciousness and of material realities that might seem to care little about whether consciousness perceives them or not. It steers a path between a romantic view of the subject as being able to determine the course of history by exerting its will upon realities on one hand, and a pessimistic view that accepts that the world does not exist 'for us' or 'for consciousness' at all.[17]

In our time, for a philosopher such as Meillassoux, the simple fact that the world existed prior to human consciousness (the universe long pre-dates the emergence of the human, a fact that yields what Meillassoux calls 'ancestrality')

---

[16] Gustave Courbet, 'Le Réalisme', in *Exhibition et Vente de 40 Tableaux et 4 Dessins de l'Oeuvre de M. Gustave Courbet*, (1855), reproduced in James H. Rubin, *Courbet* (Phaidon, London, 1997), 156-8 (trans. mine): 'j'ai voulu tout simplement puiser dans l'entière connaissance de la tradition le sentiment raisonné et indépendant de ma propre individualité . . . Être à même de traduire les moeurs, les idées, l'aspect de mon époque, selon mon appréciation.'

[17] See Quentin Meillassoux, *After Finitude* (trans. Ray Brassier; Continuum, London, 2008).

is clear evidence that there does exist (or at least that there did exist) a material reality that can be independent of consciousness. Against this, the nineteenth-century artist would respond by noting that even the very awareness of ancestrality is, now and as it arises, a matter for the present human consciousness. In time, this will work itself out in literature in theories regarding the persistence of inheritance, be it that of wealth (as in, for example, the classic example of Galsworthy's fictions that make up *The Forsyte Saga*) or of physical determinism (as in Zola's explorations of heredity in the *Rougon-Macquart* series).

For Courbet, attentive to an ancestral 'tradition' and simultaneously alive to the 'here, now', the question becomes one of an illustration of attitudes, inclinations, dispositions: *ethos*. Further, this attitude or *ethos* – the ethics of painting – is, above all, determined by the combination of the social and political conditions of the world that is to be depicted along with the angle from which the artist himself looks at the world. It depends upon an inflection of what Meillassoux will later call the 'correlation' between the demands that we exercise and extend human possibility set against the constraints on that possibility that are exerted by the realities of the material world.

This combination of a focus on bare material conditions with the artist's expression of an individuality – what T. S. Eliot would call, in 1919, 'tradition and the individual talent' in fact – is a key element in the constitution of aesthetic modernity: realism operates precisely as a mode of critique, and it does so by claiming to present a reality that usually lies occluded under existing social and political norms that are uncritically accepted as the determinants of human life and possibility. In literature, those norms are norms that are governed by language.

It is clear that as early as 1850, Flaubert sees something grotesque in the very fact of adequate representation itself. Importantly, he also saw that his writing had a very specific relation to the law. When he discussed his *Dictionnaire des Idées Reçues* in his correspondence with Louise Colet, he indicated that by writing it in the style that he favoured, 'no law could touch me although I would attack everything'. He is already aware of the potential difficulties that writing faces when operating in a jurisdiction whose legal system expects certain decorous norms. He goes on to explain the reason why he would be immune to prosecution, telling Colet that the contents of the dictionary 'would be the historical glorification of everything generally approved'.[18] In short, Flaubert proposes to avoid censorship by presenting the linguistic account of reality in

---

[18] Flaubert, letter to Louise Colet, 16 December 1852, in Steegmuller, *Letters of Flaubert*, 175.

its most commonly accepted forms. By writing down public opinions, he will expose them in all their fatuous vacuity and thoughtlessness. He will be utterly compliant with everything that is regulated under the law; and he will do this essentially by presenting everything that is taken for granted as 'reality', no matter how grotesque it will be, under cover of its decorousness. He will write an endless stream of cliché, whose vacuity will be obvious precisely because it will be presented as if we should take it seriously.

In this, he is a forerunner of Roland Barthes a century later. Barthes famously described his entire project of semiotic analysis as, essentially, the exposure of cliché to scrutiny. In his Introduction to *Mythologies*, he explains that 'I resented seeing Nature and History confused at every turn, and I wanted to track down, in the decorative display of *what-goes-without-saying*, the ideological abuse which ... is hidden there'.[19] Flaubert intends simply to present in its purest form – that is, to *say* – everything that passes as *what-goes-without-saying*. By expressing what-goes-without-saying as the reality of how people speak and think, and even to glorify it by writing it down, he sees that a realistic presentation of linguistic norms exposes those norms to critique. Realism and critique go together here, intrinsically and even umbilically linked. There can be no doubt that, for Flaubert, as for Barthes, 'the essential enemy' is 'the bourgeois norm', nor can there be doubt that that norm is itself governed and guaranteed by the mechanics of everyday speech and linguistic commerce.[20]

It is the realistic presentation of cliché that will scandalize everyone and that will criticize every existing social norm; and Flaubert will be untouchable by law – notwithstanding the fact that he will be criticizing every existing political and juridical value – precisely because he is simply being utterly realistic, and presenting 'reality' as the social customs and norms that underpin the law would have us see it and describe it. Given this, it is logical for Flaubert to write in simple realistic terms those very scenes in *Madame Bovary* that would, in fact, bring him to stand before the law, charged with offences against public morality. To Flaubert, the very fact of being prosecuted is both illogical (because he is simply presenting the world-that-goes-without-saying, presenting the given or what we take for granted) and also utterly predictable (because the law itself acts as a cover for social and cultural hypocrisy).

So this realism turns out to be the best vehicle for the avoidance of censorship, at least in theory if not in historical fact. That becomes the paradox that surrounds

---

[19] Roland Barthes, *Mythologies* (1957; trans. Annette Lavers; Granada, London, 1973), 11.
[20] Ibid., 9.

the trial: the naïve presentation of the world as it really exists for everyone is precisely the reality that the world cannot accept and which it must expunge. Flaubert saw it as hypocrisy; but for us, as far as an understanding of realism is concerned, it is simply and fundamentally a paradoxical aporia.

Flaubert told Colet that in the projected work, with its endless invocation of cliché, 'I would demonstrate that majorities have always been right, minorities always wrong'. In the political realm, populist majoritarian politics would be ostensibly validated; but this simple statement, with its implicit censoring of minority views (and thus of social critique), would thereby not only reveal its mindlessness but would implicitly call for resistance to the very populism that it ostensibly celebrates. In aesthetics, 'I would show that in literature, mediocrity, being within the reach of everyone, is alone legitimate, and that consequently every kind of originality must be denounced as dangerous, ridiculous, etc'. As in the political sphere, so also in the aesthetic: conformism would censor thought and invention; and, again paradoxically, this censoring calls forth resistance.

> I would declare that this apologia for human vulgarity in all its aspects . . . was aimed at doing away, once and for all, with all eccentricities, whatever they might be. That would lead to the modern democratic idea of equality. . . . It would include, in alphabetical order and covering all possible subjects, 'everything one should say if one is to be considered a decent and likeable member of society'.[21]

Flaubert comes here to the core of the question, in which the *legality of censorship* comes up against the *legitimacy of critique* and of resistance to all social norms.

The key to his avoiding censorship or constraining himself derives from the simple fact that, as with much literary modernity, the book would be very impersonal and would be composed entirely of quotations: 'There would not be a single word invented by me in the whole book.' The outcome, however, would be extraordinary: 'If properly done, anyone who read it would never dare open his mouth again, for fear of spontaneously uttering one of its pronouncements.'[22] As with speech, however, so also with actual and material behaviour: 'And a concisely written list of types could be included, to show not only what one should *say*, but what one should *seem to be*.'[23]

---

[21] Steegmuller, *Letters of Flaubert*, 175–6.
[22] Ibid., 176.
[23] Ibid.

4

Bouvard et Pécuchet is not usually regarded as Flaubert's most important work, an accolade that most often goes to either *L'Education sentimentale* or to *Madame Bovary*. However, its fundamental shape and ideological drive is utterly consistent with those novels, and it reveals its guiding intellectual principles perhaps more obviously than the more celebrated texts. All three texts here share a kind of Balzacian disenchantment with the *illusions perdues* of their respective protagonists.[24] They are novels of disappointment, of romances and hopes dashed, of optimism coming up against a material world – realism – that refuses to concede or to give grounds to fantasy or to imaginings.

Bouvard et Pécuchet, further, finds our two disillusioned protagonists eventually contemplating suicide, in a setting that is incipiently prescient of Beckett, the writer who thematizes disappointment as itself constitutive of reality as such. Flaubert's two clowns, his version of what will become in more recent literature Vladimir and Estragon, finally reach the end of their tether. Pécuchet rushes out of the room in which they are having what looks like their final argument, and heads for the garret, where they have set up a pair of nooses. Bouvard follows, after a very Beckettian difficulty in opening the door of the garret that Pécuchet has slammed behind him – farce puncturing tragedy here, as would be typical in Beckett. 'The candle was on the floor, and Pécuchet was standing on one of the chairs, with the rope in his hand.' But, as in *Godot*, 'The spirit of imitation got the better of Bouvard', so 'Wait for me!' he says, jumping up onto the other chair. Then, stopping suddenly, he says 'Hang on, we haven't made our wills!' Pécuchet replies, 'Wait, yes, that's right.' This prefigures the scene in *Waiting for Godot* where Didi and Gogo are pondering hanging themselves, but face the problem that they don't have a rope. They come up with the idea of using Gogo's belt, with Didi hanging onto Gogo's legs as he drops; but then Didi asks, 'And who'd hang onto mine', to which the dispirited reply, arresting the plan, is Gogo's 'True', a word used at many points through the play every time that some positive-sounding plan is proposed and then stymied. In *Bouvard et Pécuchet*, our two central characters are, in the same way, diverted from the task – and rope – in hand. They can't go on; they must go on; they'll go on.[25]

---

[24] The *Dictionnaire des Idées Reçues* gives the cliché around 'illusions' as: 'claim to have many, and complain that you've lost them.' See Flaubert, *Dictionnaire*, appended at end of Flaubert, *Bouvard et Pécuchet* (Garnier-Flammarion, Paris, 1966), 360.
[25] Flaubert, *Bouvard et Pécuchet*, 256 7 (trans. mine). Cf. Samuel Beckett, *Waiting for Godot*, Act 2, with Vladimir and Estragon trying to work out the logistics of suicide by hanging; and cf. Beckett, closing passage of *The Unnamable*.

In passing, and because of this structural or thematic repetition between Flaubert and Beckett, it is worth teasing out what ghosts this context as a tacit reference here to Marx. At the start of the *Eighteenth Brumaire*, Marx suggests that he re-presents Hegel, but without knowing exactly and precisely what part of Hegel it is that he mirrors or rehearses: 'Hegel remarks somewhere', he writes. What Marx can recall is the content of the remark: 'all events and personalities of great importance in word history occur, as it were, twice.' History, according to this, is structured by repetition and mirroring: the present repeats something from the past, the here-now repeats an ancestral moment, an individual and new talent rehearses and re-heats a tradition. What Marx adds to this is instructive: 'He [Hegel] forgot to add: the first time as tragedy, the second as farce.' This is Marx's way of introducing the contest, as he sees it, between the human subject's exercise of free autonomous agency and the resistance to that agency presented by the material conditions of history. Famously, 'Men make their own history, but they do not make it just as they please; they do not make it under circumstances chosen by themselves, but under circumstances directly encountered and inherited from the past. The tradition of all the generations of the dead weighs like a nightmare on the brain of the living.'[26]

The realism of Flaubert, at least in *Bouvard et Pécuchet*, works by collapsing the temporal and historical division here between first and second times, between present and representation. It takes the representation (the farce) and gives it *as* the presentation (tragedy). In doing so, it deals with the 'ancestry' issue described by Meillassoux, by showing the ancestral *as* the present, and thus by indicating that there is no escape from the past, from the ancestors, from heredity, or from the constraints of society as it currently exists. Any attempt to escape – which here means any attempt at finding an authentic speech or an authentic autonomous subjectivity – is seen as farcical, fundamentally 'improper' and thus a forerunner of the fundamentally 'absurd' a century later. As the later Beckett has it, or as he puts it in the mouth of Estragon wrestling with the recalcitrant material reality of his boots – Beckett's version of Courbet's *Stone Breakers* – 'Nothing to be done.'[27]

Flaubert's novel looks backwards in time in order to show this interjection of farce into tragedy. The whole of *Bouvard et Pécuchet* reads, in many ways, like a continuation of Voltaire's satire on philosophical (and sentimental) optimism, *Candide*. Bouvard and Pécuchet come up with endless schemes for leading

---

[26] Marx, *The Eighteenth Brumaire* (second edition, 1869), 9.
[27] Samuel Beckett, *Waiting for Godot* (Grove Press, New York, 1954), 2.

whole and fulfilled lives; and every such scheme ends in a kind of disaster, as their romantic ideas come up against reality. Our eponymous heroes experiment with agriculture (chapter 2), and fail; then turn to chemistry (chapter 3), and fail; so they move onto archaeology (chapter 4), and fail; then literature (chapter 5), where they mistake Walter Scott's realism for reality – and fail; and so on. This is a novel that sits, as it were, midway between Voltaire and Beckett.

Representation is thematized as an issue and as a structural principle right from the start, as the two come upon each other and see that they both have inscribed their names in the inside of their hats. Like a prefiguration of contemporary comedy duos, like Laurel and Hardy, they arrive at the same time, from opposite directions, at a bench beside the Saint-Martin canal. As they sit down beside each other on this hot day, they simultaneously remove their hats to wipe their foreheads, simultaneously lay their hats down on the bench, and simultaneously notice that each of them has written their names in the inside rim of their hats – and for the same reason, being that the hats can be identified as theirs when they are in the office.[28]

Once they are established as belonging together in chapter 1, Bouvard and Pécuchet go into their garden at night, candle in hand; and there, sometimes, 'a spider would scamper suddenly over the wall, and the two shadows of their bodies appeared magnified, repeating their gestures'. In this text, the real is always doubled, becoming real or realized only when the singular presence of a person or of an event is re-presented.

Alongside this internal structure of representation, it is also entirely possible that this text is, in its entirety, itself a kind of representation of Voltaire's satire on silliness masquerading as knowledge, the satire on stupidities or *sottiserie* depicted in *Candide*. This invites the question as to whether the French State's attempt to incriminate Flaubert in 1857 over *Madame Bovary* – years before this particular novel, *Bouvard et Pécuchet*, is published – is itself a kind of belated substitute for the State's feelings regarding Voltaire himself, the Voltaire who advocated a strict division of church and State, whom the State did in fact prosecute for his advocacy of free criticism of the State, and who resisted censorship. Of course, Voltaire had indeed suffered directly from State censorship, having seen his *Lettres philosophiques* burnt in public in 1734, and having been imprisoned and exiled as a direct result of various of his writings.

From this account of *Bouvard et Pécuchet*, we might see that Flaubert's much-vaunted 'realism' consists in this: the material world exists in order to

[28] Flaubert, *Bouvard et Pécuchet*, 31–2.

flout and to frustrate the free flow of imaginary ideas and ideals. Realism is what representations and the 'spirit of imitation' come up against, for his two protagonists. It is surely not accidental that these are two characters whose actual and material careers are themselves fundamentally based in imitation: they are copyists, like their American predecessor of 1853, Melville's Bartleby the scrivener. When they meet, their daily existence is entirely governed by representation. The entire text – stemming from its originating moment in that nomination scene – is a quite literal exercise in the 'politics of identity': it is identification – perhaps the most extreme form of representation – that unites them in their project. But the project is doomed.

Flaubert, then, shocks his readers with a series of texts that, in their determination to seek the realities of actually lived conditions, pierce through the decorum that constitutes public opinions and public morality. He introduces, as it were, the grotesqueries of private impropriety into the public domain, as if he is making public the actual content of his *Carnets*. It is perhaps, therefore, not entirely surprising if his readers actually get the point, and see, in Emma Bovary, a public characterization of France that they wish to render invisible, through the powers of the law courts.

The relation of realism to law is our next logical reference point in the argument.

4

Legislating reality

Law, religion and education

1

Something very specific and important happens in European writing in the middle of the nineteenth century. For the first time, a new mode of value is proposed; and this value is associated not with finance but with something that, on first glance, appears to be resolutely less material than money or capital, but which is actually designed to replace the currency of money with something that is deemed to be yet more 'real'. The category of 'the literary' is established, and given great institutional and cultural power. The thing about literature, in this context, is that it is often characterized as having a greater value than does money, for it speaks to something that is supposedly less superficial than finance.

The fundamental difference is simple. An individual's property or wealth exists at a remove from what the period considers as the essential self. Property and wealth, especially in the form of capital, operate as proxies for the individual's reality. This is a characterization that is both celebrated and satirized by Jane Austen, many of whose characters – male and female – are identified with their financial status; but the point that Austen's novels make is that this is always, for some reason, inadequate as a description of the very selfhood of the characters. The self escapes such a superficial identification, for the texts work to ask whether there is something more fundamental to the selfhood of her characters than their money. What makes Austen's texts 'literary' is precisely the raising of this question. It sets money against value. In doing so, it essentially undermines the prevailing idea that money – capital – constitutes a material reality. It indicates that the ostensibly less material idea of 'value' may, in fact, give a reality with which an individual is more intimate than she or he can be with their wealth.

Against the 'financial self', the writings that we start to identify in the period as 'literature' propose various ideas of selfhood that are more 'real' because more intimate, with that different centre: value instead of what Thomas Carlyle attacked as 'the cash-nexus'. So, literature asks – for the Austenian example – whether something as personal and intimate as sexual desire be an adequate answer to the wants of a self that is identified by wealth. It asks – via Dickens, say – whether a self based in sentiment is of greater value than one based in the supposed realpolitik that would prioritize private wealth over social good. These kinds of question all operate on the idea that there is a self with which an individual is deeply intimate: a 'reality' of selfhood that needs no proxies to operate in the material conditions of history.

That self is variously described in the period. For some, it retains a religious dimension, and the self is a soul of some kind; for those who wrestle with the relations of religion to emergent sciences, like Arnold, it is a 'best self'; for those who are directly politically engaged, it is a self that identifies with and as a 'national character'; and so on. In all cases, however, the 'real' self is something immediate, 'present-to-itself' as we might now say, identified as an experience that is felt along the pulses in residual Romantic fashion. This intimacy of selfhood addresses the real, whereas money can be counterfeit – a proposition that would be explored in depth by Gide in his *Les Faux-Monnayeurs* of 1925, by which time the issue had become absolutely central to the formation of culture and of civic and civil life.

Behind this new predicament concerning reality and its re-presentations lies a statement made, famously, by Shelley: 'the poets are the unacknowledged legislators of the world'; and what is happening in the middle of the nineteenth century is that some formal acknowledgement of this is actually now being proposed. Poetry – as literature – is deemed to have the power to establish social and even legal norms, usually ethical or civic norms, which become constitutive of the material conditions in which people live actual lives: working, establishing social relations, dying. It is therefore vital that we attend to the power of poetry and literature over the public for, after all, in this formulation, poetry and literature make the laws. Literature, from this moment, claims a quasi-parliamentary function: it is a parliament for the everyday reader, a parliament for those who have neither the time nor the expertise to engage directly in the making of formal laws for a jurisdiction; but it can claim to transcend those law-makers for the simple reason of its validation through the court of 'public opinion'.

At issue here is the relation between, on the one hand, literature, and on the other hand, the courts of both public opinion and of law. In what follows here, we will see how this plays out in the deployment of law in the years around 1857, and what are its consequences for the establishment of realism as a specifically 'modern' and even modernist aesthetic and politics.

2

It was in 1821 that Shelley made his celebrated claim regarding the relation of poetry and law. The occasion was one in which he was writing a riposte to Thomas Love Peacock, defending a specific idea and ideal of poetry. The claim, which comes at the close of his text, is an enormous one, and should be taken seriously. The claim is, of course, testimony to the high value that Shelley placed on his writing; but it is more than this, for it places literature and law in close intimacy.

Peacock's essay, 'The Four Ages of Poetry', was ostensibly rather playful, but it nonetheless contained much that was matter of high seriousness; and it was this that allowed Shelley, Peacock's close friend and literary confidante, to raise the issues to a level where they become extremely relevant to our concerns here. Peacock's essay also begins, in fact, by placing literature in direct relation to law. He argues that what he calls the first or 'iron age' of poetry is appropriate to times in which 'the great practical maxim of every form of society, "to keep what we have and to catch what we can," is not yet disguised under names of justice and forms of law, but is the naked motto of the naked sword, which is the only judge and jury in every question of *meum* and *tuum*'. This is poetry as realpolitik, although that term had not yet been coined when Peacock was writing.[1]

Peacock goes on to identify poetry also with issues of commerce, claiming that 'the origin of poetry . . . like all other trades, takes its rise in the demand for the commodity, and flourishes in proportion to the extent of the market'.[2] Although the whole essay is tongue-in-cheek, these relations between literature, law and commerce are themselves entirely symptomatic of their historical moment.[3] Peacock's essay appeared in Charles Ollier's first number of his *Literary Miscellany*, and Shelley's response was scheduled for the second issue; but the magazine failed, and Shelley's *Defense* remained unpublished until after his death, appearing in published print only in 1840.

[1] Thomas Love Peacock, 'The Four Ages of Poetry', in *Peacock's Four Ages of Poetry; Shelley's Defence of Poetry; Browning's Essay on Shelley*, ed. H. F. B. Brett-Smith (Basil Blackwell, Oxford, 1921), 3. I write in detail about Realpolitik and its origins in the 1853 work of Ludwig August von Rochau, *Grundsätze der Reulpolitik* in Chapter 9.
[2] Peacock, 'Four Ages', 4.
[3] For more detail, see my *Literature and Capital* (Bloomsbury, 2018).

By that point in 1840, the readership that Shelley's essay found was markedly different from the readership that could not sustain the *Literary Miscellany* back in 1820. The England of 1840 was different in many respects from that of 1820. One key difference lay in the rising rates of literacy in the period. Discussions around how to measure literacy rates in the mid-nineteenth century are vigorous, with a whole series of differing tools and dates. However, there is one issue on which there is general agreement, and that is that a rise in State-provided education, however scant and underused it might be, generated a rise in English literacy from around 1830 onwards.[4] Indeed, in the three or four decades following the 1830s, there were a series of great political interventions into the provision of widespread education and literacy. The work of Matthew Arnold through the 1850s in particular is testimony to the importance that the matter assumed in the cultural mind of the times. By 1862, the Palmerston administration decided it was time to assume governmental control of education, and Robert Lowe produced the *Revised Code*, which tied education and literacy firmly to the economy, instituting a system of payment-by-results to schools.[5] It was at this same time – the 1850s – as we have seen, that Alfred de Falloux had introduced a system in France that tied State education firmly to religion. In both cases, the governments of the day are clearly trying to control the parameters within which increased literacy can be encouraged: religious in France, commercial in England.

The issue of such control is important for the polities of these States. When more people can read, then, logically, it follows that there is the possibility of a new form of social assembly, perhaps even more powerful than that which I described in Chapter 1. This is the moment when the 'public sphere' that had emerged in the bourgeois coffee-houses in the eighteenth century begins to become more fully demotic, and when increasingly it threatens to become even democratic. It threatens the existing authority of the State, further, precisely because this new mode of assembly does not need to form itself in direct personal and material terms. It can be dispersed and, in its dispersal, become that much more difficult to contain. Oddly, the material threat to privilege starts to come from a force that now assumes a profound reality while itself becoming less obviously materially 'present' in one place and moment.

---

[4] For a good survey, see Devone Lemire, 'A Historiographical Survey of Literacy in Britain between 1780 and 1830', *Constellations* (online: available at: 18862-Article Text-44744-1-10-20130129.pdf (accessed 16 July 2019).

[5] The text of the *Revised Code* is available at: https://books.google.co.uk/books?id=1SRcAAAAQAAJ &printsec=frontcover&source=gbs_ge_summary_r&cad=0#v=onepage&q&f=false (accessed 6 December 2019). For more on this, see my book *For the University* (Bloomsbury, London, 2011).

When we look to the horizon where we can see the new age of people gathering together in large numbers to await the arrival of the next instalment of a Dickens novel, for instance, then we have essentially established a regime of debate and discussion that involves many more people in the formation of social mores than ever before. A readership of well in excess of 50,000 people is a readership that the State had to start taking seriously. The new challenge for the State arises from the fact that this new crowd does not need to be easily identifiable in one specific material locale. A dispersed assembly can be more powerful than one that has to gather together in one location in order to show its force: force is now being more widespread. The combination of literacy-education and print changes the disposition of political control: in short, it changes the very constitution of the realities with which literature and the other arts engage. The State thus feels the increasing need for new laws if existing privilege is to be maintained.

As Shelley starts to move towards his grand claim in the *Defence*, he argues that poetry 'strips the veil of familiarity from the world, and lays bare the naked and sleeping beauty, which is the spirit of its forms'.[6] This is a forerunner of a certain Russian Formalist idea of defamiliarization: a 'making strange' of the everyday world, in a way that reveals to our perception its underlying and usually occluded reality, as if for the first time. In doing this, it radically empowers its reader, for 'it . . . creates for us a being within our being', and this new being is one that enables a fundamental re-making of the world. Poetry, Shelley writes, 'creates anew the universe, after it has been annihilated in our minds by the recurrence of impressions blunted by reiteration'.[7] In short, by waging war on cliché (as Flaubert does in *Bouvard et Pécuchet*), and on the general social acceptance of the world 'as it is', poetry offers the possibility of material change to historical realities. So, when Shelley makes his closing claim for the power of poetry, he is really indicating that there exists a political power – a parliament of readers, as it were – that sits alongside established political power in the Houses of Parliament. This is a rival body of law-makers; and the *Defense* is thus a radical challenge to the political establishment.

It is not long after this that we see literature and the law coming into direct confrontation with each other.

---

[6] Percy Bysshe Shelley, 'A Defence of Poetry', in Brett-Smith (ed.), *Peacock*, 56.
[7] Ibid.

3

In 1840, Shelley's formulation, then, went well beyond the range of the exclusive coterie of readers whose lives were marked by social and political privilege. That world – the world of privilege – no longer constituted the sole 'legitimate' reality for everyone; and reality was now a site of some contestation. Above all, it was a contestation not just over value (and values) but over the realization in material, historical and substantial terms of values that rivalled those of the upper privileged classes. The text essentially found a readership that had in some ways 'graduated' from the high point of artistic Romanticism and that considered itself to be focused on the real conditions of everyday material life. Just five years or so after Shelley's text was published – but in conditions that were obviously now propitious for the serious analysis of the relation of law to the culture of everyday life – Marx and Engels wrote *The German Ideology*. This is a central and foundational text for cultural and political modernity, and a text that started from the principle that we reject any form of idealism and replace that with reality: the 'real conditions' of everyday life, as Marx and Engels famously put it.[8] Clearly, several new ideas – relating to the reality of politics and, by extension to the cultural politics of realism – were circulating at this time, especially in an English context. For it is here that we will see what happens to this shift towards reality as a key principle for the legitimate construction of cultural norms and beliefs.

At the centre of this is education, which now becomes fundamentally and almost intrinsically politicized. Law and education start to become enmeshed one with the other in both France and England; and, at stake in that mixing of these two institutions is the question of control over what constitutes legitimate reality, leading to a contestation over realisms in literature.

We have seen how, in France in the 1850s, there was a keen political interest in the management of education, under the Falloux Laws. Those Laws helped reinstate religion as the cornerstone of all education; and the point of the exercise was to ensure that the poor saw their future security in Christ and not in overthrowing their rich and powerful oppressors in the State. The thing about Falloux was that, via Thiers, he put a claim for absolute certainty and truth at the cornerstone of all thought, and tied this to the fundamental purpose of education. The church would determine what constituted reality, however

---

[8] It is important to note that *The German Ideology* was not published in book form until 1932. The text was 'composed' and constructed from several manuscripts; and these manuscripts all date from 1845 to 1846.

false it may be in doing so. Here was an absolute authority that was supposedly unquestionable because it was based in a transcendental law: the law as given in the text of the Christian Bible. England, too, was beginning to realize that, with increasing literacy rates, especially among the poor, there had to be a mechanism for protecting the privileges of the wealthy. The way to do this was to control the institutions of law and of education. As in France, however, this would not go uncontested. Between 1853 and 1854, two extremely popular texts appeared, both by Dickens. He tackled the institution of the law in *Bleak House* first, before turning next, and quickly, to the conditions of education in *Hard Times*.

Much has been written about the personal investment that Dickens had in addressing questions of the law when he wrote *Bleak House*. There is no doubting the importance of that. However, in terms of the question of the politics of realism, it is more rewarding to consider the novel in the historical context I have just outlined here. Part of the point in *Bleak House* is to demonstrate the ways in which the law impedes the living of real lives, while at the same time making a claim that it is the law and the law alone that can determine how it is that people must live. *Bleak House* marks a specific turn in Dickens, away from novels shaped almost fully by humour, towards a much darker vision of the world and its ills, especially in London and England. Indeed, his friend John Forster described the novel as containing much that was 'too real to be pleasant'.[9] The reality in question here, of course, is the reality of the conditions of life for everyone shaped by Jarndyce and Jarndyce, the case in the Court of Chancery.

Caught up in the interminable waiting for Jarndyce, the lives of the characters are essentially put on hold; but the result of this is that the characters have two lives each, in a prefiguration of the two realities and two worlds that we saw as central to the issue of political imprisonment in the case of Ahmet Altan in Chapter 1. The first of these is that which depends upon the Jarndyce case; the second is the life that the characters actually live while waiting for their post-Jarndyce life to begin. This casts a question over where reality lies: does it lie with the law, or does it lie with lived reality? To take one example, and make it stand for all, we could consider the ostensibly relatively minor character of Mr Gridley.

Because of the simple fact that Jarndyce touches on his very existence, even if in ways that we never actually find out, Gridley gradually finds himself close to complete personal ruin. This is a character who, in fact, prefigures the kind of situation that we find so characteristic of the world of Kafka, some seventy years

---

[9] For details, see Claire Tomalin, *Charles Dickens: A Life* (Penguin, London, 2012), 245. The statement came in an unsigned review in *The Examiner*, 8 October 1853.

or so later. Gridley is the man who is actually seeking to *enter* the law, as it were; and each day, he finds himself standing – like a nineteenth-century 'Josef K.' – 'before the law' and being denied access. We might therefore expect that his life is, in material terms, *untouched* by jurisdiction over realities of life. Yet this is not the case: his life is straitened by law every bit as much as that of Richard Carstone and Ada Clare, for examples, the central characters whose lives are utterly and entirely enmeshed in the Jarndyce case.

Gridley's relation to the law, therefore, brings the novel's anxieties about the law into profound relief. It is not that he is caught up in the case; rather, his difficulty is that he cannot persuade the Judge in Chancery to listen to his plea in the first place. Nonetheless, standing outside the law like this brings him, as if by paradoxical necessity, *into* the law; and, more importantly still, brings the relation of law to reality extremely close indeed. As is well known, the character of Gridley is based on a real and historical individual in a specific legal dispute. After the first instalment of *Bleak House* was published, William Challinor sent Dickens a copy of his pamphlet entitled *The Court of Chancery: Its Inherent Defects, by a Solicitor*; and Dickens acknowledged grateful receipt of it on 11 March 1852. One of the cases detailed in the pamphlet (but with names of participants withheld) related to Joseph Cook. Cook's father, Thomas, had bequeathed £300 to Thomas, payable on the death of Mary (Thomas's wife, Joseph's mother). After Mary's death, Joseph duly began a case in Chancery to receive the money; but the case dragged on for years without result, meanwhile costing Joseph around £900 in costs.[10]

Like the real-life individual Joseph Cook, and modelled on him, Dickens's fictional Gridley is gradually worn down by the delays in the case and by its constant prevarications and irresolution; and he is ruined financially and personally, his health failing to the point where he simply dies. The law, in short, not only 'imprisons' Gridley in its grip; in the end, it kills him. He has sought entry into justice; but the law grips him in its bureaucracy, in its offices. His 'official' life – the life determined by his place in law and determined by the law's officers – supplants and replaces his material life, which now effectively becomes a clandestine and unofficial existence. As 'unofficial', it has no material standing: it barely exists, as with the life of a prisoner removed from the social and public

---

[10] For details, see: https://www.british-history.ac.uk/vch/staffs/vol7/pp210-216 (accessed 10 December 2019). See also Graham Storey, Kathleen Mary Tillotson and Nina Burgis, eds, *The Letters of Charles Dickens, Vol 6: 1850-1852*, available at: https://0-www-oxfordscholarlyeditions-com.pugwash.lib.warwick.ac.uk/view/10.1093/actrade/9780198126171.book.1/actrade-9780198126171-div1-1204 (accessed 10 December 2019).

sphere, removed from assembly. Here, recall again the real-life cases of Ahmet Altan or of Chen Guang, described in my previous chapters: this nineteenth-century fiction is prophetic of contemporary political realities in many diverse ways. What begins in Dickens as a parenthetical interruption into a life properly lived breaks out of the parentheses to the point where it subsumes and negates that life. Law shapes and perverts the realities of a life, with the sole exception of the fact that it brings about a premature death for its victims.

4

Bleak House opens with a difficulty in seeing things: fog obscures everything in and around Chancery. On the one hand, of course, the fog is a simple metaphor for the whole Jarndyce and Jarndyce case, the intricacies of which no one seems able to see clearly. This legal institution is one that stands above historical actualities while also determining the realization of those actualities in material human lives. In this, the law itself stands not just as court of final appeal over what constitutes reality, but in a position akin to that which Joyce's Stephen Dedalus will later famously ascribe to the ideal writer: 'The artist, like the God of creation, remains within or behind or beyond or above his handiwork, invisible, refined out of existence, indifferent, paring his fingernails.'[11]

France had Falloux to place God at the centre of education. That did two things. First, it underpinned all education with an absolutist and fundamentalist certainty: what the God-teacher said was true and not subject to question – unless you wanted to question God, a position that was unthinkable or that would immediately render your position illegitimate. Secondly, the fundamentalist authority thus established worked to contain, control and constrain the people, to ensure that no rival voice to that of the theocratic State could legitimately exist: any such voice would be akin to that of a biblical Satan.

In England, something similar is happening, but with a significant inflection and a substantial difference. The difference derives from a textual device. England had a system of law that acted with an omnipotence that was allegedly grounded in its omniscience. The law knew things that those 'outside the law' could not; and this knowledge gave it power over the lives of those who were required to observe the law's norms and power. This has an effect on the production of the

---

[11] James Joyce, 'A Portrait of the Artist as a Young Man', in *The Essential James Joyce*, ed. Harry Levin (Penguin, London, 1969), 221.

literary text. As it translates into literary artifice, it consolidates and endorses a very specific view of realism, one that is displayed through the literary device of the omniscient narratorial voice. Historically, of course, literary criticism has treated this voice as something that is akin to a theological principle. Jonathan Culler has pointed out that 'the basis of "omniscience" appears to be the frequently articulated analogy between God and the author: the author creates the world of the novel as God created our world, and just as the world holds no secrets for God, so the novelist knows everything that is to be known about the world of the novel'.[12]

There is, then, a view of realism in nineteenth-century English fiction that produces a specific set of political norms. By analogy with Falloux and religion, an omniscient narrator operates like a theocratic principle: knowing all, and seeing all with utter clarity. This clarity produces conviction; and I use that term itself here to indicate that this is actually a principle of law. The politics of realism is based upon such 'conviction', and its attendant corollary of a complete belief in the system of law that underpins a society and gives it its norms of behaviour and general personal and socio-political conduct. The law works like Falloux's God; and it works via an all-seeing narrative voice.

It is thus of crucial importance that *Bleak House* experiments with this, deviates from it and thereby calls the power and supposedly transcendent authority of law into question. When Dickens decided to alternate the narrative voice in his chapters, between an 'absent' but supposedly omniscient narrator and a present voice of Esther Summerson, he thereby immediately indicates that the world that is to be represented is a world in which contestations over the nature of reality are essential. A realism that claims an undisputed authority – such as that of the law – is thereby troubled. The insertion of Esther's narrative voice – a voice that is explicit in its acceptance that it cannot see all and that its view on the world is limited – works to undermine the logic of an absolutist or fundamentalist authority. In the extreme, there is a very radical consequence that follows from this: Dickens is casting doubt on the value of the very fundamentalist system of realism that underpins what Falloux had tried to establish in France. In calling into question an absolutist third-person narrative voice, Dickens here is calling

---

[12] Jonathan Culler, 'Omniscience', *Narrative*, 12:1 (2004), 23. Interestingly, Culler begins this article with by distancing himself from the politics of George W. Bush, who 'manifestly thinks he has nothing to learn from anyone' (p. 22), and also by referring to Virginia Woolf who, in considering Eliot's religious conversion, found something 'obscene' in omniscience. The point of his article is to cast doubt on the usefulness of the idea of omniscience as a tool for understanding the operations of narrative. For a full response to Culler, see also Barbara K. Olson, '"Who Thinks This Book?" or, Why the Author/God Analogy Merits Our Continued Attention', *Narrative*, 14:3 (2006), 339–46.

into question the value, for realism, of absolute certainty: he casts doubt on the very function that Falloux was ascribing to God. This is a politics of realism that entertains radical doubt, an acceptance of the fact that any vision of reality can be clouded. This may explain why it is so appropriate that *Bleak House* opens in fog.

The fog in this Dickensian London – the London of 1830 when the story is actually set – prefigures an image made by Monet in 1871, of *The Thames below Westminster*, in which we can barely see the Palace of Westminster, shadowed as it is in the fog-ridden background of the canvas. Dickens had been a parliamentary reporter, frequenting the Palace of Westminster for his work, right up until 1834 when the Palace was devastated by fire (on 16 October that year). Monet's painting is of the re-built Palace. In it, the Palace itself is rendered vague and in the background; but the foreground of the painting is labour: workers dismantling scaffolding that had been erected to allow the construction of the Victoria Embankment, as part of the new arrangement of the land after the fire. Such an attention to labour is something that Monet inherits from Courbet. This painting prefigures several others that Monet will do in 1903–4, of the Houses of Parliament becoming more and more spectral, seen – hardly seen – through mist or fog. While Monet began his series of these fog-bleakened images, Zola – as we will see later – was also working on the *Rougon-Macquart* series of novels, in which labour is a central driving force and in which, also, a narrative device of screening (by fog and other means) helps to consolidate a way of seeing the world that reshapes the politics of realism.

On 29 January 1854, shortly after completing *Bleak House*, Dickens visited the town of Preston, where a strike – a withdrawal of labour in the cotton industry – was under way. The strike had begun the previous October, so it was a bitter and prolonged contestation over who had control of the labouring body in the cotton weaving industries that were so firmly tied to England's imperial power at the time. The confrontation between organized labour and capital became the primary ground for Dickens's new and expressly political – even propagandistic – novel, *Hard Times*. We will see the same attitude to research on the part of a novelist in the case of Zola, who would base a good deal of the narrative in *Germinal* on documentation that he discovered when he visited Anzin, near Valenciennes in northern France. Anzin was the site of a prolonged mining strike, and Zola visited and stayed, gathering materials for his novel, for around a week from 23 February 1884. Both novelists, then, were clearly interested in the ways in which labour struggles and the withdrawal of labour would provide materials for the new kinds of writing that they were engaged in.

In *Hard Times*, moreover, Dickens stages an opposition between two ways of understanding the real conditions of everyday life; and the site in which his characters are to learn such understanding is the school and the institution of education. It is there that his characters will discover the difference between an official and legitimized account of reality on the one hand, and an unofficial and somewhat clandestine – but nonetheless more fundamentally real – account on the other hand. As was the case in *Bleak House*, the narrative strategy involves a doubling of ways of seeing the world, and thus an invitation to what is now a widening readership to consider, critically and sceptically, the legitimacy of that view of reality that is proposed by the offices of the State as true and normative. Where *Bleak House* cast doubt upon the validity of the institutions of the law as guarantors of a real account of everyday life, so now *Hard Times* proposes similar doubts over the value of the offices of State education.

It is often thought that *Hard Times* is an odd departure for Dickens. It is seen as a crude fable, a crude allegory whose rawness and obviousness takes the text away from realism and into propaganda. In fact the relation between realism and propaganda is itself complex, as I will argue later (in Chapters 6 and 7) when I discuss the emergence of 'documentary realism' in the twentieth century. Here, however, the point is quite simple: the text is an exercise in realism precisely because, like *Bleak House*, it operates as a mechanism for calling into question the idea of a single authoritative account of what constitutes reality itself. These two novels by Dickens are powerful precisely because they politicize realism itself, and reveal that any account that proposes itself as totalizing, single and unquestionable is itself profoundly evasive of the real conditions of human living. There is, as it were, no one law that can safely and wholly account for human reality. Likewise, there is no single and authoritative education in the laws of biological existence, as the arguments over Bitzer's description of a horse at the opening of *Hard Times* reveals.

Law and realism – the laws *of* realism – start here to be aligned in very specific ways. Yet it is in France that we will see texts standing before the law in 1857 in very precise detail.

5

We should remember, first of all and as I argued in the previous chapter here, that it is only in this historical moment in the European mid-1850s that 'literature' starts to gain a cultural standing, as a specific mode of writing that is distinguished and set apart from the generality of written texts, and that is thereby given a particularly high social and cultural value. Further, this emergence of the category of the literary as such is consistent also with the entry into cultural modernity, in societies that start to understand the need for social 'progress' and for regulating the inequalities of wealth and health that had started to disfigure other great modern invention: the city as the dominant organization of social life.[13]

In 1857, between January and August, the Paris law courts provided the stage for two dramatic trials, in both of which literature is placed in the dock. The trials were those involving Flaubert and Baudelaire, whose texts are now, today, themselves the staple of any educational course of study that focuses on civilization. That is to say: these texts are now 'available' to a culture that has a different 'way of seeing' from that which prevailed in the French 1850s. New worlds have become visible; and they have become visible precisely because of the writings of Baudelaire and of Flaubert, because of the paintings of Courbet, and because of the ways in which some English writers (above all Dickens) or German thinkers (Marx) took on the troubling questions of how law engages with the actual reality of human lives.

The prosecutor in both of the Paris literary trials was the same man, Ernest Pinard. When he opened his case for the prosecution of Flaubert, on 29 January 1857, Pinard took the high moral ground, charging Flaubert – on behalf of the State in the Second Empire – with 'offending public morality and religion'. His case rested on the claim that the presentation of Emma Bovary's adultery – and one specific example of that adultery, with Léon – would inevitably have a substantial effect on the novel's reader, leading to the reader's literal 'demoralization and corruption'. This is the argument, by now familiar in these arguments, that certain modes of representation operate like a medical infection, threatening the health of the reader or viewer. As Dominick LaCapra puts it, in his account of the trial, for Pinard and for the prosecution, 'The novel is literally poison.'[14]

As is always the case with this metaphor, the person making the prosecution – here Pinard – is deemed to have immunity from the poison that allegedly intrinsically infects and corrupts the text's reader. At the same time, and notwithstanding this exceptional status, Pinard presents himself as the mouthpiece of a supposedly unified and single 'public opinion'. The actual public need not be consulted in this; it is simply taken for granted as something

---

[13] For more on this, see my study of *Literature and Capital* (Bloomsbury, London, 2018).
[14] LaCapra, *Madame Bovary on Trial*, 38.

that 'goes-without-saying' that the official representative of 'the law' is also and equally a representative of 'the people'. Pinard takes it upon himself to speak for those who – it is claimed – find themselves potentially traduced by the writer who menaces them – 'offends' them – with the disease of obscenity.

Yet, behind this, there lies another unstated fear, and that is the fear felt by established law, power, authority and privilege in the face of the public as such. The unstated question is this: 'What if the interests of the people do not coincide with the interests of those who control the State through its laws?' In these cases, and with this fear in the background, the law actually seeks to construct the very 'public morality' that it ascribes to the people who constitute society at large, as if that morality were naturally occurring. The mechanism that will enable this is the constructed 'scandal', the scandal caused by a literary text or other artistic work. The scandal constructs public morals by setting up a literary text as the thing that will threaten that very morality, a morality whose very shape and substance depends upon the text that allegedly offends it. Public morality here is defined retroactively through its supposed openness to assault; and it asserts and thus identifies itself in defiance of its supposed – and imagined – attacker.

The issue is yet more fundamental than this, in fact, because what is now at issue is the question of how 'real' public morality actually is. If it can be constructed, then it may not have been there as a reality in the first place. So, it follows that we have a fundamental conundrum here: Does the law fundamentally make, shape or determine reality and the real conditions of material lives for people; or does the law reflect the reality of a pre-existing public opinion whose status is independent of any matters of legal status? Who determines what it is that constitutes the 'real' state of affairs in any situation? Who determines what constitutes the 'reality' of any particular state of affairs in a specific polity or jurisdiction? In short: Who controls what it is that we determine to be 'real' and therefore to judge what is realistic? The real anxiety of the law is that it is literature – rather than the State and its authorities – that is actually constructing reality, or at least shaping the norms that govern reality. In this respect, literature is seen by the State as a direct rival in the formulation of 'public morality'. Literature may, in fact, be handing over the construction of public morality to a public assembly; and this means that the State and its privileged central power no longer asserts control over the underprivileged in its assembly.

At this point, bear in mind also that religion, after Falloux and Thiers, has been placed at the heart of French education; and we see that literature is also a threat against what the State regards now as the norms that are established by the institutions that govern how we think, how we determine right from wrong and how we shape our norms for living. Simply put: literature – or art in general – potentially threatens the standing of the State as such because, unless it is straightforwardly an affirmation of the State's existing condition (a condition endorsed by formal religiously inflected education), it menaces the position of those in privilege who control the State and its norms or laws. It is clear, then, that by the mid-1850s, the State in France (as in England but for the different reasons that we saw) was profoundly aware of how precarious its standing is, in the sense that it can no longer simply assume that it is in full control of the reality of everyday lives of citizens. It should be no surprise, then, that the State now takes extremely seriously this peculiar activity called 'writing' as well as its odd product, 'literature'.

In 1857, although the dominant and prevailing modes of aesthetic criticism might not yet see the full import of the politics of literature, the State certainly does. Against those dominant modes of criticism, however, in England and in France, a new mode of literary criticism starts to appear at this moment. This newer form of criticism, a criticism of the highest seriousness, is found in the thinking of Arnold and of Taine respectively. These are among those in the world of education who have started to realize the full political potential of literature, and its ability to disturb and discombobulate a society's norms in terms of morality, politics and religion. That year, 1857, saw Arnold elected as Professor of Poetry in Oxford, where he opened his professorial lectures up to an audience by delivering them in English (as opposed to the tradition of giving them in Latin). He also then started to work out the principles that governed his *Culture and Anarchy*, to be published a decade or so later. Meanwhile, in France, Taine, who had been a provincial schoolteacher, had started by 1857 to develop the thinking that would lead to his determination to abjure what he called 'official banality', and he started writing his series of *Essais de Critique et d'Histoire*. In place of the prevailing official banality (or cliché), he argued in a famous series of formulations, the serious critic should attend to the historical moment of a work's production, the culture in which it found an audience and – most importantly for present purposes – the 'national characteristics of its author'. As is well known, Taine thought that the foundation that lay under any literary production came from the confluence of three forces: 'la race, le milieu, le moment'.[15]

---

[15] For a good introduction to Taine, see Hilary S. Nias, 'Hippolyte Taine', in *The Cambridge History of Literary Criticism*, vol. 6, ed. M. A. R. Habib (Cambridge University Press, Cambridge, 2013), 393–405. The quoted words here come from p. 394.

Pinard, then, stands in the Paris Court to present himself as a representative of public morality and of the people. However, according to the logic of Taine's critical philosophy, so too does the artist. As Taine put it, 'the social and intellectual condition is the same for the public as for artists' and while it may be the voice of the artist that we hear, there is, 'beneath this living voice . . . a murmur, and, as it were, a vast, low sound, the great infinite and varied voice of the people'.[16] The contest that Pinard is presenting in court, therefore, is really about where we find the real and material living conditions of the public, and who best represents those: State-law, or free literature.

The logic of Pinard's case is complex, though presented straightforwardly. He uses exactly the same tropes – based on a supposed interest in public health – that Campbell would use a few months later in England, when Campbell was making his case for legislating the Obscene Publications Act. Campbell, we recall, described the obscene materials that he had seen as being 'a poison more deadly than prussic acid, strychnine, or arsenic'.[17] Four months before Campbell deployed that metaphor, Pinard had used it in the Paris courts. Flaubert's text is poisonous, claimed Pinard; the common people are susceptible to its dangers; Pinard will protect the people by criminalizing the text, and ensuring that it won't be read.

The complexity of the matter derives from the fact that Pinard – as proto-censor – claims an immunity from the disease, an immunity that stems from the fact that he himself is exceptional, an exception to the common order of things. The people menaced by the text are intrinsically weak, and need him to speak for them, because they are of the lower social orders; but the real fear is that the poison in this case might spread to the inherently strong superior orders – and it is these therefore, logically, that Pinard is actually representing in court. This is why the book must be censored. Disease knows no class; and, if enough of the lower orders imbibe and succumb, the danger is to the standing of the superior classes, who become vulnerable precisely because they pronounce themselves immune and have failed to take protection. They must therefore be protected, by the full force of a censorious law, a law that protects the privileged by eliminating the disease that is carried by the weaker and lower social classes. This disease, this poison, is, fundamentally, criticism itself: the realization that an account of reality that is presented by the privileged upper classes and protected by State

---

[16] Hippolyte Taine, *The Philosophy of Art* (2nd edn; trans. John Durand; Holt and Williams, New York, 1873), 20–1.
[17] Roberts, 'Morals, Art, and the Law', 609–29.

legislature and education might be open to question. The poison is the poison of the voice of assembly.

If the poison gets a grip of enough people, then – the argument as presented goes – even those who think themselves immune will also be affected. However, these people – the class that stands in power and in control of 'what-goes-without-saying' – will not, of course, succumb to the poison. Rather what they (and Pinard) see at stake is the possibility that they lose their privilege of deciding what it is that constitutes public and social and personal health and well-being. They lose their power to construct 'public morality' or – as it will later be called within sociology – public opinion. They might also thereby lose money, as well as their existing cultural capital. It is not the loss of health, moral or physical, that they fear; rather, what they fear is the loss of their money, privileges and the social hierarchization – status – that puts them at the top of the social order.

In France, as in England in this year of turbulence for literary activity, it is class, wealth and privilege that are at the core of the censorious impulse. Those in power in the jurisdiction deploy the metaphor of public health in order to demonstrate their supposed care for the weak and for generally good living conditions for all, especially the poor. However – and this is always a corollary of the adoption of the metaphor – the prosecutors then open themselves to the charge of acting with a hefty dose of pious hypocrisy (a charge that goes unacknowledged, since it can only come from those outside of this class and who, by definition of that class position, go unheard, their voices not legitimized). At the same time, the metaphor itself makes it difficult to resist the censorship, since any such move makes it appear that one cares little for the weak, or for public health, or even for the social health of the political and public sphere as a whole. In this way, 'public opinion' is co-opted into an opinion that was never actually shared by the public in the first place, but that is instead a construction by the privileged class who wish to retain their privileges in the face of an art – fiction, painting, even music in some cases – that calls such privilege into question or that doubts its legitimacy, even while having to accept its legality.

Had Pinard been operating in our own historical moment, he might have expected himself to be assailed by writers and intellectuals deploring censorship in explicitly liberal terms, as an assault upon free expression and similar ethical and political principles. However, there was no such outburst against him in 1857. In fact, there appeared to be broad support among the liberal intelligentsia for the kind of punitive State intervention that Pinard was endorsing. To explain why this is so, it is important to keep in mind the political and cultural context in which the idea of a limitation on publication of new ideas had become an accepted norm. It looks, in fact, as if Flaubert himself was out of step with the liberal intelligentsia of the moment. Indeed, this is why the realism of Flaubert is so noteworthy: it runs counter to established norms in literature and in society.

When he appeared in court Flaubert was not alone in the dock, for the charges extended beyond the targeted writer, and encompassed the mode of production of the text: publisher and printer. Laurent Pichat (the publisher) and Paul Dupont (the printer) stood beside him, facing the same charges. It was not just the writing, but also the publishing and the printing of *Madame Bovary* that allegedly offended public morality and religion. It is not just the book or the offending passages in it; rather, it is an entire industry that is here indicted.

Flaubert had been publishing the novel in serial form in the *Revue de Paris*. The instalments had come to the attention of the State because the State had taken a keen and critical interest not initially in Flaubert but rather in the *Revue* itself, which it saw as being too provocatively liberal and republican. The *Revue* was altogether too 'progressive' for the liking of the political State authorities of the Second Empire, whose angle of vision on the world was substantively different from the way that same world looked to the editors of the magazine. The magazine tried to render visible many ideas and propositions that the State preferred to keep under wraps, and that the State wanted to delegitimize essentially by ensuring that such progressive ideas remained invisible, unpublished or literally 'unavailable' to the public. By extension, the actual textual contents of the *Revue* would also be potentially marked in the same way as the editorial policy itself was marked, as far as the State was concerned.

Individuals within the State's authorities and operational apparatus therefore read those contents with a keen eye for anything that might be construed as a potential threat to the values, the legitimacy and even the very existence of the Second Empire. They would then use legal procedures to undermine the legitimacy of those other political positions, different political propositions and controversial ideas. The thrust is to avoid controversy itself, because controversy breeds discussion; and in turn, discussion breeds assembly; and, in a further turn, assembly breeds the possibility of concerted actions – by a real public – against the interests of those who control and give authority to the State.

In his examination of the trial around this novel, Dominick LaCapra makes a key opening observation that many will find completely non-controversial and even obvious. He writes that 'A regime based on censorship is not constrained by the rules that operate in a polity legally recognizing civil liberties'. Under the Second Empire, censorship was indeed formally established as a legitimate arm in the weaponry of the State. However, as LaCapra also notes, it was only very haphazardly brought into effect; and so there was, among artists, writers and others with a potential audience beyond their immediate circle, a more or less routine testing of the limits of what might be said or seen.[18] In these conditions, the *Revue* sat precisely – and precariously – at the interface between culture and politics, between legitimacy and legality.

The trial put the *Revue* itself into an existential predicament. Flaubert and his co-defendants themselves faced prosecution, certainly; but the journal faced formal and statutory closure. The same kind of political approach persists right up to our own time, of course, and is visible in many jurisdictions where the State has moved formally to close down newspapers or other organs that are deemed to be critical of the State's positions.[19] Being critical of the State, in all such cases, actually means claiming that the version of real living conditions presented by the State is a false one. It is always this that is at issue: what are the real conditions of life for citizens, and who controls the presentation of that reality? From this historical moment, it starts to appear that a very specific form of writing that we call 'literature' somehow intrinsically calls the State's authority over this into question; and it does so by presenting an image of the real – really existing conditions but presented in imagined form – that the State finds troubling.

During the French Second Empire, the authorities governing the regime operated a 'three strikes and you are out' kind of policy in relation to the publishing industry; and the *Revue* had already clocked up two warnings before Flaubert came to trial. Quite apart from the politics, there is also, therefore, a commercial matter at hand here; and this commercial problem would not only pose complications for any ethics regarding free expression, but also have repercussions well beyond the existence of one journal. This is the case because the entire commercial practice of publication was itself organized and brought within the ambit of the law by a formal and State-sanctioned licensing system.

As a consequence of the 'legalization' of publication through a licensing system – determining by the operations of law what images or accounts of reality might be available for the public – the loss of a license for one journal inevitably had an effect right through the entire ecosystem of publishing: it was not as if there was an endless open forum for publishing the kind of materials that

---

[18] LaCapra, *Madame Bovary on Trial*, 18. LaCapra here also cites F. W. J. Hemmings as an authority for this claim. See F. W. J. Hemmings, ed., *The Age of Realism* (Penguin, London, 1974) for a still outstanding engagement with the history of European and Russian realisms.

[19] For up-to-date details on the extent to which press and media freedoms are jeopardized by the State, see the website of Reporters without Borders, at: https://rsf.org/en (accessed 2 April 2019).

found a comfortable home in the *Revue*. Licensing meant that publication was essentially rationed, right from the start. The 'permission to publish', as it were, depended upon a certain amount of rigour and propriety, to be articulated in forms of commercial and State control of the very activity of publishing. This means that the simple amount of materials published could be limited, as it were; and this rationing was perceived, however falsely, as being a kind of quality control.

Flaubert's position as an author in the *Revue* is similar, structurally, to the position in which Courbet found himself with the Exposition of 1855. There, the practical concerns regarding the size of his paintings gave the organizers reason to reject them and exclude some of what Courbet saw as his most important work. For him, this was political, not practical. In terms of publishing, the State can say that it is limiting the *quantity* of publications, the better to ensure high *quality*; but it is actually the substantive qualities of some journals and texts that are its real – political – quarry. The politics of censorship (a qualitative issue) hides beneath the pragmatic (an administrative issue). This is an eminently recognizable legerdemain through which actions that should be controversial – the censorship of legitimate but dissenting ideas or talk – can become 'realistic' because they are presented as being merely pragmatic. In this, censorship becomes uncontroversial, paradoxically precisely because it is 'official', a matter of administrative efficiency or routine practice.

Very importantly, the qualities that are being controlled by licensing are themselves political in nature. Christine Haynes has shown how publishers, printers and writers all saw the financial benefits of having a strictly controlled and licensed system, in which the publishers were 'sentinels' guarding public morals by monitoring and assuming a share of responsibility for what they published; but this meant that they could also face prosecution – with attendant jailing or fines – as a daily condition of their work and existence.

We might – not entirely jokingly – suggest that Napoleon III echoes the Platonic notionally ideal republic, in that he endorses the idea of a very strict control on what might be represented and distributed within his ideal society or empire. Indeed, this kind of view was rather the norm, such that the publisher Paul Dupont goes so far as to describe the printer as one who should be 'a censor as enlightened as he is judicious'.[20] Haynes demonstrates conclusively that the commercial fundamentals had priority over any and all ethical or political

---

[20] Christine Haynes, 'The Politics of Publishing during the Second Empire: The Trial of "Madame Bovary" Revisited', *French Politics, Culture and Society*, 23:2 (2005), 1–27. The quotation is from p. 17.

concerns. Business ideology – and the demand for commercial and financial gain and profit – trumped any idea of what we might call disinterested 'common good' publishing. 'Publishers . . . sought economic freedoms, rather than political or intellectual ones,' she writes.[21] This is the triumph of economic liberalism, under which social or cultural liberalism will disappear: public morality succumbs to the demands of finance and capital.[22]

All in the publishing industry were united in the idea that, through this means and with these priorities, literature should serve 'order' – all, that is, except a writer such as Flaubert, or a painter such as Courbet. The 'order' in question, it is clear, is an order based on the absolute centrality of finance and business at the core of politics, an intimacy of business and the State that stands at the centre of many forms of modern political corruption.[23] Such an order is entirely consistent with the emergent norms of capital in the period; and culture is being co-opted by the State in endorsement of those norms. Some writers and artists, however, find themselves at odds with this, notwithstanding any need that they might have to actually make a living.

Many commentators have followed Flaubert's own claims, that his novel is a proxy for the State's real opponent: the republican progressivism of the *Revue de Paris* itself (though, as I have already suggested, the displacement activity here might also refer us back to the State's much earlier problems with Voltaire). In fact, the passages published in the *Revue* had themselves already been heavily redacted by Pichat and Maxime Du Camp, the journal's editors, because they envisaged precisely the kind of prosecution that might ensue had the original versions gone ahead and into print. Their redactions proved pointless, however; and, in any case, Flaubert explicitly dissociated himself from the versions that they published. Notwithstanding such a repudiation, he still found himself charged and standing before the law.

Yet the key and determining factor behind all this derives, fundamentally, not just from the existence of the text but rather (and, structurally, primarily) from the conditions of its publication: that system of licensing. When licenses are restricted so too are the numbers of publishing houses and journals. This restriction leads to the concentration, in few hands, of the commercial profits to be gained through the publishing business; and it aligns the 'realities' associated

---

[21] Ibid., 18.
[22] For a fuller exploration of the relation of literature to moral capital, see my *Literature and Capital* (Bloomsbury, London, 2018), 153-64 and *passim*.
[23] For the financier and philanthropist George Soros, an intimacy between business and government is a major characteristic of Fascism. See Soros, *Open Society: Reforming Global Capitalism* (Little, Brown & Co, New York, 2000), xi-xii.

with the movement of capital to social reality itself, subsuming the social as merely one aspect of the financial or economic – as Marx will reveal more fully.

It is this that is really at issue in terms of an understanding of how State censorship operates in social and cultural terms. It is also this that goes some way towards explaining why writers and intellectuals themselves do not flock to Flaubert's defence with the raising of highly moral and politically serious questions about the improprieties of censorship and State intervention in the processes here. They know the commercial game; and the demise of the *Revue* simply offers them a new group of consumers in a restricted and controlled market. The potential punishments faced by Flaubert as he defended his right to write what he chose, including his realistic presentation of adultery by Emma – and even in his presentation of Emma as a sexual being in the first place – mattered little in this mentality.

It is important to stress again the veracity of the claims demonstrated by Haynes, that 'Publishers . . . sought economic freedoms, rather than political or intellectual ones'. Further, accepting their public stance as 'sentinels', all publishers intrinsically accept that their role is partly to sustain and extend discipline, law and a specific social order within their societies. They thus constitute, at least tacitly, an arm of the disciplinary and ordered State, and they are 'obeying orders' from that State when they censor. The process is all the more sinister when the State is not explicit about giving such orders, and where publishers and writers have to intuit what *might* attract censure. Thereby, writers and intellectuals become more circumspect in what they write and say; and the State exerts power whimsically and unpredictably. No one is safe.

Perhaps paradoxically, and certainly perversely, it is the very increase in social and cultural authority vested in the publishers and printers that leads to a *reduction* in the range of what can be said, a sclerotic narrowing of what can be presented as realistic. By characterizing the publisher and printer as a kind of guard – like a Platonic Guardian, in fact – the range of what can be legitimized through publication is severely curtailed. The real, now, is real only insofar as it has been given licence to be real.

6

Pinard's arguments over the power of poison, it seems, are essentially beside the point in the Flaubert prosecution. In fact, as is well known, Pinard lost this particular case, and Flaubert was acquitted. Along the way, however, the politics of the case becomes almost as clear as the economics. It is right to see Flaubert as a scapegoat here, although it would be wrong to see the entire case in those terms, given the importance of the economic background I have laid out. There is no doubt that the place of publication, the insurrectionary *Revue de Paris*, is an important element in the determination of the State to pursue this particular trial, with Flaubert's text merely the convenient and instrumental vehicle through which the journal, as the State's real quarry, can be pursued.

It would be too direct – too confrontational and nakedly revealing of its political force – for the State to attack the *Revue* directly and as a whole. The policing aspect of State control of law and order always works best when it is taken as a condition of 'normality' and of the 'everyday routine'. It thus needs the occasional generated scandal if it is to hold in check any political order that will operate as a rival to its own. It is here that the function of scapegoating operates most effectively and efficiently. In producing a scapegoat, the State – in this case the Second Empire – shows its determination to keep itself 'pure', honest, and on the side of everyday law and order: the commonly agreed 'public morality' (an 'agreed' reality that is, in fact, a coercively enforced one, as I have shown). The structure here is exactly the same as we saw operational in England, when we saw the deployment of an Indian scapegoat as the means through which to establish a supposed English 'moral' civility.

The scapegoat can thus inadvertently reveal the exact nature of the State's anxiety and insecurity regarding its own power. Yet that remains too general. We need to focus on what it is that this 'power' consists in. In the case of an obscenity trial – such as the Flaubert example (or in British obscenity laws) – it seems clear that the fear is about the fragility of sexual power, a sexual power that is given by the compliant observance of what the State describes as 'propriety' and decorum regarding a woman's sexuality. Specifically, the trial's unstated ground lies in the State's fear that the social ritual of marriage might fail to control female desire and sexuality.

When Emma Bovary is adulterous, the text of the novel opens to view the possibility of sexual adventure that the nineteenth-century French marriage ritual and the norms that it governs are meant to prevent. It makes visible that which the State prefers to occlude and which it thereby deems to be illegal; and, in doing so, the novel makes actions that the State wishes to restrain not only possible for validation but also available as a wedge to drive into the closed doors of State power and control. Such openness to sexual adventure, however, is seen by the State not as an end in itself; rather, it is seen as being symptomatic of a more general trajectory in which powers can be articulated and released in ways that will call into question – and that might even fracture – the power of the State itself.

It follows from this that censorship is always very highly *specific* in its practical application, even when the precise particular of what is censored has an applicability well beyond the specific writing or painting. It is not necessarily – at this stage of the argument at least, or at this historical moment – all representation as such that is feared. Rather, the content of the matter to be censored is specific to its historical and cultural moment; and this factor shapes the precise determination of the modes of censorship in each case, and gives it a local colour, flavour and set of tropes. It has a significance that is highly localized, certainly; but that local application is but a symptom of a much broader cultural and political condition. The State in Flaubert's case is not worried about Emma; rather, it is concerned about the hierarchical structure of sexual relations, and their fundamental underpinning in property rights. 'Propriety' and its disruption – 'offending public morality and religion' – is what is at issue.

The State's appropriation to itself here of both religion and the identification of what constitutes public morality is a major aspect of the claim that the State can apply legality over legitimacy; and this finds a very specific inflection in the case of Emma Bovary, where a woman's adultery is being literally 'ruled out of court'. The State is trying to present female adultery as something that cannot be validated as a thing that could have any reality; yet it is, of course, only because it is a really occurring reality that the State uses the law to delegitimize its actual existence in this way. The State's logic is that if it can be deemed to have no reality in law (if it is not recognized as legal) then it can have no reality in fact (it can have no legitimate existence). If the State has a theocratic principle on its side, as it does in this moment through the Falloux Laws, it thereby claims an absolute right to act as it alone sees fit. Further, if such religion is tied to public morality via State education, the State co-opts 'the public' on the side of its claimed rights and powers and privileges – even when those privileges are not shared by the general public at all.

So, in 1857, Flaubert becomes the scapegoat for a more general set of anxieties about the power of the *Revue*, a power that might endorse anti-imperial feelings and actions. Crucially, the actual scapegoat in any such situation must be characterized as being a kind of 'enemy of the people', a figure whose views and values are 'other' than those endorsed as normative by State powers. It is thus not purely and simply the case that Flaubert attacks norms; rather the principle of scapegoating ensures that things work the other way around, but they do so covertly. By picking on Flaubert in the way it does, the State actually *creates* the norms that it says it wants to defend, and then ascribes the validity of those values by attributing them to a co-opted general public and by underpinning them with theological certainty: reality itself. Those norms were not there, and were not articulated as such, in the first place; it is the activity of scapegoating that gives them such reality as they have.

7

Pinard used similar arguments as those that he had tried in the Flaubert case when he returned to the same Paris court some six months later to prosecute Baudelaire. Six poems from *Les Fleurs du Mal* were cited as evidence of religious immorality, obscenity and outrageous offence against public morality. This case was heard and judged in one day: 20 August 1857.[24] Baudelaire faced charges that were very similar to those levelled at Flaubert. This time, however, although Baudelaire together with his publisher and printer were all found to be innocent of religious immorality, the charges of obscenity and outraging public morality were upheld; and they were all fined substantial sums.

What does the difference in these two cases signify? The first thing to note is that Baudelaire is cleared of the charge of religious immorality. We might, then, see this year – 1857 – as the start of a period when the effects of the Falloux Laws begin to weaken, at least as far as their relation to a general culture is concerned. The secularization of State education would come much later, of course; but in 1857, in the Baudelaire case, we see a situation in which poetry escapes, at least in this instance and at least momentarily, from the clutches of State-sanctioned religious norms.[25]

That is an indication also of what else is going on between the cases of Flaubert and of Baudelaire here. After Flaubert is cleared, the State reasserts its claims to control over 'public morality'. There is obviously a struggle going on between January and August of this year over who has the right to determine what constitutes the norms of public or civic life in France. Michèle Hannoosh describes this situation correctly when she describes the situation in Baudelaire's

---

[24] The allegedly offending poems were 'Lesbos', 'Femmes damnées', 'Le Léthé', 'A celle qui est trop gaie', 'Les Bijoux' and 'Les Métamorphoses du Vampire'.
[25] Of course, it is also the case that arguments over religious schools, secular education and *laïcité* remain an ongoing issue even to the present day in France, as in other jurisdictions. In almost all cases, religion is the acceptably presentable pious face of what would otherwise be politically unacceptable political positions.

case as one where 'on 20 August 1857 a crowded courtroom awaited a duel between "modern" literature and that of the reigning "bourgeois"'.[26]

The issue in the courtroom was not just the content of the six poems, with their obvious interest in lesbianism: rather, it was the condition of sexual morality and liberated behaviour as an indication of the emergence of modernity itself. We might go so far as to say that what was at issue was the very status of the law and of the courtroom itself. The unstated question in the trial – but its nonetheless fundamental question – was whether the State authorities had any right to legislate on these matters at all, or whether the State had the right and indeed duty to intervene into private lives in order to regularize and constrain sexual and other desires. A fear of an emergent modernity – identified here with what the State saw as the disruptive power of female desire – might be one reason why the court ruled against Baudelaire on this particular count.

That emergent modernity is one that raises two very pressing questions. The first indicates the emergence of a contestation over what constitutes the proper relation between private and public affairs: who has the right to calibrate the relative interests of the private individual and the public citizen; and how does imaginative literature, with its figures of imagined realities, intervene in this? Secondly, it raises questions about the relative status and authority of law and of literature. 'Public morality', this new modernity suggests, is something that is to be determined by the real experience of citizens in the lived conditions of their daily existence and practices, practices that are legitimized by those individuals themselves. It is not something to be determined formally and legally *a priori* by the State, especially when the State uses the mechanism of a constructed 'public morality' or 'public opinion' as the means whereby the State will delegitimize real and really lived experience. The legitimacy of experienced reality is set against a legally constituted reality in this.

In the case against Baudelaire, while the State might relinquish the support of religion, it nonetheless reasserts its rights to determine what is permissible and what might count as 'real' sexual desire, thereby denoting any and all other modes of sexual desire to be aberrant or 'deviant': illegitimate *and therefore* illegal. The State in the Paris courtroom in the Baudelaire case asserts the primacy of law over legitimacy; it *reasserts* the primacy that was potentially lost in January when the State lost against Flaubert. Emma Bovary's adultery was one thing; but lesbianism is, for the State, quite another thing entirely; and this 'other thing' is properly identified as the emergence of modernity, with an entirely different

---

[26] Michèle Hannoosh, 'Reading the Trial of the *Fleurs du Mal*', *Modern Language Review*, 106:2 (April 2011), 374.

relation between State and citizen from that which prevailed in the first half of the nineteenth century.

Five days after the Baudelaire case in Paris, and on the other side of the Channel, Campbell's Obscene Publications Act passed legislation and was fully inscribed into English law. Recall that M. J. D. Roberts characterizes the Bill for this Act as 'a clear example of that recurrent Victorian pastime – the attempt to legislate morals'. That description catches precisely what was also happening in France: the contestation between law-as-rule and what the public might accept as proper conduct, based primarily upon their real and actual practices of life. However, that epithet 'Victorian' then allows Roberts to mischaracterize what is at stake in England at the time, for he goes on to say that the Act shows Victorians grappling 'with one of the most intractable ethical problems of their time – the problem of reconciling the claims of a libertarian ethic of individual responsibility with the claims of an ethic of paternalistic social concern'.[27] This latter formulation tends to domesticate the issue, and to circumvent the fact that it is fundamentally a contest between the law as made by established Parliament and the life on the streets that is at issue; and, when we remember this fact, we see that what is at stake is the control over what constitutes reality itself.

In one sense, of course, a religious society is one where reality has always been called into question. Most religions – and certainly Christianity in England or France – make the claim that what we consider to be reality (the material conditions of our experiential life) is simply a shadow or foreshadow of a greater or higher or more fundamental reality (that which is given in the immaterial conditions of an after-life, an after-life that is unavailable for empirical presentation and unavailable to sense-perception). In the mid-nineteenth century, we can find in the attitude to imaginative literature a particular way in which the societies start to attempt to release themselves from the theocratic grip that calls historical existence into question. This is what the prosecutions of Flaubert and of Baudelaire showed in the French context. The courts find a middle ground between the absolutes of divine revelation regarding reality and the purely material conditions of living women and men: it places law as the fulcrum between those orders. Law is then to operate as a kind of surrogate divine register, and we are expected to conform to its norms. Literature, however, says that this is always contestable, always amenable to debate.

---

[27] Roberts, 'Morals, Art, and the Law', 611.

8

Bleak House, we might say, is a direct attack on the prerogatives of law and on the competence of the legal order to determine what constitutes reality. The cases of Flaubert and of Baudelaire actualize this in real historical legal activity. Realism now emerges as endowed with an entirely new politics: it has little to do with how accurately a representation of the world matches some primary-order material reality. It goes much deeper than this: realism is precisely grounded in a depiction of the contest over who controls and shapes and describes reality itself, in fact.

Immediately the world is presented in different points of view, reality is called into question. It is this, of course, that makes Henry James – the acknowledged 'master' of point-of-view narration – such an important novelist of an emergent modernism and modernity. A contestable reality is no longer a stable reality, no longer a reality that is under the control of the law as such: no longer 'regular' or subject to rule. This is what *Bleak House* explores in fiction; and it is what Pinard explored in fact in the Paris courts.

The central thing about Jarndyce and Jarndyce – and we should note that doubling of the name itself – is that the *conduct* of the case in Chancery proceeds entirely by its own arcane procedures, to which the public have no real access. It seems that if we want to understand the intricacies of the case, we would need to enter the inwards-spiralling discourse spoken by the lawyers in Chancery. It seems as if the law is simply divorced from the realities of everyday life of the people who are subject to it. Yet, at the same time, the law here clearly does have a massive effect on the lives of ordinary citizens, caught up in its web: Mr Gridley from Shropshire dies, worn out; Jo dies; Richard will die, also worn out notwithstanding his 'legal' victory. Even Tulkinghorn, the man at the centre of law in the novel, dies, murdered by Hortense, Lady Dedlock's former maid. In his presentation of Chancery, Dickens is showing that the law operates as a bureaucracy: it merely pretends to control an external social reality, while concentrating instead on policing and monitoring the coherence of its own internal logic. In so doing, however, innocent people die.

Tulkinghorn becomes the fulcrum figure in this. It is he who tries to manipulate the real conditions of the lives of those touched by his legal practice. He is constantly at pains to try to ensure that reality does not escape his grip. He 'buys' Hawdon's letters from Smallweed, but on strict condition that Smallweed denies that they even exist – he rules the documents out of reality while holding them himself, denying the material existence of letters held in his own hand. Justice in this text does not operate in terms of social rectitude at all; rather (and this is usual in Dickens, of course) justice is contaminated by money. It is debt that shapes law throughout this text; and thus it is also the reality of financial debt that determines human conditions. Dickens cuts directly to the quick of real human conditions in nineteenth-century England, in which law itself is but a cover for the protection of unearned financial privilege.

Where Courbet had shown reality to consist in the material facts of labour, death and sex, Dickens shows that governing all three of these key realities is something that is, 'really', yet more fundamental: money and economics. *Bleak House* was not well received at first: readers and critics 'expressed disappointment that [Dickens] had abandoned humour for the grotesque and contemptible'; and as I noted earlier, even his close friend and supporter, John Forster, hesitated over it, finding it 'too real to be pleasant'.[28]

In his critique of the legal system in *Bleak House*, Dickens did several things. He demonstrated the inadequacy of the justice system to engage properly with the fundamental economic injustices that scarred the England of the 1850s. Through this, he indicated that, while the institution of the law (operating as an arm of the State) claims a fundamental right to determine what constitutes legal conduct, it nonetheless fails entirely to deal with issues of legitimate claims that people have to determine autonomously their own conditions of life. To that extent, he demonstrates that law is divorced from reality precisely at the moment when law claims to constitute the very ground and underpinnings of human and material reality itself.

The object of Dickens's critique here is what we have learned to call, in very recent times, 'capitalist realism', that sense that reality is real only to the extent that it conforms to the norms of a prevailing capitalist ontology. Dickens would qualify, in these terms, as an example of what Mark Fisher calls 'naïve utopianism'. *Bleak House* proceeds *as if* a critique of such capitalist realism might change things. However, 'a moral critique of capitalism, emphasizing he ways in which it leads to suffering, only reinforces capitalist realism', Fisher writes. 'Poverty, famine and war can be presented as an inevitable part of reality'.[29] Against this, however, is the simple historical fact that, after *Bleak House*, reform of the law did indeed take place. We might say that, while he did not manage to undermine capitalist realism, Dickens did undermine the claims of the law to determine the reality and norms that would shape the lives of individual citizens, especially when that system of law was designed, at the connivance of the State, to protect existing privilege and wealth. He could change the law; he could not, yet, change reality. The execution of that task is, in fact, Dickens's legacy.

---

[28] Tomalin, *Charles Dickens*, 245.
[29] Mark Fisher, *Capitalist Realism* (Zero Books, London, 2009), 16.

Part II

Making the real

5

Science and modernity

Vision, force, Turgenev and Russian Formalism

1

A significant number of Shakespeare's plays present their drama around issues of law. In almost all cases, the plays pitch the question of formal legality against moral or social legitimacy. Obvious examples include *The Merchant of Venice* and *Measure for Measure*. However, it is in another play, *Othello*, that we see a significant version of this that opens the way to a specific figuring of modernity, a modernity that will base some of its propositions concerning our understanding of reality upon empirical science.

The key scene occurs in Act 3. It is the longest scene in the play, and one in which Iago taunts and tempts Othello by implanting deep seeds of sexual jealousy in his mind. The scene has many twists and turns; and, at times, Iago has to work hard to keep a firm hand on the control of Othello's imagination and, by extension, to inaugurate the terms that authorize the murderous action that will follow when Othello kills Desdemona. The moment that clinches this, for Iago, is a moment that brings science and empirical inquiry into direct alignment with fiction. Having planted the suspicion in Othello that Desdemona has been unfaithful to him by having sexual relations with Michael Cassio, Othello finds himself unable to bear the kind of doubt and uncertainty from which, a few decades later, Descartes will found the entirety of modern philosophy.

Tormented by doubts, Othello turns on Iago and demands that key element in any court of law: proof. In an extraordinary moment, he tells Iago 'be sure thou prove my wife a whore'. Then, the demand for empirical and evidentiary proof immediately follows this: 'Be sure of it. Give me the ocular proof. . . . Make me to see't'. Othello trusts to his own eyes, and it is when he sees the reality of something that he will escape from his doubts and believe it without further hesitation. He will then be able to act upon this certainty. He wants an image; and this is exactly what Iago then paints for him, asking what is it that will satisfy the demand for proof: 'Would you, the supervisor, grossly gape on – / Behold her topp'd?' With this, essentially an imagined painting – and, perhaps, a key moment of a kind of pornography in Shakespeare, inviting Othello *and the audience* to see Desdemona and Michael Cassio naked and engaged in a sexual act together – Othello *sees*. Seeing here is then tantamount to believing that this imaged and imagined sexual congress is, in fact, reality.[1]

It is the bringing together here of imagination (a representation) with science, in the 'ocular proof', that we find one of the bases of modernity. By the time of the nineteenth century, this is playing out in the interrelations between painting and literature. In what follows here, we will see how this develops into a specific inflection of realism; and, where, for Shakespeare and the later Descartes, these issues are resolved at a personal and ethico-philosophical level, the nineteenth century sees them being worked out in the more public and thus political domain. Central to this is the manufacture of something that will come to be called 'the court of public opinion'. The phrase enters into political discourse proper with Rousseau, and it rapidly becomes 'regarded as a tribunal from whose disapproval one must protect oneself'.[2] For Rousseau, the anxiety about public opinion is an anxiety about 'the threatening aspect of publicity', an anxiety quite simply about 'being seen' or giving ocular proof to some phenomena that can then be called 'reality'.

This may go some way to explaining the prevalence of visual metaphors in the theories of realism that emerge in the nineteenth century, from Stendhal's mirror walking along a road, via Zola's construction of the idea of the screen or 'écran réaliste', on to Henry James's house of fiction with its many windows, and eventually into Virginia Woolf's demand that we 'look within' for an account of what constitutes reality. We can trace some of this movement here.

---

[1] For an outstanding history of performance of *Othello*, see Julia Hankey's Introduction in Julia Hankey, ed., *Othello: Shakespeare in Production* (Cambridge University Press, Cambridge, 2005). The discussion of *Othello* in the mid-nineteenth century (pp. 46–62) is especially relevant to the issue of the visibility – and nationalist politics – of race and the associated cultural perception of Othello himself. See also Lois Potter, *Othello: Shakespeare in Performance* (Manchester University Press, Manchester, 2002), 29–47. Potter's history pivots on the instance of Paul Robeson and his black actor predecessor, Ira Aldridge. Against these compelling accounts, see also James Hirsch, '*Othello* and Perception' in *Othello: New Perspectives*, eds Virginia Mason Vaughan and Kent Cartwright (Fairleigh Dickinson University Press, Madison, 1991), 135–59 which, oddly, seems not to notice the visible ocular evidence of Othello's difference.

[2] Elisabeth Noelle-Neumann, *The Spiral of Silence: Public Opinion – Our Social Skin* (2nd edn; University of Chicago Press, Chicago, 1993), 80.

2

I wrote in my opening chapter on 'Assembly' about the importance of the Falloux education laws. These were laws enacted in 1850 to reinstate the power of the church and the clerisy essentially allowing the church not only to control French national education but also, through that, to ensure that citizens knew that the church would monitor their public behaviour. The laws work – like many laws – without the necessity of continual intervention: in cases like this, the church can rely on a coerced public to monitor and censor themselves, with each citizen knowing that she, he or they is/are under the tacit surveillance of all neighbours. The Falloux Law, therefore, was controversial. In fact, this Law subverts the usual operation of a free assembly, in that it operates precisely to police, control and subjugate such a free assembly to the power of an overarching and superior monitoring eye, that of the church (and, by implication, that of an omnipotent and omniscient being, a god).

Louis Hachette, the founder of the Hachette publishing house and bookstore, was one opponent of the laws and of their intrinsically censorious powers. Among the publications that Hachette brought to the public domain were several that were explicitly critical of the kinds of censorious attitudes that the Falloux Law enshrined, including a journal that was explicitly opposed to those laws and to their social and cultural effects. One such key effect included making the church into an arm of the State and, worse, coercing the State into becoming a subservient arm of the church, and thus becoming incipiently a fundamentalist and tacitly theocratic State. Hachette was decidedly liberal, sympathetic to 'enlightenment' in general as well as philosophically precise terms, and keen on reform while remaining opposed to the violence that usually accompanies revolution.

On 1 March 1862, Hachette employed a young man – a would-be writer who had spent the immediately preceding years leading a rather bohemian existence – in its publicity department. Five years earlier, in 1857, this young man, the seventeen-year old Émile Zola, had been about to move from Aix to Paris with his mother, Emilie. They had fallen on hard times in Aix after the death of Zola's father, François, a decade earlier. They made the move, definitively, in 1858, a decisive and formative moment in Zola's life and career as a writer. That year, he would fail his baccalaureate, and would thus have to find ways of making a living. In due course, four years after this decisive failure, he found employment in Hachette, dealing with publicity; and in this employment, he quickly rose to a position of some influence.

By 1862, then, Zola had found an appropriate place to begin his proper literary apprenticeship, in a publishing house that was a republican bastion against Napoleon III. Among his earliest writings we find his art criticism, central to which is an admiration for – among some others – Courbet, by this time a celebrated artist and one identified with an explicit new Realism. We should be precise here: it is not realism as such that Zola admired in Courbet, but rather what he saw instead as a commitment to truth, a concept that is closer to science. In 'Proudhon et Courbet', written in July and August 1865, Zola criticized the way in which Proudhon used Courbet's work as a mere vehicle through which Proudhon advanced a political argument. As Zola saw it, this was inappropriate, and essentially dismissive of the very painting that it supposedly celebrated, for it saw the painting simply as an allegorical presentation or illustration of Proudhon's preferred politics.

As Zola worked his own critical position through carefully, he would subsequently be very clear on this. 'Realism', he wrote on 11 May 1866 in 'Les Réalistes du Salon', 'for many people ... consists in the choice of a vulgar subject'; but if you want to be a serious realist, 'paint some roses, but depict them as living things'.[3] In short, his argument is that the artist must search for a truth – an organic reality – in the presentation of the world: fact becomes central to his understanding of what constitutes 'reality', partly because this will replace doubt with some basic element of the true grasp of our predicaments and material historical situation, our 'living things'.

Disavowing his own membership of any 'school', Zola at this time argued that what he valued was 'truth, if you will, life, but above all flesh and different souls each interpreting nature differently'. He went on to add here that 'The definition of a work of art can be nothing other than this: *a work of art is a corner of creation seen through a temperament*'.[4] This – which recurs as a much-repeated phrase in Zola's writings – made its first appearance as a response to Proudhon who, in his posthumously published 1865 text, *Du principe de l'art et de sa destination sociale*,

---

[3] Émile Zola, *Le Bon Combat: de Courbet aux Impressionistes*, ed. Jean-Paul Bouillon, présentation et préface de Gaëtan Picon (Hermann, Paris, 1974), 67 [trans. mine: 'Le réalisme, pour bien des personnes, consiste dans le choix d'un sujet vulgaire'; 'Peignez des roses, mais peignez-les vivantes, si vous vous dites réaliste'].

[4] Ibid., 69 ['de la vérité, si l'on veut, de la vie, mais surtout des chairs et des coeurs différents interprétant différemment la nature. La définition d'une oeuvre d'art ne saurait être autre que celle-ci: *Une oeuvre d'art est un coin de la création vu à travers un tempérement*']. It should be added here that Zola's positive view of Courbet was not entirely uniform: he did find things of which he could be adversely critical, as in his 'Les chutes' of 15 May 1866, written less than a week after 'Les Réalistes du Salon'. We should compare André Gide, in *Journal des Faux-Monnayeurs* (Gallimard, Paris, 1927), 13, where he argues that he should 'Ne jamais exposer d'*idées* qu'en fonction des tempéraments et des caractères'.

had argued that art is 'an idealist representation of nature and of ourselves, in view of the physical and moral perfection of our species'.[5]

Zola's reply, then, frequently revisited, should be understood as one that argues for a realism that is based on truth itself, and not upon the deployment of representation for ideas. It does not mirror a pre-existing empirical reality; rather, it attends to the truth of how things stand in the material world. To that extent, his 'political writings' in the fictions – the realities of labour and of a strike (*Germinal*), the issue of prostitution (*Nana*), the scourge of alcoholism for working-class people (*L'Assommoir*) and so on – are not intended as allegorical: they are the 'living roses', but as seen through his own specific individual perception, or as seen via his *écran réaliste*.

While working in the offices of Hachette, Zola met a number of important figures, including Hyppolite Taine, whom he saw as an embodiment of a modern spirit, embracing scientific analysis and objectivity; and, thanks to Taine's influence, he also discovered the writings of Stendhal and of Flaubert, and of English fiction. Taine's *Histoire de la littérature anglaise* appeared in 1863, shortly after Zola's arrival in Hachette, and it is obvious how Zola would have found Taine's scientific approach to a kind of proto-sociology of literature – with its famous emphasis on *la race, le milieu, le moment* – to be congenial. Science could help provide access to truth, via empirical observation and an awareness of social context. This, for Zola, would help endorse his own emerging political aesthetic.

In passing, we should note also the importance of my attention to *Othello* in terms of a structure of feeling that shapes modernity here. In that play, 'ocular proof' is not just fundamental to the erosion of doubt: it also serves to place the very character of Othello himself in a specific position with respect to his social world. The play rests a good deal of its intrinsic structural tensions on the fact of the visible difference between Othello the Moor and the rest of the European characters, above all Desdemona. The issue of a perception of supposed racial difference and racial hierarchies is, itself, basic to the emergence of European modernity. It plays a key role in the nineteenth century's construction of eugenics, and that same period's construal of the supposed self-evident superiority of certain ethnic characteristics. This, of course, is what we saw as a determining factor in the construction of the 1857 Obscene Publications Act.

---

[5] As cited in Zola, *Le Bon Combat*, 51. For the original, see Pierre-Joseph Proudhon, *Du principe de l'art et de sa destination sociale* (1865; repr. Rivière, Paris, 1971), 68.

Zola's own first published fiction in 1864 was *Les Contes à Ninon*, a collection of short stories that had been individually published in magazines since 1859 and that he now collected together in single volume form. The following year, 1865, saw the publication of his first novel, *La Confession de Claude*. The novel caused a scandal and, as a literary publicist, Zola saw the positive commercial side of this. It also gave him his first confrontation with the law and the censors as a result, for the book would be banned in the United States. In France, even the liberal and republican Hachette felt discomfited by the book, whose subject matter was what ostensibly caused the problem: it is about a student in love with a prostitute. It is important for us to grasp what underlies Hachette's discomfort here. In 1865, it is entirely possible and legitimate to stand in opposition to Napoleon III and the Second Empire; but the terms of opposition and critique are themselves carefully circumscribed and limited. Even an opposition has to follow protocols that are written by the dominant order, the order that determines what constitutes legitimate (and thus acknowledged) reality. That order remains, still, that tacitly fundamentalist marriage of religion and State. Such a social order of things must adopt a pious pose, in which it claims to be scandalized by this kind of novel. The force of this is strong, for what is at issue relates directly to realism itself.

The State's officers are not in fact scandalized by prostitutes as such, though they must pretend to be so (indeed, many of those officers doubtless engaged directly with prostitutes); rather, the State takes a stance that proposes that 'the public' must be 'offended' even by the merest acknowledgement of the real existence of prostitutes. Official discourse attempts to screen the prostitute out of existence, censoriously to render her 'unreal', placing her empirically beyond visibility. Given the political culture of a society operating under Falloux, with its tacit empowerment of 'public opinion', even those opposed to the dominant forces and order of the State – like Hachette – are nonetheless required to take their stand within the bounds set by the official discourse if they are to have any legitimacy. More than this: they must take this stance if they are to continue to enjoy any legal existence: the censorious State can, quite simply, close Hachette or any other opposition down.

However, the subject matter is not the most important issue here. It is, rather, what Zola does with the subject matter that is most significant. Essentially, the novel is an exposé of some troubling aspects of bohemia, done in such a way as to show 'the author's attempt to achieve or strengthen the illusion of reality by deliberately reversing typical Romantic plots or situations'.[6] The influence

---

[6] John C. Lapp, 'The Critical Reception of Zola's *Confession de Claude*', *Modern Language Notes*, 68: 7 (1953), 460.

of Taine, both in terms of Zola's increasing admiration for Flaubert and in his determined identification of modernity with the priorities of scientific objectivity, becomes clear. The consequence is the assault upon an entire social and political mentality that finds its rationale in romanticism, a romanticism that had in fact largely conditioned the fey wistfulness of the stories in his *Contes à Ninon*.[7] Zola essentially aims to replace this with a determined new set of priorities. Those priorities are characterized as modern, and as realistic in their concern for exposing and stating a truth that is always occluded – rendered unsayable – by the officially permitted discourses in the State. It is here that we find the real reason behind the shock of Zola.

The importance of that shift for Zola himself is fundamental. Among other things, it constitutes, as I note, a repudiation of the romantic elements of his earliest writings in the *Contes à Ninon*. Indeed, a decade later, when he published *Les Nouveaux Contes à Ninon*, he drew explicit attention to the changes. He wrote then, in his prefatory address to 'Ninon', that 'a man cannot always remain tied to a young girl's skirts. There comes a time when your flowers are too cloying. Can you remember that wan autumn evening, the evening when we parted? It was when I came out of your fragile embrace that truth took me into its hard hands. I became crazed by precise analysis.'[8] Zola was clear about this great new development, and his turn to this now very precise scientific realism. He gave his own account of *La Confession de Claude*, in a prefatory note addressed to his friends, Paul Cézanne and J.-B. Baille, where he wrote that

> This story is naked, raw truth. Those of a delicate disposition will rebel against it. I haven't felt the need to cut a single line, so sure am I that these pages are the complete expression of a heart in which there is more light than shade. They have been written by a nervous loving child who has given of himself entirely, with quivering flesh and leaping soul. They are the sickly demonstration of a particular temperament that has the bitter need for reality and the deceptive and sweet hopes of the dream. The whole book is there, in that struggle between dream and reality.[9]

---

[7] See Émile Zola, *Contes à Ninon* (Fasquelle, Paris, 1955), *passim*. The opening address to Ninon sets the tone: 'My dear soul, you made ever sweeter the sadness of our melancholy evenings' ['Ma chère âme, tu me rendais plus douces les tristesses des soirées mélancoliques', p. 9]. The whole of the stories continue in that vein.

[8] Zola, *Les Nouveaux Contes à Ninon*, available at: https://beq.ebooksgratuits.com/vents/zola-ninon2.pdf (accessed 2 August 2019), 11 [trans. mine: 'Les hommes ne peuvent rester toujours dans les jupes des filles. Il vient une heure où vos fleurs sont trop douces. Tu te rappelles la pâle soirée d'automne, la soirée de nos adieux ? C'est au sortir de tes bras frêles, que la vérité m'a emporté dans ses dures mains. J'ai été fou d'analyse exacte].

[9] Available at: https://beq.ebooksgratuits.com/vents/zola-claude.pdf (accessed 1 August 2019), 20–1 [trans. mine: 'Cette histoire est nue et vraie jusqu'à la crudité. Les délicats se révolteront. Je n'ai pas

The terms that Zola uses here are instructive: he is both associating realism with an attack upon the prevailing modes of romanticism that would glorify bohemia and also suggesting that realism needs a story that is stripped bare, with truth given and measured essentially by its nakedness, rawness or crudity. As in the case of Othello imagining Desdemona naked in the sexual embrace of Michael Cassio, so also here we have an image that yields a complex relation to empirical realities. The real opposition is then between fantasy and reality, between the bitter need for the real and the deceptive and sweet hopes that arise in the dream. Othello, of course, chose wrongly in trying to resolve this complexity; Zola encourages us to choose rightly by a stripping bare that involves us looking behind what the State and its theological drivers permits us to see. The truth is screened, and he will deploy a metaphor of the screen to explain his logic.

In the specific case of his own fiction, Zola now argues that he is firmly on the side of stripping things bare. It is the nudity of the tale in its telling, not the nudity of a prostitute, that shocks his critics and the society. As with Courbet, it is not the reality of nudity – the painting of naked bodies – that is shocking; rather, it is the very fact of sex and of sexuality, the truth that humans exist through sex (and labour, both existing defiantly – 'living roses' – in the face of death) that constitutes the truth and material realities of our existence. The trouble with this, for a State that is theologically driven by a moralistic and censorious 'public opinion', is that sexual activity and its fundamental drives exist well beyond the State's direct control.

It is in his famous letter to Antony Valabrègue on 18 August 1864 that Zola outlined the metaphor of the screen in detail. First, he writes there that 'every work of art is like a window opened onto creation' ['toute oeuvre d'art est comme une fenêtre ouverte sur la création'], thereby prefiguring Henry James, as I noted earlier. However, within the frame of this window, there is always a half-transparent screen through which objects appear deformed, changed in some more or less perceptible way in their lines and colours; and such deformations are produced by the very nature of the screen ['il y a, enchassé dans l'embrasure de la fenêtre, une sorte d'Écran transparent, à travers lequel on aperçoit les objets plus ou moins déformés, souffrant des changements plus ou moins sensibles dans leurs lignes et dans leur couleur. Ces changements tiennent à la nature de

> pensé devoir retrancher une ligne, certain que ces pages sont l'expression complète d'un cœur dans lequel il y a plus de lumière que d'ombre. Elles ont été écrites par un enfant nerveux et aimant qui s'est donné entier, avec les frissons de sa chair et les élans de son âme Elles sont la manifestation maladive d'un tempérament particulier qui a l'âpre besoin du réel et les espérances menteuses et douces du rêve. Tout le livre est là, dans la lutte entre le songe et la réalité'].

l'Écran']. Note here the importance of the fact that even this description is taken as if from painting: line and colour being the determining issues. What follows from this is Zola's version of Taine, for the logic is that in any work, we see the world through the point of view of a person, a temperament, and a personality.[10]

Zola delineates three types of screen: the classic ('un verre grandissant' – an aggrandizing glass of sorts); the romantic (a prism that breaks all light up and refracts it in a dazzling and vertiginous shimmer); and, finally, Zola's own preference, the realist. The last yields images that are as faithful to actuality as it is possible to have, notwithstanding the fact that they are screened from us. This realist screen essentially eliminates its own actual existence ['L'Ecran réaliste nie sa propre existence'].[11] Zola advocates a medium that aspires to the condition of immediacy before the facts, as it were. He wants us to see, in his writings, the world in its fundamental structure, its true condition: not the naked body, but the structure of sex shaped by capital that produces prostitution; not the man at work, but the structure of labour under capital that exploits the human body as a resource to be devoured by the very earth that the labourer works for a living; not the alcoholic, but the structure of working-class life and its necessary social relations that make people avoid too great a consciousness of that hard reality through drink-soaked oblivion. That realism, then, shares some definitive overlap with what we have seen in Courbet: the three key areas of physical being as manifest in death (or the unconscious), sex and – as much conventional criticism would have it, above all in Zola's case – labour.

3

It is perhaps the condition of labour, in these years, that determines the politics of realism as it now takes its definitively modern shape. This is happening not just in France, where the 1857 economic crisis had hit Paris especially hard, with the consequence that the danger of a major crisis akin to that of 1848 was considered as a serious possibility.[12] Perhaps most obviously, the structure of labour conditions is undergoing its most significant change in Russia in these years, with the proto-revolutionary agitation that would lead to the 1861 Emancipation. It

---

[10] Émile Zola, *Correspondence I: 1858–1867*, ed. B. H. Bakker (Presses de l'Université de Montréal; Editions CNRS, Paris, 1978), 375.
[11] Ibid., 378, 379.
[12] Ibid., 63, from 'Introduction historique' by Jeanne Gaillard: 'le danger d'une crise noire analogue à celle de 1848 est conjuré'.

is in this milieu and moment – shortly before he strikes up a deep personal and professional friendship with Flaubert – that Ivan Turgenev is also making the same shift that we have seen in Zola, a shift away from romanticism to realism, from *First Love* to *Fathers and Sons*.[13]

The key historical determinant of Turgenev's *Fathers and Sons* is the disruptive political condition in Russia; and this disruption is essentially a contestation over the relations between, on the one hand, labour that works the land and, on the other hand, land ownership. It will be resolved by the massive political shift brought about through the Emancipation of the Serfs. The novel's structure is given essentially in two parts: first, we have Arkady hosting Bazarov in Arkady's family home, with Arkady's father, Nikolai Petrovich and his uncle, Pavel; and second, we move to Bazarov's family home, a kind of mirror-image of Arkady's, except that Bazarov's parents, Vassily Ivanych and Arina Vlassyevna, are poorer. Both families, however, are facing a re-organization of the social and political relations on their land. Nikolai's first words, on the arrival of Arkady and Bazarov, are to the effect that 'The peasants are giving me a lot of trouble this year' because 'They won't pay their tithes', and at the same time the hired men 'are being set against me'.[14] Bazarov's father, self-consciously 'modern', says 'I have put my peasants on the rent system and have given up my land to them in return for half the crops'.[15] The structural divide here is shaped, further, by Nikolai's domain as one that is old-fashioned, still under the influence of aristocratic ideologies, given over to aesthetics, art, poetry, music, while Vassily's domain is avowedly committed to modernity, configured as commitment to science.

Structurally, however – and formally determining for the actual content of the tale – between these two domains governed by labour relations and the contest of modernity with tradition lies that arena circumscribed entirely by the sexual interest: primarily the infatuation that is indulged by Arkady and Bazarov over Mme Anna Sergeyevna Odintsov, but additionally, the interest in Yevdoxia as the 'emancipated woman' and in Fenichka, Nikolai's mistress. The contestation that structures Nikolai versus Vassily, then, is given yet deeper formal power because it is refigured and presented in two related ways: first, as the intergenerational conflict between an old (and largely aristocratic) determination of social realities

---

[13] Turgenev met Flaubert at a dinner in Paris on 28 February 1863, attended also by Edmond de Goncourt and Sainte-Beuve. For details, see Barbara Beaumont, ed. and trans., *Flaubert & Turgenev: A Friendship in Letters; the Complete Correspondence* (Athlone Press, London, 1985). It was in 1869 that Flaubert would introduce Turgenev and Zola to each other, inaugurating what would become, after April 1874, the more or less weekly '*dîners chez Magny*'.
[14] Ivan Turgenev, *Fathers and Sons* (trans. Rosemary Edmonds; Penguin, London, 1965), 22; see also ibid., 24–5.
[15] Ibid., 139.

and a newly emerging view associated with youth (and with what the older generation thinks of as nihilism); and second, as the contest between a staid tradition and the newer science and its association with enlightened thinking. Bazarov calls Pavel, Arkady's uncle, 'an archaic survival'; and in response, Pavel says that Bazarov 'has no faith in principles, only in frogs', in a reference to Bararov's scientific interest in dissection.[16] Bazarov tells Pavel that 'a decent chemist is twenty times more useful than any poet' and that the only art he acknowledges is 'the art of making money or of advertising pills for piles'.[17]

In the midst of this – essentially an argument that derives from the emergent political pressures in his contemporary Russia determined by shifting attitudes to labour – Turgenev presents this labour-struggle also as an erotic struggle, a struggle over sexual relations; and these latter even become seen as basically scientific matters, focused on the material facts of whatever love might be. Thus, the key determinants that we saw as the shaping forces of the emergence of realism in Courbet play a fundamental role here in giving this novel its basic significance.

According to Edward Said, Bazarov is the model in fiction of the figure of the newly emerging phenomenon of 'the intellectual', a man shaped by 'the sheer unremitting force of his questioning and deeply confrontational intellect'.[18] It is interesting to place this alongside V. S. Pritchett's description of Bazarov, as 'the anarchist, even the incipient terrorist of today'.[19] That tacit suggestion – that to be a thinker is to be, incipiently, a terrorist – is itself a powerful and lingering conservative political position, pertinent even to our contemporary moment. It suggests that any thinking that might controvert an existing depiction of the value of the reality of the world as it currently exists is damaging, terrifying and thus to be criminalized.[20]

The terms in both Said and Pritchett themselves are important – though not necessarily in the way that Said (or Pritchett) meant them. 'Force' itself – the force of an intellect and also as the scientific basis of physical reality – is a major issue in the novel. At a key moment, Turgenev plays science off against art almost crudely: Bazarov de-romanticizes nature, describing it as 'not a temple, but a

---

[16] When he sees Anna, Bazarov doesn't fall into aesthetic terms to describe her, but instead thinks 'What a magnificent body! . . . Shouldn't I like to see it on the dissecting table' (Turgenev, *Fathers and Sons*, 97).
[17] Ivan Turgenev, *Fathers and Sons* (1862; trans. Rosemary Edmonds; Penguin, 1865), 30, 38–40.
[18] Edward Said, *Representations of the Intellectual* (Vintage, London, 1994), 12.
[19] V. S. Pritchett, 'Introduction', in Ivan Turgenev, *First Love* (trans. Isaiah Berlin; Penguin, London, 1978), 6.
[20] For a fuller argument detailing this, see my study *The New Treason of the Intellectuals* (Manchester University Press, Manchester, 2018).

workshop' and stating that 'man's the workman in it'; but this is interrupted and potentially undermined by the sound of Nikolai playing the cello. Nikolai then hears Bazarov patronisingly calling him old-fashioned, mocking his reading of Pushkin, and saying that he should instead read *Stoff und Kraft*, a highly controversial book written by Ludwig Büchner, brother of the revolutionary playwright Georg Büchner.

The actual title of the book is *Kraft und Stoff*, or *Force and Matter*; and it argues, among other things, that force and matter are inextricably linked, one being the manifestation of the other. 'No force without matter – no matter without force!' wrote Büchner, introducing the work. He goes on, 'We know in the physical world of no instance of any particle of matter which is not endowed with forces, by means of which it plays its appointed part in some form or another, sometimes in connection with similar or with dissimilar particles.'[21] This book is usually regarded as a primary work in the development of scientific materialism; and is thus determining of a particular attitude to reality, one that considers reality in purely empirical and material (scientific) terms, but also as a reality that is shaped by force and its exercise. Reality, thus, is matter as manifested – given 'ocular proof' – by force; or force is realized in empirically observable and self-evidencing material realities, or matter. That, for Büchner, has a universal applicability.

It follows that thought itself – the work of the intellectual – is purely material, and not divorced from the forces of a physical or empirical reality: 'As there is no bile without liver, no urine without kidneys, so is there no thought without a brain: mental activity is a function of the cerebral substance.'[22] Thinking itself, according to this, is now fully encompassed by labour: it, too, has a very specific reality and can be manifest as force. Developing this further, in what is an extraordinary chapter on 'Free Will', Büchner essentially argues that the character of each and every individual is determined by the material reality or condition of her or his physical environment, and most specifically, by her or his relation to the land (and even to the physical facts of ecology, such as the prevailing weather systems that shape the environment). This leads Büchner to the succinct statement that 'Man is free, but his hands are bound.'[23] That position, of course, is a different formulation of the famous opening sentence – made four years earlier – of Marx's 1851–2 *Eighteenth Brumaire of Louis Napoleon*

---

[21] Ludwig Büchner, *Force and Matter* (1855; eighth edition, 1864; ed. and trans. J. Frederick Collingwood; Cambridge University Press, 2012; e-publication), 2.
[22] Ibid., 139.
[23] Ibid., 245.

that 'Men make their own history, but they do not make it just as they please; they do not make it under circumstances chosen by themselves, but under given circumstances directly encountered and inherited from the past'.[24]

To see the significance of this for a developing politics of realism in the European nineteenth century, we should return first to the fundamental contestations that shape *Fathers and Sons*. As I have noted, this is a text that focuses precisely upon the ways in which a contemporary reality is shaped by how sons inherit the circumstances of the past, and upon the forceful and material realization of that inheritance, as it is given by labour relations and by the political ecology of land-control and capital ownership, including ownership of the labouring body itself. In *Fathers and Sons*, the historical disruption represented by the rise of the new intelligentsia – itself existing alongside Emancipation and in dialectical relationship with physical labour – focuses on the simmering opposition in world views between Bazarov and Pavel. Finally, that opposition comes to a head not through argument. Rather, the only way to resolve their arguments, it seems in the end, is by a duel: force and violence. The duel, which is actually about the fundamental political shifts of the time, takes its form, however, in the displacement of political activity – labour reform – onto sex: they duel over Nikolai's mistress, Fenichka. Bazarov flirts with, and then kisses, Fenichka; but is seen doing so by Pavel. Pavel issues the challenge of the duel, ostensibly because he is defending an idea of honour (Fenichka is the mistress of his brother, and Bazarov's behaviour is dishonourable), but actually, it becomes clear that Pavel himself – unstated at this moment – is besotted with her, and that this is a duel shaped by that erotic interest rather than by moral principle.[25]

The duel itself, however, is marked by irresolution. Pavel is injured, but not mortally; and the two duellists end up sitting together on the ground, more or less amicably discussing again the condition of the Russian peasant, as 'the mysterious Unknown that Mrs Radcliffe used to talk about so much. Does anyone understand him? He does not even understand himself'.[26] They agree that they will hide the truth of what brought them to duelling together, especially from Nikolai.

As the novel nears its completion, Bazarov and Anna Sergeyevna meet again; and they agree to 'forget' what had actually passed between them as the basis of an unrealized affair, because, after all, says Anna, 'love . . . is a purely imaginary feeling'. Thus it is that we reach a kind of final statement by Turgenev regarding

---

[24] Marx, *The Eighteenth Brumaire*, 9.
[25] Turgenev, *Fathers and Sons*, 170–6.
[26] Ibid., 186.

realism; and it is one that shifts our attention away from a concern for 'the real' and – as in Zola – towards an interest in 'the true'. Both Anna and Bazarov agree on this description of love as image only, 'and they both believed they were speaking the truth'. But 'was the truth, the whole truth, to be found in their words? They themselves did not know, and still less does the author'.[27] This, as we will see now, is the new turn in the political interest in realism.

4

We can situate this more fully historically. As Victor Erlich points out, the 'new cultural formation' of 'the plebeian intelligentsia' in 1860s Russia took, as a founding position, an 'impulse . . . to reject the cultural heritage of the leisured classes', and the inauguration of a specific 'social utilitarianism' as the basis of literary and cultural criticism. These critics had little interest in matters of aesthetic form, instead reading literary works for their 'progressive' or 'reactionary' social content. Thinking of themselves as modern and governed by scientific impulses towards objectivity, they were what we might call crude reflective realists, looking to praise only those works that offered a clear and didactic political message and image.[28]

To subscribe to this, however, is essentially to erase the very medium in which literary work exists: it circumvents the language for a supposed unspoken yet governing message in any text. The scientific materialism of Büchner – subscribed to by a character such as Bazarov – would require, by contrast, an explicit acknowledgement not only of the materiality of language but also of its force. Words effect *and* affect reality. It is not an entirely unexpected development, therefore, that Russian criticism moves into an exploration of form, and thus accepts the eventual emergence of a movement of thinking that will lead to Russian Formalism as we now know it.

For the moment, we can leave aside the obvious ways in which Russian Formalism rose and fell between about 1915 and 1930 in the light of its own historical and political situation. That is itself an important historical and political story; but it is not quite the core issue in the question of the politics of realism. More important, for present purposes, is the matter of the Formalist understanding of consciousness and its relation to reality. One of the key

[27] Ibid., 204.
[28] Victor Erlich, *Russian Formalism* (3rd edn, Yale University Press, New Haven, 1981), 20–1.

foundational – and most influential – texts that shaped Russian Formalism was Shklovsky's 'Art as Technique', written and published in 1917, while he was actively engaged in the February Revolution and, subsequently, serving the Provisional Government. It is worth mentioning this simple fact of Shklovsky's political engagements, lest anyone consider that Russian Formalism is constructed while its thinkers are divorced from historical fact.[29] These facts, indeed, help explain some of his critical positions.

As is well known, probably the most rehearsed and fundamental elements that shaped Russian Formalism as it developed were *literaturnost'* and *ostranenie*, usually translated respectively as 'literariness' and 'defamiliarization' or 'making strange'. It is the second of these – making strange, described most fully by Shklovsky – that is of most importance here, given that it is also a key indicator of the moment when we enter the field of 'literariness' itself. *Ostranenie*, as I will show here, is fundamentally about consciousness. Indeed, we might go so far as to suggest that it can be described as 'the political conscious' in relation to the issue of Realism.[30] 'Making strange' – as a means of awakening a reader into consciousness, quickening the reader back into life from an allegedly habitually unconscious state – assumes its role alongside labour and sex as key issues in the formulation of political realism as it develops through the latter half of the nineteenth century and on into the revolutions of the early twentieth. *Ostranenie* is a formal procedure that reawakens our consciousness, a consciousness or perception (aesthesis) that, according to Shklovsky, has been literally anaesthetized – rendered unconscious, asleep, as if dead – by habit and cliché.

The logic is straightforward. We survive everyday existence by a subscription to habit. Were we to be fully alert to everything that happens to us, we would have difficulty in getting out of bed in the morning. We would be too aware of the feeling of our body, the sheets around us, the air whether warm or cold, the slight ache in that specific corner of the left shoulder where we slept too heavily, the person or persons alongside us, their smell, our own smell, the sound of the traffic and so on and on. In order simply to survive the day, we need to ignore many of the things that constitute our material reality and conditions of living.

---

[29] Almost immediately after writing 'Art as Technique', Shklovsky would learn that his brother had been executed, and that his sister had died of hunger in what was then Petrograd. Another brother would be executed in 1938.
[30] The allusion here, of course, is to Fredric Jameson's *The Political Unconscious* (Routledge, London, 1981).

In this way, we fail to attend properly and fully to that reality, and we no longer sense or experience it in some fundamental ways.

Shklovsky puts it in stark terms, arguing that 'as perception becomes habitual, it becomes automatic' to the point where we no longer really have perception at all. Habit, he argues, 'devours works, clothes, furniture, one's wife, and the fear of war'. Against this forced lapsing into what is essentially the death-of-perception that is unconsciousness, 'art exists' and it does so in order that 'one may recover the sensation of life; it exists to make one feel things, to make the stone *stony*'.[31] Far from it being the case that the Formalists turn their back on material realities into the pure and technical niceties of prosody or genre, say, these arguments indicate that, for Shklovsky at least, the point of art is to return the world to us – work, clothes, furniture, 'one's wife', fear, war, and so on – in all its material and empirical realities. Central to this is the fact of perception itself, the living condition of Zola's rose, as it were; and Shklovsky is clear that it is the fact of perception – aesthesis – that is paramount. 'The purpose of art,' he writes, 'is to impart the sensation of things as they are perceived and not as they are known.'[32]

In this, we see an important nuance. Formalism is not interested in truth, but in perception. It does not matter what aspect of the world is experienced; what is important is solely that fact of the experience and of our re-awakening into consciousness of the perception itself. It is like an awakening into naivety. In this regard, although Formalism may be seen to have its roots in, and to emerge from, the politics of the Russian 1860s and the plebeian intelligentsia, its aims differ markedly from those associated with the rise of science. It wants to put literary criticism on a secure and quasi-scientific footing (hence the attention to technique and to technical issues in literature), but its aim is not to get at any underlying truth of the conditions of material existence, only to let us see (or, in general, experience) the world as if for the first time. Its key trope is the pleasure of surprise, not the work or material change of revolution.

This is why Trotsky, for the most obvious example, finds it easy to dismiss Shklovsky; and it is why, by 1924 when Trotsky writes *Literature and Revolution*, the position of the Formalists in post-1917 Russia starts to become fraught. Trotsky acknowledges the usefulness of technical analysis (even if he satirizes it as 'the counting of repetitive vowels and consonants, of syllables and epithets'); but his case against the Formalists is that 'to them verbal art *ends* finally and fully

---

[31] Viktor Shklovsky, 'Art as Technique', in *Russian Formalist Criticism: Four Essays*, Lee T. Lemon and Marion J. Reis, introduced and trans. (University of Nebraska Press, Lincoln and London, 1965), 11–12.
[32] Ibid., 12.

with the word, and depictive art with colour'.[33] For Trotsky, such an investigation is merely a beginning. The Marxist, unlike the Formalist, wants to *know* and not just to *feel*, so to speak. The key questions, once technique has been quickly engaged, are different. 'To which order of feelings does a given artistic work correspond in all its peculiarities?' The answer to this requires development into the next and more probing question: 'What are the social conditions of these thoughts and feelings?'[34]

Like Zola, for whom realism was not conditioned by the choice of a 'vulgar subject', so also Trotsky argues that 'It is not true that we regard only that art as new and revolutionary which speaks of the worker, and it is nonsense to say that we demand that the poets should describe inevitably a factory chimney, or the uprising against capital'.[35] This said, Trotsky is clear that the artist does not make her or his art in a social vacuum, divorced from the real conditions of the world. Art can only draw upon really existing facts of life, even if it does not perfectly duplicate them. He concedes that 'artistic creation . . . is also a deflection, a changing and a transformation of reality'; but that reality is twofold. It is at once 'the world of three dimensions' (and Shklovsky would no doubt agree with this), but it is also and simultaneously 'the narrower world of class society'. It is this latter (according to Trotsky) that Formalism ignores – to its cost and detriment, for in ignoring it, it also ignores the desire or need to ascertain what it is that constitutes historical truth, the truth of 'what happened, when; what *really* happened, when'.

For Trotsky, the materialist approach amounts to what he might call a subscription to political 'totality': the material conditions of life, of the living rose, have one basic and overarching explanation or true foundation, as given essentially by Marxist philosophy. The Formalists, by contrast, are critics whom he condemns as 'idealists' because, in their attention to the particularities of language, they treat language as a system that exists independently of all other phenomena in the totality of the actual conditions of the world: they fail to see how the language is itself a product of the fundamental world-condition. They thereby miss the truth, and fall back into the real, a real that can be considered as 'an abortive idealism applied to the question of art'. The difference here is

---

[33] Leon Trotsky, *Literature and Revolution* (trans. Rose Strunsky; University of Michigan Press, Ann Arbor, 1975), 163, 164 (stress added).

[34] Ibid., 169. In some ways, this is the fundamental position validated by Jameson in his *The Political Unconscious*, in fact. Jameson's position might be (crudely) summed up in these words from *Literature and Revolution*, 178: 'Marxism alone can explain why and how a given tendency in art has originated in a given period in history; in other words, who it was who made a demand for such an artistic form and not for another, and why.'

[35] Trotsky, *Literature and Revolution*, 170.

that 'The Formalists show a fast-ripening religiousness. They are followers of St. John. They believe that "In the beginning was the Word". But we believe that in the beginning was the deed. The word followed, as its phonetic shadow'.[36]

That closing formulation, while looking definitive, merely serves to reiterate the fundamental issue with which we began in this chapter when we considered Iago making an image, in words (a 'phonetic shadow'), of a deed that Othello could *see*, and thus take as the truth, whether or not it *really* happened. In the closing part of this chapter, now, we can seek to find a way beyond this.

5

That clash or contestation between the world as it is – a 'real' world – and the world as it can be – an imagined world – is at the cornerstone of what we now call literary modernity: the relation of the material world to its phonetic shadow, the 'portrait' of a lady (James) or of an artist (Joyce) or of a painting (Wilde) and so on. Zola is one of its key initial figures; and at the core of his thinking is the foundation of realism in writing. It has a philosophical counterpart that will find its best articulation, later, in the thinking of Hannah Arendt, as I will show later.

The most celebrated discussion of Zola's own position regarding realism comes, as I pointed out earlier, in the often-cited letter that he wrote to Antony Valabrègue on 18 August 1864, where he proposes the idea of the screen. In the light of this, it is interesting to note, in passing, how often his novels begin with someone hanging out of a window or looking through an open doorway, onto a scene that is sometimes bare, sometimes a crowd. *L'Assommoir* – the novel that really allowed him to start making a living from his fiction – opens with Gervaise waiting for Lantier, who, for the first time, has not actually returned home. Gervaise soothes the children and then 'she turns back to lean out the window, taking up her night vigil again, her eyes scouring the pavements, far into the distance' ['elle retourne s'accouder à la fenêtre, elle reprit son attente de nuit, interrogeant les trottoirs, au loin'].[37] At the opening of *La Bête humaine*, we find 'the station second-in-command, who having opened a window, leans out on his elbows' '[le sous-chef de gare, [qui] ayant ouvert une fenêtre, s'y accouda'].[38]

---

[36] Ibid., 183.
[37] Émile Zola, 'L'Assommoir', in *Les Rougon-Macquart II*, ed. Armand Lanoux (Pléiade, Paris, 1961), 376.
[38] Émile Zola, 'La Bête Humaine', in *Les Rougon-Macquart IV*, ed. Armand Lanoux (Pléiade, Paris, 1966), 997.

La Curée opens with Renée first of all looking out from a caliche door, then, 'as her sight was poor, she took up her pince-nez, a man's pince-nez' ['comme elle voyait mal, elle prit son binocle, un binocle d'homme'].[39] *Pot-Bouille* opens with Octave lowering 'the window of a door' ['la glace d'une portière'] in his hackney cab.[40] *L'Oeuvre* begins with Claude looking *into* the windows of the apartments he passes in the rain, all lit up and clear.[41] *L'Argent* has Saccard entering chez Champeaux, 'in the white and gold hall, whose two high windows looked out onto the square' ['dans la salle blanc et or, dont les deux hautes fenêtres donnent sur la place'], before going to sit at one of those windows, 'monitoring the passers-by on the pavement' ['épiant les passeurs du trottoir'], staying there to enjoy the view.[42] Virtually every novel in the Rougon-Macquart series opens with the description of a scene that is in fog or mist or smoke, and where seeing through and seeing clearly is an issue for the characters and narrator.

James acknowledged the power of Zola ('the coarse, comprehensive, prodigious Zola') almost as much as he admired Turgenev ('this beautiful genius'). It is perfectly possible that he had such scenes as this in mind when he wrote his 'Preface to *The Portrait of a Lady*', because it is there that he speaks openly not just of Turgenev but also of the 'house of fiction'. This house 'has in short not one window but a million. . . . Every one of which has been pierced . . . by the need of the individual vision and by the pressure of the individual will'. Yet more obviously, 'at each of them stands a figure with a pair of eyes, or at least with a field-glass, which forms, again and again, for observation, a unique instrument, insuring to the person making use of it an impression distinct from every other'.[43]

The underlying principle that governs the entire structure here, the entire 'way of seeing' through these windows, glasses or screens, is one that suggests that reality is always hidden from direct view, and that the purpose of the writing is an act of a kind of unveiling, the establishment of the right kind of screen, a perspective or way of seeing that will allow us to adjudge the truth of what might be visible, or quite literally to 'prove' what is given to the eye or to sensual experience. It is taken that actual reality as such is always screened, and maybe even that it must be screened from view, in some way.

---

[39] Émile Zola, 'La Curée', in *Les Rougon-Macquart I*, ed. Armand Lanoux (Pléiade, Paris, 1960), 320.
[40] Émile Zola, 'Pot-Bouille', in *Les Rougon-Macquart III*, ed. Armand Lanoux (Pléiade, Paris, 1964), 3.
[41] Émile Zola, 'L'Oeuvre', in *Les Rougon-Macquart IV*, 11.
[42] Émile Zola, 'L'Argent', in *Les Rougon-Macquart II*, 11.
[43] Henry James, 'Preface to "The Portrait of a Lady"', in *The Art of Fiction*, introduced by R. P Blackmur (Charles Scribner's Sons, London and New York, 1962), 31, 44, 46.

But Zola wants Valabrègue to be alert to nuance. If he prefers the realist screen, it is not, after all, because it reveals directly the truth of things. It, too, deforms and disfigures; but in doing so, it disfigures in a way that makes a work of art: it makes art from the materials of the real, while hinting at the truth behind the deformed image, a truth that may not itself be amenable to immediate self-evidencing. So, he writes, in what now appears as a prefiguration not just of James but also, surprisingly, of Trotsky (when did we ever expect James and Trotsky to be aligned?) 'My preference is for that Screen which, holding closest to reality, is happy to permit of just enough falsification in order to allow me to sense the presence of a man in an image of creation' ['je préfère l'Ecran qui, serrant de plus près la réalité, se contente de mentir juste assez pour me faire sentir un homme dans une image de la création']⁴⁴ (Letters, 380).

Yet it was perhaps his first 'working-class novel', *L'Assommoir*, that set the scene for what would be the characteristic depiction of Zola. He initially published this novel in serial form in 1876; but the serial publication was unsteady, because the government authorities of the day interfered with the publication. The government ostensibly responded to an establishment's sense of scandal in the face of sex and alcoholism: these were not matters to which the bourgeois wanted to draw attention. More than this, however: in 1876, French politics and society were haunted still by the reverberating echoes of the 1872 Commune, 'when the people of Paris had repudiated their national government and set up their own'.⁴⁵ The fear that provoked the governmental intervention was, once again, the fear of the assembly of people and of the authority that the very fact of such assembly might give to those people.

That fear, felt by the ruling political class, does not necessarily generate explicit prohibitions and censorship. Much more powerful and much more effective is the generation instead of what Elisabeth Noelle-Neumann characterized as a 'spiral of silence'. The establishment of a dominant 'public opinion' works to establish political norms; and this in turn yields a situation in which to speak against such norms is potentially to isolate oneself, to remove oneself from 'the public' and thus to become essentially illegitimate socially, culturally and politically. The consequence is that the oppositional voice falls into an ever-deepening spiral of silence, at the very least as a mode of self-protection or of sustaining oneself as an acknowledged human individual within the society. 'The fear of isolation

---

⁴⁴ Zola, *Correspondence I*, 380.
⁴⁵ Brian Nelson, 'Zola and the Nineteenth Century', in Nelson, *The Cambridge Companion to Émile Zola* (Cambridge University Press, Cambridge, 2007), 9.

seems to be the force that sets the spiral of silence in motion.'[46] Those who are effectively silenced in this way are no longer 'the people'; and it is in this way that a ruling political elite can co-opt those whom it oppresses and can make the underprivileged and disenfranchised complicit in their own further oppression. Now, any view that is critical of the political ruling class is also a view that is opposed to 'the people'; and a principle of 'realism' is established, by the political ruling class, as the means by which this is effected. To oppose or criticize is now to be 'unrealistic' or – as Trotsky puts it against Shklovsky and the Formalists – 'idealist'.[47] This now establishes the terms of future debate over the politics of realism. At its root is the function of the 'idea', a word that in its etymological root is linked firmly to the image: the question is how to adjudicate the values of an 'idea of reality' on the one hand and a 'reality-without-idea' on the other hand; and at the core of this is the status of the visual and the empirical.

Insofar as the ostensible scandal over Zola's work was related to sexual matters, it is more precise to note that the real issue was 'the sheer force and candour of his representation of the squalor of slum life' combined yet more offensively with 'the graphic portrayal, unprecedented in French fiction, of the workers' physical being, their bodies'.[48] It may have been unprecedented in fiction; but the model existed, as we have seen, in Courbet's realist painting of *The Stone Breakers*. The now manufactured 'public opinion' conspires to eliminate the worker's body itself from public view: it is not simply the sexual aspect of being human that is silently censored here; rather, it is the fact of a bodily existence itself. The labouring body itself is to become no longer a 'suitable' or even permissible element of literary or artistic culture. No wonder Trotsky would later be deeply concerned over this kind of aesthetic and political turn.

The political conditions prevailing around the publication of *L'Assommoir* prepare the ground in turn for *Germinal,* some eight years later. This novel's story is set at a time of economic crisis in France, precisely the time when Flaubert and Baudelaire were being prosecuted, in fact. Indeed, it is right to see that the crisis is linked to those prosecutions: the fear among capitalists is the fear that people will assemble in ways that capital itself cannot control. We might thus see that one of the primary functions of capital here is precisely the control of 'public opinion' itself. This is the purpose of a strike as well, in some ways: it deliberately calls into question the limits of the power of capital to control material realities.

---

[46] Noelle-Neumann, *The Spiral of Silence*, 6.
[47] Trotsky, *Literature and Revolution*, 183: 'The Formalist school represents an abortive idealism applied to the questions of art.'
[48] Nelson, 'Zola and the Nineteenth Century', 9.

Germinal is a novel about work in an age of unemployment, an age characterized by the absence of work – and then by the determined absenting of the worker from her or his labour during the strike. Work itself comes again to the fore here in fiction, as with Courbet in painting.

However, there is a significant development in Zola's moment. In *Germinal*, Etienne's first conversations are with 'Bonne-mort' the grandfather in the Maheu family, called Bonne-mort because he has 'died' three times in mining disasters. Importantly, Bonne-mort is a direct descendant of the people who actually first found the mines, the coal seams, in Montsou 106 years earlier; but somehow, this land has been taken by the Compagnie des Mines, and is no longer owned by the people who work the earth and who mine the resource or the wealth. Bonne-mort's death-and-resurrection, as it were, hints at the life-and-death struggle that the miners have not just with the earth but with capital and with the ownership of the earth. A significant part of the point here is that this struggle is profoundly individualized, in this character of the aged grandfather, the character who links the current struggles with a pre-history.

The miners in the novel are hungry, almost all the time; but so is the mine. Le Voreux is consistently described as a monstrous eating machine, swallowing the miners as they disappear down its shafts in regular mouthfuls: 'For half an hour at a time, the shaft devoured them like this, gulping them down more or less voraciously, depending on the depth to which they'd go . . . but without a pause, always ravenous, like a huge gut that can easily digest a whole people' ['Pendant une demi-heure, le puits en dévora de la sorte, d'une gueule plus ou mois gloutonne, selon la profondeur . . . mais sans un arrêt, toujours affamé, de boyaux géants capables de digérer un peuple'].[49]

In some ways, this is an uncanny prefiguration of the great cinematic screen exposition of the working of capital, Chaplin's *Modern Times*. In this 1936 film (it started production in 1933, in the immediate aftermath of the economic disaster of the Great Depression, and the year that Hitler came to power in Germany), Chaplin plays 'the Worker', robotically tightening bolts on a factory production line. In the attempt to boost efficiency, his boss tries out a machine designed to feed the Worker as he works, so that the machinery of capital never stops. However, the body of the Worker interferes with the smooth operation of the machine, and won't be fully complicit with its demands, producing only mess and chaos. His body is out of step with the rhythm of the machine, and it is as if he experiences time itself differently from the clockwork routine. In his regular

---

[49] Émile Zola, 'Germinal', in *Les Rougon-Macquart III*, 1154.

work, the Worker starts to fall behind the pace of the machines that he operates and, in trying to keep up, ends up being more or less devoured internally by the entire production machinery.

In what is the most famous image of this film (and, perhaps, of Chaplin himself as a cultural icon), we see Chaplin caught up in the machinery, as if it is both eating him and also producing him. This is the future that Zola had foreseen in his own metaphors of the voracious mine. Etienne himself becomes assimilated, as later Chaplin will be, in the machinery: 'As time passed, he [Etienne] became accepted, regarded as a true miner, in that crushing of habit that reduced him, day by day, to becoming a mere function of the machine' ['Au demeurant, il était accepté, regardé comme un vrai mineur, dans cet écrasement de l'habitude qui le réduisait un peu chaque jour à une fonction de machine'].[50]

The persistence of this kind of struggle can be witnessed further, and closer to our contemporary moment, in William McIlvanney's 1975 novel, *Docherty*. At the centre of this is the character of Tam (or Thomas) Docherty, a miner who is profoundly aware of the political realities of his life and that of his family. McIlvanney describes Docherty's love for his daughter: 'His love ... was fuelled by odd, apparently disconnected fragments from other parts of his life, his rage at the man-made predestination that loomed over them, his contempt for the acceptance of it in others, his dread that they would none of them have the chance to be what they might have been.' All of this 'was gathered into and consumed by the irrational belief in the worth of people which was as intense as a flame in him.'[51]

McIlvanney, indeed, points directly at the historical link back to the nineteenth century, when he points out that 'the mystique of habits' that these people practiced 'went beyond reflexes conditioned by capitalist oppression, came closer to primitive rites for exorcising the power of the bastard god, economy, originated in an impulse that antedated Factory Acts'. In lines that render something like Zola's concern for justice for workers very directly, McIlvanney goes on to say that 'they had endured long enough to acquire the sense not just of the unmerited privileges of others but of their essential worthlessness as well. Many of them, like Tam, felt militant in the face of these injustices.'[52] This will serve, in fact, as a good description of Zola, who, a century earlier, repeatedly stresses the intimacy of justice with his demand for truth as the condition of his writing and politics.

---

[50] Ibid., 1249–50.
[51] William McIlvanney, *Docherty* (1975; repr. Canongate, Edinburgh, 2016), 90.
[52] Ibid., 268.

Germinal also yields a superb and subtle comparison between the Maheu family and the wealthy Grégoires, as they awaken. This is Zola's account of Courbet's *Sleep*, as it were; and, as with his account of labour, there is a significant turn. In the Maheu household, there are not enough beds to accommodate all the inhabitants; but their potential predicament is solved by the fact that they work shifts, and thus also sleep shifts. Thus, when Zacharie and Jeanlin get up to start their day, it is more or less just as the grandfather, Bonne-mort, is returning from his night's work in the mine; and they have warmed the bed for him. There is a constant turnover, as it were, with the bed itself now part of the shift-pattern of clockwork that organizes the mine itself and its input and output of labour.

Catherine is the first to rise in the Maheu household; and as she does, we find a specific attitude to the sexed body as it awakens from sleep. When she wakes Zacharie, his nightshirt has lifted above his stomach, revealing his genitalia, 'and he pulled it down, not because he was coy, but simply because he wasn't warm' ['et il la baissa, non par pudeur, mais parce qu'il n'avait pas chaud'].[53] There is nothing sexual about all this: it is simply a matter of the naked bodies of a family; but they are again realized as individuated bodies, not drawn as a kind of abstraction of sexual or gender difference. Again, this marks an advance on Courbet's image in *Sleep*. The text then offers a contrast between this and the household of the Grégoires, when La Maheude, the mother, goes there to beg for financial help. The breakfast scenes in the two houses are markedly different, and Zola is inviting the comparison here, a comparison that reveals gross inequality. Where the Maheu family rise at 4 am, Cécile Grégoire is having a long lie-in in bed, much to the careless and self-indulgent amusement of the family. Where sleep is sexualized in Courbet, here is it politicized in terms of the issue of labour and wealth inequalities.

6

Courbet, I argued, painted labour *as such*. Zola's turn – from what he considered to be the claims of realism and towards the claims instead of truth – takes us from this generalized abstraction to present us with individual labourers. It is as if we see the distinct faces of the stonebreakers. This new turn in fiction is one that determinedly individualizes those that the ruling political class prefers to identify as 'the masses'. The force of work as such that we saw in Courbet becomes

---

[53] Zola, 'Germinal', 1164.

instead the force of these masses, with a new emergent identification of 'the people', a people without individual identities, an anonymous people-without-persons, so to speak. It is to counter this very tendency towards the falsifications made by such an abstraction that Zola writes at all. It will find its eventual and most celebrated form in his defence of Dreyfus, where – notwithstanding his calling-out of the scandalous anti-Semitism of the French State and its ruling class – his case rests upon the identification of Dreyfus as a specific individual and not simply as the abstract representation of the figure of 'the Jew-as-such'.

The case against Dreyfus, Zola realized, was built upon a prejudice whose foundation rested in the collapsing of Dreyfus's individuality into the figure of a representative, and thus as a 'type'. In this case he was not a representative of 'the people', but rather simply of 'the Jewish people'. The political figure of 'the people' is here clearly seen by Zola as a means of mobilizing a general public opinion against Jews; and, in doing this, Jews have to be represented themselves not simply as a homogenous single identity ('the Jewish race') but also as enemies of 'the people'.

First, though: Zola demands truth and the justice that will accompany it. In his famous open letter, Zola describes the acquittal of Esterhazy as 'a supreme insult to all truth and justice'; against which he claims that he, Zola, will 'dare to tell the truth'. The conspirators – Generals Mercier, de Boisdeffre and Gonse – 'seem . . . to have given in to the religious bias of their milieu and the prejudices of their class'. With Dreyfus tried behind closed doors, the most extravagant rumours were spread and 'the public, naturally, was taken in. . . . The people clamored for the traitor to be publicly stripped of his rank'. The perpetrators, Zola claimed, 'stirred up all of France' but 'hid behind the understandable commotion they had set off', 'sealed their lips while troubling our hearts and perverting our spirit'. Of this kind of whipping up of public opinion, Zola says, 'I know of no greater crime against the state'. One key element in the State's subsequent attack on Zola is precisely due to the fact that, here, he is breaking out of the spiral of silence that the State imposes by it control of public opinion. In the Dreyfus case, further, the State's interest in the maintenance of capital inequalities is tied firmly also to the State's military functions and institutions.

Zola argues that Dreyfus is a victim of 'the "dirty Jew" obsession that is the scourge of our time'. The newly appointed minister of war, General Billot (who had replaced Mercier between the trials of Dreyfus and the investigation into Esterhazy), 'had the authority to bring out the truth', but 'he did not dare, no doubt in terror of public opinion'. By the time that Esterhazy was being investigated, public opinion against Dreyfus had been completely mobilized;

and the key instrument of this was the press, operating essentially in the service of the General Staff (and, by extension, operating also as an arm of the State). For a manufactured public, a manufactured version of 'the people', reality was now that which is given by this complex triad of State-General Staff-press. This, for Zola, is a complex that not only elides the truth from reality but also arraigns those who – like him – try to realign the real with the true.

He writes that 'it is a crime to have relied on the most squalid elements of the press, and to have entrusted Esterhazy's defense to the vermin of Paris, who are now gloating over the defeat of justice and plain truth'. He goes yet further, because 'it is a crime to lie to the public, to twist public opinion to insane lengths in the service of the vilest death-dealing machinations. It is a crime to poison the minds of the meek and the humble . . . by appealing to that odious anti-Semitism that, unchecked, will destroy the freedom-loving France of the Rights of Man'. Against all this – where public opinion is mobilized by the combination of State and army – ensconcing 'the sword as the modern god' – Zola calls upon modernity and science, arguing that while 'science is tiling to achieve the coming era of truth and justice', we can see that 'truth is on the march, and nothing will stop it'.

Zola himself has learned the rhetoric – that reference to 'poison' – that was operational in the cases of the English Obscene Publications Act and in the prosecutions of Flaubert and of Baudelaire in 1857. Now, however, he has realized that such a rhetoric can be deployed – *must* be deployed – this time *against* the State. It is the State that is now poisoning the minds of the general population, through the deployment of anti-Semitism. Predictably – he himself predicted it – the State prosecuted Zola. Where Dreyfus had been exiled to Devil's Island, Zola exiled himself, to England. The law made him an outsider – and yet, at the same time, he was integral to a specific determination of French national identity, precisely by his challenge to the existing coercive spiral of silence that constituted his milieu and moment, a milieu and moment shaped – like Shakespeare's England, like the 1857 English State that determined the Obscene Publications Act in the light of the Indian Mutiny – by specific attitudes to race.

7

We have seen throughout this chapter the various ways in which theories of realism, especially in writing, rest upon notions of the screen (Zola) or window (James); and we have seen how this fuses with a moment of dramatic political change (from Turgenev to Russian Formalism). It is useful, in the light of the foregoing, to consider some of the work of two painters working in the middle of this later moment: Berthe Morisot and Gustave Caillebotte. These are painters who, at this time, draw especially on the placing of windows or mirrors in their work, in ways that have a direct relevance to the arguments I have made around the trajectory of realism.

In 1875, Gustave Caillebotte made a painting that is, in some ways, an updating of Courbet's *Stone Breakers*. Caillebotte painted *Les Raboteurs du Parquet* (or *The Floor Scrapers*).[54] As with Courbet, the emphasis here is on hard physical labour; but there are some significant new shifts of emphasis. Courbet painted his workers from behind, and absorbed in and by the work; by contrast, Caillebotte's three figures face us. They are certainly absorbed in the work, scraping vigorously at the floorboards; but they are also, very clearly, in conversation with each other. Zola saw the painting, and, while suggesting that its academic mimetic accuracy rendered it essentially 'bourgeois', nonetheless admired its technical accomplishment. It was, however, rejected by the 1875 Salon on the grounds of its supposed vulgarity. Three figures of the new urban proletariat, stripped to the waist, are using tools to plane the floor of what looks like a plush apartment. A bottle of wine is in the hearth, with one filled glass awaiting the moment when they will slake their thirst. Their work, however, is not the entirety of their substance: as they make their way towards us across the floor, on their knees, two of them are in earnest conversation, the angle of their head suggesting that they are seeking some concordat between them, while the third catches them up. This, then, is the start of an assembly of the urban workers, heading directly towards us, and talking with each other while ignoring us, the viewer.

Behind them, a window with veranda casts light into the room from the world outside. However, nothing of that world is visible. We have here an image of workers engaging with each other, without any intervention from any outside forces. It is a genuine assembly of the workers in that respect; yet they are working together precisely in the shadow cast by the light from that world, which imprints itself, from that window-frame, on them and across the floor that they are scraping. That same year, Caillebotte also painted *Jeune homme à sa fenêtre*, where an obviously well-to-do man (actually, Caillebotte's own brother, René) stands with his back to us, looking out from a plush apartment, onto the city streets below. There, he sees a single woman standing midway between two horse-drawn carriages. The man's own reflection is shown in the windowpane

---

54 To view an image of this painting, see: commons.wikimedia.org/wiki/File/Caillebotteraboteurs.jpg.

and, just behind him, a comfortable chair is placed, no doubt waiting for him to sit and meditate on what he sees.

Between these two paintings, we find two kinds of structural opposition that shape the politics of realism. First, the *Raboteurs* gives us an image of the reality of work for the urban proletariat, while hinting at the potential revolutionary power of a class that is now able to speak to itself, in the shadow perhaps of an outside world but nonetheless quasi-autonomous with respect to it, turning their backs on it. Secondly the *Jeune homme* gives us an explicit opposition between the world of the interior self (the young man on the inside, his chair awaiting his further self-reflection and introspection) and the world of the exterior (marked by commerce and the potential for sexual encounter).

These paintings can be placed alongside the paintings from the same period of Caillebotte's friend, Berthe Morisot. In 1872, Morisot painted *Le Berceau*, where her sister, Edma, sits with her infant daughter, Blanche, in her cradle. The child is partly veiled, seen only through a semi-transparent net curtain that hangs over the cradle while, behind Edma, another lacy curtain blocks our view of anything beyond the two figures. The point here is to establish an intimacy: Edma is entirely absorbed in the relation with Blanche, and even uses her arm to hold the net curtain in place, as if to veil her from view. The effect is to set up a chain of intimacies: the construction of the image draws us to concentrate attention on Edma who, in turn, concentrates fully on Blanche.

This is an interiority in its most profound and intimate sense. It prefigures the theoretical position of Virginia Woolf who will tell us that, if we seek reality, we must not concentrate on the material objects of the world that are exterior to consciousness, but rather we must always 'look within'. In her 1925 essay 'Modern Fiction', Woolf argues against the dominant modes of popular realistic fiction (in Wells, Bennett and Galsworthy), writing that 'There is not so much as a draught between the frames of the windows, or a crack in the boards', going on to ask 'And yet – if life should refuse to live there?' Against this, she tells her audience to 'Look within' where we will find that life itself is very different from the world given by the exactitude of mimetic accuracy of external matters.[55]

In 1875, three years after making *Le Berceau*, Morisot paints another image of *La femme à sa toilette*. Here, we have a figure, viewed from behind, sitting before a mirror in which we cannot really see her reflection, pinning her hair.

---

[55] Virginia Woolf, 'Modern Fiction', in *Selected Essays*, ed. David Bradshaw (Oxford University Press, Oxford, 2009), 7, 9.

She is not stripped like Caillebotte's *raboteurs*, but her dress is off her shoulder, revealing her naked back to us. Everything in the image, apart from the woman herself – and especially her naked flesh – is imprecise and vague: we can see very little detail of the world beyond this scene in which the woman is intimate with herself. We become like a voyeur, trying to spy into the woman's own deep self-reflection and introspection. Once again, the message is 'look within'. A year later still, in 1876, in *Psyché* or *The Cheval Glass*, another woman stands before a mirror, preparing herself before going out, her left shoulder again revealed as she ties her dress at the back. She may have looked within; but she is now readying herself for an engagement in and with the world outside, hinted at again in the window that is visible at the right hand side of the canvas.

In all of these, a contest is being staged between an interior and an exterior. This is the ground on which a good deal of literary modernism will be founded, where writers will contend that reality is individuated, that it is a world constituted by the interior of the self, by the interior of our consciousness (and even of our unconscious). Yet this is always set against a world of material realities that constantly impinge upon or at least exert a pressure upon that interior.

When he lectured on 'Hamlet and Don Quixote' in 1860, Turgenev divided humanity into two types. On the one hand, there was the Don Quixote type, who searched always for fulfilment in an engagement with the world beyond the confines of the individual self. On the other hand, there was the Hamlet figure, who searches for similar fulfilment but wants to find it always by looking within and exploring the recesses of a self divorced from material circumstance. In fact, however, as he and Flaubert knew, there is always a dialectic between these two. The consequence, in their writing, is that indecision that one sees explicitly in Turgenev, when the author claims that he does not know what is the reality of the world his characters inhabit. As Barbara Beaumont puts it in her introduction to the Turgenev-Flaubert correspondence, 'Their approach to the function of reality for the artist' is that 'it should be no more than a starting point for the novelist, who must not try to reproduce the real world, detail by detail as a photographer does'. At the same time, 'they were both concerned to base their literary works on observation and research'.[56]

Socially, it is a story of the construction of insiders and outsiders. That is why the issue of race has played such a key role throughout the development of this structuring of realism and reality. The question that the art seeks to pose is one where it asks where indeed reality is to be found: inside, outside, or in

---

[56] Beaumont, *Flaubert & Turgenev*, 29, 31.

the dialectical contestation of the two. The only possible outcome of this is a politics of realism that is grounded in ideas not just of identity and difference (inside and outside) but also a politics that – from the point of view of a society or political State – is grounded in the idea of the manufactured identity of an entirely new political phenomenon: 'the people'. The observation and research on this new phenomenon is where we can now turn. In one form, aesthetically, it will eventually offer a theory of impersonality such as we see it noted in T. S. Eliot; but in its more troubling political form, it becomes the reality of 'the will of the people', which will take very unpredictable forms in the century to come.

6

Realism changes reality

Revolution, documentary and socialist realisms

1

In 1892, Henry James wrote a brief story, called 'The Real Thing'. At the core of this story is an exploration of the relations between art, money and representation. Fundamentally, the tale explores the relation of aesthetics to economics, and places the issue of the representation of reality – most specifically the reality of the human body at work and in gainful employment – at the centre of that relation. The narrator is an artist who, like many artists, cannot make an entirely comfortable living from his portraits; so he also does illustrations – his 'pot-boilers' as he calls them – for use in magazines and fictions. When Major and Mrs Monarch visit him one day, he mistakenly assumes that they want their portrait done, in oils and on canvas; but, in fact, they want to offer themselves as models for black-and-white images that can then be sold on for magazine circulation. They, too, although of a certain social class, are ageing and need money. The text cagily circles round the embarrassment that the need for making a living actually causes, as if 'making a living' is itself a rather vulgar thing to do.

As if to clarify the inherent vulgarity, James gives us another of the artists' models, Miss Churm. Miss Churm arrives at the studio by public transport and on foot; she looks 'a trifle blowsy and slightly splashed', 'only a freckled cockney'. She can't spell, she loves beer, the theatre 'and seven sisters', but 'has not an ounce of respect, especially for the *h*'. Sitting, for Miss Churm, is a job; but she is extremely good at it, able to 'represent everything, from a fine lady to a shepherdess'.[1] Miss Churm may indeed be working class, vulgar and 'common'; but she is able to make a living from her labour. The work involves becoming other than she

---

[1] Henry James, 'The Real Thing', in James, *The Aspern Papers and other Stories*, introduced by S. Gorley Putt (Penguin, 1876), 116.

is: representation certainly, but always the representation of something that she most explicitly is not. Representation is enmeshed thoroughly and necessarily in misrepresentation, as it were, such that the artistic copying of something works precisely by hiding 'the real thing' beneath the art, beneath the representation.

It is here that James finds his fundamental theme: identity, specifically the identity of the material fact of the human subject with her or his equally material but different manifestation of that identity in society.[2] The subject of the tale is the identity of identity with difference, as a Hegelian or a proto-deconstructor might have put it. Miss Churm is good at being other than herself (identity shaped by intrinsic difference and openness to all that is other); Major and Mrs Monarch seem to be unable to escape from their very specific identity (identity as a closed self-reflexive system of identity with itself). The paradox, of course, is that the Monarchs are anything but stable in their identity, given what seems to be their precarious financial or economic position. When another model, Oronte, also shows up out of the blue – 'a young man whom I easily perceived to be a foreigner and who proved in fact an Italian acquainted with no English word but my name' – our artist decides to employ him as a model in return for Oronte's acting as a domestic servant, a double-edged economic relationship. Mrs Monarch is amazed when she sees the drawings for which Oronte has modelled, simply because the man she sees before her own eyes is not recognizable from them. By contrast, 'Now the drawings you make from *us*, they look exactly like us', she says, to which the artist thinks 'and I recognized that this was indeed just their defect'.[3]

In relatively quick time, the Monarchs fall further into becoming useful in the studio, and end up doing the kind of things – humble housework chores – that they found so distasteful and vulgar when they were done by Miss Churm or Oronte. They start washing up the crockery, tidying up (a rather significant change of status for a 'monarch', of course). 'They had accepted their failure.' However – and here is the fundamental point of this fable – 'they couldn't accept their fate. They had bowed their heads in bewilderment to the perverse and cruel law in virtue of which the real thing could be so much less precious than the unreal', writes James; and he immediately, acerbically, adds, 'but they didn't want to starve'. The economic conditions of labour – no matter how distasteful, no

---

[2] In passing, we should note that this discovery of the theme of 'identity' is more or less exactly contemporaneous with the moment when Arthur Conan Doyle also focuses the question of realism on that 'case of identity' in the 1891 short story of that title. Where the fictional Holmes 'solves' the case of identity, James presents it as a fundamental quandary and problem concerning the relation between empirical and material realities and their representations.
[3] Ibid., 125.

matter how much one wants to avert one's Jamesian eyes from those facts – are determining of biological survival.

The issues that James raises here are threefold. First, representation is re-thought in terms of misrepresentation: the problem with the Monarchs is that they are just too much 'the real thing'. Secondly, 'the real thing' itself is reconfigured here as something available not through reality but through an engagement with a certain unreality. Thirdly, we have the question of economics, re-thought here in terms of where we locate value: Is it to be found in the sphere or art and aesthetics, where we value the 'precious' nature of the unreal; or do we find it instead in the sphere of material life and the body's needs, where the Monarchs need money to live and do not want to starve, and so have to 'realize' themselves as labour, as bodies whose reality is materialized in work, even in 'vulgar' work?

In respect of the political economics of realism, James here is in alignment with Zola. Zola was clear about the pragmatic need to make money from art; and he tied this, further, to the issue of free speech. He was adamant that writing was a form of labour, and that it was thus tied to the operations of capital: 'It is money', he wrote, 'the legitimately earned proceeds of [the writer's] work that has delivered him from every humiliating patronage, and which made the former court-jester and the former ante-chamber comic into a man who stands on his own feet'. With money, Zola went on, the writer 'dared to say everything, took his analysis everywhere, right up to the king, to God, without the fear of losing his daily bread. Money set the writer free, and it was money that shaped modern writing' [C'est l'argent, c'est le gain légitimement réalisé sur ses ouvrages qui l'a délivré de toute protection humiliante, qui a fait de l'ancien bateleur de cour, de l'ancien buffon d'antichambre, un citoyen libre, un homme qui ne relève que de lui-même. Avec l'argent, il a osé tout dire, il a porté son examen partout, jusqu'au roi, jusqu'à Dieu, sans craindre de perdre son pain. L'argent a émancipé l'écrivain, l'argent a crée les lettres modernes].[4]

Alongside this issue of capital, both formally and thematically James's story of 'the real thing', written in 1892, is a dramatic forerunner of an entire series of theoretical issues and problems to do with the changing shapes of realism in the next century. It prefigures, among others, the themes and arguments in a number of significant later texts: André Gide's 1924 *Les Faux-Monnayeurs*;

---

[4] Colette Becker, citing Zola, in her 'Introduction Biographique' to Zola, *Correspondence I* Please re-insert deleted matter. This is the first reference to this work in the present chapter, 51. Zola asserts the right of a writer to call the monarch into question. It is a moot point – but an interesting speculation – as to whether there is a subterranean link between this thinking and that of James.

Walter Benjamin's 1936 'Work of Art in the Age of Mechanical Reproduction'; Antonin Artaud's *The Theatre and Its Double* in 1964; Clément Rosset's *L'Objet singulier* of 1979; Jean Baudrillard's entire *oeuvre*, from *The Mirror of Production* through at least to his *Evil Demon of Images* in the period from the 1960s through to the 1980s; Umberto Eco's consideration of *Faith in Fakes*, which likewise covered work from the 1960s onwards. This is work that will reach a logical culmination in our own contemporary issue around 'fake news' and the deployment of artificial intelligence and associated advanced technologies to present persuasively realistic presentations of entirely faked 'realities'. That is an issue that is itself shaped by the determination of the already privileged to control 'their' economic and political reality, a reality that is not to be scrutinized or subjected to criticism of any kind. However, this said, the important thing for present and immediate purposes is primarily the issue of the politics of realistic misrepresentation.[5]

In its own moment of 1892, James would likely himself have seen his story as an interesting contribution to debates over truth in painting and, through that, debates over the kind of turn that Zola had made when he started to think of realism in terms not of a representation of the real but rather as a proclamation and assertion of truth itself. Further, since the advent of photography in the nineteenth century, painting itself had had to change, given the supposed 'truth' of photographic representation. What happens to a truth when it is repeated? How is it ever possible to 'represent' the truth, given truth's absolute uniqueness, and given that any worthwhile or valuable representation must, in fact, deviate in some way from 'the real thing' if it is to be understood in its status as a *re*-presentation at all? As before, the status of the image in representation is important in this writing. That is about to take a very dramatic new turn, however, in the decades that follow James's story, decades that brought about formal revolutions in aesthetics and political revolutions and wars that would shape an emergent modern world.

2

While Zola was awaiting his second trial after his *J'accuse* public and open letter – and while his lawyers and supporters were thinking he would have to go into exile in England – Jane Anthony Grierson gave birth to her first son (and fourth

---

[5] The issue of 'fake news' is addressed in more detail in later chapters here.

child) in Deanston, a tiny one-street hamlet near Stirling in Scotland. John Grierson was born on 26 April 1898, in a location that was almost certainly completely unaware of the political issues around Zola and Dreyfus; yet John would go on to become a figure who took Zola's underlying concern for truth and justice into the new medium of film, and in so doing, transforming entirely our understanding of the politics of realism.

Twenty-four years later, in 1922 and while studying at Glasgow University, Grierson saw Robert Flaherty's *Nanook of the North*, and was amazed at its power and at its mode of presentation of the world. Watching more of Flaherty's relatively sparse output – specifically while watching *Moana* – he coined the new term 'documentary' to describe this new genre of film-making. In doing so, he – consciously or not – gave a currency to Zola's historical interest in the status of the document as a basis for artistic production. Grierson believed that Flaherty was making a film that would stand as a 'document' in itself – and this, as we now know, is a judgement that has proved to be accurate, historically. Flaherty's films are themselves documentary evidence vital to any understanding of the social, cultural and political themes (presciently, these themes are profoundly environmentalist and governed by an interest in ecology) that they address.

Grierson actually lifted the word 'documentary' from an original French source. The term was first used in 1924 to describe films that were educational and instructive (often early versions of travel films, giving information and images of 'elsewhere' locations),[6] either simply showing documents or basing themselves on events and realities that had not been pre-prepared or 'staged'. The French dictionary, *Le Petit Robert*, cites a first usage in this sense by André Gide, when Gide adopts an adjectival usage: 'Marc tâche de filmer des scènes documentaires' [Marc sets himself the task of filming some documentary scenes]. For Grierson, the distinction from the staged and anything 'stagey' or theatrical was fundamental: 'The significant thing to me now,' he wrote, describing his childhood Scottish community's first experience of film, 'was that our elders accepted this cinema as essentially different from the theatre. Sin still, somehow, attached to play-acting, but, in this fresh new art of observation and reality, they saw no evil.'[7] The people in these films were, so to speak, 'absorbed' in and by their work and life, a description that should recall briefly here the

---

[6] Such was the basic proposition governing Grierson's famous TV documentary series, *This Wonderful World*, running from 1957 to 1966 on UK television, broadcast from the Theatre Royal in Glasgow.
[7] John Grierson, 'The Course of Realism', in *Grierson on Documentary*, ed. Forsyth Hardy (Faber and Faber, London, 1979), 70. 'The Course of Realism' is also available in Charles Davy, ed., *Footnotes to the Film* (Lovat Dickson Ltd, London, 1937), 137–61, which was, in fact, the place of its original publication.

terminology of 'absorption and theatricality' that we deployed when discussion the emergence of realism via Courbet in painting.

As Zola knew, the status of the document is crucial in the determination to seek truth and justice. Zola knew this, of course, for the simple reason that the document was fundamental to his scientific understanding of the operations of art and of social and cultural criticism that is embedded in art. *Les Rougon-Macquart* is a researched series of fictions, and much of the research stems from the explorations of historical and factual documents that give access to the real conditions of life for the kinds of characters described by Zola. In preparing *Germinal*, for instance, Zola not only read a substantial number of books and articles about mining and strike action, he also visited Anzin immediately after a strike broke out there in February 1884, for the explicit purpose of taking and making factually based notes for his novel.[8] Of course, it is almost certainly not necessary here to stress again the importance of the document – and the question of authenticity or authentic realities – in his exposure of the skullduggery in the Dreyfus case, where forged writings and signatures on fake documents proved to be central to his task, a task that exposed some *faux-monnayeurs*, as it were.

Grierson's 'observation' as such, however, is not scientifically neutral: the '*art* [stress added] of observation and reality' is, above all, an art: it is one that is sinful but not evil, in Grierson's terms. Grierson inherits his terms of reference here from two different sources. The first is that early modern English moment that I explored earlier, in which theatre was cast as the site of sin, but where the religious veneer covered a political fear of people gathering in riotous assembly against privileged central powers. The second source is a certain dour religiosity – itself based in a combination peculiar to modern Scotland of Presbyterianism and Calvinism – that was suspicious of anything that gave the mildest hint of bodily or sensual pleasure, or that would permit a human to experience the reality of her or his body via any pleasing material sensuousness. It would be especially suspicious of a psychology that considered such pleasure as the basis of the reality of the human condition.

A certain dour neo-puritanism triumphs over the mildest hint of Epicureanism, which would be regarded as sybaritic luxury wrongfully indulged precisely when the human individual should be realizing that we are on earth and given a physical body for the primary purpose of suffering. In this mentality – a mentality that is a signal of political thinking – 'realism' equates with the

---

[8] For an indication of the substantial range of books and articles he consulted, see, for instance, Colin Smethurst, *Zola: Germinal* (Edward Arnold, London, 1974), 21–2.

experience of a pain that is to be based on a representation of Christian bodily pain: an *imitatio Christi* that focuses on crucifixion. When Grierson makes that distinction between sin and evil, however, he is finding a nuance that both acknowledges that cultural reality while at the same time seeing an escape route from it. That combination – fundamentally a condition in which sin exists as a tempering force against evil (in the same way as pain inhabits and interrupts pleasure, or 'reality' intrudes upon fantasy) while still being involved and enmeshed thoroughly within it – is of the essence of the dialectic of criticism itself (being enmeshed in a reality while not being entirely of it or contained by it); and for Grierson, the resulting critical attitude or ethos is fundamental to documentary.

It is important to realize, at the outset then, that the documentary movement inaugurated and informed by the work of Grierson is not at all concerned to present reality in some innocent and neutral fashion. Such a presentation might be valuable; but that would be matter for the newsreel, according to Grierson. Instead, he insists always on two things: first, the documentary film must go beyond mere representation of reality in order to seek the founding conditions that make that reality not only possible but materially realized (this is the 'art' that is inscribed in the basic observation, allowing the viewer to see beyond the superficial); and secondly, the documentary is always inscribed with a profound educational impulse, and is concerned primarily and above all with civic – and civilizing – education and with the issue of how to be an active citizen in a modern world and environment (and this is the 'art' of reality that the documentary reveals).[9] Not for him a 'doubling' or mere representational duplication of reality or of 'the real thing' via film: he is aware that value lies not in 'the real thing' but rather in the art that gives a kind of defamiliarization – like a Russian Formalist *ostranenie*, like James's Miss Churm or Oronte – that analyses and educates simultaneously. These matters, he knows, are shaped by economics.

There is no evidence that Grierson knew the work of the Russian Formalist literary critics directly; but he did know early Russian film.[10] Indeed, while he was in the United States and meeting Flaherty for the first time, he prepared

---

[9] It is worth recalling here also Joseph Conrad's famous formulations in his 'Preface' to his 1897 novel, *The Nigger of the 'Narcissus'* (Penguin, London, 1979), 11–13, where he argues that the function of art is to 'make the reader see', while also ensuring that the line of sight is itself always directed by a pedagogical consciousness.

[10] See, for example, his extraordinarily detailed critical commentary on Eisenstein, Turin, Dovjenko, Dziga Vertov, Fridrikh Ermler, Pudovkin and others in his 'Summary and Survey: 1935', in Grierson, *Grierson on Documentary*, 52–69, esp. pp. 64–6.

Eisenstein's 1925 film, *Battleship Potemkin*, for its first ever US viewings in New York (in December 1926); and, indeed, he even had to edit the film in the face of New York State's censorship laws.[11] When Grierson premiered his own first documentary, *Drifters*, in London in 1929, he programmed it alongside *Potemkin*, which was just emerging from UK censorship at the time. He also knew thoroughly the films and philosophy of Dziga Vertov. Like Grierson himself, Vertov was suspicious of the emergent tendency to narrative film, writing (like Shklovsky in Formalist literary criticism) that when it turns to narrative and its sentimentalities 'the body of cinema is numbed by the terrible poison of habit'.[12] This will turn out to be important as we consider both documentary realism and 'Socialist Realism' as these emerge through the 1920s and beyond.

Vertov operated in line with the thinking of Lenin, who had told Anatoly Lunacharsky, Lenin's Commissar of Education, that film was the most important of all the arts in the revolution and that it must reflect Soviet actuality. For Lenin, this meant that newsreel was fundamental – but fundamental to the purpose of State education in what constituted Soviet actuality or the realism of the new Bolshevik State. Grierson, while less committed to newsreel, did indeed see the purpose of documentary as being firmly tied to education and –though this will sound controversial in today's lexicon – documentary was also intimately tied therefore to propaganda. It was as if, for Grierson, documentary film did not 'reveal' or even 'present' reality; it actively propagandized for it. Interestingly, when Grierson considered Lenin in relation to both propaganda and education, he described him almost as if he were a kind of political Formalist, committed to education precisely as a process of defamiliarization. He wrote that 'Lenin justified his case by arguing that particular groups of individuals in a reactionary society were so bound to false ways of thinking that they were either conscious or unconscious enemies of the good life. He urged that their enlightenment should be continuous and unremitting.[13] The Formalist and Shklovskian attack on 'habit' is here recast as an attack upon a consciousness that is 'bound to false ways of thinking' and that needs the unmasking that comes with enlightenment. To pierce through this requires a mode of education that looks very like the action of propagandizing for a reality that is occluded under falsehood.

This yields a very specific and new idea of what the 'art of observation and reality' now means for a theory of the politics of realism. It seems to differ from, and to make a marked advance on, the thinking that has shaped the politics

---

[11] Eric Barnouw, *Documentary* (Oxford University Press, Oxford, 1983), 85–6.
[12] Dziga Vertov, as cited in Barnouw, *Documentary*, 54.
[13] Grierson, 'Propaganda and Education', in *Grierson on Documentary*, 142.

of realism throughout the modern period. Fundamental to this shift is the idea, given to us via James in 'The Real Thing', that 'the real' – and the artist's relation to it – is formed and, more precisely, 'deformed' by class and money. This is also exactly what lies behind the forged documents that were used to incriminate Dreyfus, of course. Now, however, arriving at a perception of the real requires that, above all and following Zola, we adopt a principle of negation – a thundering of the word 'No!' – in response to an existing state of affairs. Realism engages us in a negation of what the Formalists called the force of habit that dulled our perception of reality; and it engages us equally in response to what Lenin thought of as a false consciousness that misled people in to a quietist acceptance of a bogus account of the real state of human relations and of force.

From now on, and in these circumstances, realism – both in Grierson's documentary realism and in Soviet Socialist Realism – will be about changing reality, not innocently accepting it and certainly not slavishly reiterating or re-presenting it. This means that education now plays a role in the formation of a realist way of seeing the world; and it also means that the State, which governs education, enjoys a fundamental and even determining relation to the politics of realism.

3

'Art', Grierson said, 'is not a mirror but a hammer',[14] making thereby a definitive break with the prevailing metaphors of realism that he had received from literature in the previous century. He 'importuned his staff', while making their documentary films at the Empire Marketing Board, 'to avoid the "aestheticky." He told them they were propagandists first, film makers second'.[15] To contemporary ears, this may sound more than a little awkward. And it is. That, in fact, is part of Grierson's own extremely radical point. The point here is that education – which is central to the changing of reality – depends upon a circumvention of the prevailing economics that govern representation, especially in cinema. If the existing habit of perception is based in a falsifying mode of representation, then it is ipso facto based in a mode of propaganda (fake news). If education is to circumvent this – as it must do if it is interested in truth and justice, as in Zola

---

[14] See Roger Blais, 'Grierson' (1973). Documentary film made for the National Film Board of Canada, available at: http://latetedelemploi.nfb.ca/film/grierson/ (accessed 4 October 2019). Obviously, this recalls Nietzsche's *Twilight of the Idols; or, How to Philosophize with a Hammer* of 1889.
[15] Barnouw, *Documentary*, 90.

– then the documentary maker must engage in what is essentially a different propaganda, even a counter-propaganda.

We can begin to comprehend the justification for this more fully by starting from Grierson's economic analysis. When film and cinema began, it was cheaper to film out of doors, where lighting was given free and naturally; and so, in the early films – of Lumière, say, filming the workers leaving Lumière's own factory and streaming out of the building into the streets – 'there was fresh air' and 'more importantly, there was some reflection of ordinary life in the drama'. However, technological advances in cameras and production then combined with what was emerging as the basis of the 'star system' as we would now call it. 'Big names and celebrated subjects brought attention, and attention brought money'; and so film moved indoors where 'the high falsehood of trickwork and artifice was in, and reality and the first fine careless rapture were out'. Thus it was that cinema was 'driven by economics into artifice',[16] and away from everyday reality. Once this economic foundation is asserted, censorship also follows. Indeed, censorship becomes an active component part of the same economic priorities that directed cinema and representation (or images in general) towards capitalist profit. It follows from these economic conditions that 'it is not surprising that [the censor's] slogan of "No Controversy" – which to philosophy and all the world is "No Reality" – is abjectly obeyed'.[17]

Grierson's own aesthetic philosophy is also clear. He firmly believed that beauty is at its most honest and just whenever it 'has come to inhabit the edifice of truth', found most clearly in those films that are 'patient, analytic and in the best sense observant'.[18] The example from Grierson's own work is his 1929 *Drifters*, with its theme of 'the ardour and bravery of common labour'. With this model in mind, Grierson contended that, in every documentary that he and his team made, 'we have been able to rely . . . beyond renter and exhibitor alike, on the people, and their superior taste in realism'.[19] That taste was – as the censor and the political establishment, identifying fully with the capitalist motivational principles of private profit, feared – potentially a taste for social and political change.

It is perhaps unsurprising that such a film as *Drifters* caused political and cultural controversy when it was shown in 1929 and 1930, in the wake of the

---

[16] Grierson, *Grierson on Documentary*, 70, 71, 72; cf. Grierson in Davy, *Footnotes*, 138–40.
[17] Grierson in Davy, *Footnotes*, 141. This passage is omitted from the version in Grierson, *Grierson on Documentary*.
[18] Grierson in Davy, *Footnotes*, 145; cf *Grierson on Documentary*, 73.
[19] Grierson in Davy, *Footnotes*, 151; cf *Grierson on Documentary*, 76–7.

opening shocks of the Great Depression. The political establishment of the time might have found it difficult to link the film and that particular economic disaster; but it wasted no time in aligning Grierson with Bolshevism, which proved a very convenient method of diverting attention from the political and economic realities to which Grierson's film of ardent and brave labour drew the attention of the movie-going general public. As Grierson wrote, 'The thought of making work an honoured theme, and a workman, of whatever kind, an honourable figure, is still liable to the charge of subversion.'[20]

The subversion in question, of course, was nothing more or less than the shock of historical change itself. A conservative world view, such as that which dominated the censors' office in 1929, say, is designed primarily – as the name suggests – to conserve existing material and social conditions of life. In this case, that meant a determination on the part of the political establishment to preserve existing privilege and political states of affairs as they existed – 'really' – under capitalism. Notwithstanding the shock of the Great Depression, capitalism still equalled or equated to realism; and the political establishment believed that any challenge to capitalism and its modes of life must be forestalled. This 'capitalist realism' is what Grierson's documentary challenges, through its art of observation, an art that is an analysis and a revelation of the underlying and otherwise hidden conditions that subtend contemporary reality, or that make any material reality possible at all. Grierson may have been alert to all that the Bolshevik Lenin had done in Russia; but he was much more in tune with the aims of Lunacharsky, the Commissar for Education. The reason for this is that, as far as Grierson is concerned, art itself is primarily in the business of education as such; and at the heart of this education was the construction of a civil sphere and of a people able to survive and thrive within it.

Citizenship education was at the heart of Grierson's realist project. While it might not need a sickle to achieve this, it certainly did require a hammer, a hammer that would be taken to the existing metaphor of art as a mirror or screen of nature and of reality. Anatoly Lunacharsky would have provided a useful model. On 29 October 1917, he had argued that 'The laboring masses ... thirst after education'; and the role of the State, faced with this thirst, would be simply to provide the means whereby 'the people themselves, consciously or unconsciously, must evolve their own culture'.[21] Grierson was explicit that 'our British documentary group began not so much in affection for film as in

---

[20] Grierson, in Davy, *Footnotes*, 152; cf. *Grierson on Documentary*, 77.
[21] See Sheila Fitzpatrick, *The Commissariat of Enlightenment* (Cambridge University Press, Cambridge, 1970), 26.

affection for national education', an education in what citizenship might mean and how people might most fully enjoy such citizenship in the modern world that could be known through the new media. Looking back at his own childhood community, in which coal mining was central to life, he saw that 'true leadership in education . . . had in fact passed to the miners themselves'.[22]

Grierson described himself as a man who had been born into and formed thoroughly by strikes, long strikes, nine-month-long strikes; and this real-life experience, reminiscent of *Germinal* and of a number of nineteenth-century 'working-class' English novels, such as Elizabeth Gaskell's great fictions (*Mary Barton* in 1848, her 1854 *North and South*, *Wives and Daughters* in 1866), not to mention the obvious precursor of Dickens, or the sociological work of Harriet Martineau (as in her 1849 text on *Household Education*) remained with him throughout. While Flaherty would go to the extremes of the earth for his material, Grierson found it all closer to home and to the everyday living realities of the domestic scene. He recalled telling Flaherty, 'You do the savages at the end of the earth; I'll do the savages in Birmingham'.[23] This was important for him, as a corrective to the ways in which film is misleading – mis-educating – his audiences.

As Grierson saw it, the culture of his contemporary England 'is divorced from the actual': the dominant mode of seeing is shaped and controlled by the gentleman class. That culture 'is practised almost exclusively in the rarefied atmosphere or country colleges and country retreats'. Those who live in such places enjoy a certain assuredness in which they prove their hierarchical status, in control of society's norms, by presenting an exotic account of all others. 'Our gentlemen explore the native haunts and investigate the native customs of Tanganyika and Timbuctoo, but do not travel dangerously into the jungles of Middlesbrough and the Clyde', he wrote, adding that 'Their hunger for English reality is satisfied briefly and sentimentally over a country hedge'.[24] Lunacharsky's 'thirst' and Grierson's 'hunger' for education determine the function of realism as an instrument of popular education, and as a legitimizing force for popular culture and a solid account of actuality.

Lunacharsky was to become embroiled in a series of controversies over the nature of education in the new Soviet State. While acknowledging what he saw as the need for the people more or less to determine their own education, through

---

[22] Grierson, 'Education and the New Order', in *Grierson on Documentary*, 125.
[23] See Blais, *Grierson*, available at: http://latetedelemploi.nfb.ca/film/grierson/ (accessed 12 August 2020).
[24] Grierson, 'Flaherty', in *Grierson on Documentary*, 32.

the autonomous determination of their own culture, he nonetheless valued extremely deeply the history of an earlier high culture. For him, then, education was not something that could simply be assumed: the people had to be given the means through which they could pursue their cultural self-determination; and this entailed an awareness of the very cultural practices and norms against which they were supposedly in revolt. The logic, for Lunacharsky (supported in this by Nadezhda Krupskaya, Lenin's wife), led to his 'Declaration' on education. In the Declaration, he proposed a philosophy of education that was very close to the schemes that John Dewey had been developing in the United States: 'anti-authoritarian, non-scholastic', roughly similar to Dewey's 'activity school'.

While being anti-authoritarian, such an education could nonetheless be authoritative, based on an existing notion of seriously important cultural norms; and, as Sheila Fitzpatrick points out 'The shadow of Tolstoy' hangs over this scheme (and, we might add, also that of Turgenev whom we examined in the previous chapter here).[25] At the centre, notwithstanding the attention to literary history, is the idea of the 'labour school', and it is this that ensures that education is tied firmly to the ideas and dignities of the labouring body. Crucially, for both Lunacharsky and his various rivals in the formulation of the new schooling, 'Schools had to drop religious instruction ... and introduce labour and aesthetic training and physical education' into the curriculum, with aesthetic education dedicated to 'the systematic development of the organs of perception.'[26]

We thus have the emergence of a system that is directly opposed to what had happened in the previous century in France, where the Falloux Law had placed religion at the centre of education, using that religion thereby in order to firm up State control of individual social and political realities. In place of religion, and also equally in place of the institution of law that was subjected to critique in the English case, labour will now occupy this role. For Grierson, however – with that peculiar Scottish religious temperament that I described earlier – propaganda is itself intimately related to religion and, indeed, to law. He points out that the very word 'religion' derives etymologically from a root meaning 'a bond'. The bond that he has in mind, however, is not so much a bond between an individual and a god, as a bond among individuals themselves: a social bond or even a kind of 'social contract', as political philosophy usually construes it. He notes that, in his time, people have lost religious faith, and have thereby lost 'that complex of loyalties and attitudes by which men's needs are first appreciated and then

---

[25] Fitzpatrick, *Commissariat*, 30.
[26] Ibid., 48, 32.

fulfilled'; and he stresses that he is making the same point as those who 'have recently deplored the separation of education from religion'.[27]

This, however, is no revival of a Falloux-style thinking. Grierson has no time for piety, but insists instead that religion – and education – should be tied to real and material conditions and needs. The bond that he has in mind is more like the bond of social class, cognizant as he is that the world's 'reality' is actually the world deformed by the class interests of the already privileged, at the cost of the worker. Further, 'education is activist', and must be conditioned by the real material need for change. It is 'the key to the mobilization of men's minds to right ends or wrong ends, to order or chaos'.[28] What this meant for Grierson is clear: 'nothing less than a drastic spring cleaning of the concepts we teach and the sentiments by which we govern our action'.[29] Documentary realism exists primarily to effect this kind of change.

It is instructive to bear the Russian example in mind as we seek to grasp the idea that realism is no longer about representing the world but rather about changing it: realism means changing reality, not showing it. In Russia, Lunacharsky had both rivals and enemies working against his proposals for the new education agenda. Teachers initially refused to carry out the new programme; and the university sector in particular mounted stringent opposition. They were supported in such opposition by a group known as the *Proletkult*, who were much more iconoclastic – and who, although they shared the teaching profession's opposition to Lunacharsky and Krupskaya, did so for entirely different political reasons. While the teachers and professors wanted to rest their case on traditional ideas of the autonomy of the university and on the rights of teachers to determine the school curriculum, Proletkult essentially set out to destroy all previous educational principles and values in what was a form of anarchy – a proto-Maoist 'cultural revolution' – suspicious of intellectuals and determined to pretend that it was possible to hand over the construction of all realities to 'the people'.

Proletkult wanted, for example, what they called a proletarian theatre, in which non-professional actors would carry all the roles. This is something that would be taken up seriously, later, by Italian neorealist cinema (especially de Sica and Rossellini) and also – much later – by UK-based cinema directors such as Mike Leigh or Ken Loach. In the early days of the new Soviet State, however, the use of such non-professionals became enmeshed in larger-scale

---

[27] Grierson, 'Education and the New Order', 130–1.
[28] Ibid., 122–3.
[29] Ibid., 123.

ideological issues. Platon Kerzhentsev, a leading figure in Proletkult, 'believed that proletarian theatre would be created through rejection of the past and not – as Lunacharsky thought – through mastery and development of traditional forms'.[30] Lunacharsky's position, as described here, is an extremely highly politicized version of T. S. Eliot's ostensibly much milder argument on his 1922 essay on 'Tradition and the Individual Talent', in which an argument for artistic innovation (expressed in the individual talent) relies upon a profound immersion in the tradition. However, where Eliot was interested in formal innovation and aesthetic novelty, Kerzhentsev and his Proletkult supporters were interested in the construction of new social, cultural and material realities. Kerzhentsev found his ally in Vsevolov Meyerhold who, having been appointed by Lunacharsky to assume national directorship of new Russian theatre, promptly abandoned Lunacharsky's philosophy and instead favoured 'the abandonment of literature, psychology and representational realism' in the theatre.[31]

These arguments over education eventually devolve onto the central argument around what we have since come to call 'Socialist Realism'. Sheila Fitzpatrick describes the fundamental issue around this account of realism succinctly. She writes that 'in the discourse of socialist realism, a true representation of a society that was in the process of building socialism involved the depiction not only of "life as it is" but also of "life as it is becoming"'.[32] This is expressed, in different terms, by Grierson's descriptions of what he admires in Flaherty. In *Moana* or in *Nanook of the North* or in *Man of Aran*, Grierson saw 'the power of poetry or of prophecy', not just the kind of precisions that we find in poetic description, but also a foreseeing of how things will be.[33] In his own documentaries, he would give us that form of realism which, 'with its streets and cities and slums and markets and exchanges and factories, has given itself the job of making poetry where no poet has gone before it'; but, as with the Marx of *The Eighteenth Brumaire*, this would be an intimate realization that 'the social revolution' of the twentieth century, like that of Marx's nineteenth, 'cannot draw its poetry from the past, but only from the future'.[34]

When Georg Lukács explored *The Meaning of Contemporary Realism* in 1957, he argued vigorously for the proposition that realism has always 'assumed change

---

[30] Fitzpatrick, *Commissariat*, 146.
[31] Ibid., 151, citing T. Knyazhevskaya, *Yuzhin-Sumbatov i sovetskii teatr*.
[32] Sheila Fitzpatrick, *The Cultural Front: Power and Culture in Revolutionary Russia* (Cornell University Press, New York, 1992), 236.
[33] Grierson, 'Flaherty', 41.
[34] Marx, *The Eighteenth Brumaire*, 13.

and development to be the proper subject of literature.'[35] My own contention here is that this has not in fact always been the case; rather, it is a new development, and one that follows from the documentary research of Zola in literature and of Grierson in film. Indeed, Lukács presents realism as a mode that exists primarily in opposition to modernist literature, which, he claims, is focused on the 'static apprehension of reality' that he sees as being fundamental to the ideology of modernism.[36]

At the same time – and notwithstanding his argument that a key starting point for his work is 'the antithesis between realism and modernism' – Lukács asserts that the real opposition that structures his thinking 'is not between socialist realism and bourgeois modernism, but between bourgeois critical realism and bourgeois modernism'. That is what will allow him to acknowledge that the writer who rejects socialism as a quasi-inevitable necessity 'closes his eyes to the future' and 'gives up any chance of assessing the present correctly'.[37] It is in this context that Lukács makes his sole reference to Zola, 'who said that whenever he set out to tackle a new problem he always came up against socialism'.[38] Such socialism is, of course, based upon change. 'Clearly,' writes Lukács, 'there can be no literature without at least the appearance of change or development', and 'as the ideology of most modernist writers asserts the unalterability of outward reality . . . human activity is *a priori*, rendered impotent and robbed of meaning'.[39]

Throughout this book, Lukács needs a model of literature against which he can assert the primary value of what is essentially a socialist realism; and modernism is usually precisely the model on which he calls for this purpose. Essentially, he is troubled by work that seems to prioritize formal experimentation over serious content; and he identifies modernism with just such formalism. However, and also throughout the work, his descriptions of this quasi-formalist modernism have to work very hard to fit into his required preferences. Throughout, he notes precisely how modernist writing does indeed engage with change; but, in extremis, he will say that such change is at best superficial, that it is concerned only with the interiority of consciousness, and that it fails to grasp precisely

---

[35] Georg Lukács, *The Meaning of Contemporary Realism* (1957; trans. John and Necke Mander; Merlin Press, London, 1962), 35.
[36] Ibid.
[37] Ibid., 60.
[38] Ibid., 59. Note also his claim that 'The struggle between socialism and capitalism is still – as it has been since the 1848 rising of the Paris proletariat – the fundamental reality of the modern age', ibid., 13. This rehearses Zola's own words about *Germinal*, that it presented 'la lutte du capital et du travail' which would also be 'la question la plus importante du XXe siècle' Ebauche for *Germinal* in Émile Zola, *Les Rougon-Macquart 3: Pot-Bouille, Au Bonheur des Dames, La Joie de Vivre, Germinal*, ed. Armand Lanoux, notes par Henri Mitterand (Bibiliothèque de la Pléiade, Gallimard, Paris, 1964).
[39] Lukács, *Meaning*, 36.

the kind of change – change in the world external to consciousness – that he wants to bring about: the move to socialism. His argument ends up being purely prescriptive (when it describes, it actively mis-describes) and thus, paradoxically, unrealistic.

The conditions that I have described as prevalent around Lunacharsky and Grierson – in their respective different contexts but in their similar concern for education – allow us now to see what is essentially a new stage in the politics of realism in the early decades of the twentieth century. We have seen realism being defined in terms of a mimetic adequacy over the fundamentals of labour, sex and death (Courbet as paradigmatic example). It then mutates into a new stage where realism is measured by its commitment to and revelation of whatever constitutes truth and justice (Dickens and Zola). Now, in this new stage, realism is measured by its propensity to change the real itself: 'realistic' here, in this new context, means a kind of misrepresentation of the world as it is in order to bring about a new world, a world as it might or must be. We might call this 'realism as propaganda'.

And this is how Grierson saw it as he developed documentary realism. For him realism was tied firmly both to education and to propaganda: art as a hammer, and not as a mirror.

4

Grierson took the view that a cinema that was dedicated to the prioritization of aesthetics was a symptom not only of decadence in a polity, but also a confirmation of an existing economic structure of mass inequality and mass injustice. He argued that 'the self-conscious pursuit of beauty, the pursuit of art for art's sake *to the exclusion of jobs of work and other pedestrian beginnings* . . . was always a reflection of selfish wealth, selfish leisure and aesthetic decadence' (stress added).[40] Further, not all documentary manages to avoid such decadence. He distinguished realist documentary from what he called 'romantic documentary', a form of documentary that he regarded as 'symphonic', a form that was 'concerned with the pure orchestration of movement as such'.[41] Flaherty's screen, he argued, 'is not a stage to which the action of a story is brought', as in some theatrical representation. Instead, it is 'a magical opening in the theatre

---

[40] Grierson, 'First Principles of Documentary', in *Grierson on Documentary*, 41.
[41] Ibid., 43.

wall, through which one may look out to the wide world'. As it does this – and as if incidentally – it leaves us 'overseeing and overhearing the intimate things of common life which only the camera and microphone of the film artist can reveal'.

Such 'intimate things of common life' are the kinds of thing we saw prefigured in Zola's description of a family rising in the morning, unashamed in their near-nakedness, the showing of 'a body and soul laid bare' ['un corps et un coeur dans leur nudité'], in the phrase he used when describing *La Confession de Claude*. In time, the incidental eavesdropping on such intimacy will itself become less incidental and more conscious. Indeed, it will become determining of a principle of realism, especially in theatre and film, and especially after 1968's ending of theatrical censorship when stage nudity and the near-pornographic depiction of sexual and erotic relations becomes more and more routine: 'the intimate things of common life', certainly laid bare and openly displayed. As we will see later, however, nudity already plays a role in political propaganda as early as the 1930s, when Leni Riefenstahl makes her famous documentaries that are supportive of Nazism.

Yet, with all his high seriousness, Grierson was by no means immune to aestheticism. In fact, we can go so far as to say that he saw it as an important aspect of documentary film, and a serious element in its importance. He was clear that, in almost all filming of everyday realities, there are 'strange moments of beauty', such as 'some accidental pose of a character or some spontaneous gesture which radiates simply because it is spontaneous'. These moments may be occasioned by 'some high angle of a ship, or a crane, or a chimney stack, or a statue, adding some element of the heroic by a new-found emphasis'. The emphases in question might be the result of the placing of the camera itself, as in 'some mere fore-shortening of a bollard and a rope that ties a ship to a quay in spirit as well as in fact'. Behind all this, however, there is something that the beauty in question actually occludes. The moments of aesthetic charm that he describes, he says, 'may be the bright revelation of rhythms that time has worn smooth: the hand movement of a potter, the wrist movement of a native priest, or the muscle play of a dancer or a boxer or a runner'.[42]

There is no doubt, for Grierson, that these moments are indeed beautiful. However, when we see and rest or even arrest our perception in 'rhythms that time has worn smooth', Grierson is determined, against such ease, to ensure that 'the camera is in a measure both the discoverer of an unknown world

[42] Grierson, 'Flaherty', 31.

and the re-discoverer of a lost one'.[43] In this, he is in fact not a million miles distant from Lukács, who argued that 'it is the view of the world, the ideology or *Weltanschauung* underlying a writer's work, that counts'.[44] Grierson wants a documentary format that enacts a form of defamiliarization of the habits that have 'worn smooth' our perception of what actually lies behind the body of the boxer, dancer or runner: the underlying conditions that make any such movement possible and perceptible in the first place.

Documentary realism pierces through the romance of habit to allow us a perception of a usually unknown or unacknowledged world, the world of the reality of labour – another intimate thing of common life – that Grierson is determined to rediscover. Against the spontaneity of the filmed radiant gesture, Grierson wants the spontaneity of the viewer's discovery of the material conditions that underlie the shape, rhythm and movement of the body at work, be it in boxing, dancing, running – or, as in his own documentary films, catching herring (*Drifters*) driving rivets into the hull of a ship (*Industrial Britain*), or delivering letters across the country by train (*Night Mail*). The same applied to documentaries under his leadership, as when famously we hear a woman recounting at length the story of how she and her husband managed living in slum conditions and chasing rats (*Housing Problems*), say. His aim was film that 'showed the common man, not in the romance of his calling, but in the more complex and intimate drama of his citizenship'.[45]

For this to become a reality – for a realism that would change the present to a more enlightened future – the polity needed education. Such an education, for Grierson, acknowledges two things. First, as in the thinking of Lunacharsky, it 'is activist or it is nothing'; and secondly, if it should 'detach itself from the economic processes and what is happening in the world', then it does so to its own utter detriment, rendering itself pointless, purely ornamental and – worst of all – complicit with the very system of capital injustice and social privilege about whose failings education is supposed to inform the viewer.[46]

As an example of how such activist education works, Grierson calls on the example of his own father, a great educationalist who would travel miles to bring an education to workers in many rural villages across Scotland. The education in question was traditional, and – although he will argue that, now in the midst of war, it is completely outdated, inappropriate and 'beside the

---

[43] Ibid.
[44] Lukács, *Meaning*, 19.
[45] Grierson, 'Battle for Authenticity', in *Grierson on Documentary*, 84.
[46] Grierson, 'Education and the New Order', 122, 126.

point' – it worked when his father taught because it began a process of making the workers start to think. The point, however, is this: 'thinking, they became less and less satisfied with the miserable pay they received'.[47] One might think that such a result renders education itself to be somewhat beside the social point, especially when Grierson then adds, 'What were the delights of literature when a distant judgment by a distant corporation could throw a man into six months of economic misery?'[48] This, in fact, *is* the point of an education for Grierson: it is not enough simply to enjoy the delights of Shakespeare or Burns or Flaubert or Zola; the point is not simply to understand the reality of the world as it is now, but rather to change it for the future. Documentary, he argues, 'does not teach the new world by analyzing it. Uniquely and for the first time it *communicates* the new world by showing it in its corporate and living nature'.[49]

We know, says Grierson, what are the proper ends of education – and they bear some similarity to the determinants of realism as I have outlined it: labour (or its opposite in unemployment), sex (and the constraints put upon it by 'public morality'), death (and its contrary, basic survival). When he indicates that the basic point of education is so that people can ensure and guarantee that they have 'food, shelter and the good life for everyone', he is drawing attention to the same fundamental material aspects of bio-political existence as we saw in Courbet and since, in those intimate things of common life. His claim is that our modern societies have forgotten such fundamental realities, due to the power structures of class hierarchy, structures that are enforced by our existing processes and principles of education. The ends of education, he says, 'may have been forgotten in sectional selfishness and private privilege; and the privileged ones may have allowed every kind of complacent, urbane, cynical and indifferent attitude to hide from them the primitive fact that their neighbours, national and international, have been starving and dying in their midst'. Even worse and more damning is the alternative explanation for the failures of the existing educational philosophies: 'it may be that the leadership has been depressed by the progressive difficulties of a complex world and has lost its will-power and has wearily given up the task of leadership without abandoning its privilege.'[50]

In the face of this, Grierson simply argues that the proper education that he seeks is and should be essentially a corrective to our existing institutional forms of education. The reason is that those existing modes are themselves a kind of

---

[47] Ibid., 125.
[48] Ibid.
[49] Ibid., 129.
[50] Ibid., 131.

silent propaganda: they propose privilege – and the realities of the world as presented by privilege – as normative and beyond explanation: real. They accept the way of seeing the world that has been manufactured by the privileged classes as if it were neutral and non-controvertible. The point of documentary realism is to reveal that existing false account of reality – an account that entrenches injustice as unchangeable – and thus to bring about precisely the kind of change whose very possibility the privileged class denies.

We might therefore feel easier at Grierson's endorsement of education as propaganda if we see it for what it actually is: a mode of counter-propaganda. In another essay written and delivered as a speech to the Winnipeg Canadian Club in 1943, Grierson showed what we now take more or less for granted (largely thanks to interventions such as Grierson's, in fact), that educators have already lost control of education 'to the men who govern the newspapers, films, radio, advertising and public information, few of whom have a licence to teach'.[51] It is this realization that helps explain and justify the claim that 'propaganda, far from being the denial of the democratic principle of education, becomes the necessary instrument for its practical fulfilment'.[52]

5

Grierson's key essays on education and its relation to realist documentary were all written while he was in Canada during the Second World War, and under the shadow therefore of the spreading threat of Nazism and far-right politics and not, in the first instance, of Bolshevik revolution. To link education to propaganda in this moment is obviously controversial, given the then-existing obvious example of the Nazis themselves, who took control of the media in all the territories that they claimed, and given, further, the Nazis' complete control of censorship, with the establishment of a Ministry of Popular Enlightenment and propaganda under Goebbels. Yet, what these simple facts show is that 'the politicizing of documentary was not a Grierson innovation but a world phenomenon, a product of the times'.[53] With Hitler in power since 1933, documentary as propaganda becomes almost inevitable, not as a matter of choice by the film-maker but rather because any presentation of material actuality is inherently politicized. Further, the very title of Goebbels's ministry – Popular Enlightenment – indicates the

[51] Grierson, 'Propaganda and Education', 148.
[52] Grierson, 'Education and the New Order', 139.
[53] Barnouw, *Documentary*, 100.

link established as normative during the Second World War of propaganda with what Nazism referred to as 'the will of the people'. The relation of realism to this troubling phrase is what we now need to explore.

In the period between the 1920s and 1940s, the question of a popular will was of paramount social and political importance, across Europe and in the United States and Canada. Moreover, the relation of a popular will to social and political realities was a primary site of argument and contention. The question amounts simply to whether reality can be made to conform to a popular will, or whether such a will expresses itself at all clearly through something called 'public opinion' – a notion developed especially in US sociology of the 1920s – or in a triumph of the will – as in Riefenstahl's 1935 presentation of Hitler and Nazism in the 1930s. In what follows here, we need to bear in mind the influence on Grierson of the thinking of Walter Lippmann, the Chicago sociologist whose 1922 work, *Public Opinion*, was extremely influential right through most decades of the twentieth century.

Lippmann helped found *The New Republic* in 1914; and, for its first edition on 7 November that year, he wrote an essay titled 'Force and Ideas'. War had been going on in Europe for the previous four months; and Lippmann's piece is a plea for the value of ideas over the facts of force. He warns especially of how the arts and criticism can be co-opted, when 'the best scholarship has turned press agent to the General Staff'.[54] Essentially, this is a demand for scholarly autonomy, and a warning *against* the perversion of education into State-sponsored propaganda. By 1922, he was profoundly aware of how war had transformed the usual expectations of science, research and, above all, how it had transformed our perceptions of material realities.

In *Public Opinion*, he gives the example of how it comes about that 'an Attorney-General, who has been frightened by a bomb [that has] exploded on his doorstep' starts to develop expectations about material reality that may start to replace the facts of material reality. In the light of this one experience, this Attorney-General, unsurprisingly easily 'convinces himself by the reading of revolutionary literature that a revolution is to happen on the first of May 1920'. Expectations start to supplant reality, argued Lippmann; and 'the war, of course, furnished many examples of this pattern: the casual fact, the creative

---

[54] Walter Lippmann, 'Force and Ideas', in Lippmann, *Force and Ideas: The Early Writings* (Transaction Publishers, New York and London, 2000), 3.

imagination, the will to believe, and out of these three elements a counterfeit of reality to which there was a violent instinctive response'.[55]

Central to this description of how war has transformed human consciousness – especially with regard to 'the will to believe' – is what, in a later war, will be explicitly and dangerously called the 'triumph of the will'. Between *Public Opinion* in the liberal United States of 1922 and *Triumph des Willens* and *Olympia*, the Nazi propaganda films of Leni Riefenstahl in 1935–8, we might say that human consciousness changed. At the core of this change is the relation between will and reality, between how we want the world to be and how material realities might circumscribe those possibilities. In terms of the education and propaganda that interested Grierson and others, what is at issue here is precisely this new account of the limitations and possibilities of realism in the written and in the cinematic media.

Grierson writes his key essays on education, heavily influenced by Lippmann's liberalism and early socialism as also by his pioneering work on 'public opinion' during the Second World War. At this time, he writes, 'We face one of the deepest crises in the history of human organization' precisely because of the facts of war and of how it has transformed human expectations regarding reality. In the face of this crisis, his starting point is that we must bear in mind that education 'is the process by which the minds of men are keyed to the tasks of good citizenship', a mode of citizenship that aims to serve 'the highest purposes of the community'.[56] 'Education is activist', he writes, adding that it 'is the key to the mobilization of men's minds to right ends or wrong ends, to order or chaos'.[57]

This moment – he is writing in 1941, in Canada – is a period 'when the whole basis of truth is re-examined and when the operative philosophies are revolutionized and renewed'.[58] He is rehearsing, during this 1939–45 war, the same realizations regarding the perception of material reality that were made by Lippmann in the Great War. What he adds is the determination that education is activist, participating in the war pretty directly; and the activity requires that educators 'mobilize' the will through the effect on the minds of those who are to be taught. We should note that he entertains the possibility that 'men's minds' can be mobilized towards wrong and chaos; and it follows from this that education is engaged in a struggle to make right and order prevail.

---

[55] Walter Lippmann, *Public Opinion* (1922; repr. Free Press and Collier-Macmillan, New York and London, 1965), 9–10.
[56] Grierson, 'Education and the New Order', 122.
[57] Ibid., 122–3.
[58] Ibid., 123.

Lippmann's work provides a basis for this kind of thinking. Part of his argument is that 'public opinion' is based not upon material realities, but upon a 'human picture' of those realities. 'The analyst of public opinion', he argued, begins 'by recognizing the triangular relationship' that exists among three things: 'the scene of action' (or what is materially and actually happening in the environment); 'the human picture of that scene' (essentially a fiction or, as Lippmann calls it, a 'pseudo-environment'); and 'the human response to that picture working itself out upon the scene of action'.[59] It is important to note the implication of this: the response that we make to a situation is based not upon reality but rather upon an image of that reality: that is to say, human history is motivated by images of reality and not by the material facts of reality. As Lippmann put it, 'what is propaganda, if not the effort to alter the picture to which men respond, to substitute one social pattern for another? What is class consciousness but a way of realizing the world?'[60] This is one reason why Grierson is so concerned with the basic premise that the documentary image essentially operates as a mode of educational propaganda: it provokes and extends human actions and activity, and in doing so, brings about social change.

Education, for both Lippmann and Grierson, is about the preparation of attitudes that will allow us to adapt our existing moods and dispositions to the emergence of new material facts. New concepts must enter our educational framework if we are to keep up with material change 'and we shall find ourselves dramatizing [such new concepts] so that they become loyalties and take leadership of the Will'.[61] The problem is, of course, the disturbing realization that the change wrought in this way might be detrimental to human life and even damaging to the very fabric of social and political realities. The obvious case in point is provided by the Nazi documentaries of Leni Riefenstahl. In these films, we might find that 'the triumph of the will' depends upon the power of images not just to present 'the intimate things of common life' but also to grasp that the most intimate such thing is the will itself; and the propaganda machinery here is one that is tied firmly to labour, sex and death in the manufacture of 'the will of the people' as supposedly constitutive of the new social and political order. That is not so much the poetry of the future, as the catastrophe that sees the totalitarian State in complete and censorious control of anything that might resemble poetry at all.

---

[59] Lippmann, *Public Opinion*, 11.
[60] Ibid., 16.
[61] Grierson, 'Education and the New Order', 128.

Part III

Making the unreal

7

Naked propaganda
'The intimate things of common life'

1

The impulse to documentary operates on the basis of a determination for a specific type of 'revelation'. Essentially, the realist documentary works on the principle that we need to investigate the obvious and everyday appearances of the world in order to find an underpinning force of real social and political forces and relations. When a documentary shows, for example, Nanook hunting a walrus (in Flaherty's *Nanook of the North*), the point is to discover, or to uncover, the way in which Nanook actually lives his life, 'clearly and simply, in terms of existence and action' and not as the construction of a 'character', as might be the case in a fiction film. For Flaherty, 'filmmaking was an art of exploration'; and, in *Nanook of the North*, he showed that the reality of human existence is for humanity to 'improve [our] lot on earth by working', thereby prioritizing labour as the condition of reality. Further, he showed that family members are 'probably [our] first and most important helpers', indicating that socio-sexual relations become the foundation of how we ward off the threat of death.[1]

Grierson essentially formalized and theorized this kind of attitude when he described the point of realist documentary in terms of its focus on those 'intimate things of common life' that are usually hidden under the protocols and regularities that govern everyday activities. His argument is that those protocols and regularities actually cover up the real social moods, attitudes and the materially real and personal play of forces that shape an unjust society and its 'values'. In some ways, Grierson's point of departure is at the root of mid-twentieth-century 'investigative journalism', a mode of journalism that has had a persistent and a percussive force up to the contemporary moment. This is,

[1] Richard Barsam, *The Vision of Robert Flaherty* (Indiana University Press, Bloomington, 1988), 19.

in fact, the only form that we have of serious journalism, the determination to record daily actuality, *jour par jour, de jour en jour*, and to question the quotidian appearance of things in such a way as to find the link between each day, to find the meaning of the present when it is tied to a past or projected to a future. The point is to get a total picture that is dependent not simply upon the local and the immediate but rather to see the immediately available in a context that explains and gives the present its meaning. Serious journalism is, of course, part of the *media*, and as such, it 'mediates' the otherwise immediate.

Increasingly, the distinction between entertainment-journalism and serious (or investigative) journalism is precisely the distinction between showing – in a fundamentally celebratory mood – the world of appearances (entertainment, veering into titillation, focusing on 'celebrity' in every sense) as against trying to find out why those appearances – despite the appearance of shiny, happy people in them – are precisely the very conditions that inform a deep unhappiness and profound injustice that is the reality of social and political life: the realities of labour conditions, socio-sexual conditions, and the public health issues that face up to the constant fact of death in its unarguable finality. Entertainment-journalism, in this sense, is there precisely to deter and even to deny – to censor out of all consideration – the realist documentary impulse: in the extreme, entertainment-journalism exists effectively to endorse existing injustice, to distract attention from such injustice and from its consequences. In this way, entertainment-journalism in all its forms is the very antithesis of realism, even and most especially when it pretends to show the realities of a life.

In many ways, this is surely one of the most fundamental realizations that shapes the profound austerity of Adorno's thinking, and that lies at the root of his occasional disjunctions with respect to Walter Benjamin who, though also very critical of the political distractions of an 'entertainment' culture, nonetheless felt the need for a certain intimate knowledge and experience of that same culture. In the 1930s and 1940s, first in Germany and then – for political reasons and governed by the need simply to survive, to keep alive at all – from exile elsewhere, Benjamin and Adorno engaged with each other in arguments over the question of realism in film.

Adorno took the more austere approach. Having witnessed the conditions of Hollywood productions, he argued that, in its mass appeal, cinema was structurally condemned to be reactionary. This, he thought, was all the more the case if the film in question was 'realistic' in its aesthetic: questions of technology and of technique, he argued, were necessarily intermixed, with some consequences that he saw as detrimental to any kind of emancipation from the capitalist norms of the culture industry. That is to say: the intrinsic industrialization of culture that made cultural forms into a commodity inevitably turned the viewer into a passive consumer, unable or unwilling to consider the 'reality' presented in the compelling screen images as something that is contingent, and therefore as something that is subject to intellectual critique or historical change. His argument was that 'the reactionary nature of any realist aesthetic today is inseparable from this commodity character. Tending to reinforce, affirmatively, the phenomenal surface of reality, realism dismisses any attempt to penetrate that surface as a romantic endeavor'.[2]

Indeed, such realist cinema, Adorno argued, produced certain modes of everyday behaviour as normative. Thus, whenever we see 'boys and girls crossing the streets . . . kissing each other unembarrassed' then we should acknowledge that 'they have learned this . . . from the films which peddle Parisian libertinage'.[3] In the broader wartime and Nazi context of this historical moment, Adorno essentially 'feared the advent of the Hollywood Studio film as akin to Nazi propaganda'.[4] For this kind of thinker, working in the immediate shadow of Nazism, there are serious questions to be raised about the politics of realism, and the relation of mass culture and entertainment films especially, that emerge from that shadow.

A serious consequential issue would follow from this in our own inquiry here: Is it the case that the entertainment aspect of any and all art is, in our contemporary circumstances, also the antithesis of realism? Does it divert us from the material conditions that shape human lives and our interrelations with each other and with the environment and polity in general? In the same way that contemporary politics has succeeded in calling into question the very idea and principle of truth, might it also be the case that the privileged classes have also managed to call into question the very idea and principle of reality itself? One major engagement with this question arises through all kinds of 'neorealist' work through the middle of the twentieth century, from cinematic neorealism (especially in Italy, as we will see in my next chapter) through to what can only be described as the degradations of reality that are found in so-called 'Reality TV' and its variants in all forms of celebrity culture.

It might seem to follow – from the idea that realism is revelatory – that I am claiming that contemporary realism depends upon a kind of 'stripping bare' of the

---

[2] Adorno, 'Transparencies on Film' (trans. Thomas Y. Levin), *New German Critique*, 24/25 (1981–1982), 202.
[3] Ibid., 201–2.
[4] Laura D'Olimpio, 'Thoughts on Film', *Educational Philosophy and Theory*, 47 (2015), 622–3.

world of appearance, showing those 'intimate things of common life' sought out by Grierson. In some ways, this is what informed the modernist drive to interiority in literature: Woolf's demand to 'look within'; Joyce's stream-of-consciousness veering eventually into the unconscious as revealed in *Finnegans Wake*; the self-reflexive and self-reflective inward turn in the modern *Kunstlerroman*; or in the structure of texts such as Proust's 'investigative' seeking after the relation of past to present in *A la Recherche du temps perdu*; and, behind all this, the extraordinary rise of the crime and detective novel throughout the latter decades of the nineteenth century (and on into our own day, in which the serious and literary espionage novel – as in John Le Carré, say – continues a similar exploration).

To put it crudely, it might seem that I am suggesting that realism depends upon a basic impulse towards nudity, upon a concentration on the extremes of intimacy. This, however, is precisely that antithesis of realism that is enabled by those who would want to maintain social and political privilege by the denial of the principle of reality. The key historical moment that determines this perversion of the realist impulse into voyeuristic titillation and triviality is the abolition of theatrical censorship in England in 1968, which was in some ways the perfect mirror-image of and riposte to the 1857 Obscene Publications Act where we started back in Chapter 1.

As is well known, Harold Wilson's Labour administration abolished censorship in the theatre when it passed the Theatre Act on 26 July 1968; and, immediately on the following day, 27 July 1968, the musical *Hair* opened in London's West End. *Hair* is best known for some of its popular songs ('Aquarius', 'Good Morning, Starshine' and so on) and it is remembered for being a musical in which the novelty of live nudity happens on stage. Yet it was primarily a piece of political theatre, aimed at agitating against US participation in Vietnam. The nude scene is extremely brief, and actors' participation in stripping off their clothes was to be voluntary in many productions. Put into that political context, the nudity makes a claim for justification as something that is more than titillation. However, in the historical context of the aesthetic agitation against stage censorship, the culturally powerful and percussive effect of the scene – that is to say, why we remember it – derives primarily simply from the fact that, for the first time, actors were entirely naked, on stage, and before a live audience: the political dynamic of anti-Vietnam protest has long been culturally relegated to minor consideration in the face of the more superficial shock-value of this aspect of the musical.

At the time, the nudity was more of a statement in and of itself: it was a reaction against establishment prudery, and it presented itself as a celebration of the human body as such. The prevailing hippie culture that shaped the musical argued that the body was not a site of shame: it was a 'natural' condition and, to that extent, the scene proposed a recognition of human reality in its naivety. Naivety itself here becomes a political stance, a neo-Rousseauvian kick against the corrupt state of political affairs. Its basic principle is that which we witness in the opening comments, two centuries prior to *Hair!*, in Rousseau's *Emile; ou, de l'éducation* of 1762: 'Everything is good as it emerges from the hands of the Creator, and everything degenerates once it is in the hands of men and women'; and 'we are born bare, with nothing' ['Tout est bien sortant des mains de l'Auteur des choses, tout dégénère entre les mains de l'homme'; 'nous naissons dépourvus de tout'].[5] Obviously, the corollary of this is the rather naïve and disingenuous claim that we can re-claim our participation in a condition or state of nature in which the human is 'pure', purged of the taint of any and all politics.[6] The fundamental infantilism of such a position is entirely at odds not just with the impulse towards realism but also with the idea that nudity is in any way related to a political activism or that live nudity is a political act or engagement, especially in relation to a drive towards realism.

A similar state of affairs pertains also to Kenneth Tynan's deliberately provocative 'erotic revue' *Oh! Calcutta!*, another immediate response to the end of theatrical censorship. In the closing scene of *Oh! Calcutta!*, the actors strip and dance, nude, on stage, fitting themselves into a series of tableaux; and there is a voice-over (provided mostly by the actors onstage) imagining and presuming to represent the reactions of 'real' people in the audience. It is this voice-over that marks the irruption of reality into the entertainment. The voice-overs ask questions that ostensibly puncture the 'entertainment' by seemingly 'investigating' the reality of the bodies on stage: 'What the fuck are they doing up there?'; 'Wonder if the guys ever get a hard-on?'; 'Gee, that girl has pretty eyes'; 'That's my boyfriend. . . . He *does* have a hard-on'; 'My God, that's my daughter up there'; 'I wonder what the girls do when they get their periods'; 'This makes *Hair* look like *The Sound of Music*'.

These interventions serve no political revelatory function: rather, they simply indicate that these are, indeed, live human bodies, nude, performing before the audience. To that extent, the nudity 'reveals' nothing beyond its entertaining

---

[5] Jean-Jacques Rousseau, *Emile; ou, de l'éducation* (1762; repr. Flammarion, Paris, 1966), 35.
[6] For the tacit source of this, consider merely the famous opening claim in Jean-Jacques Rousseau, *Du Contrat Social* (1762; repr. Flammarion, Paris, 1966), 41: "people are born free, but are everywhere in chains' [L'homme est né libre, et partout il est dans les fers']. This text appeared in April 1762, just one month ahead of *Emile* in May that same year.

artificiality. The actors are like Sartre's waiter, in the famous example from *Being and Nothingness*. In his chapter on 'bad faith', Sartre invites us to consider the existential status of his café waiter. When we look at him, Sartre says, we see a man who carries out his actions all a little bit too much like how he thinks a café waiter should behave, so that, in the end 'his behaviour throughout strikes us as an act', each gesture emphasized as the gesture appropriate to the role of café waiter. 'He is playing, amusing himself. But what, then, is he playing at? One does not need to watch him for long to realize: he is playing *at being* a café waiter' ['Considérons ce garçon de café . . . Toute sa conduite nous semble un jeu . . . Il joue, il s'amuse. Mais à quoi donc joue-t-il? Il ne faut pas l'observer longtemps pour s'en rendre compte: il joue *à être* garcon de café].[7] Tynan's actors are not naked; they 'play' at being naked. We might say that they 'act the (private) part'.

In *State of the Nation*, Michael Billington details the history of British theatre since 1945, and notes that the 'post-Churchillian world' is one where 'there was an increasing sense that all public life was an arena for performance'. People went walking around the fashionable areas of London 'in all their peacock finery as if taking part in a theatrical costume parade'. The Institute for Contemporary Arts 'exhibited a huge plastic tube which visitors entered and walked about inside as if they themselves were on show'.[8] When all the world becomes a stage in this way, then reality itself becomes elusive, even as it is allegedly being lived.

This is precisely the existential condition of 'being nude' in these 1960s post-censorship productions. The actors are not 'really' nude, but are playing at being nude; and in this way, their nudity becomes, in fact, a mode of clothing. Paradoxically, therefore, this nudity becomes itself the new censorship: in its determination to shock by showing us live nudity, it turns the possibility of investigative documentary realism – concerning Vietnam, the politics of sexuality, the coercive State and so on – into pure entertainment, pure 'celebrity culture'. It shifts – in what the same historical period identifies as existential bad faith – from reality to role-play; and there is thus nothing 'real' or realist about it. Like *Hair*, *Oh! Calcutta!* adopts the naivety of an infantilism that 'challenges' the audience to acknowledge that – big surprise – under their clothes, they and the actors are naked; and, at the same time, like some kind of contemporary Adam and Eve, it covers that nakedness at exactly the moment when it pretends

---

[7] Jean-Paul Sartre, *L'être et le néant* (nrf Gallimard, Paris, 1943), 98–9; *Being and Nothingness* (trans. Sarah Richmond; Routledge, London, 2018), 102–3.
[8] Michael Billington, *State of the Nation* (Faber and Faber, London, 2007), 165.

to show it. Nudity becomes pure titillation.⁹ Shockingly, perhaps, *The Sound of Music* was, indeed, much more politically engaged than was either *Hair* or *Oh! Calcutta!*.

Richard Rodgers and Oscar Hammerstein, composer and lyricist respectively for the ostensibly saccharine *Sound of Music*, were both from Jewish backgrounds; and, notwithstanding the sentimentalism of the cinematic version, *The Sound of Music* is a piece of musical theatre concerned centrally with the ways in which a sexual interest (between Maria Rainer and Captain Georg von Trapp) relates to – and is to some extent determined by – the Nazi *Anschluss*. The central point of the musical is a critique of Nazism, and it is highly serious in this regard. The reference to this musical, at the end of *Oh! Calcutta!*, is mocking; and Kenneth Tynan's tacit claim is that the nudity of *Oh! Calcutta!* is a realist position and a stance that he was taking against the sugary sentimentalism of the 1965 film version of *The Sound of Music*, a version that was, indeed, presented in a way that occluded or at least minimized the seriousness of the politics that drives the narrative. However, *Oh! Calcutta!*'s live nudity is itself thereby a 'performance' that is determined to remain superficial, operating at the level of celebration of appearance (the appearance of a nude body); and, as such, it is a masking of exactly the kinds of authoritarian and far-right political realities that form the backdrop to *The Sound of Music*.

Kenneth Tynan and others who suggested that nudity and linguistic obscenity were a slap in the face to previous establishment censorship turn out, in paradoxical fact, to be the new censors, the new anti-realists, because the nudity in question here operates at the level of celebrity entertainment and not at all in the spirit of documentary investigative journalism. There is nothing politically challenging to the privileged establishment about it, when nudity really simply becomes the new clothing, the new cover-up. In a bizarre reversal of the 1837 Hans Christian Andersen tale, the naked Emperor here is, indeed, fully and even gorgeously clothed and revelling in his privilege and power while pretending to be on the side of the downtrodden; and, given that this Emperor Tynan *looks* naked, it is difficult, if not impossible, to call out the unearned and illegitimate political power that he enjoys. This is nudity or laying bare as anti-realism, in all its political senses.

---

⁹ See Billington, *State*, 167 on Ed Berman's 'Ambiance Theatre' in Bayswater, London, 'where one cheerfully munched one's lunchtime sandwiches while watching various forms of sexual congress'.

2

The effects, then, of interventions such as *Hair* or *Oh! Calcutta!* are profoundly reactionary, in terms not just of the politics of realism but also in terms of politics as such. We saw that the Jamesian 'house of fiction' had its multiple windows, and that the texts of Zola and others often begin with characters looking out at the world of material social and political realities from windows or screens. After modernism, we see a situation that is markedly different, and even the reverse of this. Now, we have a situation that ostensibly construes realism in terms of a norm in which we look *into* the house and home of celebrity figures, trying to see their most intimate conditions, including above all the sexual conditions, of their lives. In such cases, realism has veered into voyeurism, the politics of which go far beyond the sexual.

However, more immediately, we can consider the more important and pressing issue of the social dimensions around the 'house of fiction'; and we can do so by examining the presentation of reality as it concerns actual houses and actual housing issues. In this, we can move from the Jamesian metaphorical house of fiction to documentary realism's facts of housing. Two key moments in documentary realism will form our focus here: 1935 saw the production of *Housing Problems*, a classic example of documentary realism in Grierson's style; and 1966 was the year when the BBC's 'Wednesday Play' showed Ken Loach's *Cathy Come Home*. The mood of the thirty-year period between these two is shaped by a number of social and political issues; but right at the heart of that time is the politics of the Second World War, in response to which we can also consider Kay Mander's *Homes for People*. Propaganda, which was a key element of Nazi politics – and, as we now know, propaganda was also at the heart of a specific attitude to the pedagogical impulses of realism – determines the mood that shapes these films, and the shifting attitudes revealed in them.

In 1935, two of Grierson's protégés from the Empire Marketing Board Film Unit, Arthur Elton and E. H. Anstey, produced *Housing Problems* under the aegis of the British Commercial Gas Association. The film is organized around a series of individuals who speak directly to camera about the conditions in which they live, in crumbling buildings, where they are plagued by vermin, and where they are badly affected by a lack of any proper or adequate sanitation. This makes it sound desperate, yet at the same time one of the film's key propaganda points is optimistic: it is at pains to show how some enlightened local authorities are addressing those issues, and how a positive governmental housing strategy can change the way in which people actually live, work and have children.

The film opens with a preliminary analysis of the problems. Slums exist, it shows, because of the movement of labour. As the very condition of labour changes, in societies where modernization displaces an agricultural economy through industrialization, people move from the country to the city; and the cities have to produce, at precipitate speed, some basic housing for them. The result is that houses are indeed provided there, built with industrial efficiency but in a shabby condition, and often barely fit for human habitation: we produce the abstract and conceptual form of a house, as it were, without the material content that could make it a habitation or a home. The reality of labour is, as it has been throughout this history of realism, at the heart of the issue. Here, this is pressing on two counts: first, there is the fact of mass movement of labour from agricultural and rural economies to newer modern industrial and civic economies; and secondly, the fundamental shabbiness of the work that went into building the houses is itself determined by the overarching demands of industrial capital that demanded mass production with quantity trumping quality at every moment.

The focus then shifts from the material condition of the buildings to the people who live in the slums. Each in turn narrates their conditions, and – having seen the realism of labour – we move instantly to the presence of mortality as a second condition of this documentary form of realism. The first to speak is Mr Norwood who pays ten shillings a week in rent to live in a house that is plagued by bugs, mice and rats. With distressing acceptance and with the understatement of resignation, he says that 'since coming here I've had no luck', by which he means that two of his children have died. Mrs Hill, Mrs Graves and Mr Burner all follow, with horrific tales of vermin, crumbling walls and stairs, and appalling overcrowding. These are the material conditions and the reality of life, of death and of labour for the people: the slums constitute their polity, one that is contaminated by the ever-present threat of further impediments to life itself.

Half-way through, the film then turns back from the talking people towards an emphasis again on the actual material conditions of our building and housing stock; and it is at this moment that it tries to find the optimistic turn, and a search for the possibility of using realist presentation to change realities. Some social authorities, all extremely well meaning in the face of such seemingly intractable bleakness, describe how they are in fact now dealing positively with the problems; and they show some idealized plans for new possibilities, such as 'cottage-estates', which can be built where 'the price of land is not too high'. If we can overcome this capital-related issue, then better things can follow: provide decent housing, and people live better lives. That is the film's basic optimism: it propagandizes for good housing, and educates its viewers as to the benefits through exposing the reality of contemporary material living conditions. This all depends on the relation of some fundamental aspects of capital – land ownership – to the organization of societies into social councils that deal with working people who are not themselves land owners.

As the film makes this optimistic turn, it focuses on Mrs Reddington, who is delighted with her new council house, because, in it, she has space and a bathroom. Most importantly, she stresses that she can now open her windows and get fresh air for her family, making them all healthier. This, in fact, stands as a symbol of the documentary-realist mode itself. Just as in earlier realist fiction, it involves an opening of windows onto the world, such that we see it afresh, such that we can breathe and live a healthier and ongoing sustainable life. We learn about the external material conditions that shape the interiority of a life shaped by labour, the lack of personal space (and thus the inhibition of personal intimacy or sex) and by the ever-encroaching proximity of death. This is the film's propaganda, in short.

In terms of my argument here, though, one further thing is vital to note. When Mrs Reddington gets her new house, she opens the windows to look out. This act shifts, and turns on its head, the shape of the film: it moves from a salacious and lubricious (even potentially voyeuristic) interest in the detriments that others suffer to an opening out of vision – looking outwards – towards imaginative, enlivening and generous expansiveness. This – rather than Tynan's crude world – is a genuinely 'permissive society'.

Throughout, the film manages to avoid that potential tendency to voyeurism that is intrinsic to its subject matter. Although it looks into the private lives of the inhabitants of the slums, it does not do this for the purposes of entertainment. Instead, the exploration and revelation of a life within the houses is instrumental in and preliminary to the opening outwards of Mrs Reddington's windows. As those windows open, the meaning of the film's realism becomes clear. It is indeed an optimistic piece, showing what might come about; and the future that it envisages and promises is one that is visible entirely as a result of the film's own structural propaganda. We can see in this documentary that Grierson's 'propaganda' is indeed an act of education, and an education in civic culture, addressed to us in the audience that stands outside of Mrs Reddington's windows. It is about a society being able, as it modernizes, to find a way of accommodating its people, such that they can properly determine the shape of their own living conditions. The education in question here is realist precisely because it looks into the very conditions, material and political – and therefore the real conditions – that make the interiority of the lives led by the slum inhabitants not only possible but inevitable; and it demands change on the part of the viewer. The point of this documentary is to change things, to find a means of showing an existing reality in order to change it. This is realism by provocation; and it is realism *as* provocation, calling for social change through the mode of the documentary film.

Housing Problems is thus entirely in line with the fundamental thrust of Grierson's entire project, as a film that deploys its realist ideology, or that deploys the techniques of realism, as a medium of social change. The point of documentary, for Grierson, is to establish a situation where realism changes an existing reality. The propaganda aspect of *Housing Problems* is directed towards the improvement of public health, through a determination to prove the necessity of making a fundamental shift in the ways in which we occupy space and place.

Four years after this film was made, many of Britain's homes – and indeed entire cities – were devastated yet further by wartime bombing. After the war, by 1945, it might have been thought that these extremely bad circumstances had made the discovery of a solution to Britain's housing problems yet more pressing. That year saw the production of a film directed by Kay Mander, *Homes for People*, another documentary that focused on similar issues to those described by Anstey and Elton a decade earlier. While Anstey and Elton had been at work on *Housing Problems* in 1935, Mander was working for an entirely different organization: she was a secretarial receptionist at the International Film Congress in Germany, under the directorship of Goebbels. By 1945, she was back in England, able to witness how the German wartime attacks had made the predicament around uninhabitable housing in Britain more general through the destructions caused by the bombing. The new government, Attlee's 1945 Labour administration, was well aware of the new reality that made the issue of the intimate things of common life – basic living standards – urgent.

Attlee and the Labour Party backed Kay Mander (who had joined the Communist Party of Great Britain in the 1930s) in the making of *Homes for the People*, a documentary film that constituted a key element in Attlee's election campaign that year.[10] Here, then, is a political party – subsequently a governing

---

[10] The film was sponsored by the left-leaning newspaper, *The Daily Herald*, and was produced by Basic Films, a company owned by Mander and her husband, Rod Neilson Baxter.

party – explicitly deploying realist documentary in the service of political change; and it wanted to garner the support of the people for that change. Although *Homes for the People* reiterates the same theme as *Housing Problems*, it marks a very significant shift in documentary realism, because it introduced into documentary some fundamental elements of narrative film. In this respect, it can be classed as the pioneering film in what subsequently became known as 'drama-documentary'.

We should recall Grierson's ambivalent attitude to such a turn towards narrative, and his sense that it threatened our engagement with and understanding of reality with too much aesthetic diversion. Mander, however, manages the narrative element in a minimalist fashion. Basically, instead of having people speak directly to camera (and with what were essentially rehearsed lines, as we had had them in *Housing Problems*), she filmed her participants while they were busy around their everyday chores and activities. For the most part, the people in this film were its five women, all of them engaged in diverse aspects of domestic labour;[11] and the film is significant not just for its structural novelty in this respect but also for this focus on the home itself as the site of productive labour, not to mention the gendering of particular work activities.

This, then, was reality – the contemporary condition of the social and political state of things – seen primarily from the point of view of women engaged in domestic labour, and in which a collocation of labour, gender and domestic economy is brought firmly to the fore. As such, it constituted another learning experience for the viewer, accustomed as she or he was to conceiving of a world as seen and dominated by the supposed 'normality' of a masculine or male perspective, and in which labour was seen as something external to the home, conditioned by industry, and the primary preserve of men. It thus shifted the dominant perceptions of what constituted political realities in this 1945 moment, and shocked the viewer into seeing the world afresh through this moment of defamiliarization.

The interior of the home is also a site of previously neglected labour: women's labour. It should perhaps be no great surprise to see this turn to female labour, given the simple fact that, during the war and with many men enlisted in the military, women had also become absolutely central to the general material and real economy of the nation, and had worked in factories and in many areas of the

---

[11] As Brian Pendreigh pointed out in his sympathetic obituary for Mander, by having working-class women speak about their work while actually doing it, Mander pioneered 'kitchen-sink' drama. See *The Scotsman*, 3 January 2014, available at: https://www.scotsman.com/news/obituaries/obituary-kay-mander-documentary-film-maker-1-3253752 (accessed 6 November 2019).

economy that had traditionally been the domain of men. With the men absent at the front, women supplied the necessary labour to sustain everyday living. Attlee, of course, needed the women's vote in 1945; and, in its prioritization of women as workers, *Homes for the People* worked as an exercise in political propaganda. It shifted attitudes. That is a necessary, if not yet sufficient, condition for effecting actual social change: changing the political conditions of the world and thereby changing reality itself through the very fact of presenting reality via the necessary manipulations and mediations that are intrinsic to the basic essence of documentary form.

Although these films did indeed change mental attitudes, there is an argument, and some evidence, that they were not entirely successful yet in changing that material reality. The fact that even after another two decades, in 1966, housing issues remained a major social and political problem in the UK – and especially in its major cities – is testimony to a political reality – the reality as established by the privileged classes in their 'containment' of the poor and weak – that proves resistant to change.[12] It was in that year, 1966, that Ken Loach made *Cathy Come Home*, a fiction film made in drama-documentary style, much of it filmed out of doors in real locations.

Although fictional, *Cathy Come Home* nonetheless focused on the truthful reality of a specific political issue; and the figures at the centre of the film, Cathy and Reg and their children, are – like the five women in *Homes for the People* – presented as typical: although individualized themselves, they nonetheless stand for many. The thinking here is that it is precisely by the very fact of *dramatizing* the political conditions of 1966 England that we will see the *material and historical facts* that inform the fiction and that give it not only its recognizable sense but also its resonance. It is less a drama-documentary and more a documentary that has been dramatized and thus quickened into emotional life for its viewer. It is to 1960s television what Italian neorealist cinema was to film in the immediate post-war period (as we will see in more detail in the next chapter).

Cathy Come Home dramatizes an inexorable slipping away from a stable life into utter – indeed, existential – precariousness. It opens with an aged grandfather being put into a care home, essentially because of issues that we

---

[12] At least in the UK, housing remains to the present day a serious social problem. In 1980, the Thatcher administration enacted the Housing Act, known as the 'Right to Buy' Act because it encouraged citizens in social housing to buy their properties from local councils at reduced market rates. The Act remains controversial: it has been seen as part of the Thatcher administration's political project of systematically transferring public wealth into private hands; and it has continued to contribute to the denigration of 'social housing' as such, with an attendant denigration of those who live in such housing. It is seen also as having worsened the public provision of housing for less financially advantaged people – precisely the issues raised by Grierson, Mander and Loach decades ago.

saw in the 1935 and 1945 examples: a lack of space in a family home. Two sons are returning home after a stint in the army; and the grandfather has to go in order that they can be accommodated. We might recall in Zola's *Germinal* that a solution to overcrowding was found in a family essentially sleeping (and working) in shifts, according to the temporality of capital. There, too, what we saw was an intergenerational problem, the solution to which was itself wrapped up in the politics of capitalist working schemes. Through shift working, capitalist machinery runs without stop; and, domestically, this is accommodated by the fact that the two young boys kept the bed warm for the grandfather, Bonne-mort, as he returned from his night shift. In Loach's film, however, the boys who have survived and lived on after their military service now displace the grandfather, who knows that in being dispatched to the care home he is essentially facing his own death: not a 'good death' and not a *bonne mort* therefore. Mortality introduces the content of this film every bit as much as it did *Housing Problems*. The removal of the elder generation is mirrored at the end of the film when Cathy's children – the future generation – are taken from her and, as the logic of the film suggests, essentially kidnapped or captured by the State for its own capital purposes.

The consequence of this – a structural stripping away of both past and future – is that the film attends fully to Cathy's *present* in all its material reality. This moment, now, stripped bare of everything, is all that there is for Cathy. This is the fully political condition of a certain 'nudity'; and it is indeed scandalous – not because it falls into entertaining or voyeuristic titillation, but because it says, explicitly, that reality is the present, or presence as such, a 'being-here-now' with no protection from anything else. Cathy, reduced here to a bare life, is a contemporary King Lear, stripped of kingdom, retinue, family and, eventually, also of clothing in the midst of a natural catastrophic storm, or like Poor Tom on the heath: a 'poor, bare, fork'd animal'.[13]

Sex, labour and death all shape the content of this film: they constitute the realities with which the characters have to deal. As they start in their downward slide – that downturn or classic tragic literal 'catastrophe' – towards poverty consequential upon Reg losing his job after a life-threatening car accident at work, Reg and Cathy remain firstly optimistic; but they cannot help but note that no matter where they may try to find a home together, conditions are always overcrowded and cramped. The consequence is that 'you can't have a married

---

[13] William Shakespeare, *King Lear*, Act 3; scene 4; on 'bare life' see also Giorgio Agamben, *Homo Sacer* (1995; trans. Daniel Heller-Roazen; Stanford University Press, Stanford, 1998) and *Nudities* (2009; trans. David Kishik and Stefan Pedatella; Stanford University Press, Stanford, 2011).

life': sex becomes constrained by circumstances, if not impossible. Their landlady in one of their early places, Mrs Alley, reveals that she has survived in the past through prostitution: sex subsumed by capital. At this stage, Cathy rejects such a notion and, when she becomes pregnant for a third time, she explains that it is all about love and 'being for life'.[14]

Still impoverished because there is no work for Reg, Cathy and he, now with children, then become subject to a series of evictions. First, the State in the form of bailiffs come and violently break into their living space – crashing in through their door, not just gazing into their windows – to throw them into the street. Next, when living in a caravan, they are attacked by local people who want to claim the land on which the caravans sit, the caravan then being set on fire while children are sleeping inside, essentially menaced by murderous activity as firebombs are thrown through the caravan windows. Having lived under sheeting as a makeshift tent, the State then intervenes ostensibly to help out, but only at the cost of separating Reg from Cathy and the children. Their small act of rebellion against this occurs at 53' into the film, when Reg breaks into the home where the State is temporarily housing Cathy and they make love together. Sex has now become effectively illegal for them, and the law and its officers of State now threaten them further with yet more risks of degradation if they attempt to do something as basic as making love to each other, or having a shared intimacy in their private lives. The film famously ends with the children being forcibly taken from Cathy as she sits alone, isolated in a presentation of reality in its purest form as sheer presence. Yet it is a presence that demands to be changed.

With this film, the genre of drama-documentary inaugurated by Kay Mander comes fully of age, and assumes its new form as documentary realized in the form of fictional drama. It demonstrates that documentary realism has now essentially become a *style*. As such, it finds a new audience, one that mixes education with entertainment, and that mixes fiction with reality. This audience is entirely savvy about the existential predicament of Sartre's waiter; but, in seeing that predicament, this audience can also regain access to a reality that sits behind and that conditions the fictional act that it watches. The audience knows this is fiction, but learns the facts – in a manner that would be approved by Grierson – that makes such a fiction credible or, as we would say, 'realistic'.

In recent times, and with the new technologies associated with the development of artificial intelligence, we can see a troubling perversion of the entire

---

[14] See Ken Loach, *Cathy Come Home*, available at: https://archive.org/details/CathyComeHome (accessed 6 November 2019), quoted passages at 17'20", at 21' and at 22'20".

drama-documentary movement. The phenomenon we have come to identify as 'deep fake' produces films that claim to show reality as such, but that work precisely by falsifying – falsifying and not changing – that reality. This phenomenon's most typical form again involves nudity. Typical examples include the case of Rana Ayyub, whose work as an investigative reporter has been important in revealing political corruption in India and elsewhere. Her face was grafted onto the body of another woman in a series of pornographic videos and images in order to try to discredit her. She received a number of death threats as a result. The attempt is to use sex to evacuate her labour of import, and to do so with the threat of death. This is a perversion of realism, but one that nonetheless essentially underlines the nexus of labour-sex-death that shapes the entire phenomenon.[15]

The blurring of lines here is something that opens this new trajectory in the story of the politics of realism to a new set of problems. Those problems are associated with the development of propaganda and its relation to film narrative. At the core of that we will find two historical phenomena: the Nazi propaganda film under Leni Riefenstahl, and the emergence of Italian neorealism. It is to these that we now turn.[16]

3

Riefenstahl's propagandist documentary of the 1934 Nuremberg rally, *Triumph des Willens*, is organized around some of the key themes that we have seen as determining of the constitution of realism. It is a paean to labour, but to a labour that is essentially militarized as a literal 'labour-force'. Further, with its formal patterns of bodies in movement, this is a labour and a force that can be 'controlled' by the geometry of calculation and of mathematical measure. It is abstract mechanical calculation such as this that is at the core of capitalism.[17] At some key moments, the film celebrates an almost hallucinatory obsession with the near-naked and eroticized ideal body as a tacit identification of political power with sexual potency; and it saves its most striking imagery for the

---

[15] For the details around these cases, see, for example, Drew Harwell's report in *Washington Post*, 30 December 2018, available at: https://www.washingtonpost.com/technology/2018/12/30/fake-porn-videos-are-being-weaponized-harass-humiliate-women-everybody-is-potential-target/ (accessed 12 November 2019).
[16] The examination of neorealist cinema demands its own chapter, following directly from this one.
[17] We see this developed yet further when industrial capitalism moves into finance capital. See, for example, the work of Thomas Picketty, *Capital* (2013; trans. Arthur Goldhammer; Harvard University Press, Cambridge, MA, 2014). I write about this in more detail in my *Literature and Capital* (Bloomsbury, 2018).

encounter with death as such. Riefenstahl also further develops these themes in her *Olympia* films, made in the immediate aftermath of the success of her *Triumph des Willens*, and equally determined to present the human body – and the body of the nation – in a highly politicized manner.

Some critics demur at the idea of calling *Triumph* a documentary at all. For these – and they would be thinkers who are at odds with Grierson on this account – the film eschews its documentary status because it is pure propaganda: indeed, it is not really even a documentary account of 'what happened' at the Nuremburg Rally, given that the rally was staged entirely for the purpose of being filmed by Riefenstahl. That is to say: for some critics – and here, these same critics would be aligned perfectly with Grierson – the simple fact that the film is entirely a 'fiction', a manufactured stage set, means that it can have no proper documentary status. Robert P. Kolker is among those who worry over how to place the film in terms of a genre or category; but, against this, Rainer Rother suggests a more complex and nuanced position. He suggests that to consider Riefenstahl's films 'purely as propaganda' fails to 'do justice to their uniqueness. They could not have developed so effectively if they had stylized a non-documentary subject'. He goes on to say that 'It is true . . . that they document more than the political significance of the Party Rally: they testify to its emotional, even erotic basis'.[18] The question for us, however, in this study, is not really to adjudicate a categorization; rather it is to consider how the film operates as a mode of realism. Yet, within that question, there lurks the abiding issue of the relation between realism and propaganda. We should remember that Nazi propaganda under Goebbels (who saw Riefenstahl as a clear rival for Hitler's attention) was considered to be so important in shaping political realities that it had its own dedicated ministry.

Triumph des Willens opens with a series of inter-titles that are designed to set a context for the film that follows, in which it will combine historical precision with the immediate *establishment of an attitude*. The attempt is to present a determinate historical reality; but also to inflect our engagement with that reality by establishing a point of view – a window or screen – upon it. The inter-titles give the date of the opening of the rally, 5 September 1934, and then situates that date historically: it is twenty years after the outbreak of the Great War; sixteen years after the beginning of Germany's suffering (referring to the aftermath of the Treaty of Versailles); and nineteenth months after Germany's rebirth (alluding to the Nazi accession to power). Clearly, this is not 'documentary' realism in its

---

[18] See, for example, Robert P. Kolker, *Politics Goes to the Movies* (Routledge, London, 2018), 41; and cf. Rainer Rother, *Leni Riefenstahl: the Seduction of Genius* (trans. Martin H. Bott; Bloomsbury, London, 2003), 63–4.

usual way: it does not present facts as they are, but rather facts as interpreted by the mediation of Riefenstahl herself.

The film then begins with the idea of a painful giving of birth, essentially to the birth of 'Hitler' as he is to appear in the film. After the inter-titles, we turn to the visual presentation. Here – and again as in some of the fictions we discussed – the film begins by looking through a window, the window of the plane that is bringing Hitler to Nuremberg. This is the screen giving a view of reality that constructs an attitude towards that reality. For some, that fact raises the question: Can it be the case that what we see is indeed reality, or are we being asked simply to conform to an attitude towards the world? The view is clouded, for the simple reason that Hitler is descending – and it is difficult to consider this as anything other than an attempt to show him as being like a god from the heavens – through the obfuscation of the clouds to the utter clarity that follows as we see the waiting earth below. That window scenario will be repeated on the opening morning of the rally, as we look out through an opening window in Hitler's hotel room, by this time aligned with the ordinary and earth-bound people of Nuremberg. So far, so like the fictions we have read. Yet this, however, is not supposed to be a house of fiction; rather, as a documentary, it proposes itself as a house of reality. The task of the film is to present events from a point of view or as construed by a specific attitude, but to occlude that attitude as much as possible and to give the sense that the presentation is neutral.

Among the speeches by Party officials, we hear that Germany under the Nazis is indeed a house: more than a house, it is a home. The Party propaganda presents politics as a matter of family throughout, with the usual ascribed gender roles producing lots of happy, smiling children; and the older those children are, the more obviously dedicated they become to this home, to its identity and to the attitude that determines the political cause whose ends the film intends to validate. It is noteworthy that women and children play a key role. In almost all the images of Hitler parading through the streets, on foot or more usually in his car, the crowds that we see are predominantly female. Given the political ideology of the time, the task that is accomplished here is one that makes Hitler homely: *heimelig* if not yet entirely *heimlich*. This is a film for and about family; and the nation is to be considered as a family at home and at ease with its father figure: *der Führer* as *der Vater*, so to speak; and an entire ideology domesticated.

Riefenstahl, in contradistinction to Grierson, certainly did want to prioritize the 'aestheticky'. After the stylized opening, with the descent of the plane, we move onto an entire series of geometric shapes, as the crowds – both still and marching – are viewed abstractly, but with all the clarity of pure shapes and pure movements. If this were Hollywood, we would be watching a whole series of nearly perfect Busby Berkeley dance sequences.[19] This is most certainly a prime example of the aestheticization of politics against which Benjamin warned us in the immediate aftermath of this film, followed almost immediately as it was by Riefenstahl's sequel, *Olympia*.

Throughout *Triumph des Willens* – as in *Olympia* almost immediately afterwards – the human body is deeply politicized. The aim is to present the body as erotically charged, but then to divert that eroticism into a celebration of force itself, as seen in the virility of actions mediated by the grace of movement. First, we have a series of close-up shots of faces, lit and chiselled to make them resemble neo-classical statues, blurring the lines between the present reality and a kind of eternal presence of classical art: this (Nazi) body is to transcend its own physical and real limitations: it will last as long as the projected Reich. The aim is to make the transience of the present (the eruption that is Nazism) into a kind of eternal necessity (an unquestionable reality, *Ananke*).

Immediately following another set-piece of geometry – with the tents in the soldiers' camp presented as a regular and rigorously measured set of triangles making a huge rectangle – we get to see the soldiers at their morning routine. The body is presented nearly naked, with the camera lingering on some idealized forms. Then, we see these men grooming each other in an unusually intimate and loving fashion, still half-naked. We move on to seeing them next as they begin their daily labour, again stripped to the waist in many cases. Finally, in this section, we see them wrestling, a playful intimation of the fighting for which they are being prepared. This combines a sexualized labour with the life-and-death struggle in its symbolic form as wrestling: it is the domestication – the housing, as it were – of naked and militaristic force. It also brings eroticism into intimate connection with death: sex as fight.[20]

This, of course, is an aestheticization of the idealized male Nazi body that is to be taken further and foregrounded in Riefenstahl's *Olympia*, with its famous opening showing, again, bodies almost as classical statues, before seeing the contemporary body mimicking the ancient Greek body engaged in the games, naked. The women's bodies, too, are stripped bare, as they dance naked before and around the games and the sportsmen and sportswomen. The concentration

---

[19] See, for example, the extraordinary sequence 'Lullaby of Broadway' from *The Gold Diggers* movie of 1933 (coincidentally the year that Hitler came to power), available at: https://www.youtube.com/watch?v=Yx6s-YReOJY (accessed 12 August 2020). The resemblance between some of the dance sequences and Riefenstahl's staged militarism is extraordinary.

[20] In Busby Berkeley, the identification is more likely to be between sex and capital: 'we're in the money', as in the popular song from *The Gold Diggers*, accompanied by highly eroticized female dancers.

is on the pure aesthetics of movement: this is a straight aestheticization of the body politic. However, the key point remains: Riefenstahl's aim is to turn what might be thought of as a mere historical passing moment – the eruption of Nazism – into the eternity of its proposed eternity of the thousand-year Reich.

What, then, is the 'reality' that this aims to show in the Riefenstahl documentary, if indeed it is still to be considered as a documentary at all? It is, of course, a reality that is mythologized; and the stylized presentation of the bodies, especially in the *Triumph* film, is determining of that myth. Alongside the mythologization of Hitler himself as some kind of demi-god, we have the farmers more or less mutating into the military (presenting their spades as if they were rifles), as the care of the earth becomes the mastery of it through a profound identification of blood with soil through the mediation of the labouring 'classical' body.

In this exercise in propaganda via film, we also have a straight description of and paean to propaganda as such, from Goebbels, in his official role as the Minister for Propaganda in the Nazi dispensation. He had been irritated, in matter of historical fact, that Riefenstahl had been given carte blanche to make her film, over his own position; but he will certainly play his assigned role. 'May the bright flame of enthusiasm never be extinguished', he says.

> Its flame lends light and warmth to the creative art of modern political propaganda. It springs from the depth of the people and to the depths of the people must it return in order to search for the source and to find its strength. It may be all very well to have power which rests on force of arms but it is better and more gratifying to win the heart of the people and to keep it.

The words are carefully chosen: the film is punctuated at almost every turn by elemental fire and flame, torches lighting the night, bonfires burning, ceremonial flames lit. They are lit, most centrally, around death. Perhaps the most stylized moment in the film comes when Hitler, accompanied by two other officers, approaches the cenotaph to honour the dead, the three figures profiled walking against an utterly enormous range of people in serried ranks, organized into geometric shapes, and leaving a broad column through which Hitler will come and go. His approach to the cenotaph is every bit as stylized as the runner bringing the Olympic flame from Athens to Munich in *Olympia*, and it operates almost as a slow-motion version of that.[21] The real has become a stage set, and politics has been reduced to ritual and role-play. In some ways, we can see in this

---

[21] In this respect, it is a forerunner of the famous slow-motion diving sequences that were to prove so effective in *Olympia*.

turn from documentary realism to pure propaganda the beginnings of what we now know as Reality TV: Nazism provides an origin for this kind of television that reveals its fundamental political dimension.

What has happened in Riefenstahl is that propaganda has usurped the documentary-realist impulse. Instead of making a documentary whose drive is towards changing an existing reality, Riefenstahl's programme is one whereby 'reality' is manufactured as a product of the filming process itself. Such a reality has no authentic ontological status: it is not so much a fiction as a myth. It is for this reason that it yields a 'present' that is supposedly transcendent of historical circumstance, as if it is eternal and unchanging or unchangeable. It is the complete opposite of 'presence' in *Cathy Come Home*, where Cathy's intense present tense is realized in its historical actuality, by its secular links to past and future. By contrast, and as a consequence of Riefenstahl's drive towards myth, in claiming to show a present reality, *Triumph* instead manages to efface reality itself and to hide it under the mythological imagery. Not only is it anti-documentary; it is also anti-reality itself. As in the Reality TV for which it will be an unacknowledged model, it yields fantasy instead of reality, even as it uses documentary-realist technique and style to do so. *Triumph des Willens* is a documentary-against-documentary, a fake realism shaped by the determination to occlude the real material conditions of Germany under Nazism and to offer a fantasy world in its place.

4

On 18 March 1936, Adorno wrote to Benjamin from London. He wanted to quibble with what he described as Benjamin's 'extraordinary' essay, 'The Work of Art in the Age of Mechanical Reproduction'. At the core of his argument is a consideration of the issue of the representation of the real in cinema. He tells Benjamin of a day he spent 'in the studios of Neubabelsberg' in 1934. Notwithstanding Benjamin's complex thinking about film technique, Adorno says that 'what impressed me most' on that occasion in the studios 'was how *little* montage and all the advanced techniques that you emphasize are actually used'. In matter of empirical fact, as opposed to philosophical theory, Adorno argues that, in the actual making of films, 'reality is everywhere *constructed* with an infantile mimeticism and then "photographed"'.[22]

---

[22] See Adorno, 'Letters to Walter Benjamin', in Theodor Adorno et al., *Aesthetics and Politics*, with Foreword by Fredric Jameson (Verso, London 1980), 124.

He will revisit this when he writes the fragments of *Minima Moralia: Reflections from Damaged Life* and when he collaborates with Max Horkheimer on *Dialectic of Enlightenment*, both written in the immediate fall-out of the catastrophe that was the Nazi regime. In his coruscating fragment, 'Wolf as grandmother', Adorno laments what he sees as the intrinsic capacity of film to convert human subjects into functions of whatever passes for the norm in the existing social structures. It does this so thoroughly, he says, that the audiences for film 'enjoy their own dehumanization as something human, as the joy of warmth'.[23] In this sense, cinema (and he is thinking really of Hollywood) operates to deprive the citizen of the consciousness needed to make any kind of properly subjective engagement – agency – in respect of an already established political condition. It deprives the subject of the very thing that might make her or him a real subject: historical agency. Those who own and control the culture industry thus also ensure that 'reality' is what they themselves say it is; and the world starts to conform to the image on the screen.

That is the logic that had led Adorno and Horkheimer to their statement that 'Real life is becoming indistinguishable from the movies'. In their chapter on the culture industry in *Dialectic of Enlightenment*, they argue that 'The sound film, far surpassing the theater of illusion, leaves no room for imagination or reflection on the part of the audience' and this, they claim, 'forces [the film's] victims to equate it directly with reality'.[24] For Adorno (and Horkheimer) it is as if all Hollywood cinema has essentially been subsumed under the ideology of *Triumph des Willens*, in the sense that all such cinema, far from representing reality, actually constructs it. The issue, however, is that this kind of film constructs reality in the form of myth, and then requires the human citizen to act as the pure function of the enabling and enacting of that myth, unable to criticize it. At this point, propaganda has disabled education; and it does so by an essential falsification of history. In fact, more than this: it actively denies the very possibility of history – the factual material of historical activities – as the basis for reality, replacing the transient moment with the alleged eternity of a Reich.

Such a position does not go uncontested, as we will now see when we turn to Italian neorealism.

---

[23] Theodor Adorno, *Minima Moralia* (1951; trans. E. F. N. Jephcot; Verso, London, 1974), 206.
[24] Theodor Adorno and Max Horkheimer, *Dialectic of Enlightenment* (1944; trans. John Cumming; Verso, London, 1979), 126.

8

Neorealism

The real as resistance

1

In their article 'Ancora di Verga e del cinema italiano', Mario Alicata and Giuseppe de Santis issued a set of propositions that read somewhat like a manifesto of a new movement. They wrote that

> We want to bring our movie camera in the streets, in the fields, in the ports, in the factories of this country; we are also convinced that one day we will make our most beautiful film following the slow, tired step of the worker returning to his home, narrating the essential poetry of a new and pure life that contains within itself the secret of its aristocratic beauty.[1]

One can easily hear, in the rhythms and phrasing of this statement, the resonant echoes of that crazed Italian Futurism that had earlier contributed so much to the drive towards violence and war. There is the same breathless urgency that is recognizable as an echo of the rhetoric of Marinetti, whose Futurist Manifesto had itself been shaped by a demand for a Nietzschean triumph of the will. In 'The Founding and Manifesto of Futurism 1909', Marinetti had written that 'we felt ourselves alone . . . alone with stokers feeding the hellish fires of great ships, alone with the black spectres who grope in the red-hot bellies of locomotives', and so on, and on, with increasing bombast through the eleven key statements of the Manifesto.[2] In terms of content and substance, however, the difference between the drives of Futurism and this new cinema could not be more significant.

---

[1] As cited in Jacqueline Reich and Piero Garofalo, eds, *Re-Viewing Fascism: Italian Cinema 1922–1943* (Indiana University Press, Bloomington and London, 2002), 85.
[2] F. T. Marinetti, 'The Founding and Manifesto of Futurism 1909', in *Futurist Manifestos*, ed. Umbro Apollonio (Thames and Hudson, London, 1973), 19.

Alicata and de Santis evoke the history of Italian literary realism, through the figure of Giovanni Verga, whose celebrated novel, *I Malavoglia*, of 1881 had initially been conceived as the founding novel of a series that was to have been the Italian version of Zola's *Rougon-Macquart* series.[3] Like Zola, Verga had started off with some romantic-style tales, but moved in his more mature writings quite quickly into a realist mode. Verga's major fictions are focused almost exclusively on the meticulously observed realities of everyday Sicilian peasant life. The fictions depict colloquial provincial (Sicilian) speech with great accuracy; and they are governed by his *verismo*, a concern for truth (exactly as we saw in Zola) or for the motivational narrative drive of verisimilitude. *Verismo* has been described properly as 'the Italian counterpart of French naturalism'; and writers working in the emergent styles of *verismo* 'concerned themselves with the presentation of the day-to-day affairs of ordinary people ... studying life and reproducing it faithfully in its most minute particulars'.[4]

In Verga's case, this drive to verisimilitude translates as a persistent attention to the life of country-folk, peasants and fishermen primarily from the single locality of Sicilia; but he has a special interest in what happens when a character from this milieu is displaced elsewhere, not just in geographical terms, but in fact particularly in terms of social class. In this way, Verga places class and its associated issues – the conditions of labour especially – at the core of his writing; and it is this that brings him to the centre of neorealist interests. This helps explain why de Santis and Alicata discuss and foreground his work in a number of articles that are determining of the conditions of neorealist cinema in the 1940s, when Italy is in a process of post-war reconstitution and reconstruction. The moment recapitulates Verga's own historical period, when the then newly united Italy was seeking its 'proper' identity; but in the shift from the medium of print to that of cinema, there are many attendant differences of philosophy and politics.

Although one might hear rhythmic echoes of Futurist manifestoes in the priorities of Alicata and de Santis, the political direction of travel is extremely different. In his 1909 Futurist Manifesto, Marinetti had praised war as 'the world's only hygiene'. War was to be a purgatorial form of cleansing, which, in

---

[3] Verga had in mind a series that would have been known as *I Vinti* (which translates roughly as *The Vanquished*), and which would have focused on the lives of the dispossessed and underprivileged, those who felt that history had beaten them and who might be tempted to give up on life. The series was never realized, as Verga turned to other writing projects after the 1880s, including the work for which he has become known, at least in opera circles: *Cavalleria rusticana*.

[4] G. H. McWilliam, 'Introduction', in Giovanni Verga, *Cavalleria Rusticana and other Stories* (trans. G. H. McWilliam; Penguin, London, 1999), xvii.

its 'scorn for woman',[5] stands completely opposed to the impulses governing the later documentary-realist movement. Grierson and those who worked under his influence all knew that there was a great need for increased health and hygiene in modern society; but, as we have seen, they placed a respect for domestic labour, carried out largely by women, at the core of that demand. Unlike the Futurists – whose praise for 'virility' had contributed to the normalization of a war-mongering mentality that was so admired and advanced by Mussolini and the Fascists – the documentary realists suggested that reality was to be found not in the eyes solely of vigorous men but rather in the everyday conditions of life as lived by labouring women, and as seen from their point of view, through their newly washed windows. In Italy, by the time that this Futurist project had been tried out, in the Fascist enthusiasm for war under Mussolini, the cultural mood had significantly shifted; and it is this shift that is most important in our understanding of how Alicata and de Santis delineate a new aesthetic of neorealism.

So, while we can hear some *semiotic* echoes of the rhetoric of a Futurist Manifesto in Alicata and de Santis, we can also see that the *semantic* content of their writing is utterly different; and indeed, neorealism is completely opposed to the Fascist ideology that had afflicted Europe for the disastrous twelve years of Nazism and its associated political movements elsewhere, including the somewhat longer Fascist period in Italy under Mussolini. Marinetti, Mussolini and their acolytes would sing the praises of the fully militarized citizen: they had an image of the citizen as soldier that was realized as an image in Riefenstahl's presentation in *Triumph des Willens* of farmers holding their spades as if they are rifles. Now, however, in the culture that is dealing with the aftermath of war, the reality of labour would be realized and imaged rather differently; and it is this that informs the thinking of Alicata, de Santis and, indeed, the whole Italian Neorealist movement that emerges as a dominant form in cinema at this post-war moment.

2

Italian neorealism is usually thought to begin with Visconti's *Ossessione*, whose central character, Gino, is a drifter: an individual whose very existence and mode of life is at odds with the Fascist ideal of the militarized and regulated citizen

---

[5] Marinetti, 'The Founding and Manifesto of Futurism 1909', 22.

under Mussolini, but who is also – unlike the characters in Verga – untethered from any specific locale. Visconti began his film career at the side of Jean Renoir in the mid-1930s, when Renoir was an active supporter of the left-wing French Popular Front; and from Renoir he gained more than just a political education. It was during that time that Renoir gave him a typescript of the French translation of James M. Cain's 1934 novel, *The Postman Always Rings Twice*.[6] This was the novel on which Visconti based *Ossessione*. It makes sense, therefore, to consider Renoir – son of the impressionist painter Auguste Renoir, whose early works (especially his nudes) were profoundly influenced by Courbet – as one key inaugural figure of neorealist cinema, and as a major influence on Visconti and subsequent Italian film.

Where better to begin an examination of realism in Renoir than in his 1937 film explicitly about the deceptions around reality, the film grounded in 'illusion': *La Grande Illusion*? By 1937, Renoir had watched the electoral victory of the Popular Front; but that victory and the leftist optimism that it had offered were soon overshadowed by Hitler's invasion of the Rhineland. By the time Renoir was making his extremely disillusioned film about the Great War, the inevitability of the drive to war once again in 1939 seemed assured. It is in this frame, with the rising threat of Nazism, that we can make sense of the film's attitude to illusions and realities.

Right at the heart of the story presented in *La Grande Illusion*, and running behind the narrative action, is the real-life historical battle of Verdun. There is shock and dismay among the French prisoners of war and hearty celebrations among the German guards when news comes through to the prison camp on 26 February 1916 that Fort Douaumont, a key strategic point near Verdun itself, had been taken by the Germans the previous day. Then, right in the middle of the song-and-dance revue that the prisoners put on, further news arrives, this time revealing that the French have re-taken the Fort. With this military reversal, the reality of the war interrupts the stage-show: Maréchal stops the revue, and

---

[6] Renoir had received his own copy from Julian Duvivier, director of the 1937 film starring Jean Gabin, *Pépé Le Moko*. See Henry Bacon, *Visconti* (Cambridge University Press, Cambridge, 2012), 14, for details. In an interesting, if controversial, examination of *Pépé le Moko*, focused on issues of colonialism, entitled "'Blame it on the Casbah": The White Male Imperialist Fantasies of Duvivier's *Pépé le Moko*', Michael G. Vann argues that the film 'works as a study of colonial urbanism. Arguably, the city of Algiers is the real star of the film'; but he also notes the position of the film's star, Jean Gabin – who also stars in *La Grande Illusion* – as a bond between working-class real life and the world of the movies. Class, and the issue of mapping terrain, as we will see, are both crucial to Italian neorealism. See: https://h-france.net/fffh/classics/blame-it-on-the-casbah-the-white-male-imperialist-fantasies-of-duviviers-pepe-le-moko/ (accessed 12 August 2020).

the orchestra and French officers sing the Marseillaise in an extremely rousing fashion.

Broadcasting this to a French cinema audience in 1937 is a very clear political statement; and it is one that attends not simply to the reality of the Great War of 1914–18, but also to the urgent sentiments around the imminent war that everyone expected to begin in the immediate future. Those sentiments included anxieties about that war, terror at the prospect of the spread of Nazism, and a plea to the realities of the French national character and nation-state as a site of resistance to such a potential political disaster. Indeed, one of the key illusions relentlessly exposed in the film is the illusion promulgated by the political classes after 1918 that the Great War would be the last. The political dimension of the film was clear in many quarters. It was banned in the nations where Nazism and Fascism were in the ascendant: Germany and Italy. The political classes in these right-wing extremist States saw very clearly the potential power of its realism, a power that they knew would operate as persuasive anti-Fascist propaganda.[7]

The film opens with the working-class officer, Maréchal, keen to get a lift into town to see 'Joséphine', a woman with whom he is having a sexual dalliance (along with many of the soldiers, it seems). However, the visit to Joséphine is immediately stymied when his fellow officer, the aristocratic Capitaine De Boeldieu, calls him in. De Boeldieu is having difficulty in understanding an image and what it really presents. It is a reconnaissance photograph, with an indistinct smudge at its centre; and De Boeldieu and Maréchal decide they must fly over the war-terrain to find out what the smudge 'really' is. In other words, this film by Jean Renoir, son of Auguste Renoir, begins by drawing attention to the failure of a photographic image to capture reality because it is too vague, too impressionistic, as we might say; and the desire to clarify this and to discover the real that lies behind the representation both breaks off a sexual encounter and introduces the two officers to the threat of death in the war.

Sure enough, in the next scene, in a setting that mirrors almost exactly the French military building with which the film opened, we meet the aristocratic German officer, Rauffenstein; and we discover that he has shot the two French officers down. At this moment, barely five minutes into the film, we discover that war is a matter of social class. Further, for Renoir here, social class more or less completely transcends the oppositions between nations that are usually at the core of war: Rauffenstein tells his men that, if any of the men he has just shot

---

[7] Mussolini, however, had his own personal copy of the film. See Bacon, *Visconti*, 9, for details.

down turn out to be officers, they are to be invited to a very hearty and convivial lunch as his guests.

Maréchal and De Boeldieu are duly brought in for lunch, and a degree of convivial camaraderie among the French and German 'enemies' is established. However, this mood is suddenly punctured by the intrusion of death itself: a reverential silence falls as a funeral wreath is brought through the room, in honour of another French officer who had been killed when the Germans shot him down. The Germans stand to attention in honour of this dead man, and are obviously and ostentatiously joined in the gesture by De Boeldieu and Maréchal. Right at the outset, then, Renoir turns the conflict of war into a conflict shaped by class; and he relates this to issues of perceptions of the real (the faulty reconnaissance photograph), sex (the interrupted encounter between Maréchal and Joséphine) and death (the honouring of the deceased French officer).

One of the many illusions that haunt this film is precisely that of the oppositions between nations. The assumed reality of national difference and conflict that is supposed to ground the fundamentals of war is called into question, in a continuation of the uncertainty over the reconnaissance photograph that initiated the action. The end of the film mirrors the opening in that Maréchal and Rosenthal, having escaped from the prison camp, cannot tell where the border is between Germany and France: it is simply an indeterminate space – a smudge, as it were – somewhere among the trees in the countryside. Against such vagueness, however, we find instead a different and prior reality: the primacy of social oppositions, based not on international war but on class. The reality of this social division is greater, the film suggests, than any actual opposition between nations. The working-class Maréchal and aristocratic De Boeldieu, both French and working in very close intimacy with each other, nonetheless cannot fully overcome their class distinctions. Simultaneously, De Boeldieu and Rauffenstein, though wartime enemies, are utterly identified with each other in terms of their aristocratic class, with Rauffenstein constantly privileging and protecting De Boeldieu against the difficulties and hardships of confinement.

It is important to note that, at the most profound moments of that shared intimacy, these aristocrats both abjure their native tongues and turn to English as an ostensibly neutral medium of communication. Yet it is also their fluency in English that marks them out as being above the national opposition of France and Germany, and far above their respective compatriots, in class terms. Linguistic incomprehension is important in at least two other moments in the film, again operating as mirror images of each other. In the first, when the French are being decamped, Maréchal tries to explain to a newly arriving English prisoner that the French have been digging an escape tunnel in barrack number seven, and hoping that the Englishman will continue the dig. The communication fails, because they cannot speak each other's language. However, this is re-worked in the final sequence of the film. The escaped Maréchal and Rosenthal find protection and refuge with Elsa, the German woman who lives alone on her farm, when they are on the run from the German forces. Although Elsa speaks no French, and Maréchal no German, nonetheless these two establish a deep erotic relation with each other. Sex overcomes language barriers; and the material realities of sexualized bodies – body language – speak more positively than the tongue itself. As the aristocrats show, the tongue is malleable and a marker of an artificial class distinction; and as Elsa and Maréchal show, the material and sexed body is more ontologically powerful.

That body language is also key to an absolutely central aspect of this film: Rosenthal's Jewishness. By 1937, the Nazis had started the institutional persecution and victimization of Jews; and this was not a matter that was yet hidden from the rest of the world. The world knew, for instance, about the Nazi passing of the 1937 'German Civil Servants' Law' that determined that Jews would be barred from holding any public or state office as civil servants; and that civil servants who had Jewish relatives would also be fired from their positions. The anti-Semitism was open, and known about. *La Grande Illusion* stages a situation in which a German woman (Elsa), a French working-class officer (Maréchal) and a French aristocrat (De Boeldieu) all worked together in an action whose effect is to protect the Jew (Rosenthal) from the Germans. Although the Great War of 1914–18 did not have Nazism at its core, and *La Grande Illusion* is about the Great War in terms of its narrative, in terms of its realism the film is really about the conditions of France, Germany and Europe in 1937, when the effects of Nazism were becoming an obvious lived reality for the Jews of Europe.

It is interesting also that there is an indirect reference to the cultural barbarism that we might associate with Nazism in the film: the burning of books that had already begun in Germany in 1933, some four years before Renoir made the film. However, it is not the Germans who burn books here; rather, it is the Russian officers in the camp who set fire to an entire casket of books, against Rosenthal's desperate desire to read. The Russians invite the French for dinner, having been sent a massive casket or hamper from home. Everyone gathers around excitedly but, as the Russians pull out the protective straw from the casket, all that is revealed is a massive collection of books, and no food. Disgusted, they start to burn the books. Reality for the Russians at this moment is a matter of the hungry material body, nostalgic for the empirical scents and tastes of their homes, and the sensation of freedom that they would have there. Reality is not a matter of imagination and art – except for Rosenthal.

When he was interviewed in 1962, Renoir said that he thought that *La Grande Illusion* (like *La Règle du Jeu*) 'is a sort of reconstructed documentary, a documentary on the condition of society at a given moment'. His argument in this interview is that what we see as an external reality 'is often the expression, the symbol, of an interior truth'; and the truth that he has in mind is one that implies that, under the naked skin, there is more that joins people together than sets them apart; and this is true even in class terms. The movement of history means that 'Certainly it's difficult now to distinguish between a Boeldieu going to the theatre on a Saturday and a Maréchal doing the same thing'. Differences certainly remain; but 'they're much more subtle, more interior, and they're gradually being wiped out'.[8]

The emergence of neorealism in cinema at this moment has its roots in this entire political (even geopolitical) complex. As in the literary examples that we have seen, and as in the movement around documentary realism, social class is fundamental as a driver of any realist narrative. Within those issues of class, however, we have the relations between the worker and the privileged running alongside and punctuated by a sexual interest and – in the case of *La Grande Illusion*, explicitly – the introduction of a new element: racial prejudice as the foundation of a state's polity. In Renoir's case, that is seen not just in the figure of the Jewish Rosenthal, but also in that of a Black officer who is in the same barracks and camp as Maréchal.

This prisoner passes the time by drawing; and he offers his completed image of 'Justice pursuing the crime' to Maréchal. In his cynical dismissal of the drawing, barely casting a glance at it and appearing completely dismissive of its Black artist, Maréchal also dismisses the reality of a potential politics as envisaged by this Black officer, whom he casually brushes aside. Of course, behind this issue of racialized perception is the fact that it is the Black man who has an accurate and real view of what underpins the politics that governed the war: the demand for justice. He also knows that it is this reality that even the working-class Maréchal cannot see or that he will not allow himself to see. Renoir's point, though, is that time and the future will resolve those differences, for society is gradually and

---

[8] Louis Marcorelles, 'Conversation with Jean Renoir, 1962', in *Jean Renoir, Interviews*, ed. Bert Cardullo (University Press of Mississippi, Jackson, 2005), 106–7.

inexorably moving towards a state of affairs in which a single perception of the world can be shared; and it is this that will constitute reality.

Realism is the search for that single perception: it is the determination to remove the smudge or – as with Renoir's own impressionist father – to accept that the smudge is itself reality, vague and imprecise, and it is always elusive – always demanding the next movie, the next approximation to realism and to a realistic portrait of the material realities of the world. Coming after the high point of literary modernism, this reality – for Renoir – is eventually to be found in the interior of the human. Neorealism, we might say, is an ongoing contest between the claims upon reality and truth that are made by the world of historical exteriors and that of an interiority of consciousness.

3

This is what influences Visconti when he makes *Ossessione* in 1942, ready for its first showing in May 1943. The war foreseen by his mentor, Renoir, was fully under way when Visconti made this film; and Mussolini had brought Italy firmly into the conflict. The film, then, is made directly under the auspices of the Fascist regime, and not just because of Benito Mussolini's bombastic war-mongering. Mussolini's son, Vittorio, was at this time the editor of the journal, *Cinema*; and he also presided over the premiere of the film. The conflict touched the lives of filmmakers such as Visconti directly, for, at the end of 1942, Alicata and others associated with Visconti had been arrested by the regime.[9]

Benito Mussolini promulgated a very specific account of what constituted legitimate Italian reality. The individual in Fascist Italy barely enjoyed the right of existence as an individual, but was instead considered to be an operative of the social and political system as such, and was therefore highly regimented in almost all aspects of life. Women were 'respected' under Mussolini's Fascism, but only as the vehicles through which a virile society of manly vigour and labouring force could be sustained, through the assigned female function of giving birth

---

[9] For Alicata especially, cinema was political above all. See Gaetano Tramontana, *Invito al Cinema di Luchino Visconti* (Mursia, Milano, 2003), 35: 'Nello stesso gruppo di "Cinema" c'è chi, come Alicata e Puccini ad esempio, intende il cinema come un mezzo di lotta politica, e tende a sceneggiature fortemente incentrate sulla raffigurazione realistica del tessuto sociale' ['Among the group around "Cinema" are those who, like Alicata and Puccini for example, consider cinema as a means of political struggle, and whose dramatic tendency is to focus extremely strongly on a realistic representation of the social fabric' (my trans.)]. On the arrest, see Tramontana, *Invito al Cinema di Luchino Visconti*, 48, 49–50.

to boys who would continue the regime's line. Sexuality was itself policed and regimented, and seen as instrumental in the propagation of more Fascists; and therefore homosexuality was rendered illegitimate (although Visconti, who was from a high-class background, escaped censure over his own homosexuality). Above all, Fascism under Mussolini was to be centred on an ideology that would recast the national character that would be 'founded upon tradition, on a rural way of life and characterized by a grandiosity inherited from the newly mythologized figures of the Renaissance and the Risorgimento'.[10] This, then, was the anti-realist and reactionary take on Verga's *verismo*, against which the more progressive tendency of Visconti and others would be pitched.

Against the prevailing Fascist account of legitimate reality – that romanticized myth of the grandeur of a simplified peasant life and its modernization into the citizen-soldier – Visconti posted *Ossessione*. However, and obviously following the arrest of his colleagues, Alicata and Puccini, during the actual filming, it would not be wise or even possible to make an explicitly anti-fascist film. Pietro Ingrao argued that 'it's not (and nor could it be) an explicitly antifascist message: but it is – for the first time – a reading of Italian society that is antithetical to fascism' ['non c'è (perche non ci poteva essere) la parola antifascista esplicita: ma c'è – per la prima volta – une lettura della società italiana che è antitetica al fascismo']. This antithesis of Fascism is manifest 'by the way in which it [the film] struck at the notion of the family, the traditional images of the worker, the representation of social relations, the actual material and physical environment of Italian life' ['per il modo con cui venivano colpiti la nozione di famiglia, l'immagine tradizionale dell'operaio, la rappresentazione dei rapporti sociali, lo stesso ambiente materiale, fisico della vita italiana'].[11]

Ossessione's central character, Gino, is the antithesis of the Fascist citizen-soldier: he is highly unregimented, a vagabond or drifter, with no home other than his own skin. Giovanna, the woman with whom he shares the passionate sexual obsession that drives the narrative, was once a woman who had to sell her body to men in return for food. By contrast, Bragana, Giovanna's corpulent husband and one-time *bersigliere*, sees and treats Giovanna – in an ideal entirely at one with Mussolini's regime – as his domestic subordinate and servant, useful primarily to take care of him and to 'make this boy', or get pregnant through

---

[10] Donatella Spinelli Coleman, *Filming the Nation* (Routledge, London, 2011), 84.
[11] Pietro Ingrao, *Luchino Visconti: L'antifascismo e il cinema*, as quoted in Tramontana, *Invito*, 49 [trans. mine].

their sexual activity.¹² The political tensions are clear. There are two competing accounts of reality and realism in this: on one side, 'official' Fascist reality, as determined by the politics of the State; on the other, a 'clandestine' and covert life, running alongside and under the official account, and striving to actualize itself in the enactment of a passion. This duplicates what we had in earlier literary engagements, between (say) Verga's account of an official 'modern' world, and the clandestine and unofficial realities of peasant culture, whose status might be less secure but nonetheless more materially and empirically real. Beyond Verga, it rehearses once again almost the entire literary history that we have examined thus far.

Just as Renoir might place an erotic charge at the centre of an optimism that could survive the war, in the relation between Elsa and Maréchal at the end of *La Grande Illusion*, so Visconti will place a sexual and corporeal passion at the core of his realism here. The realities of war and of Fascism might be the officially real world; but there is another world, and one that is constituted through lived experience rather than through the formal and bureaucratic determinations of a State. The fundamental principle governing *Ossessione* is that an erotic passion constitutes a genuine basis for real experience, but that Fascist politics will strive to deny the actualization or realization of that basic human relation. One task of neorealism is to allow a clandestine reality – here, that shaped by erotic relations and obsession – to appear and survive.

Gino's appearance at the trattoria run by Bragana and Giovanna is a sudden if happenstance interruption into the regular everyday formal and 'official' or State-sanctioned lives of those two. It is precisely the happenstance nature of the event that contributes to the fundamental realism: this 'just happens', with no obvious premeditation, for Gino drifts aimlessly and without goals or objectives. He fits into no pre-existing rules or regulations; and there is thus no Renoirean 'règle du jeu' to which he will conform. The film brings Gino and Giovanna together over music – Gino hears her singing and enters the trattoria. Music will also be instrumental in the film's narrative drive that brings Gino and Giovanna to murder Bragana, as when Bragana triumphs in the singing competition with his rendition of 'Di Provenza il mar, il suol' from Verdi's *La Traviata*.¹³ The opening of *Ossessione* thus reprises structurally the opening also of *La Grande*

---

¹² Gino had also served as a *bersigliere*, as the film makes clear; but he is utterly indifferent to his past military service, whereas Bragana vaunts his and tries to make it the basis of a comradeship or militarized homosocial unity between the two men.

¹³ In the opera, Germont (the baritone) sings this aria. It is an emotional plea made to his son, to persuade the son to leave a lover behind and return to the stability of the family home.

Illusion in which the militaristic introductory music is itself interrupted by Maréchal playing and singing along to a popular love song, 'Frou-frou'; and where a cacophony of music is deployed as the distraction within the camp that will allow Maréchal and Rosenthal to escape.

Gino and Giovanna look at each other as Gino enters the kitchen; and in that moment, reality for both of them breaks through the lives they have been leading, those previous lives that suddenly are marked by a kind of inauthenticity and – crucially – the characters' *realization* or making real of that inauthenticity of their everyday realities in the organized State (such as it exists under Mussolini). The aimless drifter finds a rock that steadies his wandering desire, in the eyes of Giovanna; the bored and downtrodden woman finds, in the erotically charged body of Gino, the insistent and charged presence of a reality that breaks through the dull routine of her domestic labour and unpleasant sexual life with Bragana. After a trick played by Giovanna concerning Gino's supposed non-payment for food, Bragana drags Gino back to work for him, as a mechanic and odd-jobs general labourer. This sets the scene for the contest in which a clandestine reality – that of erotic obsession – must strive to actualize itself.

Once again, then, we see labour and sex brought together as before; but we are now seeing this in a political context that makes the sexual desire, in particular, a profoundly anti-Fascist statement. For Bragana, sex is to be functional, a duty to produce and reproduce the next generation of Fascist soldier-citizen-workers. After winning his prize at the singing contest, his inebriated mind turns to sex and he drunkenly provokes Giovanna, asking 'when will we make this boy, then?' Giovanna has already told Gino of her horror at having to have sex with Bragana, the physically unattractive older man. By contrast, as we have seen at her very first meeting with Gino, she regards him, unlike her husband, as eminently physically desirable. Their obsession is driven by physical and material force, focused entirely on the eye as the organ of perception itself. This is a reality and not an imagined or romantic love, the real presence of the body before the eye, and not a mythic or idealized constructed image. In a neat reversal of the usual erotic roles in cinema, here it is the man, Gino, who strips his shirt off, and Giovanna admiringly observes his body, his 'shoulders like a stallion'.

The other sexual politics in the film relates to the character of The Spaniard, Lo Spagnolo. This, too, arises after a chance meeting: another random happenstance that gives an 'effet de réel', as Barthes might have it. It is an ostensibly contingent and entirely unplanned meeting, one that is not driven by necessity. Gino and The Spaniard come together on a train, after Gino has abandoned Giovanna and has leapt on board the train to Ancona with no ticket and no money (but with her suitcase). The Spaniard intervenes with the guard – the officer of the State in the Italian railways that, famously, Fascism allegedly made run on time – and pays for the ticket (and the regulation fine). The Spaniard uses that moment – and his money – to establish a congenial relation with Gino. The ensuing relation between these two is constantly presented in a tantalizingly homoerotic manner: they share a bed; they sit together in a classic image of a countryside lovers' scene; they 'buddy-up' as travelling workers; in the end, they fight, yet retain lingering looks after each other until the betrayed Spaniard walks away. Once again, the erotic interest here operates against the State's Fascist norms, and indicates the possibility of a reality of experience that goes beyond and counter to what the State will endorse as legitimate, or as officially real.

The Spaniard, of course, represents more than this homoerotic interest in the film. He is known as The Spaniard because, as he tells Gino, he has recently been 'working in Spain'. As if we needed this further political indication of the film's concerns, this is an obvious reference to his activities in the Spanish Civil War, when Republicans, among them The Spaniard, faced Franco's Fascists. The Spaniard, having survived this and come to Italy, has carved out a new career of sorts as a travelling showman, his act being fortune-telling. His future, though, is one that will not be lived by Gino, Giovanna or even Bragana: Giovanna and Bragana will both die; Gino will be arrested by the police, who have acted as the agents of a surveillance State throughout the film. The survivors will be only the homosexual Spaniard and Anita, the prostitute to whom Gino confesses his story, significantly filmed through the gauze of a veil hung over the prostitute's work-place, her bed.

Intriguingly, when Gino and Giovanna confront each other over accusations of betrayal, the scene is filmed before a towering building of some kind. High in a window, between the heads of the two front-of-shot characters, we see a woman insistently brushing her extremely long hair. This figure is only barely glimpsed, serving no function other than 'being-there' as a quasi-documentary reality. Yet it also seems clear that this is not meant to operate as simple depiction of an unscripted reality; rather, it is a reference to the fairy-tale character of Rapunzel, who sits at the centre of a folkloric tale of sexual passion or obsession and in which pregnancy brings Rapunzel and her Prince together, while also bringing about their enforced separation. But while the fairy tale ends happily, *Ossessione* will not: happiness such as Rapunzel's is matter for fictions, not for empirical realities.

Sexual obsession, then, while it operates as the driving force of an anti-Fascist politics, turns out to be an entirely necessary but simultaneously unrealizable path to political freedom. It is significant that the film closes with the car crash that kills Giovanna and the embryo – that future life – that she is carrying inside her. That crash obviously and perhaps clumsily (at least, in structural or aesthetic terms) reprises the faked crash in which Gino and Giovanna killed Bragana. However, more important for present purposes is that the crash at the close of the film happens as a result of vagueness and the difficulty of seeing reality clearly or properly. That question, concerning the clear sight or vision upon material history, is central to the film's core politics. It is important to recall here that, throughout the film, the police play a crucial role in the narrative; and that role, fundamentally, is one of State-sponsored surveillance of two ordinary and everyday people, Gino and Giovanna: looking into the interiority of lives, investigating, trying to see clearly, trying to reveal the reality or truth of what is actually going on. The entire question of realism sits behind this, for one of the key issues raised in *Ossessione* concerns surveillance in its every sense. Can we trust what we see; is the reality of our experience visible, and do we wish it to be visible to the State; and can the State itself have a view of material political conditions that is essentially naked and uncensored?

If we leave the question at that, however, we would miss the crucial point. Seeing – in a State governed by surveillance – is policed and thus always political; and this means that the real is never 'naked'. Further, in the surveillance State, the State obsessed with the allegedly hidden or clandestine political realities that obsess everyone, this applies not only to the police: it is utterly generalized. In this kind of polity, perception itself becomes thoroughly political, and any representation of what we perceive is marked as propaganda. Credibility becomes a central predicament, and is propaganda's social correlate. Under Nazism, people 'really believed that truth was whatever respectable society had hypocritically passed over, or covered up with corruption'.[14]

When this happens, we are in that state of affairs described by Arendt as the fundamental condition of Fascism: it is not a state of affairs in which we think that the truth is covered by lies; rather, it is that state of affairs where the difference between truth and lies starts to become unimportant. She describes this as a mode of modern cynicism, 'an absolute refusal to believe in the truth of anything, no matter how well this truth may be established'. When this happens, and we no longer distinguish between truth and falsehood, then 'the sense by which we take our bearing in the real world . . . is being destroyed'; and, with

---

[14] Hannah Arendt, *The Origins of Totalitarianism* (1951; repr. Penguin, London, 2017), 459.

this, we are also destroying the 'real world' – reality – as the basis for our beliefs and actions – realism.[15]

We see here the same kind of anxiety about ocular proof that has haunted everything from *Othello* through to John Campbell's reaction to pornography, and on into Riefenstahl. When Gino 'really' confesses his action, for example, it is significant that Visconti films him across a gauze veil, casting the scene into hazy shadow and a lack of clear sight. When the suitcase he is carrying (Giovanna's) bursts open in front of The Spaniard, and real female clothing tumbles out, The Spaniard draws an inference from the evidence of his eyes that we do not share; but then the two characters share a bed together. Reality is, in some ways, precisely what this neorealist film strives after – but the key point is that it strives tantalizingly in the direction of a promised reality without ever reaching it; or, rather, when it does eventually reach into reality as the lovers make their failed getaway, the only material reality left is that of the inevitability of death. This is, indeed, one of the three inescapable realities that the film shows as a matter of fact: the reality of human mortality; the reality of sexual desire; the reality of labour and its correlate, unemployment.

The closing sequence follows Gino and Giovanna in their truck, but they are filmed across the windscreen, framing them like a film within a film in a move that intrinsically and structurally calls reality as such into question, while also making it a matter of life and death. The film-within-film structure, like the modernist novel-within-novel and all such self-reflective art, serves to distance the real from its representation. It calls ontology as such into question, under the priorities of epistemology: the real is not what we experience, but what we can know.

In trying to see clearly through the windscreen, they are, in effect, also trying to escape that structured framing that separates them formally from the ontological reality of the road and countryside around them: it is as if they are trying to smash their way through the windscreen, a screen that now blocks their access to the real, rather than (as in Zola and others) giving access to it. This empirical reality is what they are trying to reach: the Italy that we have seen displayed in its geography and countryside throughout the film. The film had also opened with a long sequence filmed through the windscreen of a truck: in that case, it was the truck that brought Gino into the film, and into the world of the Braganas and their trattoria. At the end, when the camera films Gino and

---

[15] Hannah Arendt, 'Truth and Politics', in Arendt, *Between Past and Future*, introduction by Jerome Kohn (Penguin, London, 2006), 252–3; and cf. Arendt, *Origins of Totalitarianism*, 460–3.

Giovanna from outside the truck, we see their anguished faces: they know that the agents of the State – the police – are pursuing them. They cannot pass the truck in front to escape, however, because – as we see when the camera turns to film from their point of view, again through the windscreen – they are in the slipstream of a heavy haulage truck (labour on the move), and it is billowing out smoke and fumes that make it impossible to see.

This is to say: as *Ossessione* closes, neither Gino nor Giovanna can see the road ahead; and the reality of their future is increasingly and suddenly, quickly, becoming more and more vague, less and less real or realizable. They are moving in a reverse direction from the officers at the start of *La Grande Illusion*: there, it was from a smudge on a photograph towards the reality of conflict; here, it is from the sought-after reality of an erotic relation and future to a radical uncertainty under police surveillance and control. The window – that opening to realism that has dominated the literary history that we have examined, and that functions to allow us to see the realities of the world – is clouded under Fascism. Mussolini, as it were, is closing the outlook upon the real and, like Riefenstahl, replacing that reality with vague mythology. It can only end in death. It is against this that Visconti makes his film; and he closes, essentially, by demanding that the viewer provide the vision that Fascism and its state police have foreclosed.

4

'The road ahead', while perhaps invisible to Gino and Giovanna, is in many ways exactly the topic of a good deal of Italian neorealist cinema after Visconti's *Ossessione*. As critics have consistently noted, an attention to landscape is one abiding mark of neorealist style, and the neorealist camera offers many panoramic and traveling shots as it looks over the country. Usually, this is considered as a mark of the attention given to the social classes that live in the countryside, typically seen as being endangered by the modernization of civic life and its attendant industrialization (and hence the importance, for many of the earliest apologists for neorealism, such as Alicata and de Santis, of the influence of Verga). In a historic reversal, the countryside which had traditionally been associated with a certain romanticism now becomes the site of a claim to realism. What has happened here is that 'authenticity' has passed from the nakedness of a primitivism to a politics that knows about the deprivations that have followed from international conflict. After the Second World War, this takes on a new inflection; and it is one that refers us back to the very beginning of this study, when John Campbell feared for the English national character as he prepared his Obscene Publications Act. There, we should recall, issues of race and the supposed purity of the body and tribe, although never directly stated, were at the core of his concerns.

As I have just shown, *Ossessione* both opens and closes with a kind of proto road-movie sequence, filming through the windscreens of a moving car. We had the same also in the rolling train at the start of Renoir's *La Bête humaine*, his 1938 film based on the Zola novel. The first ten minutes of this film constitutes an extraordinary sequence in the history of narrative cinema. The only sound is that of the train; and for a full ten minutes or so, all we see is the rail-track and countryside ahead, occasionally punctuated by shots of the train driver trying to communicate, by hand-signals, with his mate, over the loud noise. It recalls the 1935–6 documentary, *Night Mail*, made by Grierson's GPO Unit, which also focused on the railway as a means of communication.[16] The start of that film, too, like *La Bête humaine*, focuses on railway workers, and it shares much of the same imagery, right down to the workers drinking. Both the films start, then, with a fundamental focus on communication; but it is communication across a huge geographical space, across France (Renoir) and Britain (Grierson).

There are significant differences. Grierson sticks to his documentary principles and focuses primary attention on the material facts of labour: *Night Mail* is primarily about the work involved in delivering the mail, and the film shows every stage of that process and the work that it requires. When the film attends to geography, it does so to give a map of labour in Britain, with the different modes of industrial production linked to their specific locations. As it leaves Crewe, the voice-over says: 'North – with a hundred tons of new letters to sort. The Postal Special picks up and distributes the mail from industrial England: the mines of Wigan; the steelworks of Warrington; and the machine shops of Preston'; and each of these place-names is given a passing night-time image, with all the machinery still working. The point is made: capital occupies both place and time, it knows no stops, no interruption to its operation, and the rolling train is a central part of that, instrumental as the symbolic engine of capital as such.

---

[16] When Louis Marcorelles introduced the topic of Grierson (and Flaherty) during the 1962 interview from which I have already quoted, Renoir turned attention immediately to Cavalcanti, and seemed less aware of Grierson's role. See Marcorelles, in Cardullo, *Jean Renoir*, 109: 'In England the documentary movement was created by a particular group, around Cavalcanti, wasn't it? Cavalcanti played a big part in British documentary'. In fact, Cavalcanti initially worked under Grierson, though he subsequently went on to direct several films himself, most notably *Went the Day Well?* in 1942, some years after Renoir made *La Grande Illusion*.

At Crewe also, some of the staff change over, as Scottish railway and postal workers replace some of the English crew: capital recognizes no individuals, only work-functions or human resources, as they would come to be called. Yet, against this capitalist dehumanization, Grierson ensures that we see the individual worker, showing these change-over teams joshing linguistically with each other, as the Scots finish their tea (served by the only women to appear in the film), to be greeted with 'Good morning, Jock', and with jokes about their drinking made by the departing English workers. Notwithstanding Grierson's suspicions regarding the work of capital, the definition of individuality is limited, it seems: stereotypes are there to indicate both gender roles (women as serving staff in kitchens, fuelling the workers) and national characters (all Scots are called Jock, and all are drinkers). The shift workers recall also the family of miners in *Germinal*, the new shift replacing the finished, while the machinery never stops.

By contrast with all this, the narrative film of *La Bête humaine* makes much more of the geography and the landscape, and these are given greater importance than the labour in the train driver's cabin. The driver here, Lantier – as we know from the novel (and as is suggested by the opening inter-titles of the film) and as we will find out very quickly in the film itself – suffers from alcoholism; but at this stage, little is made of this beyond a construction of working-class conviviality between Lantier and his co-worker. It is the landscape of France itself that is most insistently present, as we see not only the countryside but also the place-names on stations that they pass, stopping finally at Le Havre. Where the workers all communicate with each other throughout *Night Mail* (indeed, the soundtrack is a constant play of joshing and of comradeship, with the occasional respectful and mildly deferential silence whenever a manager passes), the opening of *La Bête humaine* is entirely done by inarticulate sound: the roaring of the train, Lantier whistling loudly to attract attention, but then having to revert to mime – the deployment of the physical reality of the material body – in order to communicate.

Landscape and communication – the communication of identity especially – is an important trait in the turn to cinematic neorealism after the Second World War; and that turn marks the politics of this new medium, this cinematic version of realism, in significant ways. As we will now see, the war trilogy of Rossellini is instructive in this regard, for in these three films (*Roma, Città Aperta; Paisà; Germania, Anno Zero*) we will see how realism is deployed in the interests of the construction not just of a national character but also of an entirely new politics in and through the reconstruction of a nation-state.

This is a simple historical fact, of course. The films that we identify under the heading of neorealism were mostly made in a country whose landscape had been largely destroyed in wartime activity, and whose countryside had therefore taken on a highly symbolic significance. Although Bazin would claim, in the words of Peter Bondanella and Federico Pacchioni, that neorealist cinema 'contained a message of fundamental human solidarity fostered by the anti-Fascist Resistance', Ennio Di Nolfo makes the more nuanced claim that 'neorealist films were more anti-German than anti-Fascist' and that this generated 'a national temper, tied more to the Resistance movement against the Germans than to militant anti-Fascism'.[17] In both cases, however, what is at issue is the construction of a cinema that will stand as a symbol of a national rebirth and a national character.

Certainly, these films are about the Italian Resistance; but they are also genuinely *acts* of resistance as well; and what they are resisting is a fundamental ideology of totalitarian control. Arendt points out, in compelling and detailed argument, that totalitarian systems of government adopt a specific attitude to reality and to realism, especially with regard to the control of masses of people in modernity. 'Totalitarian propaganda,' she writes, 'perfects the techniques of mass propaganda',[18] and these techniques had been prepared by, among other things, the fragility of the nation-state in the long historical period preceding the Second World War. Both Nazi and Bolshevik, she claims, were masters of such techniques. These techniques, again for historical reasons, then come face to face with the specifically modern construction of 'the people' into 'the masses'; and 'what the masses refuse to recognize is the fortuitousness that pervades reality'.[19]

Constructed as a 'mass', people *actively seek* the falsifications of ideology. They do this, because ideology provides total and ostensibly or superficially adequate explanations for what might seem to be random and happenstance events; and, as a mass, they are inherently suspicious of the random and 'fortuitous', suspicious of precisely what Barthes identified as 'the reality effect'. They need certainty; and it is a totalitarian ideology, providing complete explanation (however implausible) that will give this.

Thus it is that masses can buy into totalitarianism, because 'Totalitarian propaganda thrives on this escape from reality into fiction, from coincidence

---

[17] See Peter Bondanella and Federico Pacchioni, *A History of Italian Cinema* (Bloomsbury, London, 2017), 63; and Ennio Di Nolfo, 'Intimations of Neorealism in the Fascist *Ventennia*', in *Re-Viewing Fascism: Italian Cinema 1922–1943*, eds Jacqueline Reich and Piero Garofalo (Indiana University Press, Bloomington and London, 2002), 84. For André Bazin's highly influential work on neorealism, see the essays in Bazin, *What Is Cinema?* vol. II, ed. and trans. Hugh Gray (University of California Press, London, 1972).
[18] Arendt, *Origins of Totalitarianism*.
[19] Ibid., 460.

into consistency'.[20] That is to say, totalitarianism 'works' – gains its adherents – by acknowledging that 'human kind cannot bear very much reality' and, especially, by acknowledging that, once organized into masses, people become suspicious of the mysteries that seemingly lurk behind happenstance. Paranoia demands absolute certainty, even if it means explaining away the contingencies of history by turning them into the eternities of necessity.

This explains, further, that condition whereby 'the masses are obsessed by a desire to escape from reality'; and the root cause of this is, for Arendt, the fact that the masses live in an 'essential homelessness', which leaves them unable to bear the 'accidental, incomprehensible' aspects of real historical contingency. So, when neorealist film directors start to insert and prioritize the random, the happenstance, the contingent into their films, this in and of itself is an act of political resistance. In this sense, neorealism is, above all, a gesture against totalitarianism. That also means that it is a political action whose point is to *require* the viewer – like Gino and Giovanna in *Ossessione* – to seek out the reality that lies behind the fictions and myths that totalitarianism uses to maintain its grip on the masses, and to deny them the very liberation that the films aim to present.

5

Rossellini's first film in the trilogy, *Roma, Città Aperta*, was made in the immediate aftermath of the defeat at the hands of Germany. As is well known, it gets a good deal of its documentary-style feel from the happenstance that Rossellini had to work with rough cuts of film stock that he was able to cadge from various sources. He bought 'raw film stock from street photographers, splicing together unmatched bits and pieces of thirty-five millimeter film'.[21] The use of such materials gives a sense that what is being prioritized in the film is not the style itself, but the simple fact of the recording of reality, using whatever means is possible: the medium becomes part of the message, as it were, but it does so by making itself seem irrelevant to the actual world being shown. So, when Rossellini makes his most celebrated remark that 'Things are there. Why manipulate them?', the statement circumvents the fact that the material conditions

---

[20] Ibid. See also Frank Kermode, who, in *The Sense of an Ending* (Oxford University Press, 1966), 39, makes a crucial distinction in these terms between fiction and myth: 'Myths are the agents of stability, fictions the agents of change. Myths call for absolute, fictions for conditional assent.' Arendt's 'fiction' here is actually closer to what Kermode means by 'myth' – both are concerned with the myth that underpinned Nazism.

[21] Peter Brunette, *Roberto Rossellini* (Oxford University Press, Oxford, 1987), 41.

and realities of the medium themselves do the job of manipulation. Paradoxically, it is the non-style that is the style – something that we had seen centuries before in the development of a so-called 'plain style' of writing in Defoe, say. Realism starts to become an explicitly recognizable style: a signature, determined thus by its degrees of authenticity as the marker of an individual or a character.

In this case, the character is not that of a person, but rather that of a city: Rome, the film's 'chief protagonist', a single location intended to stand 'for the rest of Italy'.[22] The Rome in question here is, of course, a 'character' that has been so viciously attacked during the war years that it is now in the process of re-birthing itself. While it would be a falsification to suggest that the film is Rosselini's version of Griffiths's *Birth of a Nation*, it is equally true to say that, when he made this film, Rossellini was a director who had been working under the direct influence of Fascist ideology. This raises the obvious questions regarding the relation of neorealism with politics and with propaganda.

Rossellini's earliest forays into film were carried out under the aegis and with the friendship of Vittorio Mussolini, son of Il Duce; and those films work in the same propagandistic spirit that would be associated with the work of Riefenstahl in Germany. Ennio di Nolfo points out that 'the people [including Rossellini] who constituted the neorealist cinema community were the same ones who had constituted the cinema community in the decade preceding the fall of Fascism'.[23] He goes on to argue that

> Realist cinema was the product of the rebirth of Italian cinema after the [economic] crisis of 1923-1931. It grew as the result of the [Fascist] government's intention to use film for propagandistic purposes; but these interventions allowed sufficient space for the formation of realist currents that were not in contradiction with certain aspects of Fascist politics with respect to the masses.[24]

The difference, in 1945 when Rossellini directs *Rome, Open City*, is that by this point, the Germans are now the enemy; and, when 'Rossellini directs facts', as Bazin put it, the fact that stands before him is a devastated Rome and an Italy that needs to reconstruct its identity as a post- or anti-Fascist state.[25] This is

---

[22] Ibid., 51. Recall here Michael Vann's description of Algiers as the real hero of Duvivier's *Pépé le Moko*, noted earlier.
[23] Di Nolfo, 'Intimations of Neorealism in the Fascist *Ventennio*', 84.
[24] Ibid., 101.
[25] See André Bazin, 'In Defense of Rossellini', in *What Is Cinema? Vol. II* (trans. Hugh Gray; University of California Press, London, 1972), 100. Bazin was always clear that neorealism, while ostensibly proposing a view of reality that works as if the camera is not there and as if reality is 'unmediated', nonetheless knows that neorealism is above all a new *aesthetic*. See his 'An Aesthetic of Reality', in this same volume, pp. 16-40.

the 'character' whose reality Rossellini places before us. As a character, it does two things: it proclaims its independent and single identity *against* 'the masses', individualized every bit as much as the worker in Grierson's documentaries, so that as a city, it stands for citizenship and thus encourages the expression of the individual Italian as herself and himself; and it proposes its particularity in a specific character-trait as 'anti-totalitarian'.

However, it surely cannot be seriously argued that, in this film, Rossellini simply pointed the camera at the reality of Rome and filmed. Although some key elements in the film are based on historical fact, the film is carried by a narrative drive that is shaped at very many turns by the demands of fiction. It is certainly the case that 'the original intention was to make a brief documentary on the life of Don Morosini, the partisan priest who had been executed by the Nazis'.[26] That, however, cannot possibly explain the intervention of the comedy scenes where, for the most-discussed examples, Romoletto's bomb is juggled by Don Pietro, or where Marcello looks admiringly at the frying-pan that has been used to knock out cold an old man who might expose the existence of this very bomb to the Nazis. Nor can it explain the film's most celebrated tragic sequence when Pina is shot down and killed while running after the Nazis who have taken Francesco, her husband-to-be, into captivity. If this is seriously a primary example of neorealism, then it is so only in fleeting moments (as with the famous sequence where a stray dog ran into frame and through the prisoner-escape scene, say). We need a closer examination of what we might call a transitional moment, when neorealism starts to emerge from the traditions of film propaganda that had been central to Mussolini's Fascism, a tradition that had been exemplified by Riefenstahl in Germany.

Throughout *Rome, Open City*, we get a dominant opposition between the exteriors – the streets of Rome and the houses of the city's Italian natives on one hand – set against the interiors – and above all the interior of the offices of the German Nazi, Bergmann. The camera sits precisely in the fulcrum of these two scenarios, and it thus operates in just the same way as the many windows and screens that we have seen to be dominant in the history of literary realisms. Outside, there is devastation, rubble – and the determination of the citizens to keep a dignified home, notwithstanding the difficulties of their daily lives. This applies not just to their present, but also to their envisaged future, carried (as in the case of Giovanna in *Ossessione*) in the womb of the pregnant Pina. By

---

[26] Brunette, *Rossellini*, 42.

contrast, Bergmann's interior is characterized by a deadly order. He sits in the middle of what is essentially a quasi-religious but satanic triptych: his office at the centre; to his left, a door leading into the torture room; to his right, a door leading into the salon where the German officers sit listening to classical music and enjoying fine wines and cigars in scenes that reek of decadence despite the geometrical and highly organized order.

This is the order and highly regulated existence that shapes a particular bureaucracy that has been described by Arendt as among the most cruel kinds of political condition: cruel because of its ostensibly neutral order and organization. Arendt argues compellingly that there is an intimate link between racist ideology and the emergence of bureaucracy as a political form of organization in a society. In fact, the latter can operate as a legitimizing cover for the former: 'While race, whether as a home-grown ideology in Europe or an emergency explanation for shattering experiences, has always attracted the worst element in Western civilization, bureaucracy was discovered by and first attracted the best, and sometimes even the most clear-sighted, strata of the European intelligentsia.'[27] Bergmann uses his bureaucratically ordered files and documents – specifically the photographs of Roman citizens – to control (or at least to imagine his complete control) of the city, engaged with reality precisely by being distanced from its actuality.

The actual city – that world exterior to the office – is where Rossellini finds the everyday Italian citizen, such as Pina, struggling to find enough bread to eat, prepared to fight for it if required while at the same time generously sharing whatever bread she finds with those less provided for. Yet, to do this, Rossellini has to construct, via fictional means, an equal and opposite idea or image of the Roman and Italian from that which Bergmann constructs via the surveillance mechanisms of his bureaucratic photographic files. Thus, Rossellini constructs scenes where an Italian civil officer on one hand 'officiously' reprimands the citizens for the bakery break-in, while on the other hand accepting the reality of the need for it (and benefiting when Pina offers him some of her stolen bread); or when Don Pietro provides homilies to Pina regarding the ways of justice. By contrast, he also has to provide a characterization of Bergmann as camp and homosexual and Ingrid as lesbian; and, since Rossellini subscribed to the prevailing ideology of his time and background, both characters are thereby marked negatively, as agents of an immoral perversity.

---

[27] Arendt, *Origins of Totalitarianism*, 242.

Some of the key issues with which I opened this entire study can be seen to persist right through to this moment, almost a century later. England's Obscene Publications Act, as we saw, was partly conditioned by the determination to construct a national character who would be 'fit' to rule. Although 1857 might –*might* – have been shy of using the terms openly, this was a story about a 'master race'. By 1945, such talk had, of course, become open with the Nazis. Bergmann is clear about this, nowhere more so than when he speaks directly of the Nazis as such a master race, faced with what he sees as the degraded Italians, especially those of the Resistance who are, in his view, masters of rhetoric but of nothing else. In the film, it is precisely the intention to set up a kind of 'film-rhetoric' against such an ideology. Thus it is that Rossellini determinedly marks the Nazis as the degenerates. Crucially also, for my argument here, that depravity is seen – as was the case in 1857 England and France – in terms of sexuality, first and foremost. Where the homosexual Visconti's focus was on the power of sexuality as such to disrupt an imposed political reality (that of Mussolini's Fascism), Rossellini makes a use of sexuality to try to construct a political norm, against which he will pit a supposed sexual depravity in the Nazis.

Race now clearly enters the picture, in terms of the question of realism. Yet, at this stage, Rossellini's view of the relation of race to reality is under-developed. He starts from a resistance to the idea that a Nazified 'master race' might stake a claim upon reality at all; but he does not yet attack fully the very idea of such mastery, a mastery that gives a specific attitude a privileged access to the real. In *Roma, Città Aperta*, he sticks with the idea that there is, indeed, such a privileged point of view, a privileged camera-angle, as it were: not that of Nazism, but that of a socially conservative Christianity (inimical to homosexuality) that finds its core in Rome and in the church that places its capital and its bedrock right in the centre of that city, in St Peter's basilica. We will return to this in a more developed form in *Paisà*, because that is also where Rossellini continues his engagement with this new realism.

The intrinsic nobility that Rossellini ascribes to his Italians, via his reliance on fictional means (as opposed to a naïve realism), is given form by the combination of political resistance (Manfredi) with Catholic or Christian religious ideals (Don Pietro). The fundamental political point of the film is one that is based on a Christian idea and ideal of self-sacrifice; and we might therefore reasonably suggest that, far from avoiding myth, the film simply prefers the Christian myth over other myths, including those of Nazism or Fascism. Manfredi and Don Pietro will both die at the hands of the Germans; but their spirit will clearly live on, carried by the young boys of Romoletto's gang (including Marcello), who watch the execution of Don Pietro before returning, defiantly, to the city. That closing image is of these future citizens set against a clear Roman skyline. Although he may be crippled – like the city – Romoletto will continue the defiance of resistance to German occupation, and to what he sees as the 'theft' of his city and home, aided in this by Pina's surviving child, Marcello. The religious inflection is combined with the political message here.

The film, then, works through such oppositions in order to give birth to the future city from the ruins of the city destroyed by bombing. Yet we cannot construe this film as a primary example of neorealism, given its clear prioritization of its propagandistic (and fundamentally Christian) message. In some ways, it looks too close to the kind of strategy associated with the Fascism that had dominated Italian film-making in the previous years.

There are some turning-points in the film, also, that work against the emerging shape of neorealist norms. One of these can stand as emblematic. While Manfredi is being tortured, Don Pietro is arrested and brought into Bergmann's offices. Bergmann ostentatiously leaves the door of the torture room open, so that Manfredi can be seen. Yet the problem is starkly posed before us: this is done for the 'benefit' of Don Pietro, and is to be used to encourage this priest to betray his fellow resistance compatriots. When he was arrested, however, Don Pietro's spectacles had been broken; and the film ensures that we know that he has difficulty in seeing what is actually going on. The camera lingers on Don Pietro's face as he screws up his eyes, in an effort to see the reality of the torture. The direction of this is making it obvious to the audience that Don Pietro here cannot see what is actually going on within this Nazi environment. He has instead to infer what is going on through the noise of Manfredi's screams or groans.

In his consideration of this film, Peter Brunette makes the astute observation that the Germans throughout are seen as interlopers in Rome: they clearly do not belong there, even if they have taken the city over and declared it to be, in military terms, an 'open city'. He goes on to argue that 'the Germans are associated with all that is artificial, second-hand, cut off from the organic life of the people'. This is certainly the case, and the various fictionalized moments that Rossellini creates through the film would endorse such a view. Yet Brunette's concise conclusion following this – 'Rome is eternal, the Nazis are temporary' – covers up (or perhaps inadvertently reveals) a complexity regarding the film's claims to be a good example of neorealism.

It is the case, indeed, that the landscape of Rome – those exteriors, including the image of the dome of St Peter's that dominates the closing sequence – is presented as something that transcends its current devastation. This, however, is indicative of what it is in the film that is fundamentally *anti*-realist. Although an ostensibly historical film, detailing specific and symbolic events in the history of Italy's resistance to the forces of Nazism, *Roma, Città Aperta* nonetheless turns its fundamental message – and its eyes and camera – *away* from history. Pina laments the devastation around her, her eyes focused on the horrors of everyday life, and asks, 'Doesn't Christ see us?': she raises the question of what it is that can be *seen*, self-evidently, as reality. In reply, however, Don Pietro takes the view that, essentially, these people living in such material historical reality should instead be looking within, examining their own failings, and asking for forgiveness.

That is a classic Christian motif; but, in this context, the most important point is that it involves turning one's eyes away from what we can see as historical reality, and preferring instead to 'look within'. There – the argument goes – is where we will find a greater reality, and something that transcends the historical. Don Pietro is the character who is there precisely because, as a Christian, he turns the camera away from the reality that exists before us in historical and material terms; and his message is where the film itself comes to rest. Manfredi has been tortured while strung up in an obvious crucifixion position against the wall – and this is what the audience sees even when Don Pietro has lost his spectacles, even when he *cannot* see historical reality. The young boys of the resistance limp back to Rome after the execution of Don Pietro in the shadow of the church, the dome of St Peter's. While these boys have indeed seen material and historical reality – the execution of Don Pietro – the question is posed as to how they will respond: as followers of Manfredi and Francesco, or as followers of St Peter and Don Pietro. The film, then, closes on an ambivalence about realism, in this sense.

In its desire to transcend history, paradoxically, *Roma, Città Aperta* turns our eyes away from history, and asks us to consider that which transcends the specific historical moment. It may be that Rome is indeed an eternal city, in this regard; but as far as the film is concerned, there is a necessary turn away from documentary-style realism. It is in his next film, *Paisà*, that Rossellini will develop his cinematic modes more surely into a new form: a genuinely emergent new realism that does, indeed, focus on the material historical facts of living in the contemporary Italy.

6

Paisà opens as a straightforward documentary, with historical footage of troops landing in Sicily and with accompanying inter-titles describing the historical moment. When it turns from this to the narrative parts of the film, it goes into the first of six episodes, each of which will be punctuated by straight documentary footage. We know from the titles sequence at the beginning that this film comes in six segments; and we will see it develop essentially like a series of Verga-like short stories. These are to be linked, structurally, by one key driver of the film's movement: the map of Italy, which will appear between each episode as the setting of the stories (and the actual Allied invasion/liberation) moves steadily north. The film is primarily an act of geography, an act of the depicting and delineation of space as such. It is a precursor of the road movie in one way; more significantly, it takes the through-the-screen sequences that we saw as the opening shots in films like *La Bête humaine* or *Ossessione* and makes them the basic structural unit of the entire film.

This 'obsessively present tense movie'[28] is one where the real is governed by the issue of presence itself: each of the six episodes focuses on a kind of absolute present tense, by what can be seen in the here-and-now, and on the issue of how the real itself is constructed via the play of presence and absence. In *Roma, Città Aperta*, as we saw, there was a structural interplay between the present material and historical realities (Manfredi, Francesco, Pina, Romoletto) and a spiritual realm that allegedly transcends that reality and which, through religion, stakes a claim as a more fundamental reality (Don Pietro). *Paisà* retains one element of this, in that the fifth episode occurs in a monastery, a world of spiritual interiority that seems to be untouched by the material realities that surround it. However, in this film, such a transcendent stance is anomalous, perhaps even to the extent that the realism of the film calls into question the value or point of religion at all.

It is not that Rossellini abandons Christianity; rather, it is the case that the neorealist aesthetic demands that it assume a different status with respect to the real and material conditions of life: labour, sex and death during a time of war. Brunette argues that 'though Rossellini always deeply enmeshes his characters in a precise environment, both temporally and spatially, what he wants to portray ... is that which transcends this specificity, what is eternal, what is essential in man', and that this is essentially what governs an operative 'tension between the codes of realism and the real'.[29] We should add to this that the politics of realism in *Paisà* essentially requires that this tension starts to resolve itself in favour of the material real itself, driving the film's preferences away from the eternal or

---

[28] Brunette, *Rossellini*, 62.
[29] Ibid., 68, 70.

essential and towards a positive valorization of the specific, the here, the now: a real presence that is material rather than primarily spiritual.

The key episode for our argument is the second. In this, a Black American soldier (who, we will discover, is actually a military-police officer) is extremely drunk, and therefore unable to resist an Italian urchin who 'buys' him. The boy takes the soldier into a puppet-show, in order to hide his action (and the soldier) from the Naples police. This puppet-show is an important central motif for what the film as a whole is about, for it is fundamentally a 'scene-within-a-scene' (like a film-within-a-film) and a representation that brings into question the status of reality itself.

We should recall here the development of this significant motif right through and at the heart of neorealist cinema. Renoir's *La Grand Illusion* begins its action from the consideration of a photograph with its indeterminate image, the 'smudge' that De Boeldieu wants to investigate. Bergmann, in Rossellini's *Roma, Città Aperta*, 'explores' Rome and comes to a reconnaissance-style knowledge of its citizens through his bureaucratic files of photographic images. Now, in *Paisà*, a Black soldier, drunk and hidden from the eyes of the State police (though a military-police officer himself) watches a puppet-show in which a white Crusader fights against a Black Moor. As in the preceding examples, the question that this film poses is about the status of reality and its representations. The soldier breaks through the third wall of the theatre, as it were, and jumps onto the stage to join his racial counterpart, the Black Moor, in a fight against the white (and Christian) Crusader. Where the Christian myth prevailed in *Roma, Città Aperta*, here it is engaged instead in a struggle with a very different mythology; and it is no longer easily triumphant.

In the middle of the episode, there is a pause during which the soldier and the boy sit together while the soldier sings. The song is an old spiritual tune, later made famous by Paul Robeson: 'Nobody knows the trouble I've seen / Nobody knows my sorrow.' It is a song that attends to, and that laments, the underprivileged condition of the African American, those enslaved by the white Christians of the United States and elsewhere. Then, at the close of the episode, the soldier, now sober and fully in surveillance and policing mode as a military policeman, rediscovers the urchin who has stolen his boots. The young boy lives in abject poverty and the soldier realizes that they are both victims: he himself had not seen the troubles and sorrows of the orphan boy. The episode indicates that the causes of poverty and of degradation lie primarily in the Fascist ideology that afflicts the liberator as well as the liberated. An identity is constructed as between the Black soldier and the young impoverished and orphaned Italian boy; but the film seeks to extend that identity beyond the frame, towards the viewing audience.

How does that happen? At one level, of course, in the puppetry scene, the solider simply makes the category mistake in which he takes the representation for the real thing. In doing so, he finds a profound emotional identification with one of the show's protagonists. This is the actualization of a camera-angle, a realization of an attitude or point of view; and it is one that in fact generates an actual reality from the initial impetus of its representation: in very short order, the entire audience has also joined in the real fight, and it is no longer simply the Black soldier on stage. The representation of a fight generates an actual fight; and the structure of the film (that mise-en-abyme of film-within-film) implies that *Paisà* itself can now construct a reality in the world of *its* viewers, in the cinema who, in turn, take their struggles out onto the street.

The realism of *Paisà* is less a matter of aesthetics, and much more crucially a matter of how aesthetics shapes and even determines politics. That is to say, in this film, Rossellini starts to make the move in which neorealism turns out to be about the *construction* of a historical reality, a literal *projection* of reality. It reverses the usual idea that art represents a prior ontological reality, and instead offers us a structure in which art produces historical and material reality.

This returns us to the problem posed by Sartre's waiter, for it relates to the relation between being and acting. Further, it is here that we can properly explore the real significance of the much-vaunted use of non-professional actors in Italian neorealism.

Rossellini did, in fact, use many serious and professional actors in his films; *Paisà* stands out against this general trend, however: most of the acting in this film is done by non-professionals. In this respect, it is also like Vittorio de Sica's *Ladri di biciclette* of 1948. In that film, De Sica had two non-professionals (Lamberto Maggiorani and Enzo Staiola) to play the roles of the two central characters, Antonio Ricci and his son, Bruno. *Ladri di biciclette* is a film that is clearly driven by its narrative: an unemployed man finds work as a bill-poster advertising films, and is aided by his son; to retain his hard-found job, he needs a bicycle, and he and his wife pawn their bed sheets (a double-bed sheet, or *matrimoniale* in Italian) to secure one; while working (with his son) the bicycle is stolen; and the film follows the quest for the thief, a quest that ends with the father's disgrace as he is himself caught while trying to steal someone else's bicycle. The acting, driven by the emotional charge that shapes this narrative, is in fact persuasive in that it often resembles a classical Hollywood-style performance.

Paisà is markedly different. Its six episodes operate as the equivalent of a short-story collection; but the effect of the brevity and conciseness of each episode is one that precludes the development of 'character' as such, and the consequence is acting that looks genuinely amateurish at many (most) points. This is highly significant, but not for the reasons that criticism of neorealism usually adduces (relating to authenticity, 'real people' and so on). The significance is to be found in recalling the origins of visual realism in Courbet.

We should recall that, when Courbet made his realist turn, he did not depict individual characters. In his *Stone Breakers*, for instance, he presented not individuated labourers, but labour-as-such; in *A Burial at Ornans*, he showed death-as-such; in *Demoiselles de La Seine*, he painted sex-as-such. In one way, that attitude conformed to an ancient aesthetic model: famously, Aristotle in *Poetics* argued that, in a tragic theatre, it is plot above all that is determining: characters are there in order to fulfil the demands of the plot-as-such. This persists in a neorealist film such as *Paisà*. The amateur nature of the acting ensures that we are not diverted into a sentimental identification with any of the protagonists in the six episodes; rather, it is the general plot-structure that generates – or, as I now argue – actively *constructs* a reality: realism to be lived and experienced by the viewing audience, as it were. That plot-structure is itself given to us by a map: the actual map of Italy that punctuates the episodes and that – as in Grierson's *Night Mail* – identifies the nation. It does this in a literal sense: it identifies each separate part of the country with each other part, and thus unifies a single identity called 'Italy': the fellow-country-people of the paisà, now also including the viewer, whose task it is to realize – to actualize or make real and present – this new country and its new realism.

9

The politics of fact, and the danger of totalitarian Realism

1

We leave Italian neorealism with a new sense that post-war realism is to be defined as a kind of action-aesthetic. These films are there not so much to represent a reality that has an ontological priority and that exists, self-sufficient and whole, prior to its representations; rather, they are there to generate and to construct that reality for the first time through a provocation of the viewer into historical action. The new aesthetic is one of 'pre-presentation' and not 're-presentation'. In this respect, although the narrative focus of Italian neorealist films may be on what has recently happened in historical terms, these films are nonetheless primarily oriented to a future, and to a world-to-come; and they are focused on a more or less propagandistic effort to engage the viewer in the production of that future. To this extent, they fulfil absolutely and entirely – though by a different means – the ideology of Grierson's documentary realism: they educate the viewer by propagating beliefs that will give that viewer a norm by which to make and experience the world in the future; and such a world will differ from that which has been portrayed in the film's narrative. In some ways, it might even be a future that exists in the strictest opposition to the norms of the world that the film portrayed, as in the disavowal of injustices, unemployment and the various forms of society that Fascism or Nazism had tried to make and whose nefarious and degrading ideologies the films relentlessly expose in the narrative that they present.

If we look at the specific content of Italian neorealist films, the future is one that is to be based upon the demand for justice; but crucially, it is to be based upon a justice that acknowledges certain fundamental conditions that shape material human living: the conditions of labour (and its correlate in structural and politicized unemployment), the force of sex (and its potential political radicalism, as constitutive of events in a private sphere that, superficially at least, seem to have the capacity to escape public political control) and the inevitability of death (and how a society constructs symbols and beliefs that seem to circumvent this simple fact of human existence). The examples are fairly obvious and are clearly delineated. De Sica's *Ladri di biciclette* explores the degradation of human life that is a consequence of unemployment, and it does so by dignifying labour as such. Visconti's *Ossessione* examines how the eroticism of sexualized desire strives to construct a reality that escapes from the injustices associated with Fascism. *Roma, Città Aperta* proposes religious transcendence as a means of avoiding death; but then, as Rossellini approaches neorealism proper, his *Paisà* places the inevitability of death into a political context of resistance, with the defiant adoption of the term 'partisan' – which the Fascists had intended as a derogatory and mocking descriptor – as the dignifying headstone of a grave.

All of these films, however, end with questions: they orient us towards indeterminacy, and away from the certainties that are grounded in any fundamentalist belief-system. This makes them unsettling, for they all show that the striving after reality is something that prevailing political conditions of Nazism and Fascism always circumvent, precisely because 'striving after reality' is actually 'striving after uncertainty and contingency'. In the nineteenth century, as I showed at the opening of this book, censorship was used to divert attention from real conditions of human life, to banish these conditions from representation and from easy availability to a public assembly or society. Now, under the ideologies associated with Nazism and Fascism, there is always a screen established that, instead of giving a view on the material realities of the world (as in Zola, James and others whose interests in screens, windows and 'houses of fiction' we have seen), actually serves instead to occlude our view of it: the reality that we seek lies hidden under a fictionalized or mythic account of what constitutes the real world. The ideology of Nazism and that of Fascism – against both of which neorealism sets itself – are founded in totalitarian fundamentalism. We saw this through Arendt's analysis in my previous chapter; and it is fundamentalism as such that is at issue here.

This, we remember, is the lesson that Rossellini learns when he makes *Roma, Città Aperta*. There, he had essentially sought to place the fundamentalism of a religious creed against that of far-right politics; and it is only when he starts to abandon this, as in *Paisà* (notwithstanding its monastery episode), that he begins properly to entertain reality, by admitting into the central position in his film aesthetic a genuine historical contingency, uncertainty and the accidental as the primary conditions that govern labour, sex and death. Neorealism, we might say, is informed by the demand to give rein to the unpredictable, and to open the future to possibilities that the world as depicted in the film's narrative strives to arrest. Such an opening is an opening to the possibility of contingency and of accident; and thus it is an opening to the very opposite of the determination of reality through the power of narrative.

In essence, then, what we are seeing here is a clarification of our definition of reality itself: reality is defined as, in its essence, all that is the contingent and the accidental. It operates as a kind of openness to future possibility. This is what neorealism enables us now to discover. This would appear, superficially and at least at first glance, to be close to what a later thinker, Fredric Jameson, considers as a fundamental definition of history. 'History is what hurts,' he writes, in a formulation that might be rightly celebrated for its succinct precision. However, Jameson's view here is in fact completely the opposite of what the argument from neorealism shows. The reason for this is to be found in Jameson's own Marxist desire to subscribe to a politics that is totalizing. Having argued that 'history is what hurts', he nonetheless argues that history is also 'the experience of Necessity', which 'can be apprehended only through its effects, and never directly as some reified force'.[1] Jameson here offers with one hand what he rapidly takes away with the other: history as lived experience in all its unknowability. In its place, he offers instead an apprehension of history – a form of knowing it rather than a mode of experiencing it – which depends upon the insertion of historical accident into a narrative necessity. This is the very totalization against which neorealism operated.

Neorealism discovers that it is in Nazism and in Fascism – precisely because of their intrinsic tendency to totalitarianism – that what constitutes reality is determined for us by an established power that controls narrative, and that thus appears to control history as the enactment of a predetermined necessity. That is to say: both Nazism and Fascism conspire to make us ignore empirical and ontological reality (the realities of an intrinsically unpredictable experience), and to replace that with a specific narrative account of reality that pretends to offer total explanation of any and every accidental or contingent event, thereby rendering the events anything but contingent or accidental and reinserting them instead under the rubric of historical necessity.

This is how narrative fictions deviate into myth. It also helps explain the persuasive force of such ideologies. They are 'optimistic' in two senses. First, they propose a future in which all can be known, where all is clear, where there are no

---

[1] Jameson, *The Political Unconscious*, 102.

obscurities and no confusions in our thinking: there is only one way of seeing the world. They are also Optimistic in that they conform to a quasi-Leibnizian view of the world, in which some underlying (and invisible) force exists: a theocratic principle which can explain away any misfortune as a necessary step towards the fulfilment of the prophecy of eternal perfection.

Neither Nazism nor Fascism can contemplate the possibility of surprise. Given that, for these ideologies, reality is and has to be always-already-known, and understood through the narratives of Nazism, Fascism or, indeed, totalitarian Bolshevism – nothing unforeseen can possibly happen. In short, neorealism, by opening us up to uncertainty and undecidability, resists compliance with any and all forms of totalization. This is the real meaning of neorealism-as-resistance. It is also the reason why it prefers documentary – no matter how ostensibly 'pessimistic' it may be – over constructed narrative. The ruling powers of established totalizing politics – powers that seek to police all narratives and to give legitimacy only to one overarching account of historical necessity – are profoundly coercive; and the real impulse of Italian neorealism is to resist such coercion.

To gain and retain political control in a society is, in these terms, to gain and retain control over what counts as the narratives of necessity that go to 'explain' the world and to give that world's citizens their 'common sense', a common sense that can brook no critique or opposition. It is imperative, to those who thus control those dominant narratives, that they retain the privileges that go with such control; and they must work, therefore, to arrest any possibility that the underprivileged might claim that their historical 'hurt' (be it via impoverished unemployment, frustrated desire, unequal distributions of mortality or of bio-political life expectations) can claim its proper status.

It seems clear that what is at stake now, in this new post-war politics of realism, is revealed finally for what it has always tacitly been: control over the opinions of the public in the face of the defiant and recalcitrant material facts. Yet, paradoxically, it is the very *contingency of historical facts* that renders history recalcitrant in the first place. This essentially defines the realism of the contemporary world and its political predicaments. Yet, as the paradox here suggests, this needs to be understood with much nuance. After all, Dickens has already demonstrated that the acknowledgement of fact, without imagination, is disastrous for a social polity: that is one core principle that we can take from the very opening pages of *Hard Times*. It is, therefore, not the case that a post-war realism pays complete homage to 'fact' as some kind of necessity; rather, the point is that the new politics of realism is concerned with how we can determine what will be the facts of the future. It would be a fundamentally conservative ideology – and I include much of what passes as Marxism in this – that suggests that fact is aligned with historical necessity. Our new politics of realism, post-war, breaks the supposed intimate link between these, and instead opens fact to possibility and imagination. Against that, all conservative ideologies turn, instead, to the manufacture of opinion and of consent. This is what we need to consider as we approach some concluding observations in the argument of this book.

The politics of a manufactured 'public opinion' (or 'common sense' as accepted ideology) with its accompanying 'manufactured consent' confront the resistant realities of human being, realities that are shaped by the openness to possibility (another word for which is, of course, 'freedom'); and this – which can be concisely described as the argument over the so-called alternative facts of a Trumpian or populist post-truth society – is what constitutes the politics of realism in our time. 'Post-truth' is, of course, one particularly politically insidious and intellectually troubling version of our contemporary forms of censorship; and at its root is a determination to manufacture consent for a politics that reduces the range of possibilities that human beings can make by self-realization through work and imaginative or empathetic social relations, or – crudely put – to manufacture consent for a reduction in the scope of human freedom. This, if you will, is the new realpolitik, in which the possibility of establishing and extending freedom as a factual possibility is in danger of being devalued and re-described as mere opinion. In concluding this study, we can explore what this means for our contemporary politics of realism.

2

We can begin from 1921, and with an intervention whose strength we have already witnessed (in Chapter 6). It was in 1921 that Walter Lippmann published *Public Opinion*, a book that was hugely influential on Grierson and on many within the field of sociology. He starts from the historical moment when, as he puts it, people began to feel disconcerted by the fact that the realities of the world round about them no longer fitted into the paradigms to which they had been accustomed. The breakout of war in 1914 across Europe disrupted not just things on the ground but also in the minds of people.[2]

---

[2] In some ways, Lippmann did for sociology what Thomas S. Kuhn would do for the history of science in *The Structure of Scientific Revolutions* (1962; revised 2nd edn, University of Chicago Press, Chicago, 1970).

Lippmann starts from a neo-Kantian distinction that he takes as fundamental to all human behaviour. There is the world as it actually exists (which we can here call a world of contingency) and there is the world as we believe or 'know' it to exist (here, construed as necessity). In Lippmann's account, these two separate worlds do not always coincide, because we understand the world primarily through our determination to make sense of it. We require its 'accidental' and unexplained events to fit into an already existing narrative determination, or a kind of closed geometric shape that renders the world recognizable. We therefore prioritize our own sense of what the world is (that is to say, the world as we know it, narrate it or visualize it) over the world as it actually is (with its contingences, accidents and openness to change); and we ask that the latter conform to the former, or that contingency subjects itself to the triumph of the will of necessity. In the final analysis here, realism itself becomes aligned with necessity. In such a case, political realism now states that the world as it actually is *must* be the world as we want it to be, however false that may be as a serious political proposition.[3]

When Fredric Jameson argued in 1981 that 'texts come before us as the always-already-read,'[4] he was essentially reiterating, in relation to the text, what Lippmann had stated about the world: the world too comes before us 'always-already-known', as it were. Lippmann's key insight is essentially one – like Jameson's, in fact – that relates to ideology: we understand the world and make sense of it only because we have a prior image of it that enables us to come to terms with it. Lippmann is interested in where this prior image comes from; and the answer he finds is 'Public Opinion'. It is important for us to note here that the prioritization of 'public opinion' over historical contingency essentially censors the reality of the contingent world of history and of potential freedom out of consideration. 'Public Opinion' works by ignoring the realities of the contingent world, with profoundly damaging consequences for the condition of social and political human freedoms.[5]

In his 1921 study, Lippmann begins from recent historical events, especially the shock of the Great War as it arose and spread. He points out that 'As late as

---

[3] This position is recognizable, of course, as what Marxism calls 'false consciousness'. It also describes the increasingly fantastical world depicted by post-truth politicians, such as Donald Trump or Boris Johnson. The political danger in this becomes clear when the post-truth politician starts to make their fantasy into the only legitimate or legal reality, such as we see in oppressive regimes such as those of Viktor Orbán or Recep Tayyip Erdoğan or Xi Jinping, for typical examples, in which attempts to question the imposed fantasy result in imprisonment.
[4] Jameson, *Political Unconscious*, 9.
[5] This may be one reason why the manipulation of 'Public Opinion' is such a formidable weapon in populist politics: it seeks to reduce the doubts and uncertainties that come with political complexity down instead to the immediacy of a cliché or a simplistic political slogan.

July 25th [1914] men were making goods that they would not be able to ship, buying goods that they would not be able to import, careers were being planned, enterprises contemplated, hopes and expectations entertained, all in the belief that the world as known was the world as it was.'[6] The point he is making is that the world of fact (the material consequences of war) is about to intrude upon the world as people believed or wanted it to be. He is indicating that historical fact and circumstance can alert us to the inadequacies of the fictions by which we live our daily lives. In the case of war, those fictions simply could not accommodate the sudden real and historical experience, or the facts that changed the world as we knew it. Crudely put, the fact of war shocked people into action: they realized that their future had to be fought for, if they wanted it to assume anything like the image that they had constructed for it through their 'common-sense' normality and clichéd thinking.

If anything, this condition was made much more general in the wake of the Second World War than it was even in the Great War that had provoked Lippmann's arguments. As Tony Judt points out, 'in those countries occupied by Nazi Germany', including most of Europe, 'World War Two was *primarily* a civilian experience' and thus (unlike the Great War) a 'near universal experience' for all whom it touched.[7] Judt alludes to the prevailing images of the immediate aftermath of the war, and in doing so he reprises the deeply pessimistic bleakness that dominates the imagery of Italian neorealist cinema in words that might be a straight description of the classis neorealist films we have seen. 'Photographs and documentary films of the time show pitiful streams of helpless civilians trekking through a blasted landscape of broken cities and barren fields. Orphaned children wander forlornly past groups of worn out women picking over heaps of masonry. Shaven-headed deportees and concentration camp inmates in striped pyjamas stare listlessly at the camera, starving and diseased.'[8] This was a war that shocked the entire civilian population even more than it shocked the military. The world and our perceptions of it, and our expectations of its realities, became radically uncertain.

Lippmann argues a general rule that an expectation of what will happen supplants the reality of what does happen in our consciousness. From this, he constructs his fundamental tripartite explanation of how it is that the phenomenon that we now know as 'Public Opinion' finds its force. 'The war,' he writes, 'furnished many examples of this pattern: the casual fact, the creative

[6] Lippmann, *Public Opinion*, 3.
[7] Tony Judt, *Postwar: A History of Europe Since 1945* (2005; repr. Pimlico, London, 2007), 13–14.
[8] Ibid., 13.

imagination, the will to believe, and out of these three elements a counterfeit of reality to which there was a violent instinctive response.'[9] Historical contingency (the 'casual fact'), narrative (the 'creative imagination') and the coercions of necessity (the 'will to believe') are all at play here. They work together as a play of forces through which we do not arrive at anything like the material and empirical 'what happens', but rather, they conspire together to yield 'a counterfeit of reality'; and it is according to the logic of such counterfeits that we live (making goods that we cannot ship, and so on). As in the case of Riefenstahl's construction of images, it is as if we allow the perfection of a geometric shape (those triangles of military tents arranged into large rectangles, perfectly measured and ordered) to supplant and act as a counterfeit substitute for the actual content of the geometry (the Nazis who used such aesthetic order as a cover to divert attention from the atrocities they committed, or, worse, to propose those atrocities as themselves constitutive of aesthetic and political beauty).

In turn, that counterfeit is what underpins the construction or manufacture of public opinion in Lippmann's analysis. Lippmann's point here is that, when expectations of the real are constructed successfully – as in the case of the Attorney-General via the reading of 'revolutionary literature' to which I referred in Chapter 6 – then humans act *as if* the world necessarily conforms to those expectations when, in fact, the reality of the world passes by in what is quite possibly an entirely different fashion. The fact that people act in this 'as-if' fashion means, however, that they are essentially *agreeing* with the fiction that has been generated by the 'as-if' expectations; and in that mass agreement, we find the essence of a 'public opinion'. This is the manufacture of public opinion which in turns secures a manufactured consensual consent, consent to a political condition which, if properly scrutinized, would not in fact receive assent.

Further, it is extremely convenient to agree communally in this way, because to disagree would set us apart from what now passes as 'common sense reality'; and, thus set apart, we would find ourselves in a position that is not only isolated but also one that lacks legitimacy in the eyes of the mass, and that thus lacks purchase upon the world. 'Public opinion', based on the ascendancy of the fictions constructed by narrative necessity over historical contingency, is profoundly coercive, especially when it operates as (a fabricated) 'common sense'. The question that arises, for us, is perhaps obvious: When consent is manufactured in this way, then to what extent is it properly 'consent' at all? It is only when that question is raised that the politics of realism becomes open to the

---

[9] Lippmann, *Public Opinion*, 9–10.

possibilities of critique; it is only when the question is raised that we begin to see that a manufactured public opinion is coercive and designed to restrict real-life possibilities and material freedoms.

One of the early conclusions that Lippmann draws from his propositions is that 'it is clear enough that under certain conditions men respond as powerfully to fictions as they do to realities, and that in many cases they help to create the very fictions to which they respond'.[10] This accords entirely with Arendt's view – described earlier – that totalitarian regimes operate by the construction of 'alternative realities' that are actually fictions, based on 'alternative facts' that are simply the vehicle through which the openness to change and to future possibility is constrained. The purpose of 'alternative facts' is to give the appearance of determinate necessity to a specific (and actually contingent) political proposition: closing a geometric circle or sphere, say, instead of leaving it open to free movement.

The perpetrators and agents of those closed and restrictive fictions then work to make them so normative that not only they become credible but also – as persuasive counterfeit – so that they substitute for material realities and, most importantly, so that they preclude the possibilities of extending the freedom of human actions. In extreme cases, they do this by exerting full control over the terms of labour, over the conditions of sexual behaviour or practice – and in the end and at the extremes, they control biological survival itself.[11] Crucially, by presenting the fiction as a matter of ordered necessity, they secure compliance and complicity with the restrictive project, and thus with the restraint on human possibilities for the construction of any new and more open realities.

This is the new realpolitik of our times: power not only trumps morality and principle, but in this new version of realpolitik, power also trumps the very facts of reality, a reality whose contingency would promise freedom, if only the contingency of history would be accepted and embraced. Behind this, therefore, is the most fundamental aspect of all in contemporary politics: power precludes people extending their range of possibilities and freedoms, and insidiously coerces those very people into a condition of complicity with their own enslavement to the ideology of the existing power itself. That is totalitarianism at work; and, perilously, it proposes itself quite simply as political realism. It sometimes tries

---

[10] Ibid., 10.
[11] Examples abound. Consider, as paradigmatic examples: anti-Trade Union legislation (restricting the power of labour); all gendered legislation, from control of contraception to sequestering of activities by gender (restricting sexual activities); the murder of journalists, most obviously in the recent case of Jamal Khashoggi (restricting biological existence itself).

to dignify itself and to give itself a would-be honourable or respectable 'tradition' by calling itself realpolitik.

3

The initial coinage of the term 'Realpolitik' dates, in fact, from the historical moment with which I opened this study. Ludwig August von Rochau invented the term in his *Grundsätze der Realpolitik*, published first in 1853 following the 1848 revolutionary ferment across Europe. There, he argued that a politics based upon abstract reasoning that yielded fundamental moral principles was less effective than a politics that acknowledged that nothing could be done without power.[12] Most contemporary thinkers ascribed the first delineation of public opinion to Lippmann, but, interestingly, it was actually Rochau who described it first, under the term *Volksglaube*, meaning 'people's belief' or 'national belief'.[13] The issue facing the politics of realism in our contemporary world derives from a post-war condition in which the nation increasingly determined what constituted legitimate 'belief' for its peoples. The 'will of the people', a phrase redolent of contemporary populism, has its origins, of course not just in Nazi and Fascist ideology but also in its presentation in films such as *Triumph des Willens*; and the question facing us, basically, is whether we have ever actually properly escaped the ideology that governed the making of that film.

In his history of realpolitik, John Bew describes Rochau's position clearly, and he notes the contemporary relevance for us of Rochau's initial formulations. For Rochau, as he originally worked through the meaning of his newly minted neologism, in realpolitik 'Ideas were important in politics – increasingly so, in the democratic age – but their importance was to be judged by their political force rather than their purity or elegance'.[14] Further, the development of the term, and the necessity that called for Rochau to formulate it, dates from a moment in the mid-nineteenth century whose predicaments resemble, in some respects, those of today: 'the collision of the Enlightenment with the bloody process of national

---

[12] Rochau's work remains untranslated into English. For a detailed analysis of his thinking, see John Bew, *Realpolitik* (Oxford University Press, Oxford, 2016); and for a brief summary of the way in which the term has been used and abused, historically, see John Bew, 'The Real Origins of Realpolitik', *The National Interest*, 25 February 2014, available at: https://nationalinterest.org/article/the-real-origins-realpolitik-9933?page=0%2C4 (accessed 2 December 2019).
[13] It is perhaps important here to note that, according to Bew, *Realpolitik*, 8: 'Rochau was not concerned with the construction of worldviews but the business of politics.'
[14] Bew, *Realpolitik*, 6.

state formation and great power politics'. That world was one, like ours, where there was 'a combustion of new ideas about liberty and social order alongside rapid industrialization, class antagonism, sectarianism, the rise of nationalism ... and increasing international rivalry'.[15]

The moment was propitious for a revival of some of this when Lippmann was working over half a century later; but he engaged the pressing questions in terms of a new media age that was unknowable to Rochau. It is also an age when Lippmann has seen the power of modern propaganda, especially in relation to war. In particular, Lippmann is aware of the socio-political and cultural power of the visual image. 'Photographs,' he writes, 'have the kind of authority over imagination today, which the printed word had yesterday, and the spoken word before that. They seem utterly real.'[16] As he elaborates this, he turns to the moving image in cinema, and notes the propaganda power of D. W. Griffiths, whose *Birth of a Nation* essentially helps to consolidate the ideology of the Ku Klux Klan. In addition to this compelling power of the photographic and cinematic image, we might now add the compelling power of abstract mathematical reasoning, with its contemporary version of Nazi order: bureaucratic organization, the organigramme, or the so-called rational-economic actor of neoconservative politics.[17]

Two key features dominate here: immediacy and stereotype. Immediacy intrinsically entails the denial of the possibility of criticism. Lippmann notes that, in cinema, the images come at us seemingly 'without human meddling'; and, as a result, 'they are the most effortless food of the mind conceivable.' If there is no human meddling or mediation – that is, if they are genuinely 'immediate' and coming at speed – then there is nothing obvious with which to engage critically: the images *just are as they are* and they operate as direct representations of a world that *just is as it is*. The spectator eagerly and willingly swallows what she, he, or they sees/see, as 'effortless food'. In this, cinema images differ from other modes of slower representation, modes that, in their more leisurely pace, allow openings in and through which we can insert the possibility that we will interrupt them with independent thinking: chewing things over, as it were. 'Any description in words, or even any inert picture,' writes Lippmann, 'requires an effort of memory before a picture exists in the mind', and in that effort, we are given the possibility of our own critical intervention. By contrast, 'in the

---

[15] Ibid., 17.
[16] Lippmann, *Public Opinion*, 61
[17] I explored this in extensive historical detail in the 'Introduction' to my *Postmodernism* (Harvester-Wheatsheaf, 1993), esp. pp. 5–14.

screen the whole process of observing, describing, reporting, and the imagining, has been accomplished for you.'[18] In this account, critique is forestalled by the technology itself, for the film moves along so fast that it leaves no time or space for the independent thinking that would *intervene* to mediate its images for the viewer. Films come at us ostensibly always-already-mediated. To keep with Lippmann's metaphor, we are like the animal young whose parent has pre-digested our food for us, and we take it then straight from the parent's mouth as it is regurgitated. A certain infantilism underlies this.

Next, stereotype reduces complexity to crudity. The deployment of stereotypes enables a sense that the world we see is one we immediately recognize with an assumed familiarity: the external image simplifies and thereby permits an easy correspondence with the general image that we have in our head before seeing the film. We are as if 'at home' in the stereotype; and we are certainly at home with ourselves as we watch it: 'They [the stereotypes] may not be a complete picture of the world, but they are a picture of a possible world to which we are adapted.' This is a world where 'people have their well-known places, and do certain expected things. We feel at home there. We fit in. We are members'.[19] There is no room here for the 'defamiliarization' (that Formalist *ostranenie*) that was so important in my account of realism at an earlier historical stage of its development. In short, we have been literally accommodated; and in that accommodation lies the confirmation of compliance and conformity. We are thus co-opted into an agreement with the world as presented: it is our world, as it were, and we are at home, here, now, immediately present-to-ourselves, and thus incapable of entertaining doubts – but the inability to entertain doubt is also the inability to envisage possibility or change in us, our home, our world, our 'present'.

It is in this way that modern media can construct or manufacture public opinion. When we act in accordance with the norms that immediacy and stereotype produce, then we simply confirm the supposed validity of the world as presented. It is important to note that, in this account of public opinion, criticism – indeed, thinking as such – has been forestalled. It follows that the control of these images is an enormous aid to those who want to control the behaviour of 'the masses'. The State has a necessary interest, therefore, in public opinion, and in the manufacture and control of its norms. The new realism is aware of this state of affairs, and is structurally resistant to it.[20]

---

[18] Ibid., 61.
[19] Ibid., 63. For the full argument regarding stereotypes, see pp. 33, 54–9.
[20] On the relation of this to free speech, see Christopher Hitchens in debate with Shashi Tharoor at the Hay Festival in 2007, where Hitchens says that free speech relates simply to political maturity

4

Hannah Arendt makes a series of observations about the relation of the reality of material and historical fact to the malleability of opinion. The currency of such an opposition – one that is prevalent at the present day – is part of the terrain of totalitarianism, and is central to what we may now call 'totalitarian realism'. Totalitarianism has a fundamental resort to propaganda – and this is why we have been afraid of appealing to propaganda as part of the politics of realism, and therefore hesitant in understanding Grierson's attitude to it. After 1945, and especially after the post-war period of Stalinism, 1945–53, we have associated propaganda firmly with totalitarian rule, as something that is coercive and therefore repellent. It is indeed coercive, rather than merely persuasive. It aims to coerce reality to fit its theory, as it were: it will force the world into the shape that the totalitarian rulers decide is 'normal' by creating images of life that are normative. Thus, as Arendt points out, 'totalitarianism will not be satisfied to assert, in the face of contrary facts, that unemployment does not exist; it will abolish unemployment benefits as part of its propaganda'.[21] Obviously and self-evidently (it will claim in an example such as this), if no one is claiming unemployment benefits then, ipso facto, there can be no unemployment.

Taken to the kinds of extreme to which Stalin would take it, the Revolution could be re-written not just through the destruction of books and documents but also through the destruction of the authors and readers of those documents.[22] As Orwell knew, the 'memory hole' and its coequal political instrument of 'vaporization' were an important aspect of totalitarian politics, because totalitarianism took a version of 'realpolitik' as an absolute necessity; and abolishing memory meant not just abolishing the archive of memory (in documentary form) but also abolishing those individuals who had memories in the first place as the most extreme form of censorship.

The actual substance of propaganda, however – and its claims to realistic validity – has to be given sufficient reality through its acceptance by a mass of

---

and that therefore 'part of growing up is to say . . . I don't care about Public Opinion', available at: https://www.youtube.com/watch?v=CTPj2UEtdzA (accessed 20 December 2019). We might compare Jean-François Lyotard's suggestion that the genuine writer does not care for or seek her, his or their audience. *Öffentlichkeit* is anathema to genuine art; or, as he puts it in his dialogues with Jean-Loup Thébaud, *Just Gaming* (trans. Wlad Godzich; Manchester: Manchester University Press, 1985), 8: 'One writes only in the reader's absence. I mean not only in the physical absence of a reader; there must be a kind of absence of readers to write the way some of us wish to write. The reader's solicitation . . . must be suspended and, in a way, one must have no interest in it.'

[21] Arendt, *Origins of Totalitarianism*, 446–7.
[22] Ibid., 447.

people. Contemporary propaganda – propaganda in an age of a supposed post-truth politics – depends upon the manufactured consent and compliance of the 'will of the people'. It is this will, rather than reality itself, that a totalitarian political establishment, intent on preserving its own privileges, must now control, if it is to make the preservation of privilege and advantage and inequality become 'realistic' and thus unquestionable. However, the totalitarian State can make its own myth prevail not by persuading 'the people' that its account of reality is more 'realistic'; rather, all it need do is to abolish the distinction between truth and lies; and one important way of doing this is to reduce 'knowledge' to 'information', and to make information the newest and most economically powerful commodity-resource, as we will see later in this chapter.

Such a totalitarian State no longer needs to control reality directly; rather, it simply aims to control 'the will of the people' about a historical state of affairs that now has no basis in truth; and, consequently, totalitarian realism simply disables a criticism based upon the exposure of falsehood. It will do this by manufacturing consent for its power; and, to establish such consent, it will manufacture a world in which 'reality' itself is no longer the basis for any political 'realism'. This new political realism will simply ground itself in a manufactured public opinion, and it will bypass any scrutiny other than that of 'the people', a 'people' whose will has also been manufactured without reference to truth, to historical facts, or to the possibilities of actions that can articulate human freedoms.

This is an extremely bold move. When the material realities of the world no longer act as an anchor to underpin any description of the world, then the totalitarian State (and its agents) can act out its myths and fantasies with complete impunity. There is no longer any ground on which to contest or criticize the world that it manufactures. If we add here that the material reality of the world is itself contingent, and that such contingency is the basis of human freedom, we arrive at the dispiriting and frightening conclusion that a contemporary political realism is consistent with – and indeed is the underpinning of – the most basic attack on all those social and political actions that are the basis of human freedom. Worse still, the State has in many cases managed to coerce public institutions – including above all the institutions of education – into an almost conspiratorial compliance with this assault. This is a predicament that has not gone unnoticed in literature, the arts and the world of cultural criticism in general.[23]

---

[23] See my *Complicity: Criticism between Collaboration and Commitment* (Rowman & Littlefield, 2016) and *The New Treason of the Intellectuals* (Manchester University Press, Manchester, 2019), for extended examination of this with particular reference to the institution of the university.

5

Let us here recall the historical situation around Flaubert in 1857, shortly after the production of Rochau's analysis of realpolitik as the key determinant of political reality in this period in Europe. We know that Flaubert became a scapegoat for a more general set of anxieties about the power of the *Revue de Paris*, a power that might endorse anti-imperial feelings and actions. This structure sets an important political precedent for the succeeding historical period (right up to the present day) in the construction of a realpolitik that is concerned with the gaining and holding of power rather than with the establishment of any kind of moral integrity as the basis for a good polity. The precedent lies in the political deployment of the scapegoat.

Crucially, the scapegoat in any similar circumstance must be characterized as one thing above all: she, he or they are presented as an 'enemy of the people', which now means 'one who will question the will of the people'. That is, the scapegoat figure is one whose views and values are other than those endorsed as normative by State power, or one who is inherently sceptical about the ways in which constructed opinion masquerades as natural and spontaneous. In a word: the scapegoat is the critic; in two words, the critical intellectual.

It is not for nothing that this period in Europe marks the rise not just of institutions of learning such as the modern university, but also the rise to pre-eminence of the figure of 'the intellectual', such as we saw in Turgenev earlier. For a significant instance, Rodin's great sculpture, now known as *The Thinker*, was initially cast in 1880 and, at that time, Rodin thought of it as *The Poet*. It was modelled on Dante, cast nude and (as a constituent element in Rodin's proposed grand sculpture, *The Gates of Hell*) as if overlooking the *Inferno* of Dante's imagination. As he worked through his experiments in making this figure, Rodin read and reread Dante, but he often found that 'his vision of Dante was "not close enough to reality"'; and it was for this reason that he had to make several attempts at making his sculpture. It was only when he could afford to have live models in his studio that 'the word gave way to the reality of moving flesh, stretched muscle, arched backs, to provocative buttocks, grasping hands, collapsed bodies'.[24] This could pass as a description of Courbet, of course, or of Caillebotte; and it is what lies behind Rodin's own celebrated and famous formulation that 'What makes my *Thinker* think is that he thinks not only with

---

[24] Albert E. Elsen et al., *Rodin's Art* (Oxford University Press, Oxford, 2003), 169–70. We might here add, ibid., 170: 'His discoveries in the living bodies of men and women ... gave the sensual striving and restless despair in Baudelaire's poetry new and personal meaning.'

his brain, with his knotted brow, his distended nostrils and compressed lips, but with every muscle of his arms, back and legs, with his clenched fist and gripping toe'.[25]

This new intellectual, this 'thinker-poet' as embodied in Rodin's iconic sculpture, is clearly seen as a harbinger of material and physical change, and it is for this reason that the intellectual faces censorship almost as a matter of course. It is also for this reason that a totalitarian State wants to hive off the intellectual – and even thinking as such – into institutions that it can try to control and constrain. The university, the art gallery and, above all, the very institution of aesthetic criticism itself is just such a controlled ghetto or 'labour-camp', when considered from the point of view of a State that is concerned to protect existing privileges and to present an unjust historical condition as necessary and realistic. The more that the institution of criticism 'professionalizes' itself via such institutionalization, the more it sequesters itself from the real conditions of everyday political life. Yet it is vital to note that this 'professionalization' has been encouraged by the very institutions of criticism themselves. Professionalization is what has yielded accreditation, most obviously in the case of the higher education institutions of advanced economies.

Accreditation – which gives an individual the authority to work as an intellectual in a university, say – increasingly requires compliance with an entire suite of bureaucratic practices. Those practices take for granted certain ideological principles that are, largely, based upon what Mark Fisher has called 'capitalist realism', which he defines as 'the widespread sense that not only is capitalism the only viable political and economic system, but also that it is now impossible even to *imagine* a coherent alternative to it'.[26] Thus, for example, it is taken for granted that the relation of teacher to student is one of provider to consumer in a transactional process that is driven by a financial contract. This is one consequence of the reduction of knowledge to information, making the organic act of knowing things (which would generate democratic discussion) into a saleable commodity (which generates only commerce and financial transactions or economic activity). The contract here is designed to yield a financial surplus for the consumer, through the increased social, political and – above all – financial inequalities that it drives in a society: higher salaries

---

[25] For this much-cited phrase, see, for the most helpful example, Debora Silverman, *Art Nouveau in Fin-de-Siècle France: Politics, Psychology, and Style* (University of California Press, Los Angeles and London, 1992), 261. Silverman's account focuses at length on this idea of the physical manifestation of concept in Rodin.

[26] Fisher, *Capitalist Realism*, 2.

or wages as a so-called graduate dividend. It is important to note that this is not merely incidental: it is now a structural requirement for accreditation. It is endorsed by university leaderships who themselves seek endorsement – and advantage – by demonstrating their compliance with governmental directives. Thus it is that we arrive at a 'realism' that is entirely at odds with any possibility of criticism of establishment political power; and thus it is that this institution becomes complicit in the reduction of genuine human freedoms. The task is not to produce the intellectual; rather it is to produce the compliant consumer who will benefit personally from adherence to the norms of 'capitalist realism' in which increases in the inequalities of human possibility become institutionalized and formalized as normative.

Behind the censorious attacks that we have seen operative in the cases of Flaubert, Baudelaire and many intellectuals and artists since their day lies the tacit claim that the State is the real voice and presentation of 'the will of the people', and that it is the State that is the embodiment of public opinion as such. The critic (artist, intellectual, thinker) becomes intrinsically, if often implicitly, an enemy of the people precisely because the critic proposes to disrupt the smooth everyday operation of normative linguistic cliché. By making a writer, artist or intellectual into a scapegoated enemy of the people – as the State tried to do with Flaubert, say, and as contemporary States in advanced economies increasingly do with intellectuals in general – the State does two things: it creates, for the first time, the norms that it says it has always wanted to defend; and it manufactures and then co-opts a constructed 'public opinion' from which it claims the validity and legitimacy of those norms. We must also note here that scapegoating such as this need not be applied simply to individuals: in fact, the State can – and most effectively does – scapegoat entire regions of activity, such as the sexual, such as that of labour, such as that of cultural criticism. That is also often the basis for an entire regressive politics, a politics that determinedly seeks to limit the possibilities of human freedoms.

Reality, in this, is first of all ascribed to public opinion, and then, in a perverse logic, is shown to be under attack by an enemy of 'the people', the people whose views are contained in the public opinion that has been manufactured. In this, it is imperative that 'the people' (which may not, in fact, include or represent any particular or specific human individual at all) must be mobilized and co-opted by the forces of the privileged political class who wish to retain their control over the real conditions of everyday life. It becomes all the more forceful if that 'public opinion' can also mobilize theology, claiming that the will of the people is underpinned not by the State but rather by some theological principle of absolute certainty: reality itself as given by a god-figure or equally absolutist and fundamentalist principle – or even a charismatic individual. Self-righteousness – 'with God on our side' – becomes a key characteristic of such a version of realism; but, of course, such self-righteousness can operate with secular means just as well, sometimes obviously seen in the figure of the charismatic demagogue. That is one basic aspect of any totalitarian politics; but the key thing about it is that, in the contemporary moment, even a polity that describes itself as democratic has learnt everything from the totalitarian politics that shaped realism from the 1939–45 war onwards.

One of the most telling paradoxes here is that the State, in these conditions, no longer fears an 'assembly', in the way that we saw from the seventeenth century onwards. In fact, the State positively encourages assembly now, but an assembly whose character it controls and manipulates under the figure of 'the people' and their will. Thus, for example, a minor issue (a sex scene in a fictional text, say; or allegedly 'obscene' language) can become the locus of a major national scandal, discussed and picked over at length on as many media platforms as possible. This is what happens when Henry Miller's *Tropic of Cancer* of 1934 is re-published in 1961; it is what happens in the case of Lawrence's *Lady Chatterley's Lover* in 1962; it is what happens in the case of Hubert Selby's *Last Exit to Brooklyn* in 1964. Lest we think that we have now long passed over this kind of 'scandal', we should also consider the response to James Kelman's novel, *How Late It Was, How Late*, when it won the Booker Prize in 1994. The novel was lambasted for its liberal use of the word 'fuck', with some reviewers spending their otherwise valuable time counting the number of times Sammy, the central character, said 'fuck' or 'fucking' or 'bastard' and so on, and with one of the Booker Prize judges, Julia Neuburger, raising a major public stooshie about the 'vulgarity' of the text while ignoring entirely the political import of its substance.

The manoeuvre in question here is to manufacture a generalized public assembly that will consist of 'the people' who are co-opted into being scandalized. Yet they are being scandalized by activities in which many of them eagerly actually participate in their real lives: sex, the casual use of 'vulgar' language and so on – human realities going all the way up to and including dying. In co-opting people, or coercing 'the people' into compliance with an 'official' and authoritative discourse around texts or art such as these, the State shows that it is determined to control what can be said about a work of art (or, indeed, any activity at all), the better to instil and produce an ideological belief in a generalized public opinion, a voice or will of the people. For this, the State actually *needs* an assembly and, having learnt the power of the assembly from the seventeenth century onwards, it now makes one in its own image and voice. This is therefore to be an assembly that exists and operates only under tacit State control, its discourse limited and shaped by the language of scandal. The point is to produce an assembly whose voices will be necessarily curtailed and circumscribed by a discourse of 'norms' and 'normality', mediated as general public opinion in its everyday routinized guise as 'common sense' and 'therefore' (as if there is a logic to this) as 'realism'.

In this, there is the development of a new political imperative: the demand for utter transparency, an opening of all political windows. This yields a new inflection for realism. The logic is one whereby 'public opinion' demands that the public be informed about what their political class are doing; and such information is to be the basis on which a public assembly of manufactured opinion will be based. The very fact that such information was not always and everywhere eternally available implies that something was being determinedly hidden from the public; and the logic therefore is one that intrinsically taints political knowledge with scandal. Dave Eggers satirizes this in *The Circle* (a text whose centrality to contemporary real-world politics will be examined later). There, his character Olivia Santos is a politician who decides to 'go transparent' in the name of trust and democracy; and, once she does so, 'the pressure on those [politicians] who hadn't gone transparent went from polite to oppressive. The question, from pundits and constituents, was obvious and loud: if you aren't transparent, what are you hiding?'[27] Privacy here has been revaluated as 'hiding' and thus as something marked by the potential for scandal. As a consequence, all politics is now treated with contempt, rather than scepticism, knowledge becomes marked by scandal; and the consequence is a condition in which all social and political life is shaped by resentment. The name we have for this is 'populism'; and it is based on a specific construction of 'the people' and a commercialization of knowledge-as-commodity. Worse, 'the people' are those who are said not to have a firm grasp of reality, even as their own realities are being denied by those who manipulate their opinions.

6

In the mid-1960s, and certainly all around the Theatre Act which more or less abolished censorship in the theatre in the UK, there is a powerful display of how the manufacture of public opinion works to constrain human possibilities

---

[27] Dave Eggers, *The Circle* (2013; repr. Penguin, London, 2014), 239.

and freedoms. We have seen how the celebration of entertainment-nudity in the 1960s and since, with its consequent perversion of realism into voyeurism, helps to displace the serious political engagements that have existed around the variant forms of historical realism. As a straightforward matter of historical fact, the celebration of a supposedly radical live nudity, post-1968, provoked, as a response, a specific moralistic and religious reaction. That response was itself instrumental in diverting attention from the real conditions of material life and – as with the Falloux Laws of the previous century – it was determined to indicate that 'reality' lies beyond the facts of human life or biological existence.

The post-1968 moralist tries to rehabilitate the idea that 'reality' is to be found in a realm beyond the body, or that reality is precisely what transcends the historical and political conditions of material injustice in everyday life. It projects reality into an immaterial realm beyond labour, sex and – most crucially – death. That moral position yields the same structure that we saw operating in Zola, when he indicated – as I wrote in my previous chapter – that *La Confession de Claude* would be 'naked, raw truth', against which he noted that 'those of a delicate disposition will rebel'. It is important to note, at least in passing, that, in this religiously inflected moralistic drive, death becomes structurally thematized as the very foundation of realism. This provides, in the Christian ideology, a model that has since been followed in various extremist death-cults, from Nazism through to various kinds of fundamentalist terrorism, a good deal of which finds its supposed rationale in religion, and in religions that deny the reality of our material conditions preferring to claim that reality transcends those conditions, lying in a paradisiacal 'elsewhere' or utopia.

Opposition to the 1968 Theatre Act was swift, pious and self-righteous. The opposition to the Act did not pit a radical view against what turns out to be the intrinsic conservatism of stage nudity; rather, opposition to the Act stemmed from a politics that was much more conservative even than the pre-1968 dispensation. It was in the UK in 1965 that Mary Whitehouse set up what she called the 'National Viewers and Listeners Organization', a development of her 'Clean Up TV' organization, and thereby ascribed to herself a position and standing as arbiter not just of morals but also of real social behaviour. The organization that she headed was determined first to manufacture a supposedly authentic public opinion, and second to mobilize that for what was fundamentally an extremely – even extremist – conservative politics. A former art teacher, who also gave school lessons in sex education, Whitehouse was keen on the rhetorical use of the word 'filth' to describe things that she found uncongenial to her own fundamentalist conservative Christian politics. She would be the new agent of cleanliness and of purgation, a 'cleansing' of the national identity.

Homosexuality, for example, was 'filth', and, astonishingly, the same adjective applied to images of the liberation of Jewish survivors coming out of Belsen as more such 'filth'. This is what she would 'clean up'. What linked these two in her psycho-politics was, for her, their necessary invisibility: she did not want to acknowledge either a sexuality that was different from what she described as 'normal' (and what she wanted to be normative), nor did she want to acknowledge the historical atrocities committed by Nazism. It is interesting to consider why this might be the case, and why she was keen to describe both as 'filth', as something characterized as unhygienic. The same censorious impulse that drove Campbell or Pinard in 1857, accompanied by precisely the same rhetorical weapons, persisted as the major determinant of Whitehouse's pious and self-righteous moralism. Like her predecessors, she wanted to make that self-righteous moralism virtually obligatory; and she had recourse to law to try to ensure that her version of human 'normality' would require social and political compliance.

In her opposition to televisual reportage of the Vietnam War (for which her comments on Belsen may be a substitute), she constructed a version of the British subject, whose 'will' for defence of the nation and of national values was jeopardized by the sapping effect of the images of the reality of war. In these, it is easy to see the revival of the underlying theoretical position that drove John Campbell to advocate the Obscene Publications Act of 1857. Whitehouse had an imaginary account of 'reality', grounded in a specific myth of the British national character as one that is piously fundamentalist Christian, heterosexual, basically infantile, authoritarian, warlike and vigorously manly, and (tacitly) determined to limit the emancipation of women and of the poor. Anything that challenged this was, in her view, a dangerous filth that contaminated the pious purity of that 'reality', and should therefore be banned, rendered entirely invisible – through legislation if necessary.

Her construction of this 'reality' depended upon the mobilization of 'the people'; and 'the people' must therefore also be characterized as a mirror-image of Mary Whitehouse's own self-construction: sentimental, pious, heterosexual or asexual, fundamentalist Christian and so on. This 'people' is then construed as aspirant to a world of banal and thereby thoughtless but reassuring 'normality'. This supposed normality is actually a world in which all existing social and political privilege is protected. The protection derives from the power inhering in a governing assumption – and for Whitehouse when she turns to law, a governmental assumption – that this banal normality is 'realistic' and 'just how normal people live'. By going to court to seek to ban various kinds of representation – most famously in the case of Howard Brenton's *The Romans in Britain* – Whitehouse sought to enshrine in law her account of the national identity and its attendant account of what constitutes legitimate reality, and thereby to make her account of 'reality' not just normative but also compulsory. In that state of affairs, to oppose or even question the 'realist' status of that normal character is thereby to be, ipso facto, self-evidently 'abnormal' and thus illegitimate and even illegal.

Peter Hall commissioned Brenton's play, *The Romans in Britain*, in 1977, and it was first staged in London's National Theatre in October 1980. The period in England was marked by a good deal of industrial strife, putting the then Labour government at some substantial risk of falling. Car-workers, firefighters and undertakers were among the many groups who went on strike across the UK. The army was commissioned to replace the firefighters, and unburied corpses started to pile up across the country, some of them stored in warehouses while awaiting the return to work of gravediggers. The Irish Republican Army, or IRA, laid a number of bomb attacks in Britain. Mary Whitehouse, however, was energized by something else: a poem.

The magazine *Gay Times* had published James Kirkup's 'The Love That Dares to Speak Its Name' in June 1976. Its imagined speaker is a Roman centurion who describes his sexual engagement with the rapidly cooling corpse of Jesus after the crucifixion; and the poem makes a series of suggestions that Jesus had homosexual relations with others. By December 1976, Whitehouse had secured a copy of the poem, and immediately launched a private prosecution in the courts against the magazine and its publisher (Denis Lemon), on the familiar grounds of obscenity, but with the addition that it constituted a blasphemous libel against the Christian religion in that it 'vilified' Christ. The case was heard in 1977, and Whitehouse won.

With this legal victory behind her, Whitehouse was ready, in 1980, to continue her course of action, taking it now into the theatre. Brenton's *Romans* is a play that establishes sexual assault as a metaphor for the political relations between the UK and Ireland. Seamus Heaney had already done something similar, in fact, in his poem 'Act of Union' in his 1975 collection, *North*. One significant difference is that, in Brenton, the 'union' in the sexual congress is homosexual. Caesar's invasion of Britain is melded into the British Army's presence in Northern Ireland, and, in the scene that caused controversy, that 'invasion' is presented as the invasion of a male druid's body by a male Roman soldier. Although she never saw the play, Whitehouse pressed for legal action against the director, Michael Bogdanov, for 'procuring' a homosexual act between the two actors in the case.

The first key issue here is that Whitehouse makes the same mistaken understanding of the relation of a play to historical reality as did our Black military-police soldier in Rossellini's *Paisà*: she takes the acting of a scene for the reality of what it depicts. She proceeds, therefore, as if the play is not an account of real conditions, but instead as if the play is not a play at all: for her, the sex act is really happening. In fact, of course, the ocular proof here was not proof at all: Peter Sproule, the actor playing the Roman soldier, did not insert his penis into the anus of Greg Hicks, the actor playing the druid: Sproule gripped his own penis in his hand and extended his thumb, to simulate an erection; and he then 'jabbed this ad-libbed phallus as he straddled Hicks'.[28] Graham Ross-Cornes, the solicitor whose services Mrs Whitehouse, had solicited to see the play as her proxy eyes and ears had 'seen' what he 'expected' to see, in classic Lippmann 'public opinion' terms; but what he had seen – anal rape – had not in fact happened. He may have 'expected' to see it, and (for whatever reasons) desired to see it; but what happened was something different.

The second noteworthy fact is that Whitehouse and her lawyers completely ignored the political issue of imperialism that the play is actually about. Her attitude is not only puritanical; it is also 'purist'. That is to say, she is willing to dismiss a specific phenomenon in its entirety if it is anything less than she 'expects' – Lippmann 'public opinion' style – in all its parts. This is the same kind of politically dogmatic and purist position that afflicts any and all totalizing (and totalitarian) political positions. Although it is really quite basic to a good deal of right-wing ideology, it is also prevalent in a good deal of soi-disant leftist politics, where entire arguments can be dismissed if their proponents can be shown to be anything less than 100 per cent politically pure-left. Whitehouse adopts the same attitude, from a very right-wing political stance, and here deploys it to ignore the political dimension of Brenton and of the play's director, Michael Bogdanov, the individual against whom she took her legal case.

The third is that she hopes to enshrine in law a return to the conditions that prevailed before the 1967 Sexual Offences Act in the UK, and thereby to make homosexuality itself a criminal mode of life. It is difficult to imagine her taking any kind of similar action against Heaney, for example, notwithstanding the often very explicit suggestions in that poem that England has raped and

---

[28] Mark Lawson, 'Passion Play', *The Guardian*, 28 October 2005, available at: https://www.theguardian.com/stage/2005/oct/28/theatre (accessed 20 December 2019).

impregnated Ireland, and that the progeny of that act might take a stance that is recognizable as supportive of the position of the IRA. The male speaker of the poem, assaulting the female, speaks of the embryonic product of the rape: 'His heart beneath your heart is a wardrum / Mustering force', with the obvious menace of 'His parasitical / and ignorant little fists . . . cocked / at me across the water'. It looks as if, for Whitehouse, such vigorously male sexual violence can be ignored, provided its victim is female. It is homosexuality that constitutes, for her, the 'filth' or disease against which society must be protected.

Fourthly, she combines all of this with an assumption that UK law must primarily defend Jesus and Christians, and not UK citizens: the logical consequence of that is the belief that you cannot be a UK citizen unless you are Christian.[29] The point, in the end, is to replace independent thinking with servile faith, and, above all, with faith that relates to something that transcends death (as entry into the sacred beyond the secular), as something that polices sex, and as something that ignores the life-and-death struggles associated with conditions of labour. As for *The Romans in Britain*, it seems clear that she saw neither Romans, nor Britain, nor the issues of imperialism that the play addressed. Of course, she could not see these as she did not see the play, instead 'procuring' someone else's eyes and ears to do so on her behalf (and thus, in her own terms, endangering his soul so that her own could be preserved and saved). But she did 'see' what she 'expected' and even 'desired' to see, even if it did not happen; and from that fantasy, she built a wall of 'public opinion'.

Whitehouse's 'National Viewers and Listeners Organization' assumed and arrogated to itself the role of police, both as a kind of moral (or religious) police and also, in its basic premise, as an eventual replacement for law officers on the ground. In doing this, it also seeks conveniently to arrive at a destination where it can excuse the State from having to intervene directly in the determination to preserve existing social and political conditions: 'reality'. In doing so, it circumvents the charge that the censorious action is 'political' or politically motivated: instead, it is drawn as something 'natural', occurring as a consequence of a natural revulsion of people against a pernicious activity. The workings are simple. Whitehouse mobilizes what she and her organization can now describe as 'ordinary' people through a series of populist interventions that present such 'ordinary British people' as sentimentalized, entirely asexual, intrinsically conservative, fundamentalist Christian, driven by piety, determinedly ignorant

---

[29] Indeed, on leaving court after her case fell, she insisted that 'God would pay her costs' while the National Theatre's chaplain 'found it impossible to believe in a deity of the kind described by Whitehouse' (as reported by Lawson, 'Passion Play').

of politics and as aspirants to a world of banal 'normality' – and it rests on the 'self-evident' assumption that no one would want to self-describe as 'abnormal'. The Whitehouse 'normality' is a world in which political and social privileges are protected by the power inhering in a governing assumption that this banal normality is 'realistic' or 'just how normal people live or *should live* their lives'.

In its newest iteration, the National Viewers and Listeners Organization has reconstituted itself as more or less an explicitly surveillance operation called 'Mediawatch UK'. There, we see what is essentially the logical consequence of its basic presiding ideas. It is now primarily concerned to 'make the media work better for children and families'; and, at the time of writing, its key campaigns are entirely focused on pornography. The concern with children is important. While ostensibly (and, arguably, rightly) concerned about the protection of children, the project, as a whole, proceeds on the basis of an essential infantilization of culture as such. It is as if all culture has to be seen from the point of view of the infant; and here, the root meaning of 'infant' (as infans or 'non-speaking') reveals the fundamental premise of the Mediawatch campaigns: non-speaking is to become the new normal, unless what is spoken is spoken as if from the position of the child or from that of Mediawatch. Interestingly, the website itself is anonymous: there is no contact name and no 'who we are' tab;[30] but it claims to speak on behalf of the general public. This is the new formation of a coercive, anonymous (and therefore completely 'irresponsible') public opinion. It is public opinion as surveillance operation for the contemporary political order, an order that is intrinsically predisposed to the limitations of human freedom and growth, a kind of anti-Bildung.

7

Whitehouse envisaged her contemporary society as a dystopia, against which she would take refuge in a world beyond the secular. Paradoxically, however, she regarded the dystopian world that caused her such grief as itself unreal: reality lay instead in the realms of the sacred. As we conclude this argument, it will be worth looking at two dystopian fictions, fictions that imagine a kind of dual reality: in exposing the key elements of a dystopian world, these fictions propose the possibility of a different world, but one that remains within the ambit of the

---

[30] See: http://mediawatchuk.com (accessed 2 April 2019).

secular and thus one that is politically real. We are back with Ahmet Altan as he faces arrest in Turkey.

In Orwell's *Nineteen Eighty-Four*, the character of Winston also faces arrest in an oppressive State. He, too, has imagined a kind of doubled existence: on one hand, the public realm of the Party; on the other, the construction of a private world in his sexual relations with Julia. His view throughout is that it is the clandestine private realm, the world of actual sexual relations, that constitutes reality. The world of his work, his labour, is what the Party recognizes as real, but his job involves him in erasing things that have actually happened as he flushes them down the memory hole, and in constructing the post-truth world of 'alternative facts' that constitute a public opinion that is completely controlled by the Party. The key issue here, with respect to the politics of realism, is that the division of public and private is dismantled: the window on the world turns out to be, like the television in Winston's apartment, the medium through which the Party watches the inner life of the citizen.

This novel finds its dystopian response, properly, in 2013, when Dave Eggers publishes *The Circle*, in which once again the issue of the surveillance State becomes central to the corruption of a realist enterprise. This novel, too, begins with labour, as its central character finds new employment: Mae goes to work at The Circle, an organization that bears a striking resemblance to a kind of Google-Facebook-Amazon-Alphabet complex. Surveillance is also at the heart of this novel; but, unlike Orwell's figuration of a memory hole whose purpose is to erase historical events, 'We don't delete at the Circle'.[31] In the world depicted by Eggers, total transparency becomes the ideal, and nothing can ever be erased: instead, everything everywhere must be revealed: 'All that happens must be known'.[32] This, crucially, includes sexual activities, as when Mae unintentionally films – and simultaneously broadcasts – her aged parents in a moment that they had imagined as private, in which her mother manually stimulates the penis of her father, who is infirm and suffering from progressive and degenerative multiple sclerosis.[33]

Both texts establish a structural opposition between a kind of official and a clandestine account of the world. In the earlier text, the coming bureaucracy of a specific modernity in politics presents a threat to the sanctity of an unpredictable and contingent life, or life as it is organically lived; in the later text, contingency itself is seen by the adherents of the Circle as a menace for actual true living or for

---

[31] Eggers, *The Circle*, 203.
[32] Ibid., 67.
[33] Ibid., 369–70.

living an authentically knowable and therefore meaningful life. The consequence is that, in both depicted worlds, the question arises as to what is the status of the real itself. In Orwell, the Party decides what constitutes the truth of the real world; by contrast, Eggers explores the threats posed to reality by a world in which there is no contingency left and when a supposed ideal of complete knowledge of all things has been reached. The kind of truth that was sought in earlier accounts of political realism – Zola, Turgenev, James, Grierson, Rossellini say – is here called into question. Both texts, however, confirm the view that the real is shaped by the contingencies that yield the possibility of historical freedoms, the freedom to speak and to act. It is only when contingency becomes a reality that we can claim to be in the realm of empirically lived existence.

Eggers more or less explicitly calls upon Orwell in the making of *The Circle*. *Nineteen Eighty-Four* opens, like Chaucer and T. S. Eliot in their most iconic poems, in April; and its central character, Winston, finds what he initially thinks of as his reality with Julia, named for a later month in the calendar. Eggers has a central character, Mae, and begins his novel in June. It is as if he is filling the temporal gap – that memory hole or puncture in history itself – that structures Orwell's text. Winston believes that his sexual activity with Julia is revolutionary because it cannot be controlled by the Party; Francis, one of Mae's key sexual partners, believes by contrast that for sex to have any meaningful substance, his performance has to be encapsulated by bureaucratic and official numerical measurement: he asks to be scored out of a hundred. *Nineteen Eighty-Four* gives a world dominated by three key phrases: War is Peace; Freedom is Slavery; Ignorance is Strength. These find their corresponding motif in three phrases that shape the world of the Circle: Privacy is Theft; Secrets are Lies; Sharing is Caring. The echoes are many, and resonant.

The centre of both texts is their concern with surveillance. In the earlier novel, the surveillance is imposed by the State on its citizens; in the later, the citizens themselves – or at least the employees of the Circle – willingly embrace surveillance in the name of a moral high ground of transparency. Further, and as I indicated earlier, they follow the example of a political Congresswoman, Olivia Santos, in this. Where Winston lives surrounded by telescreens that monitor his every move, Mae establishes herself as a fully transparent 'window' – explicitly described as such – upon the realities of her lived existence.[34] Under surveillance, Winston's supposedly subversive sexual activity with Julia is witnessed by the Party, and he and Julia are arrested, betrayed by Mr Charrington. In *The Circle*,

[34] Ibid., 307.

Mae Holland films and simultaneously broadcasts to the world that sexual act between her parents; and when she has sex with Francis at the Circle, he films it – without her prior permission – on his phone. The film is then archived, always available in perpetuity.

Winston's labour involves the propagandistic modification of documentary records, up to and including the seeming eradication of those documents via a memory hole. Mae, by contrast, works in an environment where the erasure of any document is prohibited and, indeed, where every document is made as accessible as possible. In this latter case, total transparency will lead eventually to the death of Mercer, her former boyfriend. This is a death that, again, is filmed and simultaneously broadcast, in what is a horrifying harbinger of the various and atrocious mass murders that have started to appear not in fiction but in history, such as (for one example among an increasing number) the mass murder of the Muslim worshippers at the Al Noor mosque in Christchurch, New Zealand on 15 March 2019, which the murderer livestreamed via Facebook. In the Orwell case, closer to the political disappearances associated with Stalinism, various characters are 'vaporized', and both Winston and Julia are essentially hollowed out. Repeatedly, Winston notes that 'We are the dead', a phrase that itself is recorded by O'Brien and the Party and that will be brought back to haunt and taunt him.[35]

In this concluding section, we can view these texts via the framework that I have provided throughout: a politics of realism based upon the primary attention to labour, sex and death. Conveniently, Orwell himself provides the template. At the centre of *Nineteen Eighty-Four* there is another text, *the book*, which is the fundamental text written by Emmanuel Goldstein that provides a critical analysis of the Party's modes of control and, with that analysis, the means of a reasoned resistance to totalitarianism. Goldstein's text argues that 'In so far as the war has a direct economic purpose, it is a war for labour power'. Further, 'in the past . . . war was one of the main instruments by which human societies were kept in touch with physical reality', whereas now, the rulers of the State 'can twist reality into whatever shape they choose'. This is all exacerbated by the advent of print, which 'made it easier to manipulate public opinion, and the film and the radio carried the process further. With the development of television, and the technical advance which made it possible to receive and transmit simultaneously on the same instrument, private life came to an end'.[36] Goldstein indicates that there is

---

[35] George Orwell, *Nineteen Eighty-Four* (1949; repr. Penguin, London, 1982), 112, 144, 177.
[36] Ibid., 153, 160–1, 166.

nothing for the totalitarian Party to fear from the proles who 'will continue from generation to generation and from century to century, working, breeding, and dying':[37] labour, sex and death as the fundamental conditions of reality. If the Party is to establish full political control, then these are the elements over which it must establish complete mastery and power, deploying whatever technological advances are or become available.

Given this – and given, further, the proximity of the fictional Goldstein's analysis with my own here – it will be productive to consider not only the failure of Goldstein to effect political change in Orwell (and thus the limitations of my own analysis), but also how an updated account of a totalitarian society might respond to a new politics of realism in which the revival of labour or class-based politics, of sexual politics and of bio-politics might now operate; and part of the answer to this lies in *The Circle*, a novel that shows how a contemporary regressive politics in our own time, determined to limit human freedoms, can operate in a fashion that is much more insidious than anything envisaged in Orwell. The world depicted by Eggers is one in which all the negative and regressive aspects of Orwell's dystopia have become utterly normalized and interiorized, beyond the power of resistance. In the world of the Circle, it is those who are most fully enslaved who believe themselves to be most free: the impulse to resist, in the name of a better reality, is foreclosed. The character who embodies the kind of resistance that we had seen in Winston Smith, Mae's former boyfriend Mercer, dies; the character who tries to arrest the seemingly irresistible dynamic of the Circle's techno-politics, its founder Ty (or Kalden) is betrayed by Mae and by his co-founders, and the Circle progresses inexorably towards 'completion'.

In Orwell, a demand for total transparency is seen as something that would puncture the power of the totalitarian Party, whose real motivations would be rendered visible and thus open to critique and change through the operations of such a transparency. This is, indeed, precisely the principle that has governed the politics of realism historically up to the point at which Orwell writes, in the immediate aftermath of the Second World War. Opening the windows on the Ministries of Truth, of Plenty, and of Peace – and providing windows for the Ministry of Love – would offer the prospect of developing a new future reality. Eggers, by contrast, provides a world in which total transparency becomes precisely the barrier to any such change, forestalling any possibility of a critical consciousness and claiming that reality is everywhere present, at all times and places.

[37] Ibid., 169.

Winston is thirty-nine when his story opens, which means that he was born at the end of the Second World War, in 1945 or 1946. The year 1984 is also the end of the Ninth Three-Year Plan, so we can date the initiation of the regime from a vaguely described nuclear event in about 1957 (around one decade ahead of when Orwell was actually writing), when Winston's body would have been entering puberty. Right from the start, it is made clear that the physical condition of Winston's body is an issue; and the itch in his ulcerated right ankle places him in an awkward and somewhat degraded relation to the idealized body of Big Brother, whose rugged and handsome image permeates London in a series of film-star type posters. The body itself is intrinsically political here: 'Always in your stomach and in your skin there was a sort of protest, a feeling that you had been cheated of something that you had a right to.'[38] Winston's weakness during the morning's Physical Jerks routine marks him out, by number ('6079, Smith, W! Yes, *you*! Bend lower, please').[39] Winston is also aware that he must at all times police his body, right down to the expression on his face, since 'to wear an improper expression on your face ... was itself a punishable offence ... *facecrime*, it was called'.[40] This is the body as language and, as with the tongue, it too has to adopt its reduced scope, its own Newspeak. We might recall that it is the physical injury to Julia as she stumbles that initially brings them together.

Eggers reprises something similar. Mae is introduced to her desk in the Renaissance section of the Circle by Renata (the two heavy-handed references to being born again here are surely intentional). When they reach the workstation, Mae is disappointed because 'It was the first thing she'd seen at the Circle that ... bore any resemblance to the past'. Mae, though, 'knew Renata was watching her, and she knew her face was betraying something like horror. *Smile*, she thought. *Smile*.'[41] Facecrime operates here too, it seems: a logical corollary of Facebooking one's life. The desk turns out to be a faked-up version, this 'reality' of the past being a joke played by Mae's friend and colleague, Anna. Control of the body, however, is something that will be developed right through this text, especially in the case of a character like Francis, Mae's occasional sexual partner who is prone to premature ejaculation. Most obviously, Mae's father is progressively losing control of his body, through the irresistible and material realities of his multiple sclerosis, a condition that becomes political through Mae's filming and broadcasting of the sex act between him and her mother.

[38] Ibid., 51.
[39] Ibid., 33.
[40] Ibid., 53.
[41] Eggers, *The Circle*, 7.

Coming in the wake of Nazism and its idealized 'Aryan' body, Orwell's focus on Winston's body in *Nineteen Eighty-Four* indicates something profoundly political, but something that is also consistent with what we have seen historically as a political account of realism. The 'real' body is marked by imperfection, even by the kinds of ailments or disease or even physical weakness that a soi-disant 'ideal' society would wish to purge: the Circle is working on precisely such cleansing. Orwell – having seen the effects of Nazi anti-Semitism and the persecution of Romani, homosexuals and critical intellectuals – knows now exactly where the kind of censorious realism ends up. A 'realism' like that which we witnessed at the opening of this study, a realism whose politics depends on the censoring of actual living conditions (of illness, or bodily imperfection, or sex, or disease, or 'dirt' considered both materially and metaphorically) leads inexorably from the eradication of books and images to the eradication of people, usually starting from those described as somehow 'abnormal', 'deviant' or simply 'imperfect' or 'disabled' in some way.

Nineteen Eighty-Four, in this respect at least, is a plea for the profound value and political importance of imperfection, which becomes essential and necessary for anything that resembles political freedom, the freedom to live an autonomous life and to construct and change the real conditions of human, social and political life in the world. It is not just a dystopian text but also an anti-utopian one. As a text that is explicitly anti-utopian, it becomes one that is profoundly realist, concerned with the reality of the world as it is and not the idea of how it might ideally be. At its heart, then, is a significant critique of political idealism, if such idealism is based on the idea of the perfectibility of the human condition. At the same time, there is a dispiriting realization that the critique of utopia itself can be easily stymied: another 'prevention' of realism, as it were, or the prevention of realism by other means.

Winston embraces the idea of sex with Julia not just because of the act itself, but because he thinks that the sex is political, a 'political act' whose foundation in animal instinct 'was the force that would tear the Party to pieces'.[42] He believes that sex is dangerous to the Party precisely because it cannot be controlled, precisely because it is purely a physical and bodily realization of the self and, moreover, that is it open to all kinds of contaminations of purity. He especially welcomes the simple fact of Julia's promiscuity: 'anything that hinted at corruption always filled him with a wild hope'.[43] As the text shows, this is itself

---

[42] Orwell, *Nineteen Eighty-Four*, 104.
[43] Ibid., 103.

a hopelessly utopian idea, but also one that is shared by Julia, for whom 'all this marching up and down and cheering and waving flags is simply sex gone sour'.[44]

Winston's problem – shared with Julia – is that he sets up an opposition between official orthodoxy and sex, and then takes the sex as his measure of the real. In fact, in the world of *Nineteen Eighty-Four*, sex is simply a measure not of reality but of class difference that has already been accommodated within the overarching social system. There is no possibility of antagonism between classes here, because sex, far from being a subversive act, is something that can safely be handed over to the province of the proles (as Goldstein's book noted), where it will become sentimentalized and emptied of political import through trashy kitsch popular songs, while, as far as the Party is concerned, 'We shall abolish the orgasm', because the orgasm is seen as a flaw in the pure workings of the system.[45] Winston's real battle – even if (perhaps like Orwell himself) he does not realize it – is against his own class position. The overall system, given its intrinsic totalizing power, is immune to change, especially a change based upon ideas of intrinsic or class struggles; and it is certainly immune to a change initiated in the private emotions of the bedroom, no matter how turbulent or disturbing they may be. That is why, in the end and despite Winston's desires, there can be no hope in the proles or, indeed, anywhere else. In his belief that sex is subversive because it is related to dirt or contamination of the purity of all official social relations, Winston, far from critiquing the Party line, actually endorses it and thereby strengthens the Party instead of undermining it. The Party will admit of no other possible reality besides its own; and realism here means pure compliance.

Even more crucial to the politics of realism in these texts is the attitude to historical and empirical truth and to material conditions of historical events. Like many of the texts we have considered, windows and screens are a recurring motif. When Winston looks out of his window at the start of the novel, he sees a helicopter that is 'snooping into people's windows'; and, as he does so, he is himself profoundly aware of the screen in the interior of his own apartment, the telescreen that can monitor virtually every movement or sound he makes. Set against this is the building where he will eventually end up, the Ministry of Love, a building that has no windows at all. This can be set against the situation in the Eggers response-text, where all the buildings, ceilings and floors in the Circle are made of glass, and where we will eventually arrive at a situation in

---

[44] Ibid., 109.
[45] Ibid., 215, 205.

which people themselves 'go clear' or 'go transparent' as a development of the technology called 'SeeChange'. That technology depends first on the placing of micro-cameras all over the world, and subsequently on politicians and citizens starting to wear such cameras: 'SeeChange. This is the ultimate transparency. No filter. See everything. Always'.[46]

Orwell's Ministry of Love is also a building set in a city landscape that, in Orwell's description of it, resembles extremely closely the ravaged condition that we have seen in Italian neorealist cinema as the reality of the post-war European world. Towards the close of *The Circle*, Mae looks out from what has become, for her at least, the sanctuary of the Circle organization, and sees what we once called the real world with its homeless people and its issues and problems. She sees it as filthy and inefficient: imperfect. She prefers the interiority of life within the glass bowl that is the Circle. That glass bowl is itself something that we saw in Orwell's text, where it took the form of an antique paperweight, described by Winston as an essentially useless 'little chunk of history that they forgot to alter'. Holding it in his hand, Winston imagines it 'enclosing a tiny world with its atmosphere complete. He had the feeling that he could get inside it, along with the mahogany bed and the gateleg table, and the clock and the steel engraving and even the paperweight itself'.[47]

In both texts, it is as if the empirical and material reality of the world has been turned inside out, as if in a kind of three-dimensional mirror. Bailey, one of the Three Wise Men who run the Circle, argues for the perfection of 'completion', completing the circle, which will 'prevent us from feeling . . . that some distorted view of ourselves is presented to the world. . . . But a mirror can only be truthful when it's complete'.[48] Stendhal's metaphor here assumes its full import, and the consequences for the politics of realism are such that Stendhal's own understanding and ideology of representation is itself turned upside down. Meanwhile, the truth that Winston sees when he looks out of his window is that houses are 'shored up with baulks of timber, their windows patched with cardboard and their roofs with corrugated iron', and, exactly as we have seen in the films of Italian neorealism, 'bombed sites where the plaster dust swirled in the air'.[49] And, of course, we know that this is a war-site because Oceania is indeed at war.

---

[46] Eggers, *The Circle*, 69.
[47] Orwell, *Nineteen Eighty-Four*, 120.
[48] Eggers, *The Circle*, 288.
[49] Orwell, *Nineteen Eighty-Four*, 7.

The war records are crucial here, because Winston's job involves a deep engagement with documents. His treatment of the document, however, is the very opposite to Zola's. His task is to make reality always the same, especially the reality of war. This is important: the document here is not testimony to reality; rather, the document is testimony to the eternal and unending power of the Party to control reality. 'Whatever was true now was true from everlasting to everlasting. It was quite simple. All that was needed was an unending series of victories over your own memory. "Reality control", they called it: in Newspeak, "doublethink".'[50] The real war, then, is not a war with Eastasia or Eurasia: it is actually a war with the self, a war against memory and against the maintenance of the documentary records of real and empirical events. Indeed, it is what has recently been characterized as a 'war against reality' itself, as in the sub-title of Peter Pomerantsev's study of the ways in which contemporary politics deploys misinformation in order to gain and retain power.[51]

Winston is at once shamed by this and sanguine about it, because, as he carries out his tasks, he realizes 'it was not even forgery. It was merely the substitution of one piece of nonsense for another. Most of the material that you were dealing with had no connexion with anything in the real world'.[52] The key here lies in that twofold novelty: first, the absolute disjunction between real events and their linguistic representation; and second, consequent upon that disjunction, the realization that what is really most fundamental in this utopia/dystopia is not the representation of reality but its control. Such control is to be maintained through the evisceration of the very language that we can use to describe reality, an evisceration that will eradicate the distinction between truth and falsehood. Julia, after all, 'was ready to accept the official mythology, simply because the difference between truth and falsehood did not seem important to her', provoking Winston into the observation that 'You're only a rebel from the waist downwards'.[53]

8

It is important that in *Nineteen Eighty-Four* no one has ever actually seen Big Brother. His sole presence is in the form of representation. This is an image

---

[50] Ibid., 31.
[51] See Pomerantsev, *This Is Not Propaganda*.
[52] Orwell, *Nineteen Eighty-Four*, 36.
[53] Ibid., 126, 128.

without an original, as it were; and, as such, it calls to mind the interlinked phenomena of photography and cinema that Benjamin describes in his famous essay, from 1936, 'The Work of Art in the Age of Mechanical Reproduction'. With the advent of photographic technology, argues Benjamin, something very dramatic happens in the philosophy of perception. 'From a photographic negative,' he writes, 'one can make any number of prints; to ask for the "authentic" print makes no sense.'[54] The shock of this new technology derives from the shake-up it gives to our previous conception of artistic (and even personal) authenticity. This is important for contemporary political attitudes to realism.

Benjamin gives a macro-history of the development of art forms and their reproducibility. Art has always been susceptible to copy; but the big difference is that, in mechanical reproduction, we start to lose interest in the 'original' of the reproduced work. Yet, it was the very presence of the original that was 'the prerequisite to the concept of authenticity', because we were able to distinguish the original from its copies which, prior to the techniques of mechanization, would be marked as 'flawed' in some respect. Primarily, the flaw lay in the observation that the copy was not 'the real thing'. Consequently, for Benjamin, the work of art in the advanced technology of mechanization sees the withering of what he called the work's aura, the loss of 'its presence in time and space, its unique existence at the place where it happens to be'.[55] The work now is also increasingly a work that is not only made *for* reproduction; it is also a work made specifically and primarily for *exhibition*.[56]

We might recognize this phenomenon. It is a description of something we have just witnessed: the life lived by the character of Mae in *The Circle*. For Benjamin, this marks a shift in the history of presentations and representations. Prior to his technological moment, works of art were tied primarily to the cult and the ritual; and this depended on the aura of the work. Now, however, the sole remnant of this lies in precisely the image that dominates in *Nineteen Eighty-Four*, the face – the face, in this fictional case, of Big Brother. It is in these shifts – from Orwell to Eggers, from cult to exhibition – that we can find our closing observations for this study of the politics of realism, precisely as the politics of realism cedes place to the unreality of politics in our moment.

It is in the Epilogue to this, his most celebrated essay, that Benjamin makes his famous observation about the relation of aesthetics to politics, arguing there

---

[54] Walter Benjamin, 'The Work of Art in the Age of Mechanical Reproduction', in Benjamin, *Illuminations*, ed. Hannah Arendt (trans. Harry Zohn; Fontana, Glasgow, 1973), 226.
[55] Ibid., 222.
[56] Ibid., 226–7.

that 'the logical result of Fascism is the introduction of aesthetics into political life'.[57] The world of Orwell's text is a world that is controlled by an image, by an aesthetic representation in the cultish photograph of a 'person', a Big Brother whose ontological reality is never once established. Orwell was as fearful as Plato with respect to the power of such an image – an image without an original, an image without authenticity – to shape, control and pervert historical realities, and as alert as Benjamin to the perils involved in an aestheticization of the politics of realism. Through the history of the politics of representation, however, and with the more recent fiction of *The Circle* at hand, we can start to configure the contemporary question regarding the politics of realism. In fact, our contemporary predicament has led us to a state of affairs in which the more pressing question becomes not one of the politics of realism, but rather the reality – now, in the age of virtual reproduction, more precisely the unreality – of politics.

We are now living after the age that Benjamin had presciently described as an age marked by 'growing proletarianization' and 'the increasing formation of masses'. In that confluence, Benjamin saw that the new proletariat had the right to demand substantial changes to the socio-political distribution of the ownership and control of property; but he also saw clearly that 'Fascism sees its salvation in giving these masses not their right, but instead a chance to express themselves'.[58] In our contemporary moment, an age of virtual reproduction, self-expression is taken as itself a basic constituent element of political existence. Indeed, it is often taken for – and even mistaken for – democracy itself. However, what if – in the age of exhibitionism – there is in fact no original self to express? What if Beckett's famous prescription for the painter, Tal Coat, is all we have: 'the obligation to express' when there is 'nothing to express' and 'nothing from which to express'?

Express the self, at all times and in all places: this, in fact, is the new politics. It makes proles of us all, in Orwell's sense. As we express ourselves, the world goes on its merry way. As the new generalized proletariat, we are expected to content ourselves with the expression of an identity. It is not the case that we are in the realm of identity politics; rather, identity has now replaced politics. The politics of realism has been supplanted by the realism of identity, yielding a polity in which Fascism can continue, while the new proletariat joyfully sings, like the washer-woman in Orwell. With contemporary technology, a Fascism

---

[57] Benjamin, 'The Work of Art in the Age of Mechanical Reproduction', 243.
[58] Ibid.

that passes itself off as a celebration of transparency thrives, while we, as the new proletarians, watch Reality TV, as livestreamed by Mae Holland and everyone else who 'documents' their life via Facebook and other contemporary media. Politics disappears, becomes unreal; and we are governed increasingly instead by images, by 'stars' or by those other comedians who work as stereotypical caricatures of humanity. The problem we face is that these 'comedians' – Trump, Johnson, Xi, Erdoğan, Bolsanaro, Orbán, Lukashenko, Zelensky, Putin and the rest – are not funny; rather, they present a substantial threat to our possibilities of realizing our freedoms, liberating ourselves into new possibilities.

In the face of this new and emerging crisis, it is time to revive a politics of realism; and this means opening identity – especially stereotypical identity – to change and difference. The politics of realism in our time is increasingly the revival of a politics that is concerned to make a difference.

Bibliography

Adorno, Theodor, *Minima Moralia*, 1951; trans. E. F. N. Jephcot, London: Verso, 1974.
Adorno, Theodor, 'Transparencies on Film', trans. Thomas Y. Levin, *New German Critique*, 24/25 (1981–2): 199–205.
Adorno, Theodor and Horkheimer, Max, *Dialectic of Enlightenment*, 1944; trans. John Cumming, London: Verso, 1979.
Adorno, Theodor, Benjamin, Walter, Bloch, Ernst, Brecht, Bertolt and Lukàcs, Georg, *Aesthetics and Politics*, London: Verso, 1980.
Agamben, Giorgio, *Homo Sacer*, 1995; trans. Daniel Heller-Roazen, Stanford: Stanford University Press, 1998.
Agamben, Giorgio, *Nudities*, 2009; trans. David Kishik and Stefan Pedatella, Stanford: Stanford University Press, 2011.
Alicata, Mario, e de Santis, Giuseppe, 'Ancora di Verga e del cinema italiano', in Jacqueline Reich and Piero Garofalo (eds), *Re-Viewing Fascism: Italian Cinema 1922–1943*, Bloomington and London: Indiana University Press, 2002.
Altan, Ahmet, *I Will Never See the World Again*, trans. Yasemin Çongar, London: Granta, 2019.
Arendt, Hannah, *Crises of the Republic*, New York: Harcourt Brace & Company, 1972.
Arendt, Hannah, *Between Past and Future*, London: Penguin, 2006.
Arendt, Hannah, *The Origins of Totalitarianism*, 1951; repr. London: Penguin, 2017.
Aristotle, *Politics*, trans. Ernest Barker, revised R. F. Stalley, Oxford: Oxford University Press, 1998.
Augustine, *Confessions*, trans. R. S. Pine-Coffin, London: Penguin, 1961.
Bacon, Henry, *Visconti*, Cambridge: Cambridge University Press, 2010.
Barnouw, Eric, *Documentary*, Oxford: Oxford University Press, 1983.
Barré, Louis et al., Introduction to *Complément du Dictionnaire de l'Académie française*, Paris: Firmin-Didot, 1881 edition, https://gallica.bnf.fr/ark:/12148/bpt6k5834322m/f8.item.r=langue
Barsam, Richard, *The Vision of Robert Flaherty*, Bloomington: Indiana University Press, 1988.
Barthes, Roland, *Mythologies*, 1957; trans. Annette Lavers, London: Granada, 1973.
Baudelaire, Charles, *Critique d'Art*, Paris: Gallimard, 1992.
Bazin, André, *What Is Cinema?* vol. 2, ed. and trans. Hugh Gray, London: University of California Press, 1972.
Beaumont, Barbara (ed. and trans.), *Flaubert and Turgenev: A Friendship in Letters; the Complete Correspondence*, Athlone Press, 1985.
Beckett, Samuel, *Waiting for Godot*, New York: Grove Press, 1954.

Beckett, Samuel, *Company*, London: John Calder, 1979.
Beckett, Samuel, *Company / Ill Seen Ill Said / Worstward Ho / Stirrings Still*, ed. Dirk Van Hulle, London: Faber and Faber, 2009.
Benjamin, Walter, *Illuminations*, ed. Hannah Arendt, trans. Harry Zohn, Glasgow: Fontana, 1073.
Benjamin, Walter, *Selected Writings*, vol. 2, ed. Michael W. Jennings, Gary Smith and Howard Eiland, Cambridge, MA: Harvard University Press, 2005.
Berger, John, *Ways of Seeing*, London: Penguin, 1972.
Berthelot, Sandrine, 'Balzac et le réalisme grotesque. Lecture de *La Cousine Bette*', in Didier Philippot, et Fabienne Bercegol (éds), *La Pensée du paradoxe: approches au romantisme*, 147–63, Paris: PUF, 2006.
Bew John, 'The Real Origins of Realpolitik', *National Interest*, 25 February 2014, https://nationalinterest.org/article/the-real-origins-realpolitik-9933?page=0%2C4
Bew, John, *Realpolitik*, Oxford: Oxford University Press, 2016.
Billington, Michael, *State of the Nation*, London: Faber and Faber, 2007.
Blais, Roger, 'Grierson', National Film Board of Canada, http://latetedelemploi.nfb.ca/film/grierson/
Blumenberg, Hans, *The Legitimacy of the Modern Age*, trans. R. M. Wallace, Cambridge, MA: MIT Press, 1983.
Bondanella, Peter and Pacchioni, Federico, *A History of Italian Cinema*, London: Bloomsbury, 2017.
Bourdieu, Pierre, *Homo Academicus*, 1984; trans. Peter Collier, Cambridge: Polity Press, 1990.
Brenton, Howard, *The Romans in Britain*, 1980; repr. Bloomsbury, 2015.
Brett-Smith, H. F. B. (ed.), *Peacock's Four Ages of Poetry; Shelley's Defence of Poetry; Browning's Essay on Shelley*, Oxford: Basil Blackwell, 1921.
Browne, Thomas, *The Complete Works*, ed. C. A. Patrides, Penguin, 1977.
Brunette, Peter, *Roberto Rossellini*, Oxford: Oxford University Press, 1987.
Büchner, Ludwig, *Force and Matter*, 1885; 8th edn, 1864, ed. and trans. J. Frederick Collingwood, Cambridge University Press, 2012.
Butler, Judith, *Precarious Life*, London: Verso, 2003; 2006.
Clare, Janet, *Art Made Tongue-Tied by Authority*, Manchester: Manchester University Press, 1999.
Clark, T. J., *Image of the People*, London: Thames and Hudson, 1973.
Clegg, Cyndia Susan, *Press Censorship in Elizabethan England*, Cambridge: Cambridge University Press, 1997.
Clover, Charles, *Black Wind, White Snow: The Rise of Russia's New Nationalism*, New Haven: Yale University Press, 2016.
Coleman, Donatella Spinelli, *Filming the Nation*, London: Routledge, 2011.
Conrad, Joseph, *The Nigger of the 'Narcissus'*, London: Penguin, 1979.
Courbet, Gustave, 'Le Réalisme', in *Exhibition et vente de 40 Tableaux et 4 Dessins de l'œuvre de M. Gustave Courbet*, 1855.

Courbet, Gustave, *Letters of Gustave Courbet*, ed. and trans. Petra ten-Doesschate Chu, Chicago: University of Chicago Press, 1992.

Crane, Ralph and Mohanfram, Radhika, *Imperialism as Diaspora*, London: Liverpool University Press, 2013.

Culler, Jonathan, 'Omniscience', *Narrative*, 12, no. 1 (2004): 22–34.

Darnton, Robert, *Censors at Work: How States Shaped Literature*, British Library, 2014.

Davis, Lennard, *Factual Fictions*, New York: Columbia University Press, 1983.

Davy, Charles, ed., *Footnotes to the Film*, Lovat Dickson Ltd, 1937.

Deane, Seamus, *Reading in the Dark*, Jonathan Cape, 1996.

Derrida, Jacques, *Spectres de Marx*, Paris: Galilée, 1993.

Derrida, Jacques, *The Gift of Death*, trans. David Wills, Chicago: University of Chicago Press, 1995.

Descartes, René, *Philosophical Works*, trans. Elizabeth S. Haldane and G. R. T. Ross, Cambridge: Cambridge University Press, 1969.

Dickens, Charles, *The Letters of Charles Dickens, vol. 6: 1850–1852*, eds Graham Storey, Kathleen Mary Tillotson and Nina Burgis, Oxford University Press, 1974, https://0-www-oxfordscholarlyeditions-com.pugwash.lib.warwick.ac.uk/view/10.1093/actrade/9780198126171.book.1/actrade-9780198126171-div1-1204

Di Nolfo, Ennio, 'Intimations of Neorealism in the Fascist *Ventennia*', in Jacqueline Reich and Piero Garofalo (eds), *Re-Viewing Fascism: Italian Cinema 1922–1943*, 83–104, Bloomington and London: Indiana University Press, 2002.

Docherty, Thomas, *For the University*, London: Bloomsbury, 2011.

Docherty, Thomas, *Complicity: Criticism between Collaboration and Commitment*, New York: Rowman and Littlefield International, 2016.

Docherty, Thomas, *Literature and Capital*, London: Bloomsbury, 2018.

Docherty, Thomas, *The New Treason of the Intellectuals*, Manchester: Manchester University Press, 2018.

Docherty, Thomas, *Political English*, London: Bloomsbury, 2019.

D'Olimpio, Laura, 'Thoughts on Film', *Educational Philosophy and Theory*, 48 (2016): 622–37.

Duggan, Robert, *The Grotesque in Contemporary British Fiction*, Manchester: Manchester University Press, 2013.

Dutton, Richard, *Mastering the Revels*, London: Macmillan, 1981.

Eggers, Dave, *The Circle*, 2013; repr. London: Penguin, 2014.

Eliot, T. S., *Complete Poems and Plays*, London: Faber and Faber, 1969.

Elsen, Albert E., *Rodin's Art*, Oxford: Oxford University Press, 2003.

Erlich, Victor, *Russian Formalism*, New Haven: Yale University Press, 3rd edn, 1981.

Ferneyhough, Charles, *Pieces of Light: The New Science of Memory*, London: Profile, 2013.

Fisher, Mark, *Capitalist Realism*, London: Zero Books, 2009.

Fitzpatrick, Sheila, *The Commissariat of Enlightenment*, Cambridge: Cambridge University Press, 1970.

Fitzpatrick, Sheila, *The Cultural Front: Power and Culture in Revolutionary Russia*, New York: Cornell University Press, 1992.

Flaubert, Gustave, *Bouvard et Pécuchet*, Paris: Garnier-Flammarion, 1966.

Flaubert, Gustave, *Madame Bovary*, ed. Claudine Gothot-Mersch, Paris: Garnier Frères, 1971.

Flaubert, Gustave, *The Letters of Gustave Flaubert 1830–1857*, ed. and trans. Francis Steegmuller, Belknap: Harvard University Press, 1980.

Freedberg, David, *The Power of Images*, Chicago: University of Chicago Press, 1989.

Fried, Michael, *Absorption and Theatricality: Painter and Beholder in the Age of Diderot*, Berkeley and Los Angeles: University of California Press, 1980.

Fried, Michael, *Courbet's Realism*, Chicago: University of Chicago Press, 1990.

Gaskell, Elizabeth, *Wives and Daughters*, ed. Frank Glover Smith, 1864–6; repr. Penguin, 1969.

Gaskell, Elizabeth, *Mary Barton*, ed. Stephen Gill, 1848; repr. Penguin, 1970.

Gaskell, Elizabeth, *North and South*, ed. Dorothy Collin, 1854–5; repr. Penguin, 1970.

Gide, André, *Journal des Faux-Monnayeurs*, Paris: Gallimard, 1927.

Grierson, John, *Grierson on Documentary*, ed. Forsyth Hardy, London: Faber and Faber, 1979.

Guyver, Christopher, *The Second French Republic 1848–1852: A Political Reinterpretation*, London: Palgrave, 2016.

Hankey, Julia (ed.), *Othello: Shakespeare in Production*, Cambridge: Cambridge University Press, 2005.

Hannoosh, Michèle, 'Reading the Trial of the *Fleurs du Mal*', *Modern Language Review*, 106, no. 2 (April 2011): 374–87.

Harwell, Drew, report in *Washington Post*, 30 December 2018, https://www.washingtonpost.com/technology/2018/12/30/fake-porn-videos-are-being-weaponized-harass-humiliate-women-everybody-is-potential-target/

Haynes, Christine, 'The Politics of Publishing during the Second Empire: The Trial of "Madame Bovary" Revisited', *French Politics, Culture and Society*, 23, no. 2 (2005): 1–27.

Heinemann, Margot, *Puritanism and Theatre*, Cambridge: Cambridge University Press, 1980.

Hemmings, F. W. J. (ed.), *The Age of Realism*, London: Penguin, 1974.

Hirsch, James, '*Othello* and Perception', in Virginia Mason Vaughan and Kent Cartwright (eds), *Othello: New Perspectives*, Madison: Fairleigh Dickinson University Press, 1991.

Hitchens, Christopher and Tharoor, Shashi, *Hay Festival Debate 2007*, https://www.youtube.com/watch?v=CTPj2UEtdzA

Ingrao, Pietro, 'Luchino Visconti: L'antifascismo e il cinema', *Rinascita*, 13 (26 March 1976): 33–4.

James, Henry, *The Art of Fiction*, educ. Rev. P. Blackmur, London and New York: Charles Scribner's Sons, 1962.

James, Henry, *The Aspern Papers and Other Stories*, Penguin, 1976.

Jameson, Fredric, *The Political Unconscious*, London: Routledge, 1981.
Joyce, James, *A Portrait of the Artist as a Young Man*, London: Granada, 1977.
Judt, Tony, *Postwar: A History of Europe Since 1945*, 2005; repr. London: Pimlico, 2007.
Kelman, James, *How Late It Was, How Late*, 1994; repr. Minerva, 1995.
Kermode, Frank, *The Sense of an Ending*, Oxford University Press, 1966.
Klein, Naomi, *No Is Not Enough*, London: Allen Lane, 2017.
Kolker, Robert P., *Politics Goes to the Movies*, London: Routledge, 2018.
Kuhn, Thomas, *The Structure of Scientific Revolutions*, 1962; revised 2nd edn, Chicago: University of Chicago Press, 1970.
LaCapra, Dominick, *Madame Bovary on Trial*, Ithaca: Cornell University Press, 1982.
Lapp, John C., 'The Critical Reception of Zola's *Confession de Claude*', *Modern Language Notes*, 68, no. 7 (1953): 457–62.
Lawrence, D. H., *Lady Chatterley's Lover*, 1928; Penguin, 1960.
Lawson, Mark, 'Passion Play', *The Guardian*, 28 October 2005, https://www.theguardian.com/stage/2005/oct/28/theatre
Lemire, Devone, 'A Historiographical Survey of Literacy in Britain between 1780 and 1830', *Constellations*, 4, no. 1 (2013), https://doi.org/10.29173/cons18862
Lim, Louisa, *The People's Republic of Amnesia: Tiananmen Revisited*, Oxford: Oxford University Press, 2014.
Lindsay, Jack, *Gustave Courbet: His Life and Art*, London: Adams and Dart, 1973.
Lippmann, Walter, *Public Opinion*, 1922; repr. New York: Free Press, 1949.
Lippmann, Walter, *Public Opinion*, 1922; repr. New York and London: Free Press and Collier-Macmillan, 1965.
Lippmann, Walter, *Force and Ideas: The Early Writings*, New York: Transaction Publishing, 2003.
Loach, Ken, *Cathy Come Home*, https://archive.org/details/CathyComeHome
Lukács, Georg, *The Meaning of Contemporary Realism*, trans. John and Necke Mander, London: Merlin Press, 1962.
Lyotard, Jean-François and Thébaud, Jean-Loup, *Just Gaming*, trans. Wlad Godzich, Manchester: Manchester University Press, 1985.
Marcorelles, Louis, 'Conversation with Jean Renoir, 1962', in Bert Cardullo (ed.), *Jean Renoir, Interviews*, Jackson: University Press of Mississippi, 2005.
Marinetti, F. T., 'The Founding and Manifesto of Futurism 1909', in Umbro Apollonio (ed.), *Futurist Manifestos*, London: Thames and Hudson, 1973.
Martineau, Harriet, *Household Education*, Edward Moxon, 1849, https://www.gutenberg.org/files/38179/38179-h/38179-h.htm
Marx, Karl, *The Eighteenth Brumaire of Louis Bonaparte*, Peking: Foreign Languages Press, 1978.
Marx, Karl and Engels, Friedrich, *The German Ideology*, ed. C. J. Arthur, Lawrence and Wishart, 1970.
McIlvanney, William, *Docherty*, 1975; repr. Edinburgh: Canongate, 2016.

Meillassoux, Quentin, *After Finitude*, trans. Ray Brassier, London: Continuum, 2008.
Miller, Henry, *Tropic of Cancer*, 1934; New York: Grove Press, 1961.
Mitchell, W. J. T., *Iconology*, Chicago: University of Chicago Press, 1986.
Mukherjee, Upamanyu Pablo, *Crime and Empire*, Oxford: Oxford University Press, 2003.
Nelson, Brian (ed.), *The Cambridge Companion to Émile Zola*, Cambridge: Cambridge University Press, 2007.
Nias, Hilary S., 'Hippolyte Taine', in M. A. R. Habib (ed.), *The Cambridge History of Literary Criticism*, vol. 6, 393–405, Cambridge: Cambridge University Press, 2013.
Noelle-Neumann, Elisabeth, *The Spiral of Silence: Public Opinion – Our Social Skin*, 2nd edn, Chicago: University of Chicago Press, 1993.
Olson, Barbara K., '"Who Thinks This Book?" or, Why the Author-God Analogy Merits Our Continued Attention', *Narrative*, 14, no. 3 (2006): 339–46.
Orwell, George, *Nineteen Eighty-Four*, 1949; repr. London: Penguin, 1982.
Pendreigh, Brian, 'Kay Mander', *The Scotsman*, 3 January 2014, available at: https://www.scotsman.com/news/obituaries/obituary-kay-mander-documentary-film-maker-1-3253752
Picketty, Thomas, *Capital*, 2013; trans. Arthur Goldhammer, Cambridge, MA: Harvard University Press, 2014.
Plato, *Republic*, trans. Desmond Lee, London: Penguin, 1976.
Pomerantsev, Peter, *This Is Not Propaganda: Adventures in the War Against Reality*, London: Faber and Faber, 2019.
Pope, Alexander, *The Poems of Alexander Pope*, ed. John Butt, London: Methuen, 1975.
Potter, Lois, *Othello: Shakespeare in Performance*, Manchester: Manchester University Press, Manchester, 2002.
Price, Roger, *The French Second Empire: An Anatomy of Political Power*, Cambridge: Cambridge University Press, 2001.
Proudhon, Pierre-Joseph, *Du principe de l'art et de sa destination sociale*, 1865; repr. Paris: Rivière, 1971.
Reich, Jacqueline and Garofalo, Piero (eds), *Re-Viewing Fascism: Italian Cinema 1922–1943*, Bloomington and London: Indiana University Press, 2002.
Reporters without Borders, https://rsf.org/en
Roberts, M. J. D., 'Morals, Art, and the Law: The Passing of the Obscene Publications Act 1857', *Victorian Studies*, 28, no. 4 (1985): 609–29.
Rother, Rainer, *Leni Riefenstahl: The Seduction of Genius*, trans. Martin H. Bott, London: Bloomsbury, 2003.
Rousseau, Jean-Jacques, *Du Contrat Social*, 1762; repr. Paris: Flammarion, 1966.
Rousseau, Jean-Jacques, *Emile; ou, de l'éducation*, 1762; repr. Paris: Flammarion, 1966.
Rubin, James Henry, *Realism and Social Vision in Courbet and Proudhon*, Princeton: Princeton University Press, 1980.
Rubin, James Henry, *Courbet*, London: Phaidon, 1997.

Runciman, David, *How Democracy Ends*, London: Profile Books, 2019.
Rusbridger, Alan, *Breaking News*, Edinburgh: Canongate, 2018.
Said, Edward, *Representations of the Intellectual*, London: Vintage, 1994.
Sartre, Jean-Paul, *L'Etre et l.e néant*, Paris: nrf Gallimard, 1943.
Sartre, Jean-Paul, *Being and Nothingness*, trans. Sarah Richmond, London: Routledge, 2018.
Selby, Hubert, *Last Exit to Brooklyn*, New York: Grove Press, 1964.
Shklovsky, Viktor, 'Art as Technique', in Lee T. Lemon and Marion J. Reis (eds and trans.), *Russian Formalist Criticism: Four Essays*, Lincoln and London: University of Nebraska Press, 1965.
Sidney, Philip, 'Apology for Poetry', in Edmund D. Jones (ed.), *English Critical Essays: Sixteenth, Seventeenth and Eighteenth Centuries*, Oxford: Oxford University Press, 1975.
Silverman, Debora, *Art Nouveau in Fin-de-Siècle France: Politics, Psychology, and Style*, Los Angeles and London: University of California Press, 1992.
Smethurst, Colin, *Zola: Germinal*, London: Edward Arnold, 1974.
Snyder, Timothy, *The Road to Unfreedom*, London: Bodley Head, 2018.
Soros, George, *Open Society: Reforming Global Capitalism*, New York: Little, Brown & Co., 2000.
Stendhal, *Le rouge et le noir*, ed. P.-G. Castex, Paris: Garnier, 1973.
Strumingher, Laura S., *What Were Little Boys and Girls Made Of?: Primary Education in Rural France 1830–1880*, Albany: SUNY Press, 1983.
Taine, Hippolyte, *The Philosophy of Art*, 2nd edn, trans. John Durand, New York: Holt and Williams, 1873.
Todd, Emmanuel, *Qui est Charlie?*, Paris: Seuil, 2015.
Tomalin, Claire, *Charles Dickens: A Life*, London: Penguin, 2012.
Tramontana, Gaetano, *Invito al Cinema di Luchino Visconti*, Milano: Mursia, 2003.
Trotsky, Leon, *Literature and Revolution*, trans. Rose Strunsky, Ann Arbor: University of Michigan Press, 1975.
Turgenev, Ivan, *Fathers and Sons*, trans. Rosemary Edmonds, London: Penguin, 1965.
Turgenev, Ivan, *First Love*, trans. Isaiah Berlin, London: Penguin, 1978.
Vann, Michael G., '"Blame it on the Casbah": The White Male Imperialist Fantasies of Duvivier's *Pépé le Moko*', https://h-france.net/fffh/classics/blame-it-on-the-casbah-the-white-male-imperialist-fantasies-of-duviviers-pepe-le-moko/
Verga, Giovanni, *Cavalleria Rusticana and Other Stories*, trans. G. H. McWilliam, London: Penguin, 1999.
Virilio, Paul, *Défense populaire et l.uttes écologiques*, Paris: Galilée, 1978.
Virilio, Paul, *L'Horizon négatif*, Paris: Galilée, 1984.
Virilio, Paul, *Esthétique de la disparition*, 1980; Paris: Galilée, 1989.
Virilio, Paul and Lotringer, Sylvère, *Pure War*, trans. Mark Polizotti, New York: Semiotext(e), 1988.
Wall, Geoffrey, *Flaubert: A Life*, London: Faber and Faber, 2001.

Wittgenstein, Ludwig, *Tractatus Logico-Philosophicus*, trans. D. F. Pears and B. F. McGuinness, London: Routledge, 1961.
Woolf, Virginia, *Selected Essays*, ed., David Bradshaw, Oxford: Oxford University Press, 2009.
Zola, Émile, *La Confession de Claude*, https://beq.ebooksgratuits.com/vents/zola-claude.pdf
Zola, Émile, *Les Nouveaux Contes à Ninon*, https://beq.ebooksgratuits.com/vents/zola-ninon2.pdf
Zola, Émile, *Contes à Ninon*, Paris: Fasquelle, 1955.
Zola, Émile, *La Curée*, in *Les Rougon-Macquart I*, ed. Armand Lanoux, Paris: Pléiade, 1960.
Zola, Émile, *L'Argent*, in *Les Rougon-Macquart II*, ed. Armand Lanoux, 11, Paris: Pléiade, 1961.
Zola, Émile, *L'Assommoir*, in *Les Rougon-Macquart II*, ed. Armand Lanoux, Paris: Pléiade, 1961.
Zola, Émile, *Germinal*, in *Les Rougon-Macquart III*, ed. Armand Lanoux, Paris: Pléiade, 1964.
Zola, Émile, *Pot-Bouille*, in *Les Rougon-Macquart III*, ed. Armand Lanoux, Paris: Pléiade, 1964.
Zola, Émile, *La Bête Humaine*, in *Les Rougon-Macquart IV*, ed. Armand Lanoux, Paris: Pléiade, 1966.
Zola, Émile, *L'Oeuvre*, in *Les Rougon-Macquart IV*, ed. Armand Lanoux, Paris: Pléiade, 1966.
Zola, Émile, *Le Bon Combat: de Courbet aux Impressionistes*, ed. Jean-Paul Bouillon, présentation et préface de Gaëton Picon, Paris: Hermann, 1974.
Zola, Émile, *Correspondance I: 1858–1867*, ed. B. H. Bakker, Paris: Presses de l'Université de Montréal; Editions CNRS, 1978.

Films

Cavalcanti, Alberto, *Went the Day Well?*, 1942.
Chaplin, Charlie, *Modern Times*, 1936.
De Sica, Vittorio, *Ladri di biciclette*, 1948.
Duvivier, Julien, *Pépé le Moko*, 1937.
Eisenstein, Sergei, *Battleship Potemkin*, 1925.
Elton, Arthur and Anstey, E. H., *Housing Problems*, 1935.
Flaherty, Robert, *Nanook of the North*, 1922.
Flaherty, Robert, *Moana: A Romance of the Golden Age*, 1926.
Flaherty, Robert, *Man of Aran*, 1934.
Grierson, John, *Drifters*, 1929.

Grierson, John, *Industrial Britain*, 1931.
Grierson, John, *Night Mail*, 1935-36.
Grierson, John, *This Wonderful World*, Scottish Television, 1957-66.
LeRoy, Mervyn, *The Gold Diggers*, 1933.
Loach, Ken, *Cathy Come Home*, 1966.
Mander, Kay, *Homes for the People*, 1945.
Renoir, Jean, *La Grande Illusion*, 1937.
Renoir, Jean, *La Bête humaine*, 1938.
Renoir, Jean, *La Règle du Jeu*, 1939.
Riefenstahl, Leni, *Triumph des Willens*, 1935.
Riefenstahl, Leni, *Olympia*, 1938.
Rossellini, Roberto, *Roma, Città aperta*, 1945.
Rossellini, Roberto, *Paisà*, 1946.
Rossellini, Roberto, *Germania anno zero*, 1948.
Visconti, Luchino, *Ossessione*, 1942-43.
Wise, Robert, *The Sound of Music*, 1965.

Index

Adorno, Theodor W.   176–7, 195–6
Altan, Ahmet   48–9, 51, 53, 55, 93, 95, 252
Andersen, Hans Christian   181
Anstey, E. H.   182, 185
Arendt, Hannah   3, 17–18, 136, 210–11, 215–16, 219, 228, 235, 239
Aristotle   6, 12, 18, 76, 226
Arnold, Matthew   88, 90, 101
Artaud, Antonin   152
Attlee, Clement   185–7
Augustine   3–4
Austen, Jane   56, 87–8
Ayyub, Rana   190

Baille, J.-B.   125
Balzac, Honoré de   74, 83
Barré, Louis   73
Barthes, Roland   81, 208, 215
Baudelaire, Charles   13–14, 35–6, 42, 46, 52, 57, 69, 72, 77–8, 99, 111–14, 139, 144, 243
Baudrillard, Jean   152
Bazin, André   215, 217
Beaumont, Barbara   147
Beckett, Samuel   9–10, 83–5, 262
Benjamin, Walter   3–5, 152, 176, 193, 195, 261–2
Berger, John   50
Berkeley, Busby   193
Berkeley, George   78
Berthelot, Sandrine   74
Bew, John   236
Billington, Michael   180
Blumenberg, Hans   76
Bogdanov, Michael   249
Bolsanaro, Jair   263
Bondanella, Peter   215
Bouilhet, Louis   72–3
Brenton, Howard   248–9
Browne, Thomas   31
Brunette, Peter   221, 223

Bruyas, Alfred   57
Büchner, Ludwig   130–2
Bush, George W.   96 n.12
Butler, Judith   32–3

Caillebotte, Gustave   145–7, 241
Campbell, John   36–42, 102, 113, 211, 213, 247
Carlyle, Thomas   88
Castex, P.-G.   53–4
Cavalcanti, Alberto   213 n.16
Cézanne, Paul   125
Challinor, William   94
Chaplin, Charlie   140–1
Chardin, Jean-Baptiste Siméon   58–9
Chen Guang   1–5, 12, 95
Clare, Janet   30 n.8
Clark, T. J.   50, 55, 61
Clegg, Cyndia Susan   35
Clinton, Hillary   52 n.7
Clover, Charles   18
Colet, Louise   75, 80, 82
Conrad, Joseph   155 n.9
Cook, Joseph   94
Courbet, Gustave   14–15, 50, 53, 57–68, 70, 72, 75, 77, 79–80, 84, 97, 99, 106–7, 115, 122, 126–7, 129, 139–40, 142–3, 145, 154, 165, 168, 200, 226, 241
Crane, Ralph   38–9
Culler, Jonathan   96

Dante Aligheri   241
Darnton, Robert   39
Davis, Lennard J.   75
Deane, Seamus   19–20
Defoe, Daniel   217
De Robertis, Deborah   14–15
Derrida, Jacques   8, 63
De Santis, Giuseppe   197–9, 212
Descartes, René   8–9, 11, 119–20
DeSica, Vittorio   162, 225, 228

Dewey, John   161
Dickens, Charles   15–16, 88, 91, 93–9,
   114–15, 160, 165, 230
Diderot, Denis   58
Di Nolfo, Ennio   215, 217
Dreyfus, Alfred   143–4, 152–4, 157
Du Camp, Maxime   70–2, 107
Dupont, Paul   104, 106
Duvivier, Julien   200 n.6

Eco, Umberto   152
Eggers, Dave   19, 245, 252–9, 261–3
Eisenstein, Sergei   156
Eliot, T. S.   64, 80, 163
Elton, Arthur   182, 185
Erdogan, Recep Tayyip   48, 232 n.3, 263
Erlich, Victor   132

Falloux, Alfred de   16, 43–4, 90, 92–3, 95–7, 100–11, 120, 124, 161–2, 246
Fisher, Mark   115, 242
Fitzpatrick, Sheila   161, 163
Flaherty, Robert   153, 155, 160, 163, 165–6, 175
Flaubert, Gustave   13–14, 35–6, 42, 46, 52, 57, 66, 69–86, 99, 102–14, 123, 125, 128, 139, 144, 147, 241, 243
Forster, John   93, 115
Freedberg, David   23 n.1
Fried, Michael   58–61

Gabin, Jean   200 n.6
Galsworthy, John   80
Gaskell, Elizabeth   160
Gide, André   88, 122 n.4, 151, 153
Goebbels, Joseph   169, 185, 191, 194
Greuze, Jean-Baptiste   59
Grierson, John   18–19, 152–72, 175, 178, 182, 184–6, 189, 191–2, 199, 213–14, 218, 226–7, 231, 239, 253
Griffiths, D. W.   217, 237

Habermas, Jürgen   36, 45
Hachette, Louis   121, 123–4
Hall, Peter   248

Hammerstein, Oscar   181
Hannoosh, Michèle   111–12
Hardy, Ollie   85
Haynes, Christine   106–8
Heaney, Seamus   248–50
Hegel, G. W. F.   10, 84
Heinemann, Margot   31–2, 34
Hitchens, Christopher   238 n.20
Horkheimer, Max   196

Ibárruri, Dolores (La Pasionaria)   11
Ingrao, Pietro   206

James, Henry   114, 120, 126, 136–8, 144, 149–52, 155, 157, 182, 228, 253
Jameson, Fredric   135 n.34, 229, 232
Joyce, James   10–11, 95, 136, 178
Judt, Tony   233

Kafka, Franz   46, 93–4
Kelman, James   244
Kermode, Frank   216 n.20
Kerzhentsev, Platon   163
Khashoggi, Jamal   49, 235 n.11
Kirkup, James   248
Klein, Naomi   11–12
Kolker, Robert P.   191
Krupskaya, Nadezhda   161–2
Kuhn, Thomas S.   231 n.2

LaCapra, Dominick   25 n.3, 99, 104–5
Laurel, Stan   85
Lawrence, D. H.   244
Le Carré, John   178
Leibniz, Gottfried Wilhelm   230
Leigh, Mike   162
Lemon, Denis   248
Lenin, V. I.   18, 156–7, 159, 161
Lim, Louisa   1–3
Lippmann, Walter   170–2, 231–8, 249
Loach, Ken   162, 182, 187–9
Lowe, Robert   90
Lukács, Georg   163–5, 167
Lukashenko, Alexander   263
Lumière, Louis   158
Lunacharsky, Anatoly   18, 156, 159–63, 165, 167
Lyotard, Jean-François   239 n.20

McIlvanney, William   141
Mander, Kay   182, 185–7, 189
Marinetti, F. T.   197–9
Martineau, Harriet   160
Marx, Karl   7–8, 11, 15, 84, 92, 99, 108, 130–1, 163
Medvedev, P. N.   13
Meillassoux, Quentin   79–80, 84
Melville, Herman   86
Meyerhold, Vsevolod   163
Miller, Henry   244
Mitchell, W. J. T.   23
Mohanfram, Radhika   38–9
Monet, Claude   97
Morisot, Berthe   145–7
Mukherjee, Upamanyu Pablo   40–1, 42 n.29
Mussolini, Benito   199–200, 205–6, 208, 212, 218, 220
Mussolini, Vittorio   205, 217

Neuburger, Julia   244
Noelle-Neumann, Elisabeth   138–9

Obama, Barack   52 n.7
Ollier, Charles   89
Orbán, Viktor   232 n.3, 263
Orwell, George   19, 239, 252–61

Pacchioni, Federico   215
Paisley, Ian   11
Peacock, Thomas Love   89
Pendreigh, Brian   186 n.11
Pichat, Laurent   104, 107
Pinard, Ernest   99–100, 102–3, 108–9, 111, 114, 247
Plato   24–6, 28–31, 46–7, 106, 108, 262
du Poittevin, Alfred   72
Pomerantsev, Peter   20, 260
Pope, Alexander   77
Price, Roger   42–3
Pritchett, V. S.   129
Proudhon, Joseph   15, 60, 67, 122–3
Proust, Marcel   11, 178
Putin, Vladimir   13–14, 263

Renoir, Jean   200–5, 207–8, 213–14, 224
Renoir, Pierre Auguste   200–1

Riefenstahl, Leni   18, 166, 170–2, 190–5, 199, 211–12, 217–18, 234
Roberts, M. J. D.   40, 113
Robeson, Paul   224
Rochau, Ludwig August von   236–7, 241
Rodgers, Richard   181
Rodin, Auguste   241–2
Ross-Cornes, Graham   249
Rossellini, Roberto   162, 214, 216–26, 228, 249, 253
Rosset, Clément   152
Rother, Rainer   191
Rousseau, Jean-Jacques   120, 179
Rubin, James Henry   67–8
Runciman, David   28–9

Said, Edward   129
Saint-Réal, César Vichard de   53–4
Sartre, Jean-Paul   180, 189, 225
Selby, Hubert   244
Shakespeare, William   11, 119–20, 123, 126, 136, 144, 188, 211
Shelley, Percy Bysshe   88–92
Sherman, Cindy   11
Shklovsky, Viktor   133–5, 139, 156
Sidney, Philip   76–7
Snyder, Timothy   13–14, 18
Stalin, Joseph   239
Stendhal   11, 53–4, 78, 120, 123, 259
Struminger, Laura   44
Stubbs, John   35

Taine, Hippolyte   101–2, 123, 125, 127
Tharoor, Shashi   238 n.20
Thatcher, Margaret   187 n.12
Thiers, Adolphe   43–4, 92, 100
Trotsky, Leon   134–6, 138–9
Trump, Donald   12, 52 n.7, 232 n.3, 263
Tsipras, Alexis   29
Turgenev, Ivan   17, 128–32, 137, 145, 147, 161, 241, 253
Tynan, Kenneth   179–81, 184

Valabrègue, Anthony   126, 136, 138
Varoufakis, Yanis   28–9

Verga, Giovanni   198, 200, 206–7, 212, 223
Vertov, Dziga   156
Virilio, Paul   27–8
Visconti, Luchino   199–200, 205–13, 220, 228
Voltaire   73–4, 84–5, 107

Whitehouse, Mary   246–51
Wilde, Oscar   136
Wilson, Harold   178

Wittgenstein, Ludwig   63 n.27
Woolf, Virginia   11, 96 n.12, 120, 146, 178

Xi Jinping   232 n.3, 263

Zelensky, Volodymir   263
Zola, Émile   16, 80, 97, 120–7, 132, 134–45, 151–4, 157–8, 160, 164–6, 182, 188, 198, 211, 213–14, 228, 246, 253, 260